Sacred Scripture:

The Disclosure of the Word

Sacred Scripture:
The Disclosure of the Word

FRANCIS MARTIN

Sapientia Press
of Ave Maria University

Requests for permission to make copies of any part of the work should be directed to:

Sapientia Press
of Ave Maria University
1025 Commons Circle
Naples, FL 34119
888-343-8607

Cover Image: Marc Chagall, *The Lamentation of Jeremiah*
© 2006 Artists Rights Society (ARS), New York/ADAGP, Paris

Cover Design: Eloise Anagnost

Printed in the United States of America.

Library of Congress Control Number: 2006900967

ISBN-10: 1-932589-30-9
ISBN-13: 978-1-932-589-30-6

Table of Contents

Foreword

I N 1998 our present Holy Father, Benedict XVI, described the challenge posed to modern biblical studies in these words: "The exegetical problem is identical in the main with the struggle for the foundations of our time. Such a struggle cannot be conducted casually, nor can it be won with a few suggestions. It will demand, as I have already intimated, the attentive and critical commitment of an entire generation."[1]

Fr. Francis Martin, a leader in American biblical studies, has been engaged for a lifetime in precisely the task of moving the historical critical method out of the narrow confines of a Kantian epistemology and positivistic historicism into the wider world of a genuine and modern Christian philosophy and theology. In this wider world, as Cardinal Ratzinger pointed out in his 1988 conference, the genuine fruits of critical historiography can be placed profitably at the service of the Church's witness to the inspired Word of God.

In this collection of his essays, which was requested by young scholars who are moving in the direction he has pointed out to them, we find some of the hallmarks of Martin's approach: careful attention to the inspired text, a philosophical and theological sophistication, and a living faith. Those of us who taught with him and the students who learned from him, whether in Washington or Jerusalem, will recognize in these essays a sensitivity to the spiritual depths of both the biblical text and the great theologians of the past and present, as well as a firm grasp on the history of thought that has led us to the challenge described by our present pope. We will find here more than "a few suggestions." This is part of the "attentive and critical commitment" our present crisis requires.

---

[1] Conference given at the Ratzinger Conference on Bible and Church, held in New York, January 1988: Josef Ratzinger, "Biblical Interpretation in Crisis: On the Question of the Foundations and Approaches of Exegesis Today," in *Biblical Interpretation in Crisis. The Ratzinger Conference on Bible and the Church*, ed. Richard John Neuhaus, Encounter Series (Grand Rapids, MI: Eerdmans, 1989), 1–23.

Fr. Martin's work shows us that historical research has not failed, it is rather that its full potential has not been realized. Though much effort has been expended in tracing the production of a text, comparable work in understanding its reception has only begun. It is here, of course, that the Church sees the role of Tradition: the liturgical, mystical, and intellectual appropriation of the text under the action of the Holy Spirit. Careful historical work in this direction responds to the optimistic description of Pope John Paul II in *Fides et Ratio* (§71): "It is as if, moving between the twin poles of God's word and a better understanding of it, reason is offered guidance and is warned against paths which would lead it to stray from revealed Truth and to stray in the end from the truth pure and simple. Instead, reason is stirred to explore paths which of itself it would not even have suspected it could take."

Some of these new paths are being explored by younger biblical scholars, among them some of Fr. Martin's former students. In the field of textual criticism, for instance, there is a greater appreciation of the extremely intricate manner in which the tradents of a text continue to develop it within the parameters of the overall tradition until the text achieves a canonical status. Again, closer historical study of the biblical milieu gives us a greater understanding of the dynamics of precritical history and the need for critical history. Critical history can recreate for us the dynamics of this older and more profound understanding of how communal memory functions in rendering God's acts present to his people. We are witnessing as well a deeper appreciation of the nature of language and the need for a "turn to the person" in understanding the act of knowing and communicating. These and other advances in biblical studies are beginning to bring about a welcome renewal of exegesis as a theological discipline.

—AUGUSTINE DI NOIA, OP

Introduction:
The Story of a Pilgrimage

I THINK THAT the best way to introduce the following twelve essays, all of which have been published elsewhere, is to trace part of my own theological and spiritual pilgrimage. I hope in this way to illustrate the common theme that runs through these essays. This theme is the challenge known to many modern exegetes, namely, the task of integrating the ancient way of understanding the Bible with the historical methods we use today in our study of the Bible. If there are two things that personalize, so to speak, my own reaction to this challenge they would be first, the intensity of my own personal experience of the ancient approach to the Bible while at St. Joseph's Abbey in Spencer, Massachusetts, and then for the rest of my life, and second, my engagement——on almost every day since 1959—with what is called the historical critical method. I will trace this pilgrimage briefly and then present the essays in an overview.

• • •

Part One: My Personal Experience

As I have reflected on my own experience within the Catholic tradition, it has become clear to me that many facets of the ancient Catholic approach to Scripture are not explicitly articulated and were for a long time taken for granted, as it were. They stand in need of some explanation. It is for this reason that I begin with an account of my experience that embodies several facets not readily available in the post-Vatican II Church.

I was brought up in a family that prayed the rosary every night and prepared for the Sunday Mass early on Sunday morning by reading the Scripture

---

The nucleus of this Introduction first appeared as "Reading Scripture in the Catholic Tradition," in *Your Word is Truth: A Project of Evangelicals and Catholics Together*, edited by Charles Colson and Richard John Neuhas (Grand Rapids, MI: Eerdmans, 2002), 147–68.

passages that were to be read in Church. I don't remember any real accent on Scripture in my Catholic education, though I do remember a vague sense that it was "dangerous" to go off on one's own and read the Bible since that could lead you into error: It was safer to leave that to the experts and follow the teaching of the Church. Then, at the age of twenty, I entered the Cistercian Monastery in Spencer, Massachusetts, where I spent fifteen happy years (three of them in Rome doing graduate studies), and was plunged into a world that, while very much a part of the twentieth century in regard to technology, had changed but little in its basic way of life and spirituality in over 800 years.

The day, which began at 2:00 a.m. and ended at 7:00 p.m., was structured around eight periods of common prayer, all in Latin. The backbone of this was the Psalter sung or recited in such a way that the whole of the 150 psalms were prayed in the period of a week, with many being repeated several times during the week. The psalms were sung in the context of antiphons, readings from Scripture, and prayers that were composed in such a way that the ordinary days repeated themselves and the great feast days had special components. In addition there was a daily Eucharistic Liturgy, also sung in its entirety. We had helped to build the church and monastery in which this prayer took place, and it was a place of beauty and spiritual peace. The music, the Gregorian chant, sung by a group of monks considered to be among the most skilled in the country, was a constant education in the interpretation of Scripture. Let me explain.

The basic principle of Gregorian chant is that it should be "a carpet for the words of Scripture to walk upon and thus enter your soul," it is a musical exegesis of the sacred text composed in an atmosphere of prayer and fasting. Even as I write these words I can hear the Entrance Antiphon for Easter morning with its calm and powerful 4th mode melody carrying one into the world of the Mystery: "I have risen and am still with you," as the purposely double meaning of the *Vetus Latina* renders Psalm 139 (138):18. The antiphon goes on to allude to other verses: "You placed your hand upon me, your knowledge has become marvelous" (vv. 5–6). That is, "You have claimed me from the dead and revealed to all the world the inner depths of the mystery hidden for ages and now revealed in me, your Son." This psalm, an intimate dialogue of wonder at the creating power of God, passed through the soul of Christ and has become a sacrament giving access to his inner life. But there is more: The grace animating the psalmist made of his song an anticipation of the surge of joy that coursed through the heart of Christ as he was raised from the dead. The real subject of the psalm is Christ; the psalmist is an anticipatory participation in that mystery of God's plan, which is known now in its fulfillment.

In order for the words of this psalm to unfold in this way, there must be song, that is, there must be community, people together to make this song. They are gathered on Easter morning and sing what had been sung for centuries at this moment. Our song makes us one with those who sang this song before us. We are bound together by the living Christ who sings his song in us on earth and in them in heaven. It is because of this mystery, the Christ in us, the hope and fulfillment of glory, that time is no longer a neutral reality but rather something that once caught up in the life of the Body—the Christ—becomes eternal.

Other moments occur to me. The Offertory hymn that celebrated Moses' prayer to God in Exodus 32:11–14. "Moses prayed in the sight of the Lord: 'Why Lord, are you angry with your people? . . . Remember Abraham, Isaac, and Jacob, your servants to whom you swore by yourself. . . .' And the Lord repented from the evil he had spoken against his people." Once again Christ is praying in us. Moses, an anticipated partial realization of Christ, stepped into the breach, preferring to be blotted out of the book of Life rather than renounce solidarity with his/God's people (Ex 32:31). Now Christ, exercising his eternal priesthood, is always living to make intercession for us (Heb 7:25) and joins us to himself in this prayer through the words of Moses. Christ's heavenly prayer still has a historical dimension in the prayer of his Body, the Church.

In the monastic liturgy the Books of Samuel and Kings are read throughout the summer, that time "after Pentecost" that symbolizes the life of the Church, in the heat of the battle, looking to the heroes of the past whose lives are an example for us. Foremost among these, of course, is David, since Jesus, the new David, is the one Shepherd who feeds the flock of God (Ez 23:23–24). On hot Saturday afternoons, after a day of work, we met for First Sunday Vespers in the Church and at the *Magnificat* sang David's generous words of love and forgiveness: "Saul and Jonathan beloved and lovely! In life and death they were not divided. . . . The arrow of Jonathan never turned back. . . . I grieve for you my brother, Jonathan . . . your love to me was wonderful, passing the love of women" (2 Sam 1:22–27). Here is tenderness and pardon, the heart of Christ portrayed for us, not only in this magnanimous grieving for both Saul, his persecutor, and Jonathan. his friend, but even more in David's weeping over Absalom, his rebellious and treacherous son: "Absalom, my son, my son Absalom, who would grant to me that I might die instead of you! O Absalom my son!" (2 Sam 18:33). In this latter song, the melody even carries the sound of David's weeping—Christ weeping over us—and teaches us what it means to continue on earth the prayer of forgiveness of Christ himself. Finally, on a Sunday, as we approached the Lord at Communion, we sang the dialogue between Jesus and the woman taken in adultery, the confrontation of *Misericordia* and *miseria*, to quote Augustine's memorable phrase: "Has no one condemned you woman? No one Lord. Nor do I condemn you—go in peace and do not sin anymore." Once again, the melody, oscillating between calm majestic love and fearful hope, brings us into the action as participants experiencing the love of Christ even as we express it and responding with the same tremulous expectancy.

Reflections on This Experience in a More Common Context

The Liturgy

This world in which I lived and learned, I now see upon reflection taught me several basic things about Scripture and Tradition. First, I learned that the native home of Scripture is the Liturgy. Even the monastic practice of *lectio divina* (private contact with the Sacred Text for several hours a day) is a continuation of the communal prayer, which is basically the singing of the biblical text in a setting that repeated itself year after year drawing the cyclic time of the cosmos into the eternal dimension of the Resurrection.[1] Usually I read the Bible in the Vulgate translation, since this made it easier to catch all the multiple allusions to the text in the writings of the Latin Fathers. I began reading the Greek Fathers as well, and this exposure gave me a sense of the delight they mediated to us from their own contact with the Sacred Text. Henri de Lubac, whom I discovered after about three years in the monastery and who is an abundant source of understanding of the Fathers, said this of their attitude toward the Bible:

> Scripture is not only divinely guaranteed, it is divinely true. The Spirit did not only dictate it; he is, as it were, contained in it. He inhabits it. His breath perpetually animates it. The Scripture is "made fruitful by a miracle of the Holy Spirit." It is "full of the Spirit."[2]

The Spiritual Sense, or Spiritual Understanding[3]

Knowing that Christ was somehow contained in the events mediated to us in the Old Testament was not so much the result of study as it was of experience at the Liturgy. For nearly the whole of Tradition it is axiomatic that the events of the Old Testament share in the Christ event in some mysterious manner. To rec-

---

[1] In *Fides et Ratio*, Pope John Paul II accented the importance of time, that is history, in the Christian dispensation: "God's Revelation is therefore immersed in time and history. Jesus Christ took flesh in the 'fullness of time' (Gal 4:4); and two thousand years later, I feel bound to restate forcefully that 'in Christianity time has a fundamental importance.' It is within time that the whole work of creation and salvation comes to light; and it emerges clearly above all that, with the Incarnation of the Son of God, our life is even now a foretaste of the fulfilment of time which is to come (cf. Heb 1:2)" (Par. 11).

[2] Henri de Lubac, *Exégèse Médiéval. Les Quatres Sens de l'Écriture Part I, vol. 41,* Théologie (Paris: Aubier, 1959), 129. The texts quoted in this passage are from Anselm, *De concord.* 3,6 (*Patrologiae Latina* 158, 528B), and Origen, *De Princ.* 4,1,7, respectively. I am indebted for this reference to the unpublished dissertation of Marcellino D'Ambrosio, "Henri de Lubac and the Recovery of the Traditional Hermeneutic." (Catholic University of America, 1991), 147–48.

[3] This topic will be the studied at length in Chapter 12.

ognize the anticipations of the Christ event in the events present to us in the Old Testament narrative is to appreciate the *spiritual sense* of the Old Testament. It is obvious in the examples I have given above that this sense of the text was presupposed in the manner in which the Liturgy, with its nearly 2,000-year history, prayed the Old Testament. The other name given to the spiritual sense is the "allegorical" sense, which, for tradition, meant exactly the same thing, though this latter term particularly covered many extravagant interpretations.[4] There are two senses that derive from the meaning of the Old Testament once it has been sublated into the Christ event.[5] These are the "tropological" sense, which derives from the Greek term *tropos* ("way of acting"), and the "anagogical" sense, which, deriving from the Greek term *anagogè* ("ascent"), refers to the eschatological dimension. It is important to realize that for the ancients these four senses—the literal, the allegorical/spiritual, the tropological, and the anagogical—are not four meanings of the words, but four dimensions of the event that is being mediated by the words. The words are important because they are a privileged means of mediating the realities. As St. Augustine expresses it: "It is in the event itself, and not only in the text, that we must seek the mystery."[6]

In the time before the fourteenth century's move to nominalism, an era we can only imagine but not experience again (except partially in the kind of life context I described above), the accent was placed upon understanding the *reality* mediated by the words more than on the words themselves. This is the work of the Holy Spirit, bringing the mind and spirit of the reader into contact with the divine realities. As a movement of grace, such a way of approaching Scripture is very fruitful and it grounds further reflection. Theology, therefore, is a matter of perceiving the relation between *realities* by the use of reason enlightened by faith but not of drawing conclusions from texts.[7] The greatness of the Fathers of the Church consisted in their graced ability to speak of divine realities with which they were in personal contact under the guidance of the authoritative words of Scripture to which they were submitted. It suffices to trace the

---

[4] For a balanced view of this question, see Henri de Lubac, *Sources of Revelation,* trans. Luke O'Neil (New York: Herder & Herder, 1968).

[5] The process I am referring to is aptly portrayed in this description of sublation given by Bernard Lonergan: "What sublates goes beyond what is sublated, introduces something new and distinct, yet so far from interfering with the sublated or destroying it, on the contrary needs it, includes it, preserves all its proper features and properties, and carries them forward to a fuller realization within a richer context." Bernard Lonergan, *Method in Theology* (New York: Herder & Herder, 1972), 241.

[6] *"In isto ipso facto, non solum in hoc dicto, mysterium requirere debemus." On Psalm 68* (*Patrologiae Latina* 36, 858).

[7] "Yet it must always be remembered that the assent to these other truths, the various material objects of faith, presupposes the formal object as providing the authenticating force for the assent." Brian J. Shanley, "Sacra Doctrina and Disclosure," *The Thomist* 61, (2; 1997): 163–88, at 174–75 with a citation from *Summa theologiae* 2–2, 1,1c.

dogmatic conflicts of the early Church—Nestorianism, Arianism, Mono-physitism, and the rest—to appreciate the manner in which these mystics, men in touch with the Mystery, argued from Scripture. Tradition, in the Catholic understanding, is precisely this life-giving activity of the Holy Spirit, moving in the whole Body of Christ, served and guided by the prophetic action of the Magisterium, by which the realities of God and his saving grace continue to be the light and life of the People of God. This process is described well in the *Constitution on Divine Revelation of Vatican II*:

> This tradition which comes from the apostles develops in the Church with the help of the Holy Spirit. For there is a growth in the understanding of the realities and the words [note both terms] which have been handed down. This happens through the contemplation and study made by believers who treasure these things in their hearts (cf. Lk 2:19, 51), through the intimate understanding of the spiritual things they experience, and through the preaching of those who have received through episcopal succession the sure gift of truth. (*DV* #8)[8]

Tradition, as everyone agrees, is not the same as custom, nor is every habitual understanding of the text the work of the Holy Spirit. The text just cited indicates one way in which the whole body of believers, through contemplation, study, intimate understanding, and experience, as well as by accredited preachers, can use the inspired text as a corrective to what passes for tradition but is not really so. They do this in the force of the divine realities transmitted to them. As Martin Luther said: "The one who does not understand the realities cannot draw the meaning out of the words."[9]

Presence

Sometime early in the fifth century, Pope St. Leo I told his congregation:

> The visible dimension of our Redeemer has passed over into the sacraments, and that faith might be more excellent and more firm, instruction has succeeded to vision, and it is this authority that the hearts of believers, illumined by rays from on high, rely upon.[10]

That he intended by this to refer not only to the sacraments of the Church but also to the reading of the Scriptures, part of the "instruction," is evident, as

---

[8] For a discussion of this text, see Alessandro Magglioni, "Magisterial Teaching on Experience in the Twentieth Century: From the Modernist Crisis to the Second Vatican Council," *Communio* 13 (2; 1996): 225–43.

[9] *"Qui non intelligit res non postest sensum ex verbis elicere."* Tischreden, Weimarer Ausgabe 5, 26, n. 5246.

[10] *On the Ascension,* 2 (*Sources Chrétiennes* 74, 140).

we will see from others of his statements.[11] Leo's teaching, splendid in its clarity, does but sum up nearly 500 years of thinking about how the events in the life of Christ continue to have their effect in the life of the Church. I have tried, in my account of the monastic liturgy in which I was formed, to show how this is a matter of experience in such a setting and one more aspect of the ancient Catholic intuition concerning the *res* mediated by the Sacred Text. The Gospels themselves indicate how they effect such a presence. I will give examples in Chapter 5. An attentive reader will find many examples of this mode of procedure and will, if he or she will ponder the text, be drawn into its mysterious movement and the call to discipleship that Jesus, by the Holy Spirit, still proffers in and through the text.

Such an understanding of presence is also found in the ability of our predecessors to identify their lives with the narratives in the Scriptures, realizing that, while the narrative is completed, the story still goes on. Thus, the persons and events in Scripture are taken to be *figurae* of what the believers are experiencing in their own age. I will develop this notion in Chapter 1.

I consider it a singular grace of God that for fifteen years I experienced, through the Scriptures, the Liturgy, and the Fathers, the fact that my mind was borne to communicate in the saving acts of God through these sacred words and gestures. I knew that I was in touch with Reality through these instruments of mediation. I thus knew the living center of the Catholic tradition before I had the great privilege of studying Scripture according to modern methods, of seeing where this tradition had not grown where it should have grown, where it contained exaggerations, and of learning how to use the tools of historical research in order to penetrate more deeply into the Mystery contained in these precious instruments of Tradition. I would like to reflect now on that experience and the challenge that it presents to us today.

Part Two: The Challenge of Retrieval

After eight formative years in the monastery I was sent to live in the central house of the Order in Rome to do graduate work in Sacred Scripture. The basic monastic routine was retained there. After acquiring a Licentiate in theology (basically Thomistic theology), I began my studies at the Pontifical Biblical Institute and received the degree of Licentiate in Sacred Scripture two years later. Ten years later I returned to Rome and began work on the degree of Doctor in Sacred Scripture. After two years I went to live at the Ecole Biblique et Archéologique Française in Jerusalem where I continued my own work and eventually taught as well, receiving the doctoral degree in 1978.

---

[11] For places where Leo speaks of the Gospel text making the reality present, see *On the Resurrection*, 1 (*Sources Chrétiennes* 74, 123); *On the Epiphany*, 5 (*Sources Chrétiennes* 22, 254); *On the Passion*, 5 and 18 (*Sources Chrétiennes* 74, 41, 112). For the references to these citations, see Dom Marie-Bernard de Soos, *Le Mystère Liturgique d'après saint Léon le Grand* (mimeograph thesis presented to the Faculty of Toulouse on June 10, 1955).

The time of my biblical studies was a delight to me. I was trained under some of the best minds in the Church at that time, either by direct contact or through reading. I learned, once again by "instinct," that the historical methods were not enemies but friends of genuine biblical learning. Nevertheless, I began to see that the methods themselves derived from philosophical principles and presuppositions that, if not critically assessed and corrected, could deflect the faith direction of one's thinking. Work had to be done to understand these presuppositions in order to articulate what some of the best minds were doing intuitively.[12]

Thus began my pilgrimage: It has been at one and the same time a continued effort to use historical methods in biblical studies while studying the three areas of the philosophy of knowledge, the philosophy of history, and literary theory, which are implicit in the historical approach to the Sacred Text. Also, during a period of about six years, my study of feminist hermeneutics gave me a very acute sense of the need to elaborate a faith hermeneutics that was adequate to the importance of the problems being raised in feminist and liberationist theologies.[13]

Along this journey I have had contact with many who have influenced me profoundly. I cannot name them all but among them most prominently are theologians such as de Lubac and von Balthasar; historical exegetes such as Brown and Fitzmyer; many evangelical authors such as those who contributed to commentary series such as the evangelical series, the *Word Biblical Commentary*; as well as literary investigators such as my friend, the late Luis Alonso Schökel, as well as Meir Sternberg and Michael Fishbane. Finally, I wish to mention in a special way two philosophers who are close friends and whose conversation has been invaluable in my efforts to contribute to the integration the Church is seeking: Robert Sokolowski and Kenneth Schmitz.

Part Three: A Presentation of the Studies to Follow in this Book

In the title of this book I have described Scripture as the disclosure of the Word. I mean by this to point to the fact that the Sacred Text is a means of perpetuating revelation, because, as I hope to show, language is always revelatory, not representational. There is a dimension of the Scriptures that is revelatory because in it God speaks immediately to his Church and to each individual believer. As

---

[12] For an important discussion of the need for the integration I am seeking, see Josef Ratzinger, "Biblical Interpretation in Crisis: On the Question of Foundations and Approaches of Exegesis Today," in *Biblical Interpretation in Crisis. The Ratzinger Conference on Bible and Church*, ed. Richard John Neuhaus, Encounter Series 9 (Grand Rapids, MI: Eerdmans, 1989), 1–23.

[13] Much of the result of this work can be found in Francis Martin, *The Feminist Question: Feminist Theology in the Light of Christian Tradition* (Grand Rapids, MI: Eerdmans, 1994).

Aquinas will maintain, "God instructs the intellect both immediately through the sacred letters and mediately through other writings."[14]

As is the case with any author, I wish to communicate with my audience, which is an exercise of the role of teacher in the broad understanding of the term. In discussing the role of the teacher, and the same could be said of any act of communication within the world of scholarship, Aquinas first distinguishes it from the platonic notion that teaching helps another "recall" what was once known, as well as from the idea that teaching is the process by which the teacher gives his ideas to be absorbed by the student.[15] The process is basically one of *communication* in which the one communicating presents, through the use of language, the process that he or she went through in achieving the knowledge so that the one receiving the communication may follow and imitate the process and thus arrive at a personal share in what is communicated.[16]

I have borne this principle in mind in selecting and presenting these essays. As I see it, all are important in communicating what I have learned about integrating modern historical methods with the ancient sense of transcendence and its contact with the realities mediated by the text. Such an integration will not leave either of the components untouched: This is what is meant by retrieval. There is a certain progression in the studies I have selected, but it is not always linear. The same themes occur in different contexts and are thus presented in a rhythm that ebbs and flows, finally reaching a conclusion in the last chapter. There I will return to the notion of the "spiritual sense" of Scripture and use this as a focal point of the integration, as well as an invitation to move on from that point to a further consideration of the three areas already mentioned—epistemology, language, and history.

The first four chapters are reflections on method embodied in the study of a theme. Chapter 1, on the notion of *Sacra Doctrina*, presents the ancient understanding of this reality as one pole of what must be integrated in the retrieval. Chapter 2 is a discussion of some aspects of literary analysis and the philosophy of history as applied to Mark 14:32–42, the Gethsemane scene. The principal dialogue partner here is Paul Ricoeur. Chapter 3 takes the theme of the imitation of Christ and traces the way this reality is understood on both sides of the exegetical divide that began to occur in the 14th century and has resulted in a marked divergence of horizons. Much of the work here is a recounting of the history of some aspects of western thought. Finally, Chapter 4 puts the accent

---

[14] *In 1 Tim 3,* lect. 3 (Marietti ed. §812). This theme is treated in Chapter 1.

[15] This latter opinion is not far from the famous definition of a university lecture: The process by which the notes of the professor become the notes of the student without passing through the mind of either.

[16] For a complete analysis of Aquinas's thinking about communication the reader may consult Andrea Di Maio, *Il Concetto di Communicazione. Saggio di Lessicografia Filosofica e Teologica sul Tema di "Communicare" in Tommaso D'Aquino, Analecta Gregoriana 274* (Roma: Editrice Pontificia Università Gregoriana, 1998).

on the history of the reception of the Summary Statements in the Book of Acts. After locating them in their original social and intellectual context, the study moves on to consider how these texts have been operative in various communal endeavors over the centuries.

The next six chapters treat biblical texts or themes in an explicitly theological manner, seeking to serve the biblical teaching by employing various extra-biblical perspectives, often philosophical perspectives, in order to render the reality mediated by the text more intelligible. Chapter 5 studies Matthew's account of the healing of the Centurion's boy (Mt 8:5–13) using some basic principles of narratology as they apply to the unique mode of Gospel narrative that seeks to present the events of the life of Christ as they now still exist in his glorified humanity. This is a call for a theological narratology that, through the use of the historical methods, can enable us to appreciate the particular nature of biblical narrative. Chapter 6 is the study of the nuptial image in Israel with a prolonged analysis of Hosea 1–3 preceded by an analysis of Hebrew vocabulary that describes infidelity to fellow human beings and to God. Helpful here is the modern understanding of analogy, particularly in some Catholic philosophical circles, and its relevance to the biblical mode of predication.

Chapters 7 and 8 are biblical reflections on the encyclical *Veritatis Splendor*. Chapter 7 compares the teaching on the source of moral and mystical activity in the First Letter of John, applying an analysis I presented elsewhere.[17] Chapter 8 studies the themes of holiness and communion in the Scriptures and in the encyclical. The result of these studies is an appreciation of unexpected ways in which this encyclical is biblical. Chapter 9 takes seriously the paradox of Jesus' teaching on happiness and its radical and eschatological nature. This is accomplished by concentrating on the three Beatitudes in common in both the Matthean and Lucan account of the Sermon on the Mount/Plain. Chapter 10 is a study in biblical anthropology analyzing Genesis 1–3 and Ephesians 5:21–32, contesting the presuppositions and models that lie behind much historical work on the "Household Order Texts," and applying some philosophical insights to the issue of "identity and difference."

Finally, the last two chapters consider the problem of integration directly. Chapter 11 looks at the unresolved tension in *Dei Verbum* §12, which urges exegetes and theologians to avail themselves of modern historical, philological, and literary methods while at the same time retaining the basic theological outlook of tradition. A beginning is made in this chapter toward bridging the gap by pointing the way toward overcoming the anti-transcendent bias inherent in the modern methods. Chapter 12 advances the integration process by revisiting the ancient concept of the "spiritual/figural/mystical sense" of the biblical text. Without the work done in Chapter 11 this is not possible. It is also acknowl-

---

[17] Cf. "1 John," "2 John," and "3 John," in *The International Bible Commentary*, ed. William R. Farmer (Collegeville, MN: Liturgical Press, 1998), 1823–37.

edged that the advances in the historical sciences as well as philosophy must result in a more nuanced understanding of how Scripture teaches divine reality.

A word about the repetition of some quotes: I left them because I thought that they merited more than one reading. This is particularly true of Bernard Lonergan's description of what he calls "sublation." There are many places where the process so described can be enlightening. The most significant, and the most difficult, is in regard to the interrelation between historical events in what I call "economic participation." I make a beginning of the attempt to separate this from Hegel in Chapter 12, but more work remains to be done. I hope one day soon to devote a full book-length study to this and other material in the last two chapters.

It would be impossible to acknowledge adequately all the people who have been dialogue partners over the years during which these studies were written, and the number of authors who have contributed to my understanding is even greater. I would, however, like to thank Mrs. Jeannine McDonald and Mr. Damian Lenshek, who helped to prepare these studies for their present place in this book. I would like to thank as well the staff at Sapientia Press, and in a particular way Professor Matthew Levering who first proposed the idea for this book.

1   *Sacra Doctrina* and the Authority of its *Sacra Scriptura* According to St. Thomas Aquinas

SACRA DOCTRINA is an activity that begins with a divine action, revelation, and is perpetuated by that activity by which the People of God receive and pass on what God has taught. St. Thomas considers that *Sacra Doctrina* finds its source in Prophecy: "Prophecy is a knowledge imprinted by divine revelation on the mind of a prophet, in the form of teaching." This activity, far from dispensing from mental application, demands it at every level in the transmission of revelation. This can be seen by an analysis of the way in which the Scriptures bear witness to the theological activity of the prophets themselves. Thus the authority of Sacred Writings derives from the authority of God's teaching activity still present in the Church to which these Writings have been entrusted.

• • •

SACRA *doctrina, Sacra Scriptura, auctoritas:* These words ring differently, formed as they were to the medieval ear, than do our modern terms "theology," "Scripture," and "authority." In our contemporary search for a common understanding of the authority of Sacred Scripture, it will be helpful to return to Aquinas's understanding of these terms for the light that they can throw on what may be called a theory of faith-communication. I will treat each of the expressions in the light of Aquinas's view that all of these aspects of the Christian life are related in the one light of revelation, as this permeates human thought processes. I will then indicate the importance of this understanding for our modern problem of establishing criteria for the discerning of authentic Tradition.

An earlier version of this chapter appeared as "*Sacra Doctrina* and the Authority of its *Sacra Scriptura* according to St. Thomas Aquinas," *Pro Ecclesia* 10 (2001): 8–102.

Sacra Doctrina in St. Thomas[1]

In Aquinas's mind, there is something called *sacra doctrina* that is necessary for salvation. Thus, in the opening article of his mature treatment of the topic he states: "[I]t was necessary for human well being/salvation *(salutem)* that there be a kind of teaching *(doctrina)* according to divine revelation besides the philosophical disciplines which are pursued by human reason (*Summa theologiae* [hereafter *ST*] 1,1,1c).[2] *Sacra doctrina* is an analogous expression that applies to many facets of that activity by which God manifests and communicates himself and a knowledge of his plan because only in this way can we know the reason why we were created and so set our lives in that direction.[3] It includes, on the part of God, an original activity of self-manifestation that culminated in Jesus Christ, who is the revelation of God and the source of that divine gracious activity by which we can attain the end to which God has freely called us. By extension, the term *sacra doctrina* applies to all the derivative human acts, initiated and sustained by the Holy Spirit, by which this originating activity is perpetuated and made available, in many forms, to subsequent generations of God's people.

This broad description of *sacra doctrina* applies as well to Aquinas's use of the term in the first question of the *Summa theologiae*. There, as commentators rightly maintain, he is consistent throughout in his use of the term. Consistency, however, is not the same as univocity, and thus van Ackeren, who holds that the term refers uniformly to the act of teaching, and O'Brien, who sees it as a counterpoint to the body of philosophic disciplines taught at Paris, have, in my opinion, restricted the term unduly and not respected the suppleness of Aquinas's account.[4]

---

[1] Indicative of the interest that this topic still holds for modern theologians are the two articles that have appeared recently: Lawrence J. Donohoo, *"Sacra Doctrina," The Thomist* 63 (3; 1999): 343–402; and Brian J. Shanley, *"Sacra Doctrina* and Disclosure," *The Thomist* 61 (2; 1997): 163–88.

[2] Translation by Thomas Gilby in *Saint Thomas Aquinas, Summa Theologiae*, Latin text and English translation, introductions, notes, appendices, glossaries, 60 vol. (London/New York: Blackfriars in Conjunction with Eyre & Spottiswoode/McGraw–Hill, 1964–76). (Henceforth "Blackfriars" followed by volume number and page.) The translation is found on Blackfriars 1:7.

[3] See *Dei Verbum*, 2–6.

[4] Gerald F. van Ackeren, *Sacra Doctrina. The Subject of the First Question of the Summa Theologica of St. Thomas Aquinas* (Rome: Catholic Book Agency, 1952); T. C. O'Brien, " '*Sacra Doctrina*' Revisited: The Context of Medieval Education," *The Thomist* 41 (1977): 475–509. In my understanding of *sacra doctrina* I am following such authors as Yves Congar, "Le moment économique et le moment 'ontologique' dans la *Sacra Doctrina* (Révélation, Théologie, Somme Théologique)," in *Tradition: Mélanges Offertes à M.-D. Chenu* (Paris: Vrin, 1967), 135–88 (especially his opening remarks); and Jean-Pierre Torrell, "Le Savoir Théologique chez Saint Thomas," *Revue Thomiste* 96 (1996): 355–96. Referring to the term *doctrina* itself, Thomas Gilby has this to say: "*Doctrina* which is an analogical term, that is to say it always bears a common meaning variously affected by its situation,

In brief, the term *sacra doctrina* applies to several diverse realities under the aspect of what they have in common, namely the action of "causing someone to know"[5] the truth(s) they need in order to attain the goal God has set for human existence. In the expression "to cause to know" lies a whole theory of how truth is communicated, which is as far removed from our subject-dominated theories of knowledge as it is from the notion of innate ideas or the nominalism that still debilitates much of our contemporary discussion of text and authority. In what follows we will have occasion to note how Thomas's understanding of what it means to teach affects all of what may be called an epistemology of faith.

God's Revelatory Activity as *Sacra Doctrina*

In several contexts Aquinas refers to God's initial and foundational activity of revelation in terms of teaching, that is, *doctrina*. In considering God's activity in our regard we must attend to the two ways in which he teaches, and the two levels at which he teaches. First, let us examine the two ways God can be said to teach. In its widest application, the term *doctrina* refers to the act of imparting knowledge, and by implication the act of receiving it, since if no knowledge is received, none can be said to have been imparted. God imparts knowledge in a twofold manner: first by supplying someone with the light, or the capacity, to understand what is presented, and second by presenting what is to be known. In this second way God acts like a human agent.

On the human level, Aquinas likens the activity of human teaching to that of a doctor or a farmer.[6] A doctor, for instance, ministers to the vital principle of the body and assists its capacity to heal itself. Similarly, a teacher ministers to the capacity of the student's mind for knowledge and, by communication through signs, enables the mind of the student to move from what is known to a grasp of what was previously unknown. Neither the doctor nor the teacher, however, can provide the active and vital principle by which health and knowledge are acquired.

God, on the other hand, as we have said, can supply both the vital principle for the body and the light for the mind, and thus he can be said to heal and to teach in a more profound way than any human being (*ST* 1, 117, ad 1).[7]

implies knowledge generated in a give-and-take, *actio-passio,* of two or more persons mutually engaged in a living movement, and a growing in knowledge on one side." Appendix 5, "*Sacra Doctrina*" Blackfriars 1:58.

[5] Doctrina *est actio ejus qui aliquid cognoscere facit (I Analyt. 1)* cited by Yves Congar, "Tradition et '*Sacra Doctrina*' chez Saint Thomas d'Aquin," in *Église et Tradition,* ed. Johannes Betz and Heinrich Fries (Le Pye/Lyon: Xavier Mappus, 1963), 157–94, at note 10.

[6] For a discussion of Thomas's views on teaching and a list of the principal places where he treats of the subject, see van Ackeren, *Sacra Doctrina,* ch. 2.

[7] Huiusmodi autem rationis lumen quo principia huiusmodi [per se nota] sunt nobis certa, est nobis a Deo inditum, quasi quaedam similitudo increatae veritatis in nobis resultantis. Unde, cum omnis doctrina humana efficaciam habere non potest nisi ex virtute huius

The act by which God confers light on the mind is something unique to him and in this sense only God can teach. Aquinas says of this interior light of reason that it is itself a "certain participation in divine light" (*ST* 1, 12, 11, ad 3); it is, in fact, "nothing else but the imprint of the divine light in us" (*ST* 1–2, 91, 2). In addition, God can also act like a human teacher and minister to the light he himself has supplied, and this is the second way he can be said to teach. Thus, when commenting on the words of Romans 1:19, "God made it [what can be known about him] manifest to them," Aquinas speaks of God's activity in creating as that of a teacher "proposing exterior signs of his wisdom" (Sir 1:10), but also once again "conferring an interior light by which a person actually knows."[8]

Sacra Doctrina and Prophecy:
The Second Level of Divine Teaching

Much of the same terminology that we have seen applied to the natural light of reason, and the exercise of that reason in learning from God through creation, is applied by St. Thomas to *sacra doctrina*. Thus, he says of *sacra doctrina* that it is "a certain imprint of the divine knowledge" (*ST* 1, 1, 3, ad 2). This generation of knowledge is active from the side of God, while in the one who receives, it is generated or passive.[9] Thus, in conferring knowledge through revelation, God acts as a teacher. This is obvious in the case of prophecy, which is a degree of revelation the perfection of which is the beatific vision (*ST* 2–2, 171, 4, ad 2). Prophecy can be a general category, along with apostleship, by which to designate those who received normative revelation at its origin:

> [P]rophecy is a knowledge imprinted by divine revelation *(impressa ex revelatione divina)* on the mind of a prophet, in the form of teaching. Now the truth of knowledge is the same in the disciple as in the master. The disciple's knowledge is, in effect, a reproduction *(similitudo)* of that in the master, just as in things of nature the form of what is generated is a certain likeness of the form of that which generates. (*ST* 2–2, 171, 6c)[10]

It is because of this use of the notion of *doctrina* in connection with prophecy that Pierre Benoit can give the following as a primary and generic description of prophecy:

---

luminis, constat quod solus Deus est qui interius et principaliter docet, sicut natura interius principaliter sanat; nihilominus tamen et sanare et docere proprie dicitur modo predicto [human agency]. *De Veritate* 11, 1c.

[8] *Super Epistulas S. Pauli Lectura* [Rome: Marietti, 1953], *Ad Romanos*, c.1, lect. vi, §116.

[9] *On III Physicorum*, cap. 3, lect. 5 (Leonine ed. II, 113).

[10] Translation by Roland Potter, Blackfriars 45:25.

By "prophecy" St. Thomas understands essentially knowledge, supernaturally given to man, of truths exceeding the present reach of his mind, which God teaches him for the benefit of the community.[11]

There is a parallel at this second, or supernatural, level to the two ways in which God teaches on the natural level. Thomas, speaking about prophecy, appeals to God's power to provide not only what is to be known but also the light by which it is known formally, that is, in a judgment:[12]

> Now by the gift of prophecy something is conferred on the human mind over and above the powers of its natural faculty in both respects, namely in respect of judgment by the infusion of intellectual light *(per influxum luminis intellectualis)*, and in respect of the acceptation or representation of realities which is done through certain species. In this second respect, but not in the first, human teaching *(doctrina)* can be likened to prophetic revelation, for a man furnishes his pupil with realities through word symbols, but he cannot illumine from within as God does. Of these two aspects of knowledge the first is more important *(principalius)* in prophecy: because judgment is the full fruit *(completivum)* of knowledge. *(ST* 2–2, 173, 2c)[13]

Though the light, divinely given, is the principal factor in prophecy, particularly when "prophecy" is equivalent to revelation (see *Summa contra Gentiles* 3, 154), Aquinas maintains that representations of divine realities must also be supplied by God in order that the prophet's mind be rendered able to grasp, according to the nature of his mind, the truth that is being revealed. In this respect, Thomas often quotes the adage of Pseudo-Dionysius: "The divine ray cannot shine upon us except that it be veiled about with a variety of sacred veils."[14] The "variety" referred to can extend from a purely intellectual vision to

---

[11] Paul Synave and Pierre Benoit, *Prophecy and Inspiration: A Commentary on the Summa Theologica II–II, Questions 171–178,* trans. Avery R. Dulles and Thomas L. Sheridan (New York: Desclee, 1961), 60. At one place Aquinas says that broadly speaking, *"omnis supernaturalis influxus ad prophetiam reducitur." (De Veritate* 13, 13c).

[12] It is instructive in this regard to consider how Aquinas describes the two "lights" of faith: "So also in the faith by which we believe in God there is not only the accepting of the object of assent, but something moving us to the assent. This is a kind of light—the habit of faith—divinely imparted to the human mind. It is more capable of causing assent than any demonstration. . . . It is clear, then, that faith comes from God in two ways: by way of an interior light that leads to assent and by way of the realities that are proposed from without and that had as their source divine revelation. In *Boet. De Trin.* 3, 1, ad 4. St. Thomas Aquinas, *Faith, Reason and Theology. Questions I–IV of his Commentary on the De Trinitate of Boethius,* trans. Armand Maurer, Medieval Sources in Translation 32 (Toronto: Pontifical Institute of Medieval Studies, 1987), 69.

[13] Translation basically that of Potter, Blackfriars 45:57.

[14] *The Celestial Hierarchy* 1 *(Patrologia graeca* (ed. J. Migne) [hereafter PG] 3, 121).

images within and without (*ST* 2–2, 174, 3c). This need not imply, however, that all the representations must be miraculously supplied. Thus, images familiar to the prophet may be used, but these must be ordered by the help of a supernatural light if they are to be apt to mediate realities that surpass the human intelligence (*ST* 173, 2, ad 3).

There is kind of prophecy in which there are images but no light by which to understand them (Pharaoh's dreams are an example), and there is prophecy in which there is light, but no new or divinely ordered representations.[15] This second type of prophetic grace exists in those who judge with the certitude of divine truth things that are accessible to human reason, and it is characteristic of those who composed the holy writings "many of whom often spoke of things which can be known by human reason, speaking not on the part of God *(ex persona Dei)* but on their own part *(ex persona propria)* with, however, the help of divine light." (*ST* 2–2, 174, 2 ad 3). Elsewhere Aquinas considers the case of those who not only receive prophecy in the full sense—that is, there is both intellectual (or imaginary) representation and the light to judge it—but who also wrote as well.[16]

Then finally, there is the grace of understanding something revealed to someone else, the most outstanding example of which is the understanding of the Old Testament as this was conferred, upon the apostles by Christ: "He opened their minds to understand the Scriptures" (Lk 24:45). In this latter case, a greater light, that of the resurrection, is shed upon the words and images of the Old Testament and these now yield a meaning they could not have mediated until the glorification of Christ (*ST* 2–2, 173, 2c).[17] Let us pass now to a consideration of how the initial and constitutive action of God in *sacra doctrina* is transmitted.

The Transmission of *Sacra Doctrina*

In this section I wish to consider *sacra doctrina* in action, so to speak, because I think it explains the fascinating expression of Aquinas in article 6 of the first

---

[15] "Divine rays of light [referring to the text of Pseudo-Dionysius just cited] do not enlighten us in this present life without the veils of some or other images—because it is natural to men, in the condition of this life that they cannot understand without images. Sometimes, however, images drawn from the senses in the ordinary fashion are enough, nor is an imaginative vision required that is divinely procured. And so we can speak of prophetic revelation taking place without imaginative vision" (*ST* 2–2 174, 2, ad 4; translation basically that of Potter, Blackfriars 45:77).

[16] *De Veritate* 12, 13c; 12, 14, ad 5. For a discussion of this, see Synave-Benoit, *Prophecy*, 42–44.

[17] Lumen autem intelligibile quandoque—quidem imprimitur menti humanae divinitus ad judicandum ea quae ab aliis visa sunt, sicut dictum est de Joseph et sicut patet de Apostolis, quibus Dominus "aperuit sensum ut intelligerent Scripturas ut dicitur Lc 24:45, et ad hoc pertinet "interpretatio sermonum" [Aquinas is alluding to 1 Cor 12:10, but this is not really applicable].

question of the *Summa theologiae* where he contrasts that manner of judging divine things that is proper to the gift of the Holy Spirit with that manner that "pertains to this doctrine *(doctrina)* in so far as *(secundum quod)* it is obtained through study *(studium)* though its principles are obtained from revelation" *(ST* 1, 1, 6, ad 3). I take this to mean that though there are aspects of *sacra doctrina* that are not part of that wisdom, which is a gift of the Holy Spirit, there obviously is no opposition between the two.[18] In fact, though Aquinas has principally in mind that activity that we call today "theology," we must advert to the fact that *sacra doctrina* is teaching at its very origin through its successive and varied stages of transmission in the Church. Thus *studium,* or the application of the mind, characterizes all its aspects, though the human component is more prominent in some of these aspects than others. The *studium* spoken of by Aquinas is not exclusively that of the professional theologian, but that of the believer who uses his mind to receive revelation: "The act of faith essentially consists in an act of knowing. . . ."[19] This is especially true of the one who must so understand revelation as to be able to transmit it. This is the work of both prophet and teacher who must communicate what they have learned: "God reveals for this reason—that it be made known to others."[20]

This process of divinely sustained *studium* in the transmission of revelation is described by Aquinas in the following terms:

> After the level of those who receive revelation directly from God, another level of grace is necessary. Because men receive revelation from God not only for their own time but also for the instruction of all who come after them, it was necessary that the things revealed to them be passed on not only in speech to their contemporaries but also as written down for the instruction of those to come after them. And thus it was also necessary that there be those who could interpret what was written down. This also must be done by divine grace. And so we read in Genesis 40:8, "Does not interpretation come from God?"[21]

The notion that the interpretation of Scripture is a grace that belongs to the order of prophecy is frequently repeated by St. Thomas. Thus, we read:

---

18 "Wisdom is not contrasted with science as though they were opposed to each other, but because wisdom adds an additional note to science." In *Boet. De Trin.* 2, 2 ad 1, in *Faith, Reason and Theology. Questions I–IV of his Commentary on the De Trinitate of Boethius,* Medieval Sources in Translation, 32 (Toronto: Pontifical Institute of Medieval Studies, 1987), 42.

19 "The act of faith essentially consists in an act of knowing that is its formal or specific perfection; this is clear from what its object is." *De Veritate* 14, 2, ad 10. Translation is that of T. C. O'Brien in Blackfriars 31:208, n. 14. See also 1–2, 110, 4.

20 *On 1 Cor 14, lectio IV,* Marietti ed. §812.

21 *Summa contra Gentiles* 3, 154.

They are also called prophets in the New Testament who expound the prophetic sayings because Sacred Scripture is interpreted in the same Spirit in which it is composed.[22]

How Writing and Rewriting Enter into the Transmission Process

Writing, therefore, plays an essential part in the transmission of *sacra doctrina*. Though he was not reflexively aware of the particular properties of a written text as opposed to an oral text, what Walter Ong calls "the new world of autonomous discourse,"[23] Aquinas understood the normativity conferred upon communication through writing. But then, the authors of the sacred texts also understood this and exploited the potential of those written texts that had been given authority as they composed their own. This is undoubtedly true of the authors of the Synoptic Gospels regardless of what order we may consider them to have been written, and it is true of the Old Testament authors as well. I would like to give one brief example of this typically biblical style of composition, which consists in alluding to a previous authoritative text in order to further the revelation it mediates. While examples such as the rewriting of Second Samuel to Second Kings in the Books of Chronicles have long been considered, the widespread presence of this procedure has become the object of recent study.[24] In that light I wish to reflect on the process by which the promise of an eschatological outpouring of the Spirit was transmitted in the sacred Tradition by successive prophets who, through divine light applied to their studium, were able to create a development of doctrine.

An Example of *Studium* and the Interpenetration of Scripture and Tradition

My example is from the prophetic literature and the promise of a new covenant that began with Jeremiah. Jeremiah must have reflected much about Israel's radical incapacity to keep its covenant with YHWH. Probably basing himself on the Deuteronomic tradition concerning the need for a divinely circumcised heart (Dt 10:16; 30:5–6), he realized by a prophetic revelation that God would have to do still more and impress upon the heart itself the power by which

---

[22] *Ad Romanos* (on Rom 12:8) Marietti ed. §978. For the background of this principle, see Ignace de la Potterie, "Interpretation of Holy Scripture in the Spirit in Which It Was Written," in *Vatican II: Assessment and Perspectives. I*, ed. René Latourelle (New York: Paulist, 1988), 220–66.

[23] Walter Ong, *Orality and Literacy. The Technologizing of the Word* (New York: Methuen & Co., 1982). The phrase is found on p. 78.

[24] For a good example of this type of study, see Michael Fishbane, *Biblical Interpretation in Ancient Israel* (Oxford: Clarendon, 1985).

Israel could respond to him. The heart, and not stone, must be the place where God's law is written to become itself the very principle of obedience, and this would mean a new covenant. He thus prophesied, in the most daring terms, a new covenant that would enable God's people to have its power within them.

Some years later, Ezekiel, a younger contemporary of Jeremiah who knew his prophecies, perhaps even in written form, took this promise a step further by identifying the interior law with the very life breath, the Spirit, of God. To use an Augustinian phrase, Ezekiel "pondered with assent,"[25] the text of Jeremiah; his was a faith seeking understanding. His mind was raised by the divine light to understand and penetrate the revelation given to his elder fellow prophet. The symbolic mediation of Jeremiah, his *sacra doctrina*, became the means by which God instructed Ezekiel and enabled him to move to a further conclusion concerning God's remedy for Israel's infidelity.

It was probably about 200 years later than Ezekiel when another prophet was considering a weakened Israel, the prey of marauders, invaders, and slave traders. He had at his disposal the two prophetic texts we have just considered. In addition he knew of the expression "to pour out the spirit" since it is found in Ezekiel 39:29 and repeated in Isaiah 32:15 and 44:3–5 always as an expression of that moment when God would make good on all he had promised his people. This prophet knew as well of the incident recorded in Numbers 11:24–30 in which God took some of the spirit he had conferred on Moses his prophet and shared it with others. On that occasion Moses had exclaimed: "Would that all the people of YHWH [note the covenant terminology] were prophets. Would that YHWH put his spirit upon them!" (Nm 11:29). In the famous text of Joel quoted at Pentecost (Joel 2:28–32 [Heb 3:1–5]; Acts 2:17–21), we have an example in which we see how the sacred tradition was formed. The prophet sought to understand what the *sacra doctrina* of his predecessors would reveal to him of God and his plan of salvation. Aquinas's description of how the message was pronounced orally and then written down is oversimplified in most cases, but the basic principle of the interaction between prophetic light and *studium* is quite apposite.

It is interesting to observe how the same process of pondering sacred texts and alluding to them continued in Israel. This created a trajectory, bringing an understanding of what was revealed to a sharper focus, and it was this "focused" understanding that ministered to the New Testament. In the particular instance of the "new covenant" and the "outpouring of the Holy Spirit," there were no canonically incorporated developments, though we do find at Qumran allusions to the prophecies we have just considered in such phrases as: "cleansing him with the spirit of holiness. . . . He will sprinkle over him the spirit of truth like lustral

---

[25] *De Praedestinatione Sanctorum Liber ad Prosperum et Hilarium Primus,* 2 (*Patrologia Latina* 44, 963). See Aquinas's discussion of this expression in *ST* 2–2, 2, 1.

water. . . ."[26] This outlook most probably stood behind the Baptist's prophecy that the one to come would perform in Spirit what he was doing in water.

I have adduced this example of the manner in which what we call "Scripture" and "Tradition" were intimately intertwined in the process of forming the canonical Scriptures. The New Testament manner of dealing with the Old Testament, which was often in the form of allusive rewriting, was continued in the patristic writers, those whom Aquinas calls *sancti*. This was accomplished not so much by rewriting a text considered sacred but by prolonging and extending the prophetic contemplation of the mystery of Christ through the lens of the Old Testament. In this sense the Fathers did not so much comment on a text as continue its power in the community by allowing it to touch the hearts of the people. With this in mind we should look more directly at Aquinas's understanding of the authority of *Sacra Scriptura*.

Sacra Scriptura[27] *Writing and interpreting are parts of sacra doctrina.*

For Aquinas, as we have seen, writing the prophetic message and interpreting its written expression prophetically are essential parts of *sacra doctrina* and they involve the active use of the mind even while taking place under the aegis of divine grace. I would like to consider now the relation between the canonical Scriptures and *sacra doctrina*. First let us consider the way in which St. Thomas confers on Sacred Scripture a unique role in *sacra doctrina*.

> Our faith rests on the revelation made to the Prophets and Apostles who wrote the canonical books, not on a revelation, if such there be, made to any other teacher (*ST* 1, 1, 8, ad 2).

Yves Congar notes the fact that in the thirteenth century the term *Sacra Scriptura* had become a current designation for the canonical scriptures, the panoply of accompanying patristic and magisterial interpretations and even the canonical and theological teaching of the day. St. Thomas, however, clearly prefers to avoid this manner of speaking and employs *sacra doctrina* in the way we have already observed and most often uses *Sacra Scriptura* when he wishes to

---

[26] 1 QS 4, 21. Most of the material relevant to this theme of the Spirit is referred to in my study, "Le baptême dans l'Esprit; tradition du Nouveau Testament et vie de l'Eglise," *Nouvelle Revue Théologique* 106 (1984): 23–58 (English translation, *Baptism in the Holy Spirit. A Scriptural Foundation* [Steubenville, OH: Franciscan University Press, 1986]). For a study of how the text itself continued to be rewritten, see Emmanuel Tov, "The Exodus Section of 4Q422," *Dead Sea Discoveries* 1 (1994): 197–209.

[27] For a careful analysis of St. Thomas's theory and practice in regard to the authority of Scripture, see Wilhemus G. B. M. Valkenberg, *Did Not Our Heart Burn? Place and Function of Holy Scripture in the Theology of St. Thomas Aquinas*, Publications of the Thomas Instituut de Utrecht 3 (The Hague: Gegevens Koninklijke Bibliotheek, 1990).

refer to the canonical text.[28] This makes all the more significant the manner in which he can treat these two terms as in some respects interchangeable. Here are some examples:[29]

> [Singular realities are transmitted in *sacra doctrina*] in order to proclaim the authority of the men through whom divine revelation has come down to us, which revelation is the basis of Sacred Scripture or doctrine *(Sacra Scriptura seu doctrina)*. *(ST* 1, 1, 2, ad 2)
> *Sacra doctrina* should be declared a single science . . . now since *Sacra Scriptura* looks at all things in that they are divinely revealed . . . all things that are able to be divinely revealed *(revelabilia)* share in the same formal object of this science. And therefore they are included under *sacra doctrina* as under a single science. *(ST* 1, 1, 3c)
> *Sacra doctrina* is divided into the old law and the new law. *(ST* 1, 1, 4, obj 2)
> *Sacra Scriptura* argues on the basis of those truths held by revelation which the opponent admits. . . . *(ST* 1, 1, 8c)
> The theology which is transmitted in *Sacra Scriptura* . . . the theology of *Sacra Scriptura*. (In Boethius, *De Trinitate* 5, 4)

There are, however, two differences between *sacra doctrina* and *Sacra Scriptura*, and in this sense though they are used interchangeably they are not completely synonymous. First, *Sacra Scriptura* in its restricted sense signifies the canonical Scriptures and it is only of these that one can say that "their authority is the foundation of faith *(ST* 3, 55, 5c),[30] or that our faith "rests on the Sacred Scriptures" *(Summa contra Gentiles* 4, 29),[31] or again, that God is "the author of Sacred Scripture" *(ST* 1, 1, 10c). Secondly, *sacra doctrina*, which includes revelation and the writing of *Sacra Scriptura*, extends to all that mental activity or *studium* that looks to the articles of faith as to the principles of its functioning. This characteristic of *sacra doctrina*, as Aquinas considers it, can throw some light on our modern understanding of "Scripture" and "Tradition."

To discuss this, I will proceed briefly in three steps. First, I will consider what Thomas means by *auctoritas*; then I will look at the unique *auctoritas* of Scripture, and, third, I will consider the *auctoritas* of the articles of faith, which, because they are not "added to Scripture but drawn from Scripture" *(ST* 2–2, 1,9,

---

28 Yves Congar, "Tradition et *'Sacra Doctrina'*," 166–67.

29 I am indebted in this section to the work of Per Erik Persson, *Sacra Doctrina: Reason and Revelation in Aquinas,* trans. Ross MacKenzie (Oxford: Blackwell, 1970).

30 Probavit autem eis [discipulis] resurrectionem suam per auctoritatem sacrae Scripturae quae est fidei fundamentum cum dixit (Lc 24:44).

31 This latter notion, most often with the very biblical understanding of faith as something that "rests" or "leans on" *(innititur)* upon the word of God, is frequently found in Aquinas: ex. gr. *ST* 2–2, 4, 8, ad 3; 110, 3, ad 1.

ad 1), partake of some of the unique causality of *Sacra Scriptura*. This last consideration touches on the topic of tradition and the development of doctrine.

Auctoritas

Auctoritas derives from *auctor* (cause, initiator, sponsor, promoter, surety), which derives from the verb *augere* (to increase [transitive and intransitive], to enrich). *Auctoritas* first designated a surety in a transaction, responsibility for a child, or the weight of an opinion.[32] The root *aug*, thus implies a certain initiative, a causality or ability to effect something, be this an objective reality, legal responsibility, knowledge, or even confidence. The attribution of *auctoritas* to a person leads easily to considering the person himself as an authority, and finally, in case of texts, what the person writes is considered an *auctoritas*. In medieval theology the word *auctoritas* very often means a text; thus an expression such as *auctoritas Augustini* means "this text of Augustine which bears his authority." It should be noted, however, that even in this case the statement of Augustine is invoked because of its capacity to witness to an aspect of faith and thus lead to faith knowledge.

One of the great dilemmas of medieval theology was that of reconciling conflicting *auctoritates* precisely because they were looked upon not merely as conflicting verbal expressions but as symbolic communications leading the recipient to grasp the truth. Our modern practice of comparing texts merely on the basis of their words, our own form of nominalism, was foreign to the pre-Ockham epistemology of the early medieval period. In fact Aquinas himself offers a very sophisticated hermeneutic governing the reading of patristic texts, which, because of their verbal dissonance with received doctrine, must be "reverently expounded."[33] For Thomas, the intention of the author is not a psychological consideration, what "he was trying to say," but, an epistemological consideration, what his mind intended of revealed being. Thus, in the light of a better intention his word may be corrected. This simple principle is as valid in faith as in any other knowledge. Aquinas, speaking of an act of faith, says:

> Such an act [of faith] does not have a proposition as its term, but a reality, since just as with scientific knowledge, so also with faith, the only reason

---

[32] See Waldemar Molinski, "Authority," in *Sacramentum Mundi 1*, ed. Karl Rahner et al. (New York: Herder & Herder, 1968), 129–33; and most especially Marie-Dominique Chenu, "'Authentica et 'Magistralia'. Deux lieux théologiques aux XII–XIII siècles," *Divus Thomas* (Piacenza) Series 3, 2 (1925): 257–85.

[33] For a more complete treatment of this point, one may consult, in addition to the article mentioned in the preceding note, Marie-Dominique Chenu, *Toward Understanding Saint Thomas,* trans. A.-M. Landry and D. Hughes (Chicago: Regnery, 1964); "The Technical Handling of Authorities," 139–49.

for formulating a proposition is that we may have knowledge about the real. (*ST* 2–2, 1, 2, ad 2)[34]

The *Auctoritas* of Scripture

Commenting on 2 Timothy 3:16, Aquinas asks why only the Scriptures should be considered divinely inspired since, according to Ambrose, "anything true, by no matter whom said, is from the Holy Spirit." His response is that God works in two ways, one that is immediate and this pertains to him alone; such as is the case with miracles, and one that is mediate, that is through the mediation of lesser causes, as is the case with natural operations. He then says: "And thus in man God instructs the intellect both immediately through the sacred letters and mediately through other writings."[35] This is not a chance expression. St. Thomas often attributes a unique causality *(auctoritas)* to Scripture. In commenting on Pseudo-Dionysius' treatise *On the Divine Names*, he says:

> Dionysius, in his teaching *(doctrina)* depends upon *(innititur)* the authority of Sacred Scripture which has strength and power *(roborem habet et virtutem)* because the Apostles and Prophets were moved to speak by the Holy Spirit who was revealing to them and speaking in them.[36]

Again, when commenting on Hebrews 5:12–14 where the audience is told that they need someone to teach them again the "oracles" *(logiōn/sermonum)* of God, and that they need milk not solid food, Aquinas says:

> For *sacra doctrina* is food and drink because it nourishes (potat) and satisfies the soul. The other sciences only enlighten the mind, this one, however enlightens the soul. . . . This is a characteristic of the teaching of Sacred Scripture *(doctrina sacrae Scripturae)* that in it not only speculative things are handed on but also those that are to be practiced through activity *(approbanda per affectum)*.[37]

The notion that *Sacra Scriptura* is a unique part of *sacra doctrina* is a solid part of the tradition that St. Thomas is summing up. Henri de Lubac expresses that same tradition by saying:

> Scripture is not only divinely guaranteed, it is divinely true. The Spirit did not only dictate it; he is, as it were, contained in it. He inhabits it. His

---

[34] Translation by O'Brien, Blackfriars 31:13.
[35] *In 1 Tim 3,* lect. 3 (Marietti ed. §812).
[36] *De Divinis Nominibus* ch. 1, lect.1.
[37] *On Hebrews* ch. 5. lect. 2 (Marietti, §§267 and 273).

breath perpetually animates it. The Scripture is "made fruitful by a miracle of the Holy Spirit." It is "full of the Spirit."[38]

Because of this, tradition saw the words of the Scripture, particularly those
of the Gospels, as being the "body of Christ." The originator of this concept
was Origen whose views are also summed up by de Lubac:

> In the letter of Scripture, the Logos is not incarnated properly so called in
> the way he is in the humanity of Jesus . . . nevertheless, he is truly incorpo-
> rated there, he himself dwells there and not only some idea about him. . . .[39]

To speak of the Scriptures as the temple of the Holy Spirit or as being "animated by the Spirit of Christ," or as the body of Christ is an attempt to provide
a basis for and to articulate a common Christian experience, namely, that the
words of Scripture exercise a unique kind of causality in that activity by which
God teaches us here and now. About no other text is it said in the same way that
it is the word of God, no other text receives the same liturgical honors, no other
text is spoken about in the way that scripture is described.

There is a way, then, in which the *auctoritas* of *Sacra Scriptura* is unique. It
can cause knowledge immediately and, possessed of a unique power, it can have
a referential function that brings us into contact with the divine realities themselves in a way that exceeds other faith formulations.[40] Nevertheless, as human
communication in a community of human beings, it also has the authority of a
public statement that cannot be contradicted, mediating as it does the "revelation made to the Prophets and Apostles who wrote the canonical books." This is
an important dimension of *auctoritas* since, if it can be shown that an opinion is
not in keeping with what is taught in Scripture, that opinion must be rejected as
not in keeping with faith. The Scriptures, therefore, can serve as a norm as well
as a light. A decision regarding the correctness of an opinion cannot, however,
be made merely on the basis of verbal divergence from the text; there must

---

[38] Henri de Lubac, *Exégèse Médiéval. Les Quatres Sens de l'Écriture* (Théologie, 41), Part I
(Paris: Aubier, 1959), 129. The texts quoted in the text are from Anselem, *De concord* 3,
6 (*PL* 158, 528B) and Origen, *De Princ.* 4, 1, 7, respectively. I am indebted for this reference to the unpublished dissertation of Marcellino D'Ambrosio, "Henri de Lubac and
the Recovery of the Traditional Hermeneutic" (Catholic University of America, 1991),
147–48.

[39] *Histoire et Esprit: l'intelligence de l'Écriture d'après Origène* (Théologie, 16) (Paris: Aubier,
1950), 347. Translation by D'Ambrosio, op. cit. 180. The same notion is developed by
Hans Urs von Balthasar, *The Glory of the Lord: A Theological Aesthetics,* trans. Erasmo
Leiva-Merikakis, vol. I. *Seeing the Form* (San Francisco: Ignatius, 1982), 32, 529, 541.

[40] In using the word "referential" in this context, I am alluding to a statement of the Pontifical Biblical Commission in its *Bible et Christologie* (Paris: Cerf, 1984), 1.2.2.1: "The
"auxiliary" languages used in the course of Church's history do not have for faith the same
authority *(auctoritas/valeur)* as the "referential language used by the sacred authors. . . ."

always be some understanding of what the Scriptures are actually saying. As Martin Luther said: "The one who does not understand the realities cannot draw the meaning out of the words."[41]

Authenticating Tradition

We thus come upon the difficult question, one that faces us acutely today, of judging whether and to what degree teaching that belongs to the customary life of the Church is actually authored by the word of God. This problem was treated in the recent Lutheran–Catholic Dialogue and was recognized as an unresolved issue.[42] While in no way pretending that I can completely solve here this intricate question, I would like to point to the manner in which, for Aquinas, faith as a way of knowing is likened to the knowledge that results from the first principles of reason, and that recourse to these principles as received and pondered within the Church can help us in elaborating criteria for the legitimate development of doctrine. This will require a brief consideration of our third point, the articles of faith.

The Articles of Faith and the Criteria of Tradition[43]

The notion that the light of faith is to the principles of faith as the light of reason is to its first principles, the light in both cases making the principles *per se nota*, is a commonplace in Aquinas, who defines an article of faith as "a perception of divine truth that leads us to that truth itself (*ST* 2–2, 1, 6, *sed contra*).[44] The following text is particularly apposite:

> It is clear, then, that faith comes from God in two ways: by way of an interior light that leads to assent, and by way of the realities that are proposed from without and that had as their source divine revelation. These are related to the knowledge of faith as the things perceived by the senses are

---

[41] Tischreden, Weimarer Ausgabe, 5, 26, n. 5246.

[42] See Harold C. Skillrud, J. Francis Stafford, and Daniel F. Martensen, eds., *Scripture and Tradition, Lutherans and Catholics in Dialogue IX* (Minneapolis: Augsburg, 1995), especially #45.

[43] For a more complete treatment of this topic as related to the articles of faith, see Torrell, "Le Savoir Théologique," especially 377–85.

[44] *Perceptio divinae veritatis tendens in ipsam*. Aquinas attributes the definition to St. Isidore, but O'Brien (Blackfriars 31:28) assures us that it is not found in Isidore's works. That Aquinas himself agrees with this definition is witnessed to by the fact that he earlier used it without any attribution (*In 3 Sent.* d. 25, q. 1, a. 1, qa 1, obj 4). For another description of an article of faith see *ST* 2–2, 6, 1c: "[T]he object of faith is something unseen about the divine. Consequently there is a particular article of faith wherever there is something being unseen for some distinct reason. . . ." We may note that Aquinas gives here as examples various mysteries of the life of Christ. For other examples of descriptions of an article, see, *Sent III*, d. 25, q. 1, a. 1, sol 1; In 1 Cor 15, lect. 1 (Marietti ed. §896).

related to the knowledge of principles, for both make our knowledge certain. So just as the knowledge of principles is taken from the senses, and yet the light by which principles are known is inborn, so "faith comes from hearing" (Rom 10:17), and nevertheless the habit of faith is infused.[45]

The proximate criterion, therefore, of judging the authenticity of a doctrinal position or pastoral practice is its being contained in an article of faith, bearing in mind that the articles of faith are drawn from Scripture and are articulated whenever there is a particular aspect of divine truth that is being revealed. In this sense, the birth, death, and resurrection of Christ are separate articles (*ST* 2–2, 1, 6c). There are two ways in which this quality of being potentially part of an article of faith can be determined. One is by comparing what is alleged as tradition with the articles by a process that follows the laws of human thinking *(studium)*. Once again, however, this is not merely or even principally the application of logic to propositions, but rather a perception of how the two realities being compared are connected to each other: "God wills that something be because of something else, but it is not for the sake of the second reality that he wills the first" (*ST* 1, 19, 5c).[46] Thus, it is a matter of perceiving the relation between realities by the use of reason enlightened by faith but not of drawing conclusions from texts.[47] It is quite permissible to employ the results of sound philosophy in this endeavor, not as a ruling principle but as providing human insight that can be taken up into revelation:

> Those who use the work of the philosophers in sacred doctrine by bringing that work of the human mind into the service of faith, do not mix water with wine, but rather change water into wine.[48]

The second manner is by a contemplative capacity to rest in the reality mediated by its articulation and see in it all that it contains. We have seen that faith penetrating into the realities that are revealed enables these realities themselves to be the cause of knowledge. The articles of faith are enunciated in words, but it is not the proposition but the reality mediated by the proposition

---

[45] St. Thomas Aquinas, "In Boet. De Trin.," 3, 1, ad 4 in *Faith, Reason and Theology. Questions I–IV of his Commentary on the De Trinitate of Boethius,* Medieval Sources in Translation, 32 (Toronto: Pontifical Institute of Medieval Studies, 1987), 69.

[46] *Vult ergo [Deus] hoc esse propter hoc, sed non propter hoc vult hoc.* For a discussion of this text and its possible relation to the teaching of Vatican I on how reason, enlightened by faith, can arrive at an understanding of divine mysteries, see Torrell, "Le Savoir," 37–38.

[47] "Yet it must always be remembered that the assent to these other truths, the various material objects of faith, presupposes the formal object as providing the authenticating force for the assent." (Brian J. Shanley, "*Sacra Doctrina* and Disclosure," *The Thomist* 61, no. 2 [1997]: 163–88, at 174–75 with a citation from *ST* 2–2, 1, 1c).

[48] *In Boet. de Trin* 2, 4, ad 5 (Maurer, 50).

that, as an imprint of the divine knowledge, has the energy to lead the mind to judge of those things that are presented to it. It is in this sense that Yves Congar can speak of a Christian gnosis:

> As long as the human race lasts, there must correspond to that perfect act which God posited once and for all in giving the Scripture to men, an activity on God's part by which he confers upon them a growing understanding of the meaning and content of his Word. . . .
>
> The result of this divine action is the understanding of the text. The Greek Fathers, in this connection, spoke of gnosis. St. Paul asked that his faithful hearers should be filled with gnosis: he himself professed to have received this gift. By it he meant a rich and living knowledge of God's plan, the "mystery" of Christ.[49]

This theological function, while it is an act of the mind, pertains more to what Aquinas calls *intellectus* than to that of *ratio*: "That which is supreme in our knowledge is not reason, but *intellectus* which is the source of reason." (*Summa contra Gentiles* 1, 57).[50] This intuition into divine reality can only be realized imperfectly in this life. The authoritative assertion, therefore, that something is really contained in the Scriptures and the articles of faith belongs to those who are in apostolic succession and in union with each other according to the order willed by Christ. This is what is meant by the magisterium, the third of the three interrelated aspects of *sacra doctrina* as described in *Dei Verbum* 9–10:

> For Sacred Scripture is the word of God inasmuch as it is consigned to writing under the inspiration of the divine Spirit, while sacred tradition takes the word of God entrusted by Christ the Lord and the Holy Spirit to the Apostles, and hands it on to their successors in its full purity, so that led by the light of the Spirit of truth, they may in proclaiming it preserve this word of God faithfully, explain it, and make it more widely known. . . .
>
> It is clear, therefore, that sacred tradition, Sacred Scripture and the teaching authority of the Church, in accord with God's most wise design, are so linked and joined together that one cannot stand without the others, and that all together and each in its own way under the action of the one Holy Spirit contribute effectively to the salvation of souls.

---

[49] *Tradition and Traditions: An Historical Essay and a Theological Essay,* trans. Michael Naseby and Thomas Rainborough (New York: MacMillan, 1967), 387–88.

[50] Translation in Marie-Dominique Chenu, *Toward Understanding Saint Thomas,* 197, n. 60. See also *In III Sent.* d. 35, q. 1, a. 3, sol 2: *Intellectus est rationis principium et terminus.* As is well known, Pierre Rouselot developed this distinction in St. Thomas; see John M. McDermott, *Love and Understanding: The Relation of Will and Intellect in Pierre Rousselot's Christological Vision, Analecta Gregoriana 229* (Rome: Universtà Gregoriana, 1983).

Such a faith vision is the basis for Thomas's position, expressed in many ways, that "The formal objective of faith is the First Truth as this is made known *(manifestatur)* in Sacred Scripture and in the teaching of the Church which proceeds from the First Truth." Or again in the same question, "Faith adheres to all the articles of faith because of one reason *(medium)*, namely because of the First Truth proposed to us in the Scriptures understood rightly according to the teaching of the Church *(secundum doctrinam Ecclesiae)*." (*ST* 2–2, 5, 3c and ad 2). And to cite but one more text: "The formal role *(ratio)* of object in faith is the First Truth made known through the teaching of the Church" (Disputed Question, *De Caritate* 13, ad 6).[51]

It is clear that *sacra doctrina* as it exists in the Church is made up of hearing the symbolic transmission of revelation and also the infused habit of faith, which is "more capable of causing assent than any demonstration."[52] In other words, *doctrina* involves not only the pure light, which is a share in God's knowledge of himself, but also the human activity or *studium* of assimilating and articulating the divine truths according to our mode of knowing. This is the greatness and the fragility of *sacra doctrina* and its Scripture: It is the word of God in the flesh of human thought processes and words. If we ask how the prophetic word from God, that word he spoke once and for all in his Son at this, the end of the ages (see Heb 1:1–4), is to be preserved in the Church, the answer is twofold: It is to be given a written and normative *expressio*, which in turn requires the *epiklēsis* of the Spirit in order to impress itself upon the minds and souls of its hearers.

Tradition is precisely that witness of the Spirit who makes the saving death and resurrection of Christ, transmitted in the written expression of prophecy and proclamation, come alive (see 1 Jn 5:6). The Church in its preaching and safeguarding of the word is the place of the Spirit's witness. Thus, it is part of *sacra doctrina* that there be a permanent and recognizable prophetic authority who can discern and declare the witness of the Spirit. In the Catholic understanding, as is well known, that authority resides in the body of bishops who unite themselves to that one among them who has succeeded Peter.

St. Thomas insists on the need for an abiding presence of prophetic light for the understanding of Scripture and equally insists that our faith rests on "the First Truth as this is made known in Sacred Scripture and in the teaching of the Church which proceeds from the First Truth." In our search for a modern criteriology of faith, we may perhaps find in the manner in which the Second Vatican Council proceeded an example of how the Tradition was discerned in the light of the First Truth, and taught in a way that freed it from viewpoints

---

[51] An aspect of faith not treated in this study is that Christ himself as *"auctor doctrinae,"* both as God, the First Truth and as man, the privileged manifestation of that truth. See Congar, "Tradition," 173–74.

[52] See note above.

and practices that were not in keeping with revelation. The key word in this process is recognition. For almost a century before the Council some scholars had looked in a fresh way at the teaching of Scripture and the manner in which this teaching was passed on by the Liturgy and the preachers and teachers of the early centuries. Little by little, because of the faith that was in them, they "recognized" the *sacra doctrina* of these witnesses for what it was. The work of these theologians was in turn recognized as authentic by the bishops gathered at the Council who then made the teaching of these *magistri* a part of *sacra doctrina*. The whole process involved *studium* and the light of faith "which rests on the First Truth as the medium of its assent" (*ST* 2–2, 1, 1c).

Conclusion

Sacra doctrina, the whole sweep of divine teaching and divinely sustained transmission of that teaching, includes in its heart a written witness to and presence of the revealing and life-giving action of God in his Son Jesus Christ. The authoring quality of that written dimension of the word of God is such that it has a unique sacramental ability to impress immediately upon the soul of the believers the manifold action of God by which he saves us by joining us to himself now and by leading us to eternal beatitude. Again, the authority of Sacred Scripture lies in its capacity as a public ongoing witness to the truth of the Gospel message that sustains the preaching of those who have succeeded to the apostles and have the grace to maintain their witness in the Church. The practical procedures by which this apostolic preaching is authenticated need to be spelled out more completely and ecumenically. But the teaching of Aquinas on the active role of the Holy Spirit conferring on all the light by which *sacra doctrina* is truly sacred and its *Sacra Scriptura* endowed with unique authority must stand as a permanent witness to the way we must work to establish these norms.

2 Literary Theory, Philosophy of History, and Exegesis

AS THE TITLE INDICATES, this is an exegetical work that self-consciously employs literary analysis and theory as well as the philosophy of history, both in a dialogue with Paul Ricoeur, to expound the text. The heart of the study is the attention paid to the literary structure and movement of Mark's text. This is then reflected upon in the light of extra-literary principles.

• • •

ANYONE familiar with the present state of biblical studies is aware that there is a significant shift on the part of many scholars away from the historical critical method as it was practiced earlier toward methods that are based upon various theories of literature.[1] Criteria for judging the aptitude of either the historical or literary method are often established on the basis of their practical effectiveness in "yielding a meaning," particularly one that seems to serve the believing community. The difficulty with such an approach is that the philosophical principles latent in the underlying the various methods are not examined directly and are thus left to function unquestioned while the debate centers on results.

The purpose of this chapter is modest: It is to reflect critically on a concrete work of exegesis in order to see how exegesis actually proceeds or might proceed. I also wish to question some of the unexpressed epistemological principles that often operate in what biblical scholars do. Taking as a model those historians who

---

A previous version of this chapter originally appeared as "Literary Theory, Philosophy of History and Exegesis," *The Thomist* 52 (1988): 575–604.

[1] For a description of more profound aspects of this shift, see J. P. Martin, "Toward a Post-Critical Paradigm," *New Testament Studies* 33 (1987): 370–85.

have reflected philosophically on what it means to "do" history, I wish in a similar manner to reflect on what it means to "do" exegesis. Such an undertaking, it is hoped, will advance the dialogue between systematic theology and exegesis and indicate further avenues to be explored. We have arrived at a moment when it is in the interest of both disciplines to have a clearer notion of how to assess the results of biblical study.

It is becoming increasingly obvious that the central issue in biblical studies is not method as such, though discussion of what is called historical critical method, the literary method, and so on will always have its place. The core problem is that of developing a theology of human communication. This will be a theology that learns from the philosophy of language and literature and yet derives its primary lessons from the unique communication that each theologian experiences in his or her personal contact with the biblical text.

The work done by Paul Ricoeur in the field of the philosophy of language and literature can provide a point of departure in the elaboration of such a theology of communication. In addition to reflecting philosophically on many aspects of human communication, Ricoeur has expressed himself from time to time on the relation of his philosophy to biblical issues. Thus, in his essay, "Toward a Hermeneutic of the Idea of Revelation,"[2] Ricoeur speaks of biblical hermeneutic as being "one regional hermeneutic within a general hermeneutic and a unique hermeneutic that is joined to philosophy as its organon."[3] In discussing the expression of dependence without heteronomy, at the conclusion of his essay, Ricoeur goes on to say:

> . . . the experience of testimony can only provide the horizon for a specifically religious and biblical experience of revelation, without our ever being able to derive that experience from the philosophical categories of truth as manifestation and reflection as testimony.[4]

These statements, as we can easily recognize, touch upon key dimensions of the problem facing us as we attempt to locate the human communication of the Scriptures in the context of revelation. The question is that of the presence of the unique existing within the common. It is the fact that the particular and irreducible nature of the biblical witness is necessarily made in language common to all. Scripture directs itself, not to a remote and privileged sphere of "religion," but rather to the marketplace where human thoughts about existence jostle one another in a desire to be heard:

---

[2] Paul Ricoeur, "Toward a Hermeneutic of the Idea of Revelation" in *Essays in Biblical Interpretation*, ed. L. Mudge (Philadelphia: Fortress, 1980), 73–118. See, in addition, "Naming God," *Union Seminary Quarterly Review* 34 (1979): 215–27.

[3] Ricoeur, "Toward a Hermeneutic," 104.

[4] Ibid., 117.

Wisdom cries aloud in the street,
in the open squares she raises her voice.
Down the crowded ways she calls out,
at the city gates she utters her words:
"How long, you simple ones, will you love inanity,
how long will you turn away at my reproof?
Lo! I will pour out to you my spirit,
I will acquaint you with my words." (Prov 1:20–23)

Revelation, to use the expression of Walter Kasper, is a "prophetic interpretation of reality."[5] The testimony of the Scriptures makes not only meaning claims, but truth claims. It professes to portray the true perspective on reality, and this in a way that is binding on all and not merely meaningful to some. Such a witness gives a strong affirmative answer to the question posed by Jean Nabert: "Do we have the right to invest one moment of history with an absolute characteristic?"[6] It is to Paul Ricoeur's credit that he takes this answer seriously. He seeks to find a way between the pretensions of a philosophy that would arrogate to itself a false autonomy, and the pretensions of the "auxiliary language" of second-order faith statements to have exhausted the content of the "referential language" of the Scriptures.[7] Gary Comstock, in a recent study, compared this aspect of Ricoeur's contribution to that of Hans Frei.[8]

I think it is true to say that more work has been done in philosophy and philosophical theology than in exegesis in the attempt to see exactly how the uniqueness of the biblical witness actually communicates in and through common language. This situation dictates the approach I wish to take here. I will begin with the exegesis of a specific and important passage of the New Testament, the text of Mark that presents Jesus' moment of decision before his Passion (Mk 14:32–42). I wish then to reflect on how the exegesis undertaken is clarified by and in turn modifies some of Ricoeur's proposals. I will consider how this narrated event is revelation.

An Exegesis of Mark 14:32–42

This is the text of Mark in a literal translation:

32a And they came to a small estate whose name was Gethsemane,
32b and he said to his disciples:

---

[5] Walter Kasper, *The God of Jesus Christ* (New York: Crossroad, 1983), 68.

[6] J. Nabert, *Essai sur le mal* (Paris: Presses Universitaires de France, 1955), 148.

[7] The use of the terms "auxiliary" and "referential" language refers to the way these terms are used in the statement of the Pontifical Biblical Commission, *Bible et Chrisologie* #1.2.2/3. Text, in French and Latin, was published by Cerf, 1984.

[8] G. Comstock, "Truth or Meaning: Ricoeur versus Frei on Biblical Narrative," *Journal of Religion* (1986): 117–40.

32c   "Sit here while I pray."
33a   And he took along Peter and James and John with him,
33b   and he began to be overawed and distressed;
34a   and he said to them:
34b   "My soul is sorrowful, enough to die;
34c   wait here and keep awake."
35a   And going on a little, he fell on the ground,
35b   and he kept praying[9] that if it were possible the hour might pass
            from him.
36a   And he was saying:
36b   "Abba, Father, all things are possible to you;
36c   take this cup away from me;
36d   but not what I want, but what you."
37a   And he came and found them sleeping,
37b   and he said to Peter:
37c   "Simon, are you sleeping?
37d   Could you not keep awake one hour?
38a   All of you, keep awake and pray that you do not come into temptation;
38b   the spirit is eager, but the flesh is weak."
39   And again going off, he prayed, saying the same thing.
40a   And again coming, he found them sleeping,
40b   for their eyes were heavy;
40c   and they did not know how they might answer him.
41a   And he came a third time,
41b   and he said to them:
41c   "Are you still sleeping and taking your rest?
41d   It is satisfied.
41e   The hour has come.
41f   Look, the Son of Man is being given over into the hands of sinners.
42a   Rise up, let us go.
42b   Look, the one who gives me over has come near."

Historical Critique[10]

Most commentators agree that the threefold synoptic narrative (Mt 26:36–46/Mk
14:32–42/Lk 22:39–46), the use of the same basic material in John (Jn 12:27–29

---

[9] Phrases such as "kept praying" accent the use of the imperfect in the Markan text. Given
the inconsistency with which Mark uses the imperfect as a historical tense, such translations are necessarily interpretations of the author's intention.

[10] There is abundant bibliographical material available on this incident. Most of it is collected or alluded to in R. Pesch, *Das Markusevangelium* (HTKNT; Freiburg: Herder,
1984), II:396. To this add A. Feuillet, *L'Agonie de Gethsemani* (Paris: Gabalda, 1977) and
J. W. Holleran, "The Synoptic Gethsemane: A Critical Study," *Analecta Gregoriana* 191
(Rome: Università Gregoriana, 1973).

[+ 14:31; 18:11]), and the allusion in Hebrews (Heb 5:7–10) refer to a moment of crisis in the life of Jesus shortly before his arrest in which he, amid great fear, embraced the will of the Father.

We are dealing with something that "really happened." We can reduce to two the reasons for asserting that a historical event is the basis for what our sources refer to as: (1) the multiplicity of the New Testament witness, and (2) the unlikelihood that the early community would have created such a scene. It is also plausible that the synoptic location of this event is correct, both geographically, on a small estate[11] on the Mount of Olives, and chronologically, just before Jesus' arrest. John, on the other hand, places the words of Jesus' prayer of decision right after his triumphal entry into Jerusalem at an unspecified place in the city. This is a theological choice. The accent of the arrest scene in the Fourth Gospel is on the sovereign power of Jesus. In addition, the latter part of chapter 12 in John is a hinge, concluding the first part of the Gospel and joining this to the Passion Narrative. A logical place for John to present this moment of decision is in this chapter 12, soon after Jesus announces that "the hour has come" (Jn 12:23). The account in Hebrews is not a narrative, but a descriptive report that prescinds from any definite location in either time or space.

We may note that all the accounts seem to reflect a "canonical" way of narrating the heart of the event. They allude to psalms that serve to portray Jesus as the suffering just man who is "sorrowful" (Mt 26:38/Mk 14:34) or "troubled" (Jn 12:27). These two terms are found as parallel expressions in LXX Ps 41:6, 12; 43:5 (see also Ps 6:3–7). He prays "with a loud cry and tears" (Heb 5:7, see LXX Ps 37:10; 6:3–7, and so on). In addition, all the accounts stress the fact that this prayer is an expression of the filial relation Jesus has with the Father. In the four Gospel narratives, Jesus explicitly addresses his prayer to the Father (Mt 26:39/Mk 14:36/Lk 22:42, also Mt 26:44) reflecting Matthew 6:10 (despite the fact that this petition is not in the Lucan version of the "Our Father"), while John 12:28 echoes Matthew 6:9. This same prayer provides the theme of "temptation" found in the synoptics (Mt 26:41/Mk 14:38; Luke 22:40, 46: see Heb 4:15). In addition, the Gospel tradition concurs in calling this moment "the Hour." This is particularly striking in Mark (14:35b [see Jn 12:27]; 37d; 41c [=Jn 12:23]), although it also figures in Matthew 26:40, 45 (see Lk 22:53).

This well-established recourse to common sources and vocabulary is part of what I will call, using Ricoeur's terminology, a traditional interpretive "configuration."[12] As the event was reflected upon and transmitted in the tradition, a particular way of shaping the material, embodying the themes mentioned above, was established. There was a widespread consensus that the best way to

---

[11] John calls the spot a "garden" *(kēpos)*, while locating Jesus' prayer elsewhere.

[12] For a discussion of this term, see P. Ricoeur, *Time and Narrative,* trans. K. McLaughlin and D. Pellauer, vol. I (Chicago: University of Chicago Press, 1984), 64–70.

penetrate and present the inner meaning of this event was to give it a particular literary shape that indicated the relation between Jesus' definitive act of submission to the Father and the present situation of the Church.

Literary Critique

From our resumé of the results of historical criticism, we may conclude that we are dealing here with a real event in the life of Jesus, one that occurred close to the time of his arrest. The shaping or configuring of the event, however, was done according to norms and theological judgments that were widespread and pre-existed the manifold tradition we find in the New Testament. I wish now to institute a brief literary study of the text of Mark. Though a consideration of the resemblances to the other narratives and to the material in Hebrews is very useful, it will be kept to a minimum here. According to what I will call the principle of responsibility, an author must be considered responsible for what he puts in his text. No matter what pre-existing material he is using or upon which he is modeling himself, it is part of his communication. This means that once we are aware that Mark shares and exploits a widespread tradition and, in this instance, is particularly close to Matthew, we may still read the Markan text as his particular configuration of the event we are considering.

The Structure of Mark 14:32–42

There is general consensus that Mark 14:32–42 is a pericope, that is, a relatively freestanding, self-enclosed literary presentation of an event.[13] Whether Mark has inserted it into a pre-Markan Passion Story need not concern us here. There is a unity of action: Jesus arrives with his disciples at Gethsemane, urges them to pray, prays himself, exhorts them, and finally announces the coming of the hour about which he prayed and the imminent arrival of the *paradidous*, the one who will set the whole process of the Passion in movement. This unity of action is, of course, the work of the author, imposing his point of view upon the complex of activities in order to compose the event.

There are four distinct movements to the action clearly indicated in the text. The first movement (vv. 32a–36d) presents the setting, the conflict, and its resolution. The conflict and resolution of this movement is the common heritage of the whole tradition. The second, third, and fourth movements (vv. 37a–39b, vv. 40a–c, and vv. 41a–42b) are introduced by the notice that Jesus came to the disciples. The second and third movements are introduced by "came," "found," and "them sleeping." This explicitly alludes to the themes of Mark 13:36. The fourth movement continues the allusion. We can see that

---

[13] For a treatment of the distinction between pericope, episode, and incident in New Testament literature, I refer the reader to my book, *Narrative Parallels to the New Testament* (Atlanta: Scholars Press, 1988).

Mark clearly intends this means of dividing the text by the fact that no notice that Jesus went away precedes the repetition of the theme in v. 41a.

A Discussion of the Four Movements of the Text

I wish in this section to discuss the poetic function of the Markan text, that is, the manner in which the verbal texture "makes" or configures the various movements of the action by establishing links between this event and other themes and events within the Gospel and the tradition contiguous to it. In the next section, we will consider more explicitly how the text is appropriated or, to use Ricoeur's term, "refigured" by the audience.

The identification of the small estate as Gethsemane begins the narrative with a signal that Mark wishes to retell something already known in a tradition that has reached further than his immediate audience. This is true no matter how one views the question of Markan priority. The address in 32c may be an allusion to Abraham's words to his servants as he and Isaac depart for the sacrifice (Gen 22:5). If so, then we can see how the use of an expression that is already part of sacred narrative allows us to understand what is happening within the broader context of God's plan. The notice in 33a links this incident with the raising of the daughter of Jairus (Mk 5:37), the Transfiguration (Mk 9:2), and probably the eschatological discourse as well (Mk 13:3—the same three and Andrew). That is, we are in a situation of private and important revelation.

In v. 33b, we have a vivid description of Jesus' state, using two words. The first word, *ekthambesthai,* is unique to Mark and he uses it to describe an awed reaction to the result of a special divine manifestation: the crowd as Jesus comes down the mount of the Transfiguration (Mk 9:15), and the women at the empty tomb (Mk 16:5, 6). The second word, denoting a strong state of distress and disorientation, is also used by Matthew (26:27; see Phil 2:26). As I have already indicated, v. 34b serves to portray Jesus as the suffering and praying just man of the psalms. We find this theme throughout the Passion Narrative (e.g., Ps 22 in Mk 15:24, 29, 34; Ps 69 in Mk 15:23, 36).

With the instruction in v. 34c, we enter upon a more pointed and decisive use of vocabulary. The term translated here, "keep awake" *(gregorein),* occurs only in this pericope and in the exhortations and parable that conclude the eschatological discourse (Mk 13:32–37), where it occurs three times along with two other terms denoting vigilance. We will return to this shortly.

After the description in v. 35a of Jesus' distress and prostrate prayer, Mark gives a resumé of the prayer (v. 35b) in indirect discourse using the term "hour." Besides the remarkable resemblances to Johannine usage I mentioned above, we should note the phrase in Mark 13:32, "Concerning that day and the hour, no one knows. . . ." In v. 36b, we have the prayer in direct discourse addressed to "Abba, Father." This Aramaic/Greek expression is found only here in the Gospels, although it occurs twice in the Pauline letters (Gal 4:6; Rom 8:15) to describe the Spirit-inspired prayer of Christians. The use of the phrase at this point has three effects: (1) it indicates that the obedience of Jesus is that of a Son (see Mk 1:1, 11; 9:7; 15:39; compare Heb 5:8); (2) it forms an explicit link between the prayer of Jesus and that of his followers; and (3) it introduces as background the prayer recorded in Matthew 6:9–13/Luke 11:2–4, though not in Mark. Jesus addresses the Father uniquely in Mark with: "all things are possible to you" (see Mk 9:23). He is the one who "can save him from death" (Heb 5:7). This time, in common with the synoptic tradition and John (18:11), the impending suffering is described as a "cup." This establishes Jesus as the one who vicariously drinks the cup of God's wrath (see Mk 10:39).[14] The decisive movement of the action ends in v. 36c. Jesus does what he taught his disciples to do: He prays for and embraces the will of the Father. From this point, Jesus will no longer engage in decision-making, as Mark implies in v. 39b. The rest of the action has another direction and other concerns.

As we noted above, there are three further movements in this event. In each of these, Jesus is the only one to speak, and his words provide a unique resolution to the aporia of time as well as instruction concerning what is immediately to follow.

The second movement opens in v. 37a with a fulfillment of the warning given in 13:36, ". . . lest coming suddenly he find you sleeping." In v. 37b–d, we have the demotion of "Peter" to "Simon," a question about his torpor, and an allusion to the theme of "hour." This is followed by a solemn rhythmical phrase addressed in the plural (v. 38a–b), not only to the inept disciples, but also to the whole church. I propose that this phrase derives from the prophetic activity that characterized early Christian community gatherings.[15] The noun peirasmos, a word well-represented in New Testament tradition, occurs only here in Mark. It reiterates a theme from Mark 1:13, echoed in 8:11, 10:2, 12:15, as well as in 8:33, and alludes to the sixth petition of the "Our Father" (Mt 6:13 = Lk 11:4). The injunction to keep awake, repeats the allusion to Mark 13:32–37 already established. It is also a common New Testament theme (1 Thes 5:6; 1 Cor 16:13; Rev 16:15, and so on), joined here, as is often the case, to the notion of prayer (Col 4:2; 1 Pet 5:8).

---

[14] For a discussion of the background of this image and for further bibliography, see Francis Martin, "Le baptême dans l'Esprit; tradition du Nouveau Testament et vie de l'Eglise," *Nouvelle Revue Théologique* 106 (1984): 23–58.

[15] For a consideration of the role of Christian prophets in the wording of some New Testament logia, see J. D. G. Dunn, "Prophetic 'I' Sayings and the Jesus Tradition: The importance of Testing Prophetic Utterances Within Early Christianity," *New Testament Studies* 24 (1977/78): 175–98. The suggestion that Mark 14:38a–b derives in some way from the life of the community is not new. R. Bultmann, *Die Geschichte der Synoptischen Tradition*, 4th ed. (Gottingen: Vandenhoeck & Ruprecht, 1958), 288, speaks of it as *"christliche Erbaungsprache."* He also considers the pericope to have a "thoroughgoing legendary character." Even granting his particular notion of "legend," this is not, in my opinion, correct. For a resumé of other shades of opinion regarding the community source of this exhortation, see Holleran, *The Synoptic Gethsemane*, 128.

The addition of the theme of "temptation" serves to accentuate the atmosphere of the eschaton, the ultimate moment of trial (see Rev 3:10, 2:10). The most striking new element is that of a theological anthropology using terms not found in this sense in the whole of Mark. The concepts of "spirit" and "flesh" indicate not static constituents of the human frame, but rather dynamic and contrary components whose ultimate resolution will determine a person's eternal future. This thinking is broadly based in the tradition of the New Testament and finds expression, as is well known, in the writings of Paul, in 1 Peter (3:18; 4:1), and in the fourth gospel (Jn 6:63). The closest antecedent to this view is to be found at Qumran.[16]

We are certainly entitled to see in this passage a Markan use of source material, some of which he most likely derived from the liturgical life of the community. More specifically, we are dealing with a prophetic exhortation that has been incorporated into the configuration of an event in the life of Jesus. Two things are apparent here that I will discuss shortly: (1) Mark has a very particular concept of time evident in his superimposition of one dimension of the life of Christ upon another, and this involves (2) the claim of the whole Gospel that Jesus is still alive.

The third movement of the action (v. 40 a–c) seems to have but one function in the text. By using again the terminology of Mark 13:36,[17] and combining it with a word-for-word repetition of Mark 9:6 (v. 40c), Mark forges another link with the Transfiguration, which he, in turn, brings into connection with the eschatological moment. Mark intends the remark itself, along with the notice in v. 40b, that "their eyes were heavy," to show once again the inept nature of the disciples' response in the face of the suffering and glory of the Son of Man.[18] This ineptitude is not merely of human origin but has its cause in the work of Satan.[19]

The fourth and final movement (vv. 41a–42b), still using the theme of Jesus' coming and the disciples' sleeping, is for the most part a series of statements (vv. 41d–42b) that serve to give proper perspective to what has just occurred and what will occur shortly. The first of these statements, unique to Mark, remains for us unintelligible and thus provides a good illustration of the continued need for historical and philological research.[20] The announcement in

---

[16] For a good study of this, see K. G. Kuhn, "New Light on Temptation, Sin and Flesh in the New Testament," in *The Scrolls and the New Testament*, ed. K. Stendahl (New York: Harper and Row, 1957), 94–113. This line from the Hymns Scroll is particularly striking: "The walk of man is not constant except by the spirit God has created in him." (1 QH 4, 31.) Mark also uses *pneuma* in a less technical anthropological sense: Mark 2:8, 8:12.

[17] "Lest coming suddenly [at the eschatological moment] he find you sleeping."

[18] For a study of this point, see Quentin Quesnell, *The Mind of Mark, Analecta Biblica* 38 (Rome: Pontifical Biblical Institute, 1969).

[19] James M. Robinson, in *The Problem of History in Mark*, Studies in Biblical Theology 11, (London: SCM, 1959), pointed this out in general without specific reference to this text.

[20] A discussion of the possible meanings of *apechei* can be found in the commentaries, e.g., Pesch, *Markus* II, 393–94.

v. 41e that "the hour has come" refers immediately to the subject of Jesus' prayer in v. 35b, and behind that to the decisive moment in the life of Jesus and the history of the world that God has determined. Verse 41f, introduced by *idou*, indicates the fulfillment of the prophecies concerning the Son of Man in 8:31, 9:31, 10:33 borrowing some elements from each and using the key word *paradidonai*, which probably reflects New Testament use of LXX Is 53:6, 12 and which refers to the whole process of the Passion. (See Mk 3:19; 14:10, 11, 18, 21; 15:1, 10; and see as well such texts as Rom 4:25.)

In v. 42a, we have what must have been a traditional way of expressing Jesus' sense of determination as his Passion approaches: We find the identical phrase, not surprisingly, in Matthew 26:46, but also in John 14:31. The last phrase, once again introduced by *idou*, describes Judas as *o paradidous*, an epithet repeated in v. 44, and announces his imminent arrival with the same term as Mark uses for the Kingdom of God in Mark 1:15. We may compare the Johannine expression in John 14:30: "[T]he Prince of this world is coming." This immediately precedes the exhortation I referred to just above (Jn 14:31): "Rise, let us go from here."

An Interpretation of the Narrative

What we have accomplished so far, utilizing the methods of historical and literary criticism, may be termed "commentary." This is a description or a report of what the text says. There is, however, another step necessary in a total reading of the text. We may term this "interpretation": It attempts to understand what the text is talking about. When there is question of a propositional text, even a text that employs symbolic language, as do the Pauline letters, Hebrews, and others, we express our effort to understand the reality that the text discusses in a transposed set of propositions. This set of propositions is framed in "auxiliary language," which is always subordinate to the more abundant "referential language" of the Scriptures.[21]

In a text such as Mark 14:32–42, we are dealing with narrative. An understanding or reunderstanding of a narrative may be expressed in another narrative. This is often the procedure of the ancients, as I. Heinemann pointed out,[22] and we can see the procedure at work in the diverse narratives of the same Gethsemane event we are considering here. The other manner of interpreting a narrative is similar to that of interpreting propositional texts: The configured reality is described in a series of propositions. This is a discursive resumé of what results from the interaction of the reader with the text. In Ricoeur's terminology, an

---

[21] For an indication of the source of this terminology, see note 6 above.

[22] I. Heinemann, in his study of rabbinic exegesis, distinguished between "creative history" and "creative philology." By the former, he intended to describe the process of retelling an event; by the latter, the process by which a meaning is drawn out by "etymology." See Isaac Heinemann, *Darkè ha Aggadah,* 3rd ed. (Jerusalem: Masada, 1970).

interpretation is an explicitation of our "refiguring" of the narrative. There is a difference, however. Ricoeur himself has attempted an analysis of the theologico-literary procedures at work in Mark 14:32–42. His work, in my opinion, is a refiguring that does not deal sufficiently with the historical referent of the narrative.[23] This is due to a lack of attention to what a historical critical approach can and must establish. I will return to this point later.

I propose a descriptive interpretation of Mark 14:32–42, touching upon only some of its features and based upon the preceding historical and literary commentary.

There was a moment when Jesus Christ made a decision to embrace what he clearly perceived to be the will of God, his Father, for him. This moment came shortly before his arrest in Gethsemane. It was a moment of human decision. Within the confines of humanity, someone made an act of submission to God in which the Absolute is revealed in a contingent act. In the words of Maximus the Confessor, we are saved by the human decision of a divine Person.[24] Without that decision, the rest of the Passion would have been fruitless.

Because he has realized in a uniquely profound way the mystery of suffering and submission, Jesus sums up within himself in a transcendent manner the characteristics of that righteous and suffering man who has been crying out to God in his thirst for justice since the beginning of the world. What is more, his obedience reveals something of the selflessness of the relation between the Father and the Son.[25] This one punctiliar movement in the life of Jesus is itself the summing up of the temptation and the obedience that characterized his whole earthly existence. It does, however, raise them to a unique earthly existence. This is the hour. It is the moment in time when Jesus takes upon himself the ultimate consequences of belonging to "the present evil age" (Gal 1:4). It is therefore the moment of conflict between the Son of God and Satan. We are not spectators to this conflict; we are called to share in it. In the first place, the death and resurrection that ineluctably follow from this decision are the reasons we too are "delivered from this present evil age." Secondly, those things about to happen to Jesus had already been predicted as part of the future of the disciples: to be given over to tribunals, beaten, and made to stand before governors and kings. We are not to worry; what we are to say will be given us in *that hour* (Mk 13:9–11).

---

[23] Paul Ricoeur, "Le Récit Interpretatif," *Recherches de science religieuse* (1985): 17–38.

[24] The phrase of Maximus, made in the light of the Gethsemane scene, is the object of a study by F.-M. Léthel, *Théologie de l'Agonie du Christ. La liberté humaine de Fils de Dieu et son Importance Sotériologique mises en lumière par Saint Maxime le Confesseur, Théologie Historique* 52 (Paris: Beauchesne, 1979).

[25] This is developed in the study by Jurgen Moltmann, *The Crucified God: The Cross of Christ as the Foundation and Criticism of Christian Theology,* trans. R. A. Wilson and J. Bowden (New York: Harper and Row, 1974), 235–49. See the valuable remarks on this outlook by W. Hill, "The Doctrine of God after Vatican II," *The Thomist* 51 (1987): 395–418, esp. 405ff.

Yet, as the hour approaches, we see two different reactions. Jesus is at prayer, resisting temptation, and submitting to the plan of the Father. The disciples, in flagrant disobedience to the reiterated command to keep awake, are asleep, unable to watch one hour. It is at this point that a solemn warning rings out once again: "Keep awake and pray that you do not come into temptation; the spirit is eager, but the flesh is weak." These words are not the last admonition of a dead master. They are the command of the risen Lord. They are not the record of what Jesus said one night. They are the words he is speaking now to this harassed community in danger of being deceived by the forces of darkness, and of being overpowered by persecution and disappointment. This church is running the risk of totally misunderstanding the moment of revelation, of not knowing how to respond to what God is doing.

If we understand the relationship between the eschatological warning in chapter 13, and its repetition here, we see that there are two dimensions of time being conveyed. As we have said, the hour is the ultimate moment. It is characterized by being the point in human history during which Jesus overturns the forces that we can sum up under the name of Sin and which ruled over history (see Heb 2:14). It is therefore a moment of conflict between Jesus and Satan.

This is the first dimension of time. Wherever and whenever the components of the Gethsemane event are present, that point in human history may also be called "the hour," but only those moments that realize, in varying degrees, the conflict between Jesus and Satan. This is a true eschatological moment, understanding *eschaton* not as final but as ultimate. Such a moment participates not only notionally, but also in the order of being that moment when the Son of God overcomes the power of darkness.

The historically contingent manifestation of the Absolute takes place on the cross and is still present to succeeding generations because its protagonist is alive. This is the second dimension of time conveyed by the narrative. Strictly speaking, the text is not history in the sense that it is an attempt to recover the past. The New Testament is rather a proclamation that this historically contingent event is still present because Jesus Christ is risen from the dead.

How does this apply to the action narrated in Mark 14:32–42? We have here the moment of human decision, a moment without which the rest of the Passion process would have been nothing but a tragic miscarriage of human justice. Mark narrates for us the event that provides access to the "interior" of the event of the cross.[26] He endows this moment with the characteristics of the last hour because it is the ultimate moment whose full consequences will be realized in human history at that last hour when the Son of Man comes again. In the

---

[26] The manner in which the Gospels are a revelation of the interior of the events in the life of Christ receives an initial development in the study by Ignace de la Potterie, "Fondement Biblique de la Théologie du Coeur du Christ," in *Le Coeur de Jésus. Coeur du Monde* (Paris: FAC, 1982), 103–40.

meanwhile, every generation of Christians faces the same invitation: to share in their measure the messianic suffering of Jesus, that is, to die to sin and live to God (Rom 6:10–11) and, thus, to perpetuate and make known the human presence of the unique *Mysterion* in history. Mark already adumbrates this in the description of the lot of the disciples, which includes being "given over" as was Jesus (Mk 13:9, 11, 12), and he makes it explicit in Jesus' final words of his teaching concerning that day and the hour: "What I say to you, I say to all, keep awake!" (Mk 13:37). Thus, the moments of conflict with darkness occur over and over again in the ongoing life of the community. The Gospel of Mark conveys an understanding of the components of that struggle: the decision to follow Jesus "on the way" (see Mk 8:3; 10:32, 42, and so on), the temptation to be scandalized by the suffering of the Son of Man (Mk 8:32), the activity of Satan who finds in the flesh an ally in maintaining the disciples in a situation of non-understanding and inability to respond, and finally the presence of Jesus exhorting and teaching his brethren generation after generation through the words of the written text and the words of Prophecy that he delivers.

Reflections Deriving From Recent Work in the Philosophy of Literature and History

At this point, I would like to undertake a reflection on the methods involved in the steps of commentary and interpretation that we have just accomplished. My starting point is the work of Paul Ricoeur because he has published a good deal in the field of the philosophies of literature and history, and because many of his insights are helpful and congenial to the work of such reflection. However, I think there are several weak points in his presentations, in which what exegetes actually do, or should do, diverges from Ricoeur's theoretical reflections.

Methodological and Epistemological Considerations

Paul Ricoeur has always been the champion of respect for the text. He has opposed all attempts to "get behind the text" and interpret it in terms of the investigator's preoccupations rather than in terms of intersubjective communication. He has opposed the "hermeneutics of suspicion," which originated in its various forms with Nietzsche, Freud, and Marx. He has also opposed "historicism," which he defines as:

> the epistemological presupposition that the content of literary works and in general of cultural documents receives its intelligibility from its connection to the social conditions of the community that produced it or to which it was destined.[27]

---

[27] *Interpretation Theory: Discourse and the Surplus of Meaning* (Fort Worth: Texas Christian University Press, 1976), 89–90.

On the other hand, Ricoeur has not gone to the other extreme of those who seek the meaning "behind" the text or "within" the text. Ricoeur speaks of what is "in front of the text."

It must be acknowledged that much work done in biblical exegesis under the aegis of what is called the historical critical method shares, usually unconsciously, the epistemological presuppositions of historicism. The text is treated as an object that will automatically yield its meaning when one applies the proper method to it. On the other hand, in reaction to this type of historicism, other exegetes have sought the text's meaning in the application of structuralist or semiotic methods. Both approaches, historical and intratextual, are usually tempered, however, by the interpreter's desire to listen to the text. It has been Ricoeur's contribution to elaborate a theory of approaching the text that accounts for the "tempering" activity that exegetes usually exercise more on the level of common sense or instinct. This theory comes at a propitious time since the excesses of both approaches need the corrective of what I called earlier a theology of human communication.

However, as I already mentioned, there does not seem to be much room in Ricoeur's theory for the kind of activity undertaken above under the rubric "historical critique." There is a difference between getting behind a text in order to use it as a source for the history of early Christianity and as a norm for judging the meaning of a text (historical criticism), and the historical and philological study that facilitates the communicative effort of the text itself. The first makes the text a servant of extraneous preoccupations, while the second tends to serve the text. This second type of activity makes possible a deeper participation in what Ricoeur felicitously calls "the direction of thought opened up by the text."[28] It does so, however, by overcoming some of the "strangeness and distance" of the text.[29]

The very nature of revelation means that the judgment regarding the historical nature of what is being conveyed in the text is an important one. The problem of ascertaining in our text, or in any Gospel text, whether or not there is a real event being configured is not a negligible one. It affects the nature of the testimony being given to a historically contingent moment. We must ask if this is a theological notion woven into a basic narrative about Jesus, or the configuration of an event that "really happened." What are the criteria for making such a judgment?

More work is needed in order to enable us to understand the kind of literature with which we are dealing. The Gospels do not fit into any category of literature with which we modern westerners are familiar.[30] This is a good exam-

---

28 Ibid., 92.

29 For a penetrating study on the positive aspects of distanciation, see P. Ricoeur. "The Hermeneutical Function of Distanciation," in *Hermeneutics and the Human Sciences*, ed. J. B. Thompson (Cambridge: Cambridge University Press, 1981), 131–44.

30 I say this despite the considerable amount of recent research into this question. For a more extended discussion, I refer the reader to my *Narrative Parallels to the New Testament*, mentioned previously in note 13.

ple of what *Dei Verbum* §2 describes when it speaks of the "economy of revelation" taking place *"gestis verbisque intrinsece inter se connexis."*[31] I find it interesting that Ricoeur, in discussing the mutual borrowing that takes place between history and fiction, uses the term "interweaving." Origen, in his commentary on John, uses the same term *(prosyphainein)* when discussing the manner in which the four evangelists "have woven into their writing, with the help of expressions used to describe sensible things, realities evident to them in a purely spiritual *[noetos]* manner."[32] This insight deserves further study. The point I wish to make here is simply that, as far as I can tell, Ricoeur, in concentrating on withstanding the pressures of various forms of getting behind the text, has not sufficiently taken into account the legitimate role of historical investigation in determining the nature of "the direction of thought opened up by the text." This is an important, if difficult, task in New Testament exegesis.

I propose in this regard that there is a twofold hermeneutical spiral at work in historical investigation. The first spiral is the application of the historical and philological disciplines in striving to understand the utterance of the text. This is characterized, as is well known, by an oscillation between intuition and verification on successively deeper and more inclusive levels. This may be called the spiral of "explanation," and it corresponds to what we termed above as commentary. The second spiral is "understanding" and is marked by the oscillation between what is being achieved on the level of explanation and what is understood on the level of faith. In this process, the understanding of faith, while it has a directive role, must always be modified by what *the text* is stating and be able to verify its position by what is present in the text. The positing of two hermeneutical spirals merely makes explicit the fact that all historical work takes place under the aegis of some higher and broader preoccupation. In this case, faith functions not merely as a norm, a set of traditional documents against which an interpretation is to be evaluated, although this is important: It also functions as a light, as a directive principle within the mind.[33] This, I take it, is what the medieval theologians mean by "the light of faith" when discussing how theology is a science. It is the level at which what I have called interpretation takes place.

My second reflection has to do with history and poetry. We read in Volume I of *Time and Narrative* this very helpful distinction:

---

[31] I will develop this in Chapter 11.

[32] The term is found in P. Ricoeur, *Time and Narrative*, vol. I, 82. For Origen, see *Commentary on John*, 10, 5, (18), in *Sources Chretiennes* 157:394. I was first made aware of this view of Origen by the study of R. Grant, *The Earliest Lives of Jesus* (New York: Harper and Brothers, 1961), 65 et passim.

[33] Again, the question of the presuppositions operative in the historical critical method have been dealt with in the previous chapter and will be discussed at greater length in Chapter 11.

It is for this reason that historians are not simply narrators: they give reasons why they consider a particular factor *rather than some other* to be the sufficient cause of a given course of events. Poets also create plots that are held together by causal skeletons. But these latter are not the subject of a process of argumentation. Poets restrict themselves to producing the story and explaining by narrating.[34]

Using the terminology of the above quote, we must say that most biblical narrative is poetic rather than historical. There are discursive explanations given for events, as when the Deuteronomical redactor says of the fall of the northern kingdom: "This came about because the Israelites sinned against the Lord their God . . ." (2 Kgs 17:7ff.). The death of Jesus is due to "the set purpose and plan of God" (Acts 2:23) and is destined "for us" (Eph 5:1–2; 1 Tim 2:6; Gal 2:20; and so on) "for our sins" (Gal 1:4; 1 Cor 15:3, and so on) and "to destroy the devil's works" (1 Jn 3:8). But, as we can observe, the chain of causality asserted in these cases pertains to the "vertical and interior dimension" of history referred to in the previous chapter. Tradition has always accorded the Gospel writers a prophetic authority by which they poetically unfold for us the interiority of the events in the life of Jesus. They add to their narrative the dimension of testimony. In Ricoeur's terms:

> The term testimony should be applied to words, works, actions, and to lives which attest to an intention, an inspiration, an idea at the heart of experience and history which nonetheless transcend experience and history.[35]

The Markan text that forms the basis of our reflections is, by any account, a poetic text. It makes, or remakes, the event from words. It "explains by narrating." In this verbal remaking of the event, what Ricoeur calls configuration, there is a judgment made and a truth claim asserted. Mark bears testimony to an interior dimension of an event, which is at the same time the interior dimension of the whole Passion process. This dimension consists in the relationship between Jesus and the Father as Jesus manifests this in his interior decision to obey his Father's will by entering into a conflict with Sin and overcoming it. Because of the ultimate nature of this event, it is cast in terms of the eschatological moment and declared to be present as an ongoing reality in the lives of the believers. In order to grasp this, Ricoeur tells us we must interact, not with the worlds created by ourselves behind and within the text, but with the "world" by an appropriating process that Ricoeur terms "refiguration."

My question at this point is this: Is this refigured world merely a metaphor of a metaphor, as the deconstructionists would have it, or is it a genuine appro-

---

[34] *Time and Narrative,* I:186.
[35] Ricoeur, "The Hermeneutics of Testimony," *Essays on Biblical Interpretation,* 119.

priation of truth through a judgment? I am not sure that Ricoeur's description avoids the twofold criticism that David Carr on the one hand and Hans Frei on the other lay against it. Carr first questions whether Ricoeur pays sufficient attention to the intentional character of all human action, and does not rather see intentionality as the "invention" (to which Ricoeur does give both meanings) of the narrator. Secondly, Carr doubts whether Ricoeur really enters the debate among philosophers of history concerning the narrative quality of what they investigate and retell. He says of Ricoeur that "he is interested in what historical texts reveal about those who write and read them—their role in the life of culture, we might say—rather than in what they yield by way of objective knowledge of the past."[36]

Frei's objections are similar.[37] He observes how practitioners of "regional hermeneutics" "try to maintain that Jesus is the irreducible ascriptive subject of the New Testament narratives while at the same time they make general religious experience (or something like it) the 'referent' of these stories."[38] Ricoeur's remark that I quoted at the beginning of this essay shows that he attributes to biblical hermeneutics not only a place as a regional hermeneutic, but also a unique status that employs philosophy as its organon.[39] However, in the same essay, he does speak of Socrates and Jesus as examples of "a great historical archetype."[40] This returns us to genus and species thinking, although it does not necessarily exclude another form of predication in which Jesus is more than an example of an archetype.

Frei's second problem has to do with Ricoeur's reiterated statement that the role of a text, as distinguished from that of a word or a sentence, is to create a world in front of it that meets our world and opens up for us a broader world of true possibilities. Regarding the expression "in front of," Frei has this to say:

> Any "meaning" that "in front of" may have is deferred along a loosely connected potentially indefinite metaphorical axis, and in the meantime it is what it is simply by displacing that from which it differs ("meaning behind the text").[41]

---

[36] David Carr, review of *Time and Narrative*, by Paul Ricoeur. *History and Theory* 23 (1984): 357–70; citation from 363. It should be pointed out that Carr's review covers only the first volume of *Time and Narrative*.

[37] See "The 'Literal Reading' of Biblical Narrative in the Christian Tradition: Does it Stretch or Will It Break?" in *The Bible and the Narrative Tradition*, ed. F. McConnell (New York: Oxford University Press, 1986), 36–77.

[38] Ibid., 50.

[39] See note 2. I have had no access to the original French of this text, which, as far as I can tell, was never published. It must be that the possessive pronoun in "son organon" refers to biblical hermeneutics, which is joined to philosophy not as servant but as master.

[40] Ricoeur, "Toward a Hermeneutic," 113.

[41] "Literal Reading," 56.

We can partly meet Frei's objection by redressing the balance between what Ricoeur calls the ostensive and descriptive modes of reference on the one hand, and the metaphoric and symbolic modes of reference on the other. This latter mode, by the configuration of an event, creates a world, a place "I might inhabit and into which I might project my inmost powers."[42] Ricoeur states that this metaphorical reference requires the effacement of the descriptive or ostensive reference.[43] But does it? In our interpretation of Mark 14:32–42, both references contribute to our understanding. The text does not merely refashion this moment in the life of Jesus so that it opens up possibilities and exigencies of our Christian existence: It also gives us understanding of the event itself. We understand more profoundly the true dimensions of Jesus' relation to the Father, his interior decision to accept the Father's will regarding the Passion process, and the relation of that decision to the ultimate and final moment of human history. In other words, to echo Jean Nabert, there is ultimate truth revealed to us in a contingent event.

In accenting the freedom of the text from its original matrix of author and reader, and in considering the descriptive/ostensive reference of the text as needing to be suppressed in order to liberate the metaphorical/symbolic reference, Ricoeur underplays the role of the text as an instance of intersubjective *communication.* Though the perspective and contexts are different, I would offer here some words of St. Thomas Aquinas in his discussion of the role of a teacher. His insight opens a way that allows for the corrective of ostensive reference to a particular event in order to ground the metaphorical or configuring role of the total narrative act. Thomas says in effect that the role of the teacher is to produce in the student that movement of mind by which he himself arrived at the truth. His words are:

> So according to this method [by which art imitates nature], one man is said to teach another because, through symbols *[signa],* he expounds to the other that discursive line of reasoning which he himself follows in natural reasoning. And so the natural reason of the student, by means of the symbols proposed to him, instruments as it were, comes to a knowledge of unknown things.[44]

This text accentuates another aspect of human communication, namely, the influence one person has on another in the movement of the mind in grasping truth. The text of Mark is an instance of such communication. The text is independent of Mark, but it is also a series of symbols by which he still produces a movement of mind in us. This aspect of the text is safeguarded by the "servant"

---

[42] Ricoeur, *Time and Narrative,* I:81.

[43] Ibid., I:80.

[44] *De Veritate* 11, 1, in *Of the Teacher,* trans. J. P. Shannon (Chicago: Regnery, 1949), 10–11. Other aspects of the action of the teacher are treated in *Summa theologiae,* I, 117, 1.

role of the historical disciplines mentioned above. Mark is configuring an event, he is explaining by narrating, and we, as we follow his narration, are brought to share in his vision of the manifestation of what is absolute in historical contingency. Our refiguring of the event is dependent upon his configuration that exercises a real causality upon our thinking. The Markan text is not an inert phenomenon. It is a symbolic communication with a specific type of causality.[45]

Most of the elements needed to correct the "genus/species" approach to the uniqueness of the New Testament witness are already present in Ricoeur, but they are not developed. As we have seen, Ricoeur maintains that biblical hermeneutics is something more than a regional application of general hermeneutics. He has not developed this most probably because, in Lewis Mudge's words: "Ricoeur's chosen task is not the exposition of the Bible within the community of Faith. It is, rather, the rational clarification of human existence in the world."[46]

I suggest that a more philosophical modification of Ricoeur's philosophy of literature and history has to begin with a closer look at his notion of "world," which he derives from Heidegger via Gadamer, and from a more profound correction of the Kantian notion of the act of "grasping together" characteristic of the productive imagination.[47] In regard to this latter, other philosophers of history have also attempted to describe a unifying function of the mind necessary for the grasping and presenting of events. W. H. Walsh speaks of "colligation,"[48] and F. R. Ankersmit, following Walsh, develops the notion of "narrative substance" utilizing some aspects of Leibnitz's "predicate in notion" principle.[49] A clarification of this point, based on reflecting upon what exegesis of narrative actually does, is certainly in order, and will form the subject of another essay.

---

45 In treating the same subject in *De unitate intellectus*, St. Thomas explicates the type of causality involved in teaching, likening it to the function by which a medical doctor ministers to a sick body, not replacing the principle inherent in the body, but enabling it to overcome obstacles: "And just as health is achieved in a sick man not according to the power of the doctor, but according to the capability of nature; so also knowledge is caused in the pupil not according to the power of the teacher, but according to the capability of the one learning." *De unitate intellectus,* V 113. *On the Unity of the Intellect Against the Averroists,* trans. B. Zedler, (Milwaukee: Bruce, 1968), 70.

46 Introduction to *Essays on Biblical Interpretation,* 2.

47 In *Time and Narrative*, I:156, Ricoeur acknowledges his debt to an article by L. O. Mink, "The Autonomy of Historical Understanding," *History and Theory* 5 (1965): 24–47, in which this concept is applied to the narrative quality of history. Ricoeur continues to refer to this notion throughout his study: I: 41, 66, 68, 166; II: 3, 61. For another assessment of this aspect of Ricoeur's thought, see S. Schwartz, "Hermeneutics and the Productive Imagination: Paul Ricoeur in the 1970's," *Journal of Religion* 63 (1983): 290–300.

48 W. H. Walsh, *Philosophy of History: An Introduction* (New York: Harper Torchbooks, 1960), 59ff.

49 F. R. Ankersmit, *Narrative Logic: A Semantic Analysis of the Historian's Language,* Martinus Nijoff Philosophy Library 7 (The Hague: Nijoff, 1983).

A Theological Consideration

I wish in conclusion to bring together some aspects of what I have already discussed under the notion of method and epistemology and offer one of many possible theological considerations. The question I wish to address is this: How does a reading of Mark 14:32–42 show us anything about the nature of revelation and what does it permit us to say in the current discussion of "God talk"?

It is clear that in Christian antiquity, the events of the life of Christ were considered as the primary locus of revelation without much consideration given to the verbal process by which those events reached the audience. There is in this a movement "behind the text." We can see the accent on event rather than on configuration in the fact that, in the written Gospel tradition, many events received successive interpretations by being narrated several times. This was the ancient way of commenting on an event and its previous configuration, as I have already mentioned. We also see this in the list of events found in the creeds, both in New Testament (e.g., 1 Cor 15:3–5) and in later texts. The commentaries of the Fathers of the Church accented mostly this dimension, as have the meditations of believers over the centuries.

The ancient notion that each event in the life of Christ is a *mysterion* has its basis in the way the New Testament itself, in its predominantly pericopic style, presents each event. In this historically contingent reality, the Absolute is revealed. To participate in this revelation, one must accept the prophetic truth claim that the text makes. Because it is a prophetic claim, it is unique: It claims to present the interior and vertical dimension of the event and to make this available to those who accept its claim. The "world" of the biblical text, especially narrative, does not suppress the descriptive/ostensive historical referent; it transposes it by revealing its interior dimension. It is for this reason that C. F. D. Moule is correct when he speaks of the New Testament as "explanatory" rather then "primary" evangelization.[50] The role of the text is to lead those who have, at least in some manner, begun to believe into a deeper knowledge of Jesus Christ. In this connection, there is a remarkable text in which Aquinas sums up the view of his heritage regarding the need of grace in order to interpret Scripture. We may note in passing his sensitivity to the two dimensions of oral and written transmission:

> After the level of those who receive revelation directly from God, another level of grace is necessary. Because men receive revelation from God not only for their own time but also for the instruction of all who come after them, it was necessary that the things revealed to them be not only passed on in speech to their contemporaries but also written down for the instruction of those to follow them. And thus it was also necessary that

---

[50] C. F. D. Moule, *The Birth of the New Testament,* 3rd ed. (New York: Harper and Row, 1982), 9.

there be those who could interpret what was written down. This also must be done by divine grace. Thus we read in Gen 40:8, "Does not interpretation come from God?"[51]

There is as well, however, a primary evangelization. This is not done so much by the text as by living believers. The text of the New Testament also enters the marketplace and makes its claim there. The divergent approaches of Frei and Ricoeur become apparent at this point. The theologian is safeguarding the unique nature of this witness while the philosopher is insisting that by the very fact that this witness is made in language it must enter the larger realm of human communication.

The solution to this problem lies in the solution of two more basic problems: first, an understanding of how God may be said to enter into historical contingency and, second, how this event and the language that transmits it may be said to be unique and common at the same time. Both of these questions, it seems to me, hinge upon a renewed investigation of what the ancients really meant by what I might call *analogia entis historici*. The question is, obviously, too vast to be treated fully here.

A reconsideration of the manner in which Mark superimposes the ultimate and the final moments in Mark 14:32–42 may, however, contribute to the solution. In confessing that Jesus Christ is "perfect in humanity" *(teleion en anthropoteti)*, the Council of Chalcedon was implicitly declaring him to be "perfectly historical," although this was not the primary concern of the council. The condition of being perfect in humanity and, therefore, in historicity was not obliterated by the resurrection; it was enhanced. This means that when Mark presents Jesus as exhorting the disciples to vigilance, as warning about the hour of temptation, he is not commemorating a past event; he is configuring it to include the fact of the presence of Jesus Christ now to his Church. This presence still has a temporal dimension even while it goes beyond time. What history strives to do comes to a transcendent realization because of the present reality of he who suffered and died once for all. The simultaneity of the eternal and historical dimensions in Jesus is the foundation for analogical predication. Jesus is at once unique and common. In the static ontological terms of Chalcedon, he is perfect in divinity and perfect in humanity. In the historical terms in which we pose the problem today, Jesus Christ is at one and the same time the member of a past generation whose history reaches us through the witness of the text and a person present to us now. In the faith by which we allow Mark's text to preside over our refiguring of the narrated event, we are introduced into the interior and present dimension of that event. To the degree that we share in this present reality of the hour, Jesus Christ *reveals* himself to us in the unique quality of his relation to the Absolute, his Father.

---

[51] *Summa contra Gentiles* III, 154.

3 Historical Criticism and New Testament Teaching on the Imitation of Christ

BY TAKING THE EXAMPLE of the imitation of Christ as seen by two different authors, this article shows the difference in philosophical and literary outlook between the biblical and Traditional understanding of event and language. The long historical analysis of the shift from one understanding of the world to another sets the stage for an understanding of the New Testament teaching on the imitation of Christ. It also provides historical background for understanding what is positive and negative in modern historical study of the Bible and prepares the way for the further critiques to follow as well as the proposals for more explicit steps toward integration of what is true in both the ancient and the modern approaches.

• • •

WHEN Ignatius of Antioch urges the Philadelphians to be "imitators of Jesus Christ as he is of his Father,"[1] and when Jean Jacques Rousseau holds Jesus up for imitation, we are confronted with two worlds of thought that between them span the attitudes expressed in western civilization about Jesus. If we are to understand the present situation in modern exegesis, we must appreciate the nature of the journey western thought has made from New Testament times to the modern and postmodern worlds and how this journey has affected the way we interpret the Scriptures.

This chapter is an edited version of an article that previously appeared as "Historical Criticism and New Testament Teaching on the Imitation of Christ," *Anthropotes* 6 (1990): 261–87. It also appeared in French in *Revue Thomiste* 93 (1993): 234–62.
[1] Ignatius, *To the Philadelphians* 7, 2 (*Sources Chrétiennes* 10, 126).

The Event is Open

The Old Testament Witness

One of the most remarkable aspects of Old Testament thought is its capacity to interpret one event in light of another. In marked contrast to her neighbors, Israel seldom saw what transpired in her history as being the earthly counterpart of what takes place in the realm above history. Rather, the resemblance is perceived to be between one act of God and another. As Gerhard von Rad expresses it, there is "a typology based not on myth and speculation, but on history and eschatology."[2] The events of the past appeared to the prophets to have a predictive character. Thus, the prophets "looked for a new David, a new Exodus, a new covenant, a new city of God: the old had thus become a type of the new and important as pointing forward to it."[3]

So remarkable is this characteristic of biblical thought that the literary critic Northrop Frye, who, while not sufficiently sensitive to the historical grounding, can speak of the Bible's capacity for "self–re-creation."[4]

The view of reality incorporated into the text is itself dependent upon a more pervasive understanding of the relationship between God and the universe. In another essay, von Rad speaks of the "eschatological correspondence between beginning and end *(Urzeit and Endzeit)*."[5] This *eschatological* correspondence presupposes a view of God as creator, who is master of history while remaining distinct from it, who guides history but is not part of its process. Deutero–Isaiah grounds the truth of God's predictive word, one that has promised a new exodus (Is 43:16–19) by basing it on God's mastery over both "former things" and "new things,"[6] a mastery possible because "YHWH is the eternal God *('elohê 'ôlam)*, the creator of the ends of the earth" (Is 40:28).

It is of the utmost importance that this foundation of biblical thought be understood. Upon it depends all that is said regarding the capacity of the biblical

---

[2] Gerhard von Rad, *Old Testament Theology,* vol. II of *The Theology of Israel's Prophetic Traditions,* trans. D. M. G. Stalker (New York: Harper and Row, 1965), 365.

[3] Ibid., 323.

[4] "This sequence [in the presentation of the "gigantic myth" of the biblical view of reality] is connected with one of the most striking features of the Bible: its capacity for self-re-creation. . . . The dialectical expansion from one 'level' of understanding to another seems to be built into the Bible's own structure, which creates an awareness of itself by the reader, growing in time as he reads, to an extent to which I can think of no parallel elsewhere. Nor can we trace the Bible back to a time when it was not doing this." Northrop Fry, *The Great Code: The Bible and Literature* (New York: Harcourt Brace Jovanovich, 1982), 225.

[5] "Typological Interpretation of the Old Testament," in *Essays on Old Testament Hermeneutics,* ed. C. Westermann, trans. and ed. J. L. Mays (Richmond, VA: John Knox Press, 1964), 19.

[6] See C. R. North, "The 'Former Things' and the 'New Things' in Deutero–Isaiah," in *Studies in Old Testament Prophecy,* ed. H. H. Rowley (Festschrift, T. H. Robinson) (Edinburgh: T&T Clark, 1957), 111–26.

mind, including our own, to see a relationship between events and locate oneself and one's history in terms of what God has done and has promised to do. In the world of thought outside Israel, the being endowed with creative power was considered to be the highest reality in a continuum that extended from the inanimate universe up through man, the servant of the gods, to the highest gods or god. In Israel, on the other hand, there was no continuum but rather a radical distinction between the world, the gods, and YHWH. God is not created and everything else is made:

> The object of creation is without exception something outside the divine. The action of God as creator is directed exclusively to the world. God is outside creation; to be created means to be not-god.[7]

The very particular character of the Bible lies in its capacity to present the history of God's dealing with his people within two dimensions at once, dimensions, moreover, which we consider incompatible. Events move with a "horizontal logic," which is included within a "vertical logic." This grounds a very particular way of approaching the traditional text. I call this an "analogical reading," and by this I mean to designate a way of reading an expression of tradition with the conviction that what is recorded in the tradition and expressed in the text has a direct relevance to subsequent generations of readers. In rabbinic parlance, this same principle is expressed in the axiom, "The deeds of the Fathers are a sign for their sons."[8]

Many scholars using other terms have observed this characteristic. Thus, Michael Fishbane, when discussing examples of "aggadic exegesis" within the biblical text itself, speaks of the *traditum*, that which is delivered in a given text, and the *traditio*, the use of the *traditum* by subsequent generations.[9] Fishbane adduces a large number of such instances within the written expression of the biblical tradition.

In such a procedure, the author consciously inserts himself into a tradition even while he transforms it.[10] Sometimes, moreover, there is an explicit analogical use of a previous event in the description of a present or future event. This perspective goes deeper than the reuse of language and reveals the way in which

---

[7] C. Westermann, *Genesis 1–11,* trans. John J. Scullion (Minneapolis: Augsburg, 1984), 26.

[8] For a brief discussion of this phrase and its influence on Christian exegesis, see A. Levene, *The Early Syrian Fathers on Genesis* (London: Taylor, 1951), 315.

[9] Michael Fishbane, *Biblical Interpretation in Ancient Israel* (Oxford: Clarendon Press, 1988), "Introduction" and passim.

[10] I have treated this procedure elsewhere: "The Image of Shepherd in the Gospel of Saint Matthew," *Science et Esprit* 27 (1975): 261–302. Among other striking examples of the reuse of tradition pointed out by Fishbane, one could consult the manner in which Mal 1:6–2:9 reworks the priestly blessing in Num 6:23–27 (Fishbane, *Biblical Interpretation,* 332–34).

subsequent generations of readers and writers of Scripture saw themselves in profound unity with their predecessors. This was manifest in Israel's manner of composing and receiving the sacred writings. Gerhard von Rad comments on this attitude when he speaks of the continuous reinterpretation of the "old stories about Jahweh" as not only not doing violence to them but as building upon a predisposition found within the stories themselves, an "intrinsic openness to a future."[11]

To describe the stories as "intrinsically open," as von Rad does, is to appreciate them as being consciously inserted into an "open" view not only of text but also of event. Meir Sternberg, discussing the biblical expression of this conviction, accurately describes the fact that in the Scriptures God is viewed as the author both of history and of historiography, that is, that the horizontal and vertical dimensions of an event are not to be separated as though one pertained to factuality and the other to "interpretation" or fiction:

> The marriage of omniscience to fiction and of restrictedness to factual report is a much later arrival on the scene of narrative, deriving from an earthbound view both of the world and the rules for its representation.[12]

A very particular view of reality, one very different from the "earthbound view" just mentioned, underlies the analogical view of history just described. The events narrated and consequently the narratives of the events are both considered to be "open" and not "closed." That is, events are viewed not only in their context of cause and effect but also in their openness to God who is working out his plan for his people. Since God is the creator of all that is, human acts are not fully intelligible unless they are seen in relation to God and to his sovereign activity in the world.[13]

We have seen that the poetics of biblical narrative express an analogical view of reality: Subsequent generations of believers were able to see in the events of the past, as these reached them in the sacred narrative tradition, a meaning for themselves and their contemporaries.[14] This was the basis for the fact that sub-

---

[11] Von Rad, *Old Testament Theology,* 361.

[12] Meir Sternberg, *The Poetics of Biblical Narrative: Ideological Literature and the Drama of Reading* (Bloomington: Indiana University Press, 1987), 82.

[13] An excellent modern philosophical development of this point can be found in the work by J. Lacroix, *Histoire et Mystère* (Tournai: Casterman, 1962); also see W. Kasper, *The God of Jesus Christ,* rev. ed., trans. Matthew J. O'Connell (New York: Crossroad, 1988), 106–9. This aspect of the openness of events will be discussed again when treating the "allegorical" sense of Scripture in chapter 12.

[14] This is true of the whole of the biblical tradition even though not all of it is narrative. The tradition, whose foundation is narrated events, also includes praise, reflection, laws, and prophetic pronouncements, which are all treated in the same transposing manner in this literature.

sequent biblical authors—the Chronicler, for example—could rewrite the stories that formed part of the tradition in order to highlight those aspects that seemed most relevant for their own message.[15] The process was continued by the Book of Wisdom (especially chapters 11–19), Sirach (especially chapters 44–50), as well as by Philo and Josephus, the *Genesis Apocryphon*, and other intertestamental works.[16] In the process of retelling, the text was adapted by being slightly rewritten or glossed: This is the process of *traditio*.

A person is "traditional" when he or she is capable of locating the meaning of personal and collective contemporaneous existence within an inherited horizon of interpretation. Traditional is not the same as "repetitive." Meaning is not found by dwelling on the past but by transposing it creatively to the present while, at the same time, transposing oneself to the past. Thus R. Gamaliel is quoted as saying:

> In all generations it is the duty of a man to consider himself as if he had come forth from Egypt; as Scripture says, "And you shall tell your son on that day, 'It is because of what the Lord did for me when I came out of Egypt.'"[17]

The New Testament Witness

The most basic presupposition of New Testament thought regarding the interpretation of the Christ event is that the life, death, and resurrection of Jesus Christ confer upon the open events of the former dispensation their complete meaning and efficacy. The pure white light of the Mystery of Christ is refracted through the accounts of Creation, Exodus, and Covenant, as well as through the prominent figures, the sacrificial system, the wisdom speculation, and the prophetic teaching transmitted in the traditional texts of Israel.

There is a difference, however. Not only is there continuity, there is contrast. The analogy now is not between events that resemble one another because they manifest a similar divine action and intent as in the chain of events recounted in the Old Testament, but rather between all these events and that one event upon which they depend for their ultimate significance, upon which they were modeled from the beginning, and which gives intelligibility to the further history of God's people.

A vocabulary had to be found that could articulate the relationship between the uniqueness of the Christ event and the events, persons, and institutions that

---

[15] An analysis of the Chronicler's activity can be found in Fishbane, *Biblical Interpretation*, 380–407. Another example can be found in the way that Dt 1:19–36 rewrites Num 13–14.

[16] A convenient collection of examples of such retelling, particularly in the latter period of Israel's history, can be found in F. Martin, *Narrative Parallels to New Testament*, Society of Biblical Literature Resources for Biblical Study 22 (Atlanta: Scholars Press, 1988).

[17] Mishna, Pesah 10,5

proleptically shared in the nature of that event or consequently continued it. In regard to the first relation, that of anticipation, terms were pressed into service that could indicate something of the fact that there was at one and the same time continuity and discontinuity. In philosophical terms, there was analogy. In this case, however, it was an *analogia entis historici* based upon a prime analog, which, as the principle of the category "divine event," is itself beyond the category of what is compared. Christ is both the center of history and its Lord.

There was, of course, no vocabulary ready at hand to express this unique reality. Various terms deriving from various rabbinic and Hellenistic thought worlds were pressed into service, though in the process they received a new meaning. Thus, the events and persons of the former dispensation were a "type" (*typos,* 1 Cor 10:6, 11; Rom 5:14 [Heb 8:5]), less correctly, an "antitype" (Heb 9:24; cf. 1 Pet 3:21), or a "symbol" (*parabolè,* Heb 9:9 [11:19]) of the new and definitive dispensation. The contrast was presented as being that between "the shadow *(skia)* of things to come" and "the reality itself" (*sòma* in Col 2:17) or the *skia* and the "very ikon of the things themselves *(pragmata)*" (Heb 10:1). Other neo-platonic terms are also transposed from a cosmic to a historical plane, as when the Letter to the Hebrews describes various aspects of the former dispensation as a "sketch" *(ypodeigma)* to be compared with what is heavenly (8:5, 9:23, see also 4:11). Finally, Paul can employ a Hellenistic rhetorical term, using it in his own manner, when he tells us that the events concerning Sarah and Hagar should be "allegorized" (*allègoroumena,* Gal 4:24). The very wealth of this terminology indicates how early the Christian community felt the need to articulate for itself and others how it viewed the relationship between the events of Israel's history and those of its own.

In addition to the more theoretical efforts just referred to, the New Testament shows by its practice how it viewed the former events in the history of God's people. The prominence given to the Exodus event is continued in the New Testament, with the whole complex of themes and terminology associated with the Exodus transposed and using a prism with which to refract the light of what took place in the death and resurrection of Jesus. Christ is our sacrificed paschal lamb (1 Cor 5:7; Jn 19:36 et passim; Rev 7:14, 12:11), whose death effects redemption (Ex 6:6/Lk 1:68, 2:38; Rom 3:24; Col 1:14; Eph 1:7) by which we are acquired as a people belonging to God and Christ (Ex 19:5; Dt 26:18/Acts 15:14, 20:28; 1 Pet 2:9; Eph 1:14; Tit 2:13–14; Rev 5:9–10, and so on) so that, in effect, we are (or will be) saved (Ex 14:13, 15:2; Is 45:17, 46:13/Rom 1:16, 5:9–10, 8:24; 1 Cor 3:15, 5:5; Tit 2:13; and so on). We have been taken from slavery and darkness into freedom and light (Ex 20:2, and so on/Rom 8:15; Col 1:13). Now we live in a new covenant (Mt 26:28 par; 2 Cor 3:7–18; Rom 8:2–4).

Not only events but institutions, such as the temple (Jn 2:19–22; 1 Cor 3:16–17, 6:19–20) and the liturgy of Yom Kippur (Rom 3:21–26; Heb 7–10), are transposed into the Christian context. In addition, Jesus is seen as embodying and explaining in a transcendent manner the qualities and roles of Moses, David, Elijah, and others.[18]

The actual text of the Old Testament is enlisted in the process of transposition in three different ways. First, it may be explicitly quoted to indicate that something accomplished or promised has now reached its definitive goal.[19] Second, the text was slightly altered to suit the present purpose; this could sometimes be accomplished by utilizing the LXX or some other existing translation.[20] Third, phrases from the Jewish Scriptures were woven into the text in an allusive manner that provided, for those who could appreciate it, an ongoing interpretation of the prior tradition.[21]

The above examples of terminology, comparison of events, and the use of the Old Testament text hardly exhaust the ways in which the early Christian community expressed its relation to the people and events of Israel. Yet, as has already been mentioned, the New Testament looks to the future as well: Christ is the firstborn of many brethren (Rom 8:29). We will consider this at length in the third part of this study, but it will be useful to look at some examples here.

The conviction that the events of the life of Jesus continued to be the context for Christian meaning can be seen in the way these events are narrated. We find, for example, an abundant and purposefully ambiguous use of the title *Kyrios* placed on the lips of Jesus' interlocutors. Sometimes, this is overtly theological, as when Matthew never allows the term to be used by the enemies of Jesus but only by actual or potential disciples: Compare, for instance, the "Is it I, Lord?" of the disciples with the "Is it I, *Rabbi?*" on the part of Judas (Mt 26:22, 25). Again, the disciples' cry for help during the storm at sea is recorded by Mark as a moment of panic: "Teacher, don't you care that we are perishing?" (Mk 4:38), but the same address to Jesus in Matthew is couched in liturgical terms, most probably those of Matthew's own community, and still present in the Byzantine rite: "*Kyrie sòson,* we are perishing." (Mt 8:25).[22] Another example of liturgical, specifically baptismal, overtones is probably found in the phrase "your faith has healed/saved

---

[18] The attribution of qualities of earlier great men to contemporary holy men and "men of deeds" is found, without the context of transposing analogy, in rabbinic writings. See the discussion in the Introduction to my *Narrative Parallels,* ibid.

[19] An example would be the use of Ex 12:46/Num 9:12 (Ps 34:20) and Zech 12:10 in Jn 19:36–37.

[20] A good analysis of the mode of procedure in the First Gospel can be found in R. H. Gundry, *The Use of the Old Testament in St. Matthew's Gospel,* Novum Testamentum Supplement 18 (Leiden: Brill, 1967). Example: Is 7:14 (8:8) in Mt 1:23.

[21] For a recent discussion of Paul's method of proceeding in this regard, see Richard Hays, *Echoes of Scripture in the Letters of Paul* (New Haven: Yale University Press, 1989). Example, Ps 98:2; Is 51:4–5; 52:10; Hab 2:4 in Rom 1:16–17.

[22] Examples of liturgical usage as either a repetition of a Gospel formula or its source are frequent and indicate the close connection perceived by the Christians between the life of Jesus and that of his Body, the Church.

you" (Mt 9:22 par; Mk 9:52/Lk 18:42, 7:50, 17:19) since it juxtaposes *pistis* and *sozein* in a way found elsewhere in the New Testament.[23]

Sometimes the words of Jesus are so contextualized that they are obviously intended by the author to apply to future generations. This can be appreciated, for instance, in the exhortation to vigilance found in the Agony in the Garden.[24] Sometimes what has been transmitted in the tradition is changed to show its application to the contemporary situation. This is exemplified in the Matthean rewrite of material also found in Luke 13:26–27. In Luke, Jesus, as part of his warning about the narrow door, warns his listeners that even though "then" they will appeal to the fact that they ate and drank with him and that he preached in their streets, they will be rejected. In Matthew 7:22–23, the same appeal to a special claim on Jesus is now presented in terms that fit the post-Easter disciples: "We prophesied in your name, and in your name we cast out demons, and in your name we performed many works of power." The warning follows that judgment will be based on whether or not one has done the will of the Father.

Thus, for the New Testament, the Lord Jesus Christ, particularly in his death and resurrection, constitutes the center of history, giving a new and ful-filled meaning to the ancient tradition and providing a context and direction for the lives of all who come to believe in him. The New Testament frequently uses the term *mysterion* to designate this twofold openness of the Christ event. Utilizing the overtones already invested in the word in Judaism, the New Testa-ment, particularly the Pauline writings, asserts that Christ is the Mystery, the transcendent and definitive realization of what had been already adumbrated in the intimations of the Mystery in the previous tradition, and he is the living cause and exemplar of the life of each Christian who has died with Christ, been raised with him, and brought to glory.[25]

Though the Gospel texts move on a less abstract level, the things that Jesus lived through and accomplished are narrated there because the events them-selves continue to be revelation. It is the function of the narrating text to so configure the event that the "entropy" of the event may now function through contact with the "entropy" of the text.[26] Because the events in the life of Christ,

---

[23] See also Acts 14:9, 3:16, 16:31; Rom 1:17, 10:10, and so on.

[24] Cf. Mark 14:38 and Chapter 2

[25] See Raymond Brown, "The Pre-Christian Semitic Concept of 'Mystery'," *Catholic Bib-lical Quarterly* 20 (1958): 417–43; "The Semitic Background of the New Testament *Mysterion*," *Biblica* 39 (1958): 426–48; 40 (1959): 70–87. Also Karl Prümm, "Mys-tères," *Dictionnaire de la Bible, Supplément* 6 (1957), 10–225. For a study of Paul's use of the preposition syn in verbs applied to Christians, see Walter Grundmann, "Syn" in *The-ological Dictionary of the New Testament* 6:766–97, esp. 781ff.

[26] Space does not allow for a full development of this rich notion, which, in regard to the text, was expounded by J. Lotman in *The Structure of the Artistic Text*, Michigan Slavic Contributions 7, trans. G. Lenhoff and R. Vroon (Ann Arbor: University of Michigan, 1977), 25–31 et passim.

mediated to us through the Gospel narratives, are able to reveal him, they were called the "mysteries" of his life by later generations who contemplated and experienced the open quality of these events in their power to touch and change lives.

The fact that Jesus is risen from the dead makes of his humanity, in all its historicity, the transcendent fulfillment and prime analog of all that God did in the past and the exemplar and instrument of what he does now. We have contact with that humanity through faith and, as transformed by the power of the resurrection, is "the new and living" way that gives us access to the Sanctuary. (Heb 10:19–22).

The Witness of the Early Church Fathers

Sometime early in the fifth century, Pope St. Leo I told his congregation:

> All those things which the Son of God both did and taught for the reconciliation of the world, we not only know in the account of things now past, but we also experience in the power of works which are present.[27]

That Leo intended by this to refer not only to the sacraments of the Church but also to the reading of the Scriptures is evident from his oft-repeated notion that the Gospel text, when received by faith, *makes present* that which it speaks about.[28]

Leo's teaching, splendid in its clarity, does but sum up nearly five-hundred years of thinking about how the events in the life of Christ continue to have their effect in the life of the Church. The earliest church writers used the New Testament terms *typos, allegoria,* and *mysterion* when referring to the relation between Israel and Christ/the Church. In the west, the word *sacramentum* was often used to designate "mystery,"[29] while another term, *figura,* became prominent and often served to combine the notions of "type" and "mystery."[30] In actual practice, *mysterion* and *figura* indicated not only the relation between the Old Testament and Jesus, but also the relation between the events of the New Testament and those of the ongoing life of the Church.[31]

---

[27] *On the Passion,* 12 (*Sources Chrétiennes* 74, 82).

[28] *On the Resurrection,* 1 (*Sources Chrétiennes* 74, 123); *On the Epiphany,* 5 (*Sources Chrétiennes* 22, 254); *On the Passion,* 5 and 18 (*Sources Chrétiennes* 74, 41; 112). For the references to these citations, see Dom Marie-Bernard de Soos, "Le Mystère Liturgique d'après saint Léon le Grand" (Mimeograph thesis, Toulouse, June 10, 1955).

[29] See C. Mohrmann, "Sacramentum dans les Plus Anciens Textes Chrétiens," *Harvard Theological Review* 47 (1954): 141–52.

[30] For this latter term, I am greatly indebted to the excellent study by Erich Auerbach, "Figura" in his *Scenes from the Drama of European Literature* (Gloucester, MA: Peter Smith, 1973), 11–76.

[31] I will return to this in chapter 12.

The early writers continued this orientation, although some of them at times, particularly men such as Clement of Alexandria and Ambrose of Milan, tended to exploit the potential of the word "mystery" to refer to Christianity as the transcendent fulfillment of what the pagans sought for in being initiated into the *mysteria*.[32] In general, however, the earliest tradition tended to view Christ, especially in his death and resurrection, as the definitive revelation of the plan of God and therefore to see the anticipatory revelations of that plan as belonging to the mystery. The consequent experience of the Church is seen to be a series of participatory revelations of the same unique historical reality.[33]

One of the earliest and most eloquent exponents of this view, especially in regard to the anticipatory dimension, was Melito of Sardis in his *Paschal Homily*.[34] Melito speaks of *to tou pascha mysterion* (N.2) which is "new and old, eternal and temporal, corruptible and incorruptible, mortal and immortal." He goes on to discuss this mystery as present in the paschal lamb and then through-out all the history of Israel. Justin Martyr, a slightly earlier contemporary of Melito, uses *mysterion* similarly to refer to the prefiguring quality of Old Testament texts and institutions,[35] but also applies the term to the saving power of Christ's death in relation to believers.[36]

Commenting on the words of Jesus concerning his body and the explanation given by the author in John 2:20–21, Origen states:

> Thus, the resurrection of Christ which took place after the sufferings of the cross contains the mystery of the resurrection of the whole Body of Christ. For just as the perceptible body of Jesus was crucified, buried, and afterwards raised, so the Body of the saints of Christ was crucified with Christ and now lives no longer [see Gal 2:20]. . . .[37]

---

[32] See some of the remarks by Mohrmann, "Sacramentum."

[33] For some useful surveys of this material, the reader is referred to: A. Solignac, "Mystère" in *Dictionnaire de Spiritualité* 10 (Paris: Beauchesne 1980), 1861–74; A. Grillmeier, "Überblick über die Mysterien Jesu im allgemeinen," in *Mysterium Salutis* III/2 ed. J. Feiner and M. Löhrer (Einsiedeln–Zürich–Köln: Benziger Verlag, 1969), 3–22; and L. Scheffczyk, "Die Stellung des Thomas von Aquin in der Entwicklung der Lehre von den Mysteria Vitae Christi," in *Renovatio et Reformatio*, ed. M. Gerwing and G. Ruppert (FSL Hödl) (Münster: Aschendorff, 1985), 44–70.

[34] See the edition by O. Perler in *Sources Chrétiennes*, 123 (Paris: Cerf, 1966). For a convenient English translation, see Gerald F. Hawthorne, "A New English Translation of Melito's Paschal Homily," in *Current Issues in Biblical and Patristic Interpretation*, Studies in Honor of Merrill C. Tenney Presented by his Former Students, ed. Gerald F. Hawthorne (Grand Rapids, MI: Eerdmans Publishing Co., 1975), 147–75.

[35] *Dialogue* 24, 1; 40, 1; 68, 6; 78, 9.

[36] *Apology* 13, 4; *Dialogue* 74, 3; 106, 1; 131, 2.

[37] *On John* 10, 35, 229–30 (*SC* 157, 520–22).

Similar texts can be found elsewhere in Origen, in Hippolytus of Rome, Gregory Nazianzus, Maximus the Confessor and others,[38] and this same line of thought is continued in Bernard of Clairvaux[39] and Thomas Aquinas.[40]

The Consistency of the Witness Concerning Open Events

Underlying all the texts we have seen is one consistent view of the nature of history. It may be summed up in the words of Jean Lacroix:

> Mystery is that which opens up temporality and gives it its depth, it is that which introduces a vertical dimension into history: it makes of it a time of revelation, of unveiling.[41]

A biblical view of reality includes its vertical dimension. This is especially true of a biblical view of history, which sees in the fact that all human action lies "naked and exposed" (Heb 4:13) to God the Creator, the most certain guarantee of freedom. Without this dimension, there is nothing transcendent about man; he has choice but not freedom. The fundamental openness of all human activity is grounded in the mysterious dimension of that activity by which, while remaining completely human, is a dependent sharing in the divine activity.

That history is a work of God flows inevitably from the biblical teaching that the universe is a creation of God. If, however, we apply a univocal concept of causality to this notion, we find ourselves making God and man rivals. Either God causes or man causes. The truth is that divine and human causality are related analogously; they are not in competition. It is in the nature of divine causality, which freely flows from the "diffusive" quality of the divine goodness, that it create and sustain the causality proper to creatures. As Thomas Aquinas expressed it: "To deny that created things have their own proper actions is to derogate from the divine goodness."[42]

---

[38] A convenient summary of their teaching, with bibliography can be found in the article by Scheffczyk cited in note 33.

[39] See J.-M. Déchanet, "Les mystères du salut. Le Christologie de S. Bernard," in *Saint Bernard Théologien,* Actes du Congrès de Dijon, 15–19 septembre 1953, *Analecta Sacri Ordinis Cisterciensis* 9 (1953): 78–91.

[40] See I. Biffi, "I Misteri della Vita di Cristo nei Commentari Biblici di San Tommaso d'Aquino," *Divus Thomas* (Piacenza) 53 (3rd ser. 1976): 217–54.

[41] *Histoire et Mystère,* Cahiers de l'Actualité Religeuse 18 (Paris: Casterman, 1962), 7.

[42] Thomas Aquinas, *Summa contra Gentiles,* 3, 69. The text runs: "Detrahere ergo actiones proprias a rebus creatis est divinae bonitati derogare." Earlier in the same section, we read: "Si nulla creatura habet aliquam actionem ad aliquem effectum producendum, multum detrahitur perfectioni creaturae; ex abundantia enim perfectionis est quod perfectionem quam aliquid habet possit alteri communicare." For a discussion of the analogous and participatory nature of human causality, see C. Fabro, *Participation,* 488–508.

Eric Auerbach's article "Figura" is perhaps the most adequate study of the mentality that intuitively grasped the open quality of biblical events and understood how their relation to God made them a source of living and understanding one's own history. The term most often used to express this understanding is *figura*, a word preferred in the west to *typus*, also understood and used, because this latter "remained an imported lifeless sign" while the former continued to grow and exploit its roots in both popular and rhetorical language.[43]

Figural interpretation differs from symbolic interpretation in that figural interpretation establishes a connection between two events or persons, while a symbolic interpretation, popular from the time of the Reformation, connects the former historical reality with an idea, or a mystical or ethical system.[44] Figure sees events as related to one another because of their relationship to God. Symbol sees events as significant because they are expressions of a meaning. History is still in progress, and thus it is still possible to understand one's self and one's future by connecting the events in the life of the Church and one's own life to the events of the past. This view of reality is well articulated by Auerbach in the rather extended passage I now quote:

> Figural prophecy implies the interpretation of one worldly event through another; the first signifies the second, the second fulfills the first. Both remain historical events; yet both, looked at in this way, have something provisional and incomplete about them; they point to one another and both point to something in the future, something still to come, which will be the actual, real, and definitive event. . . . Thus history, with all its concrete force, remains forever a figure, cloaked and needful of interpretation. . . . [T]he event is enacted according to an ideal model which is a prototype situated in the future and thus far only promised.[45]

The aspect missing in the above description is the important distinction between the Old and New Testaments. The Christ event has made the promise present and available, though still in a manner that is compatible with the per-during presence of "this age." The definitive prototype, Christ in glory, is the exemplar and prime analog of the events that preceded him and the exemplar, prime analog, and efficient instrumental cause of the acts of God that follow. In biblical terms, the Letter to Hebrews describes the former dispensation as a "shadow" of the good things to come, while the present dispensation is an "ikon of the realities themselves" (Heb 10:1). "The good things to come" are already present. We have them by faith, which is itself the "means of possessing things

---

[43] Auerbach, "Figura," 48–49.

[44] Ibid.,54–55. This same point was made in regard to the Old Testament by Gerhard von Rad in his treatment of "Typology" in Volume II of *Old Testament Theology*.

[45] Auerbach, "Figura," 58–59.

hoped for, the means of being sure of realities not seen" (Heb 11:1).[46] Augustine described the relation between the presence of the promised realities and our position in the new dispensation by saying: "The Old Testament is the promise in figure *(promissio figurata)*, the New is the promise understood in the Spirit *(spiritualiter intellecta)*."[47]

The Accent on Horizontal Causality

At a certain point in western thought it became impossible to interpret history in a figural manner. This came about through a loss of the sense of the vertical dimension of history and this itself was part of a larger spiritual current in Europe. The story has been told many times, but only recently have the implications of this movement been appreciated as it relates to the use of the historical methods in understanding the Bible. I wish here to touch briefly on this aspect of biblical study insofar as it will help us to elaborate some basic principles needed to synthesize the legitimate horizontal or autonomous intelligibility of biblical history and its vertical or dependent intelligibility, or, in terms of our study, the relation between the imitation of Christ as extrinsic model and the imitation of Christ as interior principle of life.

The Divergence of Horizons

During a four-hundred-year period, from approximately 1300 to 1680, the accepted biblical view of the cosmos and a newer view based on observation and experimentation slowly drifted apart. It was not that no one had confronted the biblical view of history or cosmos prior to that. Origen in his day had applied the norms of Hellenistic rhetoric and history writing to the Gospels and this included categorizing its narratives as recounting events that happened, that might have happened but did not, and which never could have happened.[48] Examples of this type of thinking could be multiplied.[49]

The shift in thinking that I am describing here is not merely a matter of applying critical norms to the biblical text. It is rather the adopting of a radically

---

[46] Time does not permit me to justify here the translation of *ypostasis* and *elenchos* that I have given. My basic point would not be changed by recourse to one of the more usual translations. For a discussion of this text, see W. Thompson, *The Beginnings of Christian Philosophy. The Epistle to the Hebrews,* Catholic Biblical Quarterly Monograph Series 13 (Washington, DC: Catholic Biblical Association of America, 1982), 53–80; and O. Michel, *Der Brief an der Hebräer* 14th ed. (Kritisch–exegetischer Kommentar über das Neue Testament 13) (Göttingen: Vandenhoeck & Ruprecht, 1984), 368–79.

[47] *Sermon* 4, 9 *(Patrologia Latina* 38, 37).

[48] Origen gets this classification from the Alexandrian rhetorician Aelius Theon. See Robert Grant, *The Earliest Lives of Jesus* (New York: Harper, 1961), 65 et passim.

[49] Grant has collected some of these examples in an article, "Historical Criticism in the Ancient Church," *Journal of Religion* 25 (1945): 183–96.

different view of the reality about which the Bible is speaking. For nearly two-thousand years, the western mind had looked at the material universe through the lens of an Aristotelian perspective. The gaps and inconsistencies in this view had been noted, particularly since the early fourteenth century, but it required nearly three-hundred years of observation and experimentation to bring the data to a point of "critical mass." Then it was possible to articulate a completely different paradigm that made the so-called "scientific revolution" a factor in western history, which, according to the historian Herbert Butterfield, "outshines everything since the rise of Christianity and reduces the Renaissance and Reformation to the rank of mere episodes, mere internal displacements, within the system of medieval Christendom."[50]

The story of the impact on European thought of Sir Isaac Newton's *Philosophiae Naturalis Mathematica Principia* is well known and often told.[51] This was the first complete paradigm providing an alternative to the Aristotelian view of mechanics offered in nearly two millenia. Because it presented both heavenly and earthly phenomena as instances of an overriding set of mathematical principles, it provided, for the first time, a vision of what it would be like to understand all reality in terms of a single complex of laws.[52] Basically, such an ideal derives from a Christian view of creation, one which sees that the universe as made by God can yield an autonomous intelligibility. As Thomas Aquinas already said, created things have activities and causalities proper to themselves.

Unfortunately, the minds who first confronted the new mentality were unequal to the challenge of integrating a perfectly legitimate search for an intrinsic intelligibility of the universe based on horizontal causality with a correlative understanding based on vertical causality.[53]

---

[50] Herbert Butterfield, *The Origins of Modern Science,* rev. ed. (New York: The Free Press, 1957), 7. One may also consult with profit his essay "Dante's View of the Universe," in *A Short History of Science: Origins and Results of the Scientific Revolution* (New York: Doubleday [Anchor], 1951), 1–9.

[51] For the purposes of this aspect of our reflections, the most useful studies are: M. Buckley, "The Newtonian Settlement and the Origins of Atheism," in *Physics, Philosophy, and Theology: A Common Quest for Understanding,* ed. R. Russell, W. Stoeger, and G. Coyne (Vatican City State: Vatican Observatory, 1988), 81–102. This is a summary of a larger work, *At the Origins of Modern Atheism* (New Haven: Yale University Press, 1988). Also very useful is the study by P. Gay, *The Enlightenment: An Interpretation,* vol. I, *The Rise of Modern Paganism* (New York: Norton, 1966), and ch. 9 in Butterfield's, *The Origins of Modern Science* (ibid.), "The Transition to the *Philosophe* Movement in the Reign of Louis XIV."

[52] The foundationalism inspired by the Cartesian anxiety played a large part in framing this ideal, but it need not have done so. A good analysis of this "anxiety" is provided by Richard Bernstein in *Beyond Objectivism and Relativism: Science, Hermeneutics and Praxis* (Philadelphia: University of Pennsylvania Press, 1985).

[53] The most important study of this shift is that by Louis Dupré, *Passage to Modernity: An Essay in the Hermeneutics of Nature and Culture* (New Haven/London: Yale University Press, 1993).

There were reasons for this. The atmosphere was stridently opposed to tradition in any form and in particular to the authority of a Christian vision of reality.[54] Then, too, the universal extent of the Newtonian explanation of the universe persuaded Christian apologists to adopt Newton's optimism that the existence of the Creator could be established by the consideration of the laws of that universe. They failed to see that by abandoning any faith view of creation, they had changed it from being a word from God to being a vestige of the Prime Mover. Thus, they tacitly accepted the position that the Christian faith neither established nor defended its own first principle, namely the existence of God, but rather relied on "natural philosophy" to do that.

Modern atheism arose when it became evident that while religion needed physics to establish its fundamental principle, physics did not need religion. Thus, the Newtonian world was set on its head by men like Denis Diderot and Baron Paul d'Holbach who correctly saw that a coherent explanation of the universe could be supplied by the use of Newtonian physics without any recourse to a Supreme Being. In the words of Michael Buckley, "Atheism came out of a turn in the road in the development and autonomy of physics."[55]

Once the European mind became used to the idea that the universe was endowed with an autonomous intelligibility, the challenge of demonstrating the complementary truth, namely that the universe does not have an independent intelligibility, became more and more difficult, and remains so until our day. This is not the place to trace the history of the various currents of thought that have come to grips with this problem or to measure their success. The notion of creation was never arrived at by the use of unaided reason. It required revelation.[56] The light needed now comes from the same source if we are to appreciate the validity of modernity's stance in regard to the autonomy of the universe and to integrate that with the fact of its dependence upon the God and Father of Our Lord Jesus Christ. We must go on to see how the search for internal coherence on the level of horizontal causality affected the historical interpretation of Scripture.

---

[54] In addition to the works cited above, one should consult Paul Hazard's vivid description of the thought climate of the day in his *European Thought in the Eighteenth Century: From Montesquieu to Lessing,* trans. L. May (Gloucester, MA: Peter Smith, 1973 reprint).

[55] "The Newtonian Settlement," op. cit., 96. I am indebted in this portion of my paper to both of Buckley's studies mentioned in the above note. It strikes me that the benevolent atheism of a thinker like Stephen Hawking results from this thoroughgoing conviction that questions that move beyond the realm of physics are simply non-questions. See *A Brief History of Time* (New York: Bantam, 1988).

[56] This has been clearly demonstrated by Robert Sokolowski in *The God of Faith and Reason: Foundations of a Christian Theology* (Notre Dame, IN: University of Notre Dame Press, 1982), esp. chs. 1–4.

"The Eclipse of Biblical Narrative"

We have seen that the basic biblical view of event, a view that extended at least into the late middle ages, saw each event as endowed with an "aura," which Jean Lacroix called its "mystery" or "vertical dimension." The basis of this view was a grasp on the intrinsic relation of all created reality to God.[57] In a world in which most natural phenomena remained unexplained, the "mysterious" or vertical dimension of reality was equated with its unintelligibility on a horizontal plane. As this latter dimension of reality yielded its intelligibility, it was not a long step for some to conclude that, at least on principle, there was no more mystery in the universe.

Thus, we can trace a trajectory in the understanding of the events recounted by the Scriptures that parallels that of the understanding of the material universe: What is explained in terms of horizontal causality is sufficiently explained and derives nothing from being seen in relation to the Deity. We are fortunate in having two recent studies that trace this trajectory. One is the book whose title is alluded to by this section heading. It was written by Hans Frei, who, until his death, was Professor of Religious Studies at Yale,[58] and the other is the more recent work by Henning Graf Reventlow, Professor of Old Testament at the University of Bochum.[59]

My contention is this: As the vertical dimension of the biblical view of events faded from consciousness, the very nature of the biblical narratives themselves was misunderstood. This progressive misunderstanding paralleled the movement of thought in the physical sciences and in history more generally, though this latter remained an underdeveloped discipline until a later period.

A common outlook can be discerned in the work of Newton and the apologists who relied as well on others responsible for the fundamental shift in understanding biblical narrative. Newton's friend and admirer John Locke not only established a representationalist epistemology that was concerned with the truth of propositions, he applied this to the biblical text itself. Thus, Locke states that when God speaks to men, "I do not think, he speaks differently from them, in crossing the Rules of language in use among them."[60] Of course,

---

[57] Instructive in this regard are the remarks of Joseph Pieper in *The Silence of St. Thomas*, trans. J. Murray and D. O'Connor (New York: Pantheon, 1957) concerning the awareness of createdness implied in every judgment concerning the things of this world. See particularly pp. 57–67.

[58] Hans Frei, *The Eclipse of Biblical Narrative* (New Haven: Yale University Press, 1974).

[59] Henning Grof Reventlow, *The Authority of the Bible and the Rise of the Modern World*, trans. J. Bowden (Philadelphia: Fortress, 1985). Further bibliographical material can be found in the work of Frei and particularly that of Reventlow.

[60] *Treatise on Civil Government* I, 46. Cited by Reventlow, *The Authority of the Bible*, 276.

Locke understands these "Rules" to be in keeping with his own epistemological theory, which was basically representationalist.[61]

Locke's epistemology was applied more reflexively in the field of biblical interpretation in the work of his disciple and friend Anthony Collins. It is interesting to observe that the famous debate between Collins and William Whiston involved two men who, though strident opponents, had both embraced, each in his own way, the notion set forth by John Locke that, "no Proposition can be received for Divine Revelation or obtain the Assent due to all such if it be contradictory to our clear intuitive Knowledge. . . . Whether it be a divine Revelation or no, Reason must judge. . . ."[62]

In 1707 Whiston, a mathematician turned theologian and a close friend of Newton, gave the Boyle lectures, thus following in the line of such illustrious predecessors as Richard Bentley and Samuel Clarke.[63] His theme was the fulfillment of prophecy. Rejecting the possibility of any typological interpretation, Whiston maintained that the prophecies of the Old Testament were intended by their original authors to refer to Christ. This led him fifteen years later to publish *An Essay Towards Restoring the True Text of the Old Testament* in which he developed his thesis that the Jews of the first and second centuries corrupted the text of the Old Testament in order to undercut the use made of it by Jesus and the Apostles. This prompted Anthony Collins, in 1724, to respond with his *Discourse of the Grounds and Reasons of the Christian Religion.* Collins has already expressed his epistemological position in a previous essay in which he stated, "By Reason I understand the faculty of the Mind whereby it perceives the Truth, Falsehood, Probability or Improbability of *Propositions.*"[64] The result of Collins's attack was, in the words of Hans Frei, that:

> Under Collins's guiding hand an argument over the meaning and interpretation of biblical narratives has turned into one over the reference of these narratives. . . . A historical criterion had now come to adjudicate the meaning of the history-like narrative biblical texts.[65]

---

[61] For a discussion of Locke's notions in this regard, one may consult Frederick Coppleston, *Modern Philosophy: The British Philosophers Part I, Hobbes to Paley,* vol. 5 of *A History of Philosophy* (New York: Doubleday Image, 1964), ch. 6, "Locke (3); also, C. Gunton, *Enlightenment and Alienation* (Grand Rapids, MI: Eerdmans, 1985), 17–20.

[62] John Locke, *An Essay Concerning Human Understanding* IV, 18, 5. Cited by Reventlow, *The Authority of the Bible,* op, cit., 257.

[63] For a discussion of Robert Boyle and the important role played in the late seventeenth and early eighteenth centuries by the lecture series he founded, see Buckley, *At the Origins,* 169; Coppleston, *A History,* ch. 8; Reventlow, *The Authority,* 362ff.

[64] *Essay concerning the Use of Reason in Propositions, the Evidence whereof depends on Human Testimony,* cited by Reveltlow, *The Authority,* 354 (italics added).

[65] *Eclipse,* 84–85.

Thus, Whiston, the mathematician–theologian, and Collins, the philosopher, one coming from the world of Newtonian mechanics and the other from the world of Lockean epistemology, managed, despite themselves, to agree on one thing: Biblical statements can have meaning only as ostensive referential utterances. Their meaning is thus judged in relation to the environment in which they were pronounced and the usual sense of the words as this can be determined from common human experience. The words of prophecy or of narrative can refer either to a contemporary event or a future event, but not both. Once the possibility that the events themselves and the words used to mediate them could refer to one another analogically in view of an action of God within creation, there was no other choice. Thus, we have already begun a situation described recently by Louis Dupré as still prevailing:

> Religion has been allotted a specific field of consciousness ruled by methods of its own, but the final judgment on truth has been withdrawn from its jurisdiction and removed to the general domain of epistemic criteriology. . . . *Truth,* if still granted to religious affirmations, no longer springs from within faith but is extrinsically conveyed to faith.[66]

The attitude of the Latitudinarian (Locke) gave way to that of the Deist (Collins) as the storm center of the debate shifted from England to Germany. Actually, there was an intermediate stage, that of the Neologists such as J. S. Semler and J. D. Michaelis, who, under the influence of the English Deists, had moved from Pietism to a position called Neologism that regarded religious truth as historically manifested and appropriable but not discoverable by reason.[67] From about 1750 onward, Germany became the leader in the application of historical methods to the biblical text. The newness of this approach was not so much in a critical investigation of the biblical text, a thing even in its modern form as old as the work of Richard Simon (1638–1712) and Jean Astruc (1684–1766), but rather in the particular view of the nature of the history, which served as the basis of the critique. Briefly put, this view is that history possesses an autonomous intelligibility similar to that of the physical sciences and that any understanding of historical events is to be achieved by studying them in their chronological and "causal" context.[68]

---

[66] Louis Dupré, "Note on the Idea of Religious Truth in the Christian Tradition," *The Thomist* 52 (1988): 499–512; citation is from 509.

[67] See the opening chapter of John Rogerson's study, *Old Testament Criticism in the Nineteenth Century* (Philadelphia: Fortress Press, 1985).

[68] Giambattista Vico pointed out in 1725 the tendency of the history writing of his day to strive for the same type of exactitude as the physical sciences. His critique, however, which paved the way for Wilhelm Dilthey, is bound by the same fascination with horizontal causality and the exclusive search for autonomous intelligibility in the historical sciences. See Coppleston, *A History* (note), vol. 6, ch. 8, "Bossuet and Vico"; also J. Bleicher,

Though the elaboration of Kantian epistemology served in general to prop up the outlook initiated by Newtonian physics, Kant's own exegetical efforts in his *Religion Within the Limits of Reason Alone* (the title serves to locate him) were largely rejected. Kant argued that the biblical narratives were ideas in story form and that these ideas, when correctly (read, allegorically) understood, express the basic moral teaching of sound reason with the additional note that they also trace the movement of the subject from radical evil to the dominance of good will.[69] This seemed to ignore the historical setting of what was in the Bible altogether and most commentators, of whatever place on the spectrum, were unwilling to go that far.

The most notable achievements of the nineteenth century are to be found in the perfecting of the historical critical approach to the Scriptures rather than in any significant advance in philosophical understanding of the background and basic principles governing the approach.[70] It was during this period and continuing into the twentieth century that the historical critical approach showed its capacity to render aspects of the Scriptures more intelligible and to assure a measure of auto-correction. However, the "closed system" view of history inherited from the eighteenth century has continued to our day leaving its legacy of ambivalence. The interpretation of the text is done according to the methods governing any text, but the exclusive concentration of this general hermeneutics ignores (rather than disproves) the biblical teaching of creation and the consequent view of all human activity as having a vertical dimension. Thus, not only the Scriptures but all texts of the past are imperfectly studied. This means that the events spoken about in the Scriptures cannot be understood as they are related: They are either read as factual reports or reread as myths. Their application to the present can only be in terms of a general moral and religious experience available in other ways by the use of reason. The unique biblical mode of predication described by literary critics such as Sternberg, Frye, and Auerbach is bypassed. Success in achieving an understanding of the intrinsic dimension of reality has obscured the biblical view of creation as lying open to the action of God whose imprint can be discerned as analogously realized, with the prime analogue being Jesus Christ, in whose individual

---

Contemporary Hermeneutics: Hermeneutics as Method, Philosophy and Critique (London: Routledge and Kegan Paul, 1980), 16–17.

[69] I owe this latter observation to Frei, *Eclipse*, 263.

[70] I prefer the term "approach" to the usual designation "method." In fact the historical–critical approach involves many methods, as Martin Hengel has established in *Acts and the History of Earliest Christianity*, trans. John Bowden (Philadelphia: Fortress, 1979), 129–32. This multiplicity cannot be reduced to the service of one operation as in the definition of method given by B. Lonergan: "A method is a normative pattern of recurrent and related operations yielding cumulative and progressive results." *Method in Theology* (New York: Herder & Herder, 1972), 4.

humanity God is uniquely present in a way that completes and gives meaning to his presence within human history.

By not considering an essential dimension of human activity, the historical critical approach has restricted itself unnecessarily and has reduced its capacity to serve in an overall effort to render the biblical witness intelligible. Without a capacity to relate analogously the historical realities mediated symbolically but truly by the biblical text, investigators are left with a difficult choice. Some understand the Bible to mean exactly what it says, but conclude that what it says is irrelevant for any other age. Others, far more numerous, conclude that the Bible is expressing something that can and must be rendered understandable to us today. For some this means that the mythic expressions of a more primitive religious mind be unencumbered and allowed to speak to our age. Many scholars continue to regard the Scriptures as one classic expression among many in the world that gives symbolic expression to the mystery of human existence and points to a way of life that can yield meaning. This is a variation on the theme already enunciated by John Locke: "Hence I think I may conclude that Morality is the proper Science and Business of Mankind in general."[71] Retaining the Neologism of Semler and Michaelis, others regard the Scriptures, particularly the New Testament, as one important witness among many to the historical manifestation of some revelation. Still others accord the Scriptures an authoritative place in theology but find the narrative portions, the greater part of the Bible, difficult to interpret. There are finally still others who are attempting to appreciate the narrative, mediating mode of the Bible, but as yet have not been able to respond satisfactorily to the problem of whether we are dealing with history or fiction.

For nearly all these scholars, including many in the last named group, the past is past: The events spoken of in the Scriptures touch us only in their effects, as do any events. History writing, in the Scriptures as elsewhere, does what it can to overcome the temporal framework of human existence, but the relation of events to one another is on the level of horizontal, including eschatological, causality. The dilemma is well summed up in the famous words found at the conclusion of Albert Schweitzer's *The Quest of the Historical Jesus*:

> A curious thing has happened to research into the life of Jesus. It set out in quest of the historical Jesus, believing that when it had found him it could bring him straight into our time as Teacher and Saviour. It loosed the bands by which for centuries he had been chained to the rocks of ecclesiastical doctrine, and rejoiced when life and movement came into the fig-

---

[71] John Locke, *An Essay Concerning Human Understanding*, I, 3, 6; quoted by Reventlow, *The Authority* (note) from the edition by P. H. Nidditch. The reduction of Christianity to a noble morality was criticized by Adolf Schlatter in the early part of this century: "Atheistische Methoden in der Theologie" in *Zur Theologie des Neuen Testaments und zur Dogmatik*, ed. Ulrich Luck, Theologische Bücherei 41 (München: Kaiser, 1969), 134–50.

ure once more, and it could see the historical man Jesus coming to meet it. But he did not stay: he passed by our time and returned to his own.[72]

I believe that it is possible to move beyond the impasse so eloquently described by Schweitzer by complementing the historical critical approach to the New Testament with an "analogical" approach that seeks to recover what was sound in the basic insight of generations of believers I have already described. This insight may be called an analogy of *historical* being based on the action of God, the creator, in the world as this is supremely realized in Jesus Christ. In the third and final section of this study, I wish to present a brief sketch of how a reconsideration of the notion of the imitation of Christ can contribute to such an effort.

The Imitation of Christ

It is not my intention to develop here the rich traditional teaching concerning the imitation of Christ.[73] I wish rather to indicate how a reconsideration of this aspect of Christian doctrine as it is already present in the New Testament can, with the help of historical and literary criticism, help us recover a sense of the vertical dimension of events and thus provide the necessary complement to the approach that has characterized Scripture study for the last two centuries.

One of the issues that has served to obfuscate modern approaches to an understanding of the New Testament teaching on the imitation of Christ has been the resistance, especially on the part of Protestant scholars, to the very notion of imitation. Martin Luther was sensitive to a late medieval tendency that was later to develop into the moralizing use of Jesus as a hero to be imitated in the same way as Socrates and others. We may see this in Rousseau's comparison between Jesus and Socrates in *La Profession de Foi du Vicaire Savoyard* mentioned at the outset of this chapter, and in John Locke's contention that the role of Jesus was "for the reforming of the morality of the world."[74] Luther sought to avoid this rationalistic moralizing by insisting on a distinction between the New Testament doctrine of the following *(Nachfolge)* of Jesus and the notion of the imitation *(Nachahmung)* of Jesus. Though words related to *mimeisthai* are found almost exclusively in the Pauline literature,[75] and show

---

[72] Albert Schweitzer, *The Quest of the Historical Jesus,* trans. W. Montgomery (New York: Macmillan, 1968), 399. The last line of the translation has been emended according to the observation by Robert Maddox in his translation of Ferdinand Hahn's use of this quote in *Historical Investigation and New Testament Faith: Two Essays,* ed. Edgar Krentz (Philadelphia: Fortress Press, 1983), 27 & 33 n.18.

[73] For a valuable summary one may consult the article "Imitation du Christ" in *Dictionnaire de Spiritualité* (Paris: Beauchesne, 1971) 7, 1536–1601.

[74] *A Second Vindication of the Reasonableness of Christianity* cited by Reventlow, *The Authority,* 260.

[75] The other occurrences are 3 John 11; Heb 6:12, 13:11.

the influence of Hellenistic usage, they are being pressed into the service of a uniquely Christian concept. They have nothing in common with the "closed system" reduction of Christianity to a noble moral teaching so characteristic of the Enlightenment and its predecessors.[76] Actually, Augustine put it succinctly when he said: *"[Q]uid est enim sequi nisi imitari?"*[77]

To understand the New Testament teaching on the following or imitation of Christ requires a deeper appreciation of that dimension of biblical thinking that I have characterized by the traditional terms—analogical, figural, or typological. We have already seen some examples of the manner in which the New Testament expresses through its poetics or literary mode of procedure the conviction that the life of Jesus Christ, particularly his death and resurrection, form the center of history, resuming the past actions of God in regard to Israel and founding the Church. He is the "firstborn among many brothers" precisely because those whom God foreknew he foreordained "to be conformed to the image of his Son" (see Rom 8:29).

In the following brief discussion, I will restrict my remarks to a limited number of instances that can serve as illustrations of New Testament teaching about the imitation of Christ. I will then provide some concluding reflections.

Selections from the Synoptic Material

A striking example of the figural manner of presenting events in the life of Jesus can be found in the various vocation stories in the Gospels. First, the basic schema already found in the call of Elisha by Elijah (1 Kgs 19, 21–22) can often be discerned in the call narratives in the Gospels: (1) The Caller comes upon/sees the Called engaged at his occupation. (2) He verbally (or symbolically) calls him. [(3) There is a seeking for a delay of the call (not always present)]. (4) The Called one follows.[78] We see this schema in the call of the first four disciples in Mt 4:18–22/Mk 1:16–20; the call of Matthew/Levi (Mt 9:9/Mk 2:14/Lk 5:27–28); Luke's version of the call of Peter and the others (Lk 5:1–11). The purpose of these tightly schematized narratives is not only to resume in Jesus the prophetic authority of Elijah, it is also to present for generations of future disciples the true

---

[76] This has been clearly established by E. Cothenet in the first part of the article on "Imitation du Christ," in *Dictionnaire de Spiritualité* mentioned above. See also D. Stanley, " 'Become Imitators of Me': The Pauline Conception of Apostolic Tradition," *Biblica* 40 (1959): 859–77.

[77] *On Holy Virginity,* 27 (*Patrologia Latina* 40, 411B).

[78] It is interesting to note how Josephus (*Antiquities* 8, 13, 7) rewrites the conclusion of the call of Elisha. 1 Kgs 19:22 reads: "And he rose up and he *walked after* Elijah, and he served him." This is interpreted by Josephus: ". . . so long as Elijah was alive he was his disciple (*mathḕtḕs*) and servant (*diakonos*). See F. Martin, *Narrative Parallels to the New Testament,* Society of Biblical Literature Resources for Biblical Study 22 (Atlanta: Scholars Press, 1988), 74–75.

nature of their call. The call is a personal one, it is meant to interrupt one's worldly pursuits and attachments, it is a call to leave everything and belong to the community of those who believe in Jesus, serve him, and share in his ministry.[79] While the first disciples are portrayed as having a special ministerial role, elements of the call narratives can be found in many stories. Peter's mother-in-law, once healed by Jesus, gets up and serves *(diēkonei)* him/the disciples (Mt 8:14–15/Mk 1:29–31/Lk 4:38–39). The blind man/men at Jericho, when sight is restored, followed *(ēkolouthei)* him, "on the Way" (Mk), "glorifying God" (Lk) (Mt 20:29–34/Mk 10:46–52/Lk 18:35–43). The healed blind man in Jerusalem *worshipped* Jesus (Jn 9:38), and the women whom Jesus healed accompanied him[80] and served *(diēkonoun)* him.

There is one act on the part of Jesus that is singled out for imitation by the disciple, that is his death to this "present evil age" (Gal 1:4) in obedience to the Father. The inner circle of disciples are addressed in terms indicating a share in his "baptism" (Mk 10:38) or "cup" (Mt 20:22/Mk 10:38). However, they and all those who would follow Jesus are directly addressed in terms of his cross. The saying about taking up the cross belongs among the authentic logia of Jesus[81] though the extension of it, particularly by Mark who has it addressed to "the crowd with his disciples" (Mk 8:34), and Luke who adds "each day" (Lk 9:23), and the generalizing of it in Mt 10:38/Lk 14:27 belong to the level of early theological reflection (see Mt 16:24–26/Mk 8:34–37/Lk 9:23–25, and Mt 10:38–39/Lk 14:27, 17:33). This theological broadening of the command to include disciples of all generations is part of the figural or analogical thinking I have been referring to. No disciple, of whatever era, is above his Master (Mt 10:24–25/Lk 6:40): He must expect persecution just as Jesus endured it. That is why Luke can call all those who believe in Jesus' "disciples" (Acts 6:1, 2, 7, 9:10, 16:1, and so on).

In the theological transposition effected by the evangelists, the call to "follow" or "serve" Jesus was extended to all those generations who would come to faith in him. The Gospel writers were not attempting to convey edifying or imitable information about a dead master, they were describing for believers what it meant to live in communion with a living Lord. Every believer, each in his or her own way, is also called to preach, to live in a community with Jesus and with those who serve him, and to share his life, his commitment to the Father, his death and resurrection. To follow Jesus means for each believer that

---

[79] The difference between Jesus' call and that of the rabbis of his day is forcefully elaborated by Martin Hengel in *The Charismatic Leader and His Followers*, trans. J. Greig (New York: Crossroad, 1981).

[80] "Followed him" according to a later description in Mt 27:55 and Lk 23:49.

[81] J. Gwyn Griffiths, "The Disciple's Cross," *New Testament Studies* 16 (1970/71): 358–64; R. Pesch, *Das Markusevangelium* Herders theologischer Kommentar zum Neuen Testament 2 (Freiburg: Herder, 1984), 60.

imitation of him, which, while it involves historical activity, is no mere external repetition of the events in Jesus' life. It is, to use the phrase of Ignatius of Antioch, an imitation in activity and in Spirit *(sarkikòs kai pneumatikòs)*.[82]

Aspects of the Pauline Teaching on the Imitation of Christ

As has already been noted, "imitation" terminology is largely restricted to the Pauline literature. It would be a mistake, however, to confine our attention exclusively to those six (or seven) passages where the terminology occurs.[83] These passages, with the exception of Ephesians 5:1, all belong to that particular Pauline notion of imitating another, usually Paul, who is himself or themselves imitating Christ. David Stanley speaks perceptively of a "mediated imitation," which he describes as springing "both from Paul's apostolic authority as an authentic representative of Christian tradition and from the recognized need of those he has fathered in the faith to have an objective norm against which they can 'test' *(dokimazein)* the influence of the Spirit."[84]

Paul does describe himself as an imitator of Christ in 1 Corinthians 11:1, and he frequently holds Jesus up as an example to the believers. A closer look at some of these passages reveals a teaching on the imitation of Christ that articulates and deepens the teaching already contained in the transpositions represented by the Synoptic tradition. First, as E. G. Gulin already noted, exhortations to imitate Christ always allude in one way or another to his death.[85] In 2 Corinthians 8:9 the Corinthians are urged to be generous in their contribution for the poor in Jerusalem and are reminded of "the graciousness *(charis)* of our Lord Jesus Christ: he became poor for you though he is rich, that you, by his poverty might become rich." The recipients of Paul's letter to the Romans are told that those of us who are strong must bear *(bastazein)* with the weaknesses of less strong and not please ourselves. Rather each must seek to please his neighbor in what is good for the upbuilding of all. "Just as Christ did not please himself, as it is written, 'The reproaches of those who reproached you fell on me'" (Rom 15:1–3). Mutual forgiveness is based on Christ's forgiveness (Col 3:13), and the letter to the Ephesians urges an imitation of God as beloved children, a walking in love, "just as Christ loved us and gave himself over for us . . ." (Eph 5:1–2). Finally, unity,

---

[82] *To the Magnesians* 1, 2 and elsewhere. See E. J. Tinsley, "The *imitatio Christi* in the Mysticism of St. Ignatius of Antioch," in *Papers Presented to the Second International Conference on Patristic Studies: Studia Patristica* II, Texte und Untersuchungen zur Geschichte der altchristlichen Literatur 64, ed. K. Aland and F. L. Cross (Berlin: Akademie Verlag, 1957), 553–60.

[83] *Mimeisthai*: 2 Thes 3:7, 9; *mimètès*: 1 Cor 4:6; 11:1; 1 Thes 1:6; 2:14 (Eph 5:1).

[84] "Become Imitators," 877. This is a more correct picture than that given by W. Michaelis (*Theological Dictionary of the New Testament* 5:659–74), who still shares Luther's reluctance to see any notion of *Vorbild* in the New Testament.

[85] *Die Freude im Neuen Testament in Annales Academiae Scientiarum Fennicae* (Ser. B, Tom 26, 2) (Suomaisen Tiedeakatemian Toimituksia, 1932), 234–40.

mutual love, and humility are grounded on that act of Christ by which he emptied himself, became obedient unto death and was thus exalted (Phil 2:5–11).

The Synoptics, by their way of narrating and in their redacting the tradition of the words of Jesus, focus the Christian life on that moment of Jesus' life in which his whole attitude to the Father reached its distillation and climax: We are to take up our cross daily (Lk 9:23).[86] Paul also points his hearers in the same direction, not only in regard to the sufferings and persecution that come from living and preaching the Gospel—we were destined for this (1 Thes 3:3–4; Phil 1:29)—but in the affairs of everyday community life.

Paul, however, goes further in his articulation of the nature of this imitation. Jesus, risen from the dead and in majestic glory with the Father, is the source of the Christian's life. That act of love in which he died and in which he remains fixed forever is the event that is shared in and realized by each believer, each in his or her own way. Thus, the wounds on Paul's body are the *stigmata Iēsou* (Gal 6:17). Again, the weakness, the deprivations, the lack of social standing, the loneliness are part of the dying of Jesus that the preachers of the Gospel bear in their body so that the life of Jesus may be made manifest in this same dimension of earthly existence (see 2 Cor 4:10–11).[87] This is the meaning of the phrase "I live, though no longer I, Christ lives in me," which is intimately linked with the passion of Christ: "What I now live in the flesh, I live by faith in the Son of God who loved me and gave himself over for me" (Gal 2:19–20).

By the innovative use of verbs compounded with the preposition *syn*, Paul describes the Christian life as one that is bound up with the events in history and meta-history that define the life of Christ. To cite by a few examples:[88] We suffer with him (Rom 8:17; 1 Cor 12:26); we are crucified with him (Rom 6:6; Gal 2:19); we died with him (2 Cor 7:3 [2 Tim 2:11]); we (will) live with him (Rom 6:8; 2 Cor 7:3 [2 Tim 2:11]); we have been brought to life with him (Col 2:13; Eph 2:5); we will be glorified with him (Rom 8:17). Paul, who offers himself for imitation by those to whom he has preached, says that his greatest desire is "to know him, and the power of his resurrection and a sharing *(koinonia)* in his sufferings, being conformed *(summorphizomenos)* to his death, if only I may reach the resurrection from the dead" (Phil 3:10–11). Imitation is participation.

Conformity to the image of the Son of God, which is the goal of God's call (Rom 8:29), is thus the true meaning of the imitation of Christ. It is a process

---

[86] Paul says the same of himself in 1 Cor 15:31: "I die each day *(kath ēmeran)*. It would be wrong however to imagine that it was only the death of Christ that was imitable by the Christians. In 2 Cor 10:1 he appeals to them "by the gentleness and magnanimity of Christ." See Cothenet in the Denzinger-Schönmetzer, *Enchiridion symbolorum* article 1552.

[87] See the remarkable study by N. Baumert, *Täglich Sterben und Aferstehen. Der Literalsinn von 2 Kor 4,12–5,10,* Studien zum Alten und Neuen Testament 34 (München: Kösel-Verlag, 1973).

[88] There is a convenient list in L. Cerfaux, *The Christian in the Theology of St. Paul,* trans. L. Soiron (New York: Herder & Herder, 1966), 338.

of transformation brought about by the Holy Spirit (2 Cor 3:18) by which the Mystery, the revelation of God's plan in the death and resurrection of Christ, is made present to history generation after generation in the Body of Christ.

Some Dimensions of Johannine Teaching on the Imitation of Christ

In contrast to Paul, the Fourth Gospel does have in common with the Synoptic tradition the use of the verb *akolouthein*. E. Cothenet describes the point of view proper to John as being: "to link the time of the Church to the time of Jesus, or if one prefers, to show forth the eternal effectiveness *(actualité)* of the earthly life of Jesus."[89] In the terms of this study, one goal of the Fourth Gospel is to describe the Church's life as an analogous realization of the events in the life of Christ.

The first three uses of *akolouthein* in John trace a rhythm. Accepting the witness of the Baptist, two disciples follow Jesus, he sees them following him, questions them about their search, and then invites them into fellowship with him. Then Andrew, who is described as "one of the two who heard the words of John and followed him," announces the Good News to his brother Simon (Jn 1:37, 38, 40). Following Jesus means coming to know him, growing in fellowship with him, and making him known. Invitation to this intimate sharing of life with Jesus can be expressed by, "Follow me" (Jn 6:2, 21:22). The one following Jesus "will not walk in darkness, but will have the light of life," which is Jesus himself (Jn 8:12). Jesus is the Good Shepherd and his sheep follow him because they know his voice, and are brought into the intimacy of mutual knowledge (Jn 10:4, 14). This following of Jesus, this listening to his voice, is proper to those who are "of the truth" (Jn 18:37). To be of the truth is to be "habitually under the influence" of the revelation of the Father being effected by Jesus.[90] Those who let themselves be influenced by this revelation are able to hear the voice of Jesus, follow him, and share his life. Those who follow Jesus now are brought to understand that "the human life of Jesus, his attitude as Son, his submission to the Father, these are the translation and image, on the level of history, of the transcendent and intra-divine relationship between the Father and the Son."[91]

The disciples are to imitate Jesus in his mission from the Father and be sent by Jesus just as he was sent by the Father (Jn 17:18, 20:21). This means, according to the principle already enunciated in the Synoptic tradition that "the slave is not greater than his Lord, nor is the messenger greater than the one who sent him" (Jn 13:16; see Mt 10:24/Lk 6:40). When this principle is explicitly reiterated in John 15:20, its meaning is made clear: "if they persecuted me, they will persecute you." Identification with Jesus as a witness to the truth means identifi-

---

[89] *Art. Cit.* 1556.

[90] See I. de la Potterie, *La Verité dans Saint Jean,* Analecta Biblica, 73/74 (Rome: Pontifical Biblical Institute, 1977), II, 617, n.43.

[91] Ibid., 1011–12.

cation with him in his passion. It is precisely the role of the Paraclete to empower the disciple to bear this witness in a hostile world.[92] The one who ministers to Jesus must follow, that is imitate, him (Jn 12:26) and learn to hate his life in this life so as to keep it for eternal life (Jn 12:25; see Mt 10:37–39 par.).

But it is not only in their imitation of Jesus by participating in his function of witness (Jn 18:37) that the disciples share in his life. It is also, and primarily, in their love for one another. Just as Jesus, like the grain of wheat, must die to bear fruit (Jn 12:24), so those who are joined to Jesus, the vine, must love one another and thus bear much fruit and become his disciples (Jn 15:8).[93]

It is, finally, in regard to this mutual service that Jesus holds up his own symbolic prophecy of his passion as the "example" *(ypodeigma)* for the disciples: "You call me 'Teacher' and 'Lord' and you speak well, I am. If then I washed your feet, the Lord and the Teacher, so you should wash each others' feet. I have given you an example so that just as I have done, you also do" (Jn 13:13–15). It is in this connection that we should also include the famous text from 1 Peter 2:21–22, which is addressed to house slaves who suffer from unjust masters: "You were called to this, for Christ suffered for you leaving you an example, that you might follow in his footsteps." Christ's death was for *(yper)* them, he left them an *ypogrammon*, as a teacher leaves letters for a child to trace over and thus learn, and this "tracing" of the life of Christ consists in *following* in his footsteps. Once again the daily life of the Christian receives its meaning as a participation in, and an analogous realization of, the life of Jesus epitomized in his own death and resurrection.

Some Reflections

The teaching of the New Testament on the imitation of Christ presupposes for the most part, rather than exposes, the teaching that the life—and especially the death and resurrection—of Jesus Christ is the center of all history. Nowhere is Jesus presented merely as a model for imitation by the Christian's own moral earnestness and efforts. What transpired in Christ is now available for each believer to assimilate and express in his or her historical situation through the power of the Holy Spirit. In theological terms, the risen humanity of Christ is the instrumental efficient cause of our salvation.[94] It is to that humanity, in its

---

92 See the recent work by G. Burge, *The Anointed Community: The Holy Spirit in the Johannine Tradition* (Grand Rapids, MI: Eerdmans, 1987), 204–11. Burge is dependent to a large extent on the earlier work of R. Brown, *The Gospel According to John,* Anchor Bible 2 (New York: Doubleday, 1966/70), 685–718.

93 The relation between these two texts and their Eucharistic overtones is brought out by M.-E. Boismard and A. Lamouille in *L'Évangile de Jean,* Synopse des Quatre Évangiles III (Paris: Cerf, 1978), 367–68.

94 See J. Lécuyer, "La Causalité Efficiente des Mystères du Christ selon Saint Thomas," *Doctor Communis* 6 (1953): 91–120.

transformed historicity, that we are conformed by our external actions that-spring from a shared life *(sarkikòs kai pneumatikòs)*. The life of the Church and of each believer is an active participation in the life still available to us by the action of the Holy Spirit.

Concluding Remarks

The bedrock of our trench has turned out to be the glorified humanity of Jesus Christ. It is by being united to him, especially in the act of love in which he died and still lives, that we are able to realize in our own lives the specific energy made available to us by each of the events of his life. This is what the New Testament means by the imitation of Christ.

We have seen that this intuitive understanding of history, the possession of nearly two millennia of believers, Jewish and Christian, was the unifying factor in the way they conceived the action of God and their own relation to him. This in turn was based on an understanding of the way God relates to his creation. The presence of Christ among us, his death and resurrection, is the prime analogue that the anticipatory events of God's people foreshadowed and shared in according to what may be called a formal causality. Since the resurrection of Christ, these events themselves, and in a special way all that Christ did and suffered in his humanity, take on a new meaning. The things that Christ lived through here on earth are now, in virtue of the resurrection, not only in the category of formal cause, giving shape to our lives as disciples, they are the instrumental efficient causes that give us an actual share in the Mystery, the unfolding of God's plan in history through the life of the Whole Christ.

The difference between Ignatius of Antioch and Jean Jacques Rousseau lies precisely in the way they view the presence of Christ to history. The historical critical approach to the Scriptures has brought an enormous and precious increase in our understanding of the horizontal dimension of the text and the events it narrates. It has, however, by the use of the methods available to it, been unable to link the Jesus reconstructed by history with the one who sums up in himself all history. I have suggested that a reconsideration of the New Testament teaching on the imitation of Christ, a reconsideration that takes account of and respects the achievements of recent historical investigation, is a way of recovering that dimension of reality that slipped from view in the fascination of discovering the autonomous intelligibility of our world. Autonomous, however, is not the same as independent. This world, and especially human activity, lies open to the mysterious creative activity of God who, in his goodness, imparts the dignity of true causality to his creatures.

I submit that the intellectual challenge left to us by the era of modernity, now past, is precisely that of recovering in a new key the understanding of God's presence and saving activity in the world. The radiant center of that activity is in Jesus Christ who is at once perfectly human, therefore perfectly historical, and perfectly divine: the prime analogue of every revelation of God and yet transcending revelation by being himself the Revealed. This revelation is not judged by the autonomous vision of reality that we have secured. It is, rather, its judge, the light that gives what we have discovered its ultimate intelligibility.

The effort to articulate this reality in the postmodern world falls to Christians. We will, however, be unable to respond to this challenge unless we can integrate the two movements of thought that I have called horizontal and vertical. These are integrated in Christ and they are shared by those who participate in his life. The solution will come through those who imitate Jesus' life, death, and resurrection and from that imitation derive the interior light that enables them to articulate for our age the Mystery of Jesus Christ, who proclaims himself to be the transcendent meaning of all history: "The First and the Last, the Living One; I was dead and behold I live for ages of ages!" (Rev 1:18).

4 Monastic Community and the Summary Statements in Acts

IN SEEKING TO UNDERSTAND a biblical text, we must attend not only to the history of its production but also to the history of its reception. In this study of the Summary Statements in Acts, I endeavor to locate Luke's text within the context of its production and then trace the manner in which the text was received and lived in the early centuries of monasticism. The key to seeing continuity in this latter process is to understand that the same reality was being experienced at successive levels in such a way that the description of the early community, already interpreted and transmitted by Luke, became the inspiration and norm for further realizations of Christian community living.

• • •

YVES Congar once remarked, "The texts of Acts 4:32 and 2:42–47, dominate and inspire all beginnings or reforms of the religious life."[1] The same can be said in regard to all those religiously inspired communitarian ventures that characterized Eastern Europe in the sixteenth century and that have proliferated in the United States, particularly during the 1960s and has lasted right down to our own times.[2] The purpose of this paper is to study the three longer summaries in Acts, but most especially the first two, in an effort to determine

This chapter was first published in *Contemplative Community: An Interdisciplinary Symposium,* ed. B. Pennington, *Cistercian Studies* 21 (Washington, DC: Cistercian Publications, 1972): 13–46.

[1] "Quod omnes tangit, ab omnibus tractari et approbari debit," *Revue Historique de droit français et étranger* 36 (1958): 228–29.

[2] For a survey of the early period, see A. E. Bestor, *Backwoods Utopias: The Sectarian and Owenite Phases of Communitarian Socialism in America 1663–1829* (Philadelphia: University of Pennsylvania Press, 1950); C. N. Robertson, *Oneida Community: An Autobiography 1851–1876* (Syracuse, NY: Syracuse University Press, 1970), esp. ch. 3, "What They

what it is that is being described there, the themes that are clustered together in this description, and the theological procedure by which Luke gives a word-dimension to what was lived by the early Christian community in Jerusalem. The more one ponders these brief statements and the incessant and varied use made of them in the whole of Christianity, the more one becomes fascinated by the evocative power of this image of people living together "of one heart and one soul no one calling anything his own."

We are faced here with a very particular instance of the interaction between history and what I will call "figure." The ideal described by Acts was more characteristic of certain currents of Hellenistic thought and practice than it was of the mainstream of Hebrew spirituality, yet the community life of the believers is attributed explicitly to the power of the Spirit of the risen Jesus. The early premonastic communities of Syria, Cappadocia, and especially Egypt appealed to these texts in Acts for their justification and self-explanation, combining legend and theology in a context of historical narrative. It is hoped that a study of Luke's manner of utilizing, composing, and situating the material we now find in these summaries will shed some light on the way the early Christians used them. This in turn may help us in our reflection on these texts and our efforts to bring the healing power of the Gospel to the renewed aspiration that we experience today among Christians and non-Christians alike for an authentic common life.

This study will include three parts. First, we will analyze the themes that are present in the summary statements, touching only lightly on the question of Luke's sources. Second, we will study the common heritage within Jewish Christianity and Hellenistic thought that is reflected there. Third, we will adduce some early texts from the first five centuries of Christianity that use Luke's description as a literary and theological *topos*.

The Themes in the Summary Statements

For the sake of convenience we will give here the three summary statements from the first five chapters of Acts and will then proceed to abstract their main themes.

> *Acts 2:42–47:* They devoted themselves to the apostles' instruction *(didachē)* and the communal life *(koinōnia)*, to the breaking of bread and the prayers. A reverent fear overtook them all, for many wonders and signs were performed by the apostles. Those who believed *(pisteusantes)* were together *(epi to auto)* and held all things in common *(koina)*; they would sell their property and goods, dividing everything on the basis of each one's need. Every day assiduously they went to the temple with one accord *(omothumadon)*, and in their homes they broke bread together sharing their food in great joy and simplicity of heart; they praised God and were

---

Thought." For a modern assessment, see *Communes U.S.A.*, ed. D. Fairfield (San Francisco: The Modern Utopian, 1971).

looked up to by everyone. Day by day the Lord joined together those who were being saved.

Acts 4:32–35: The assembly of believers *(plethous ton pisteusanton)* was of one heart and mind and none of them ever claimed anything as his own, rather everything was held in common *(koina)*. With great power the apostles bore witness to the resurrection of the Lord Jesus, and great respect was paid to them all. None was needy among them, for all who owned property or houses sold them and donated the proceeds, laying them at the feet of the apostles to be distributed to everyone according to his need.

Acts 5:(11) 12–16: Great fear came on the whole church *(ekklēsia)* and on all who heard of it. Through the hands of the apostles many signs and wonders occurred among the people *(laō)*. With one accord *(omothu-madon)* they used to meet in Solomon's Portico. No one else dared join them but the people held them in great esteem. Nevertheless more and more believers *(pisteuontes)*, men and women in great numbers, were continually added to the Lord so much so that the people carried the sick into the streets and laid them on cots and mattresses so that when Peter passed by at least his shadow might fall on them. Crowds from the towns around Jerusalem would gather too, bringing their sick and those who were troubled by unclean spirits, all of whom were cured.

The two major themes in these texts are unity or communion, and the Resurrection-witness, especially of the apostles. The unity of this early community is explicitly linked to faith: In all three descriptions the members of the community are described as believers *(pisteuontes)*. Their communion is manifested in the sharing of material goods and their common accord in prayer.

In regard to the Resurrection, Acts 4:33 explicitly refers to the apostolic witness to the Resurrection describing it as transpiring "with great power" *(dunamei megalē)*. Acts 2:43 uses the classic formula "wonders and signs," while Acts 5:12 not only speaks of "many signs and wonders" but goes on to give a dramatic description of the healing power of Peter and the others.

It is interesting to note the terminology used by Luke and his sources when describing the group of believers and their unity. There are eight different words to be found in the summaries: "community" *(koinōnia* 2:42); "in common" *(koina* 2:44; 4:32); "assembly" *(plēthos* 4:32—the occurrences in 5:14, 16 are not technical); "together" *(epi to auto* 2:44, 47); "of one heart and soul" (4:32); "of one accord" *(omothumadon* 2:46, 5:12); "church" *(ekklēsia* 5:11); and "the people" *(laos* 5:12, 5:13 seems to refer to the inhabitants of Jerusalem).

Not all of the above words are equally operative in Luke's theology, but, as we will see, their presence in these summaries is significant for the light it throws on the background of the thinking and self-description of early community. Luke seems to be referring at one and the same time to the religious context of the Old Testament already given a certain slant by the Essene community at Qumran and elsewhere, and to the Hellenistic ideal of friendship and equality of goods proposed by the neo-Pythagoreans and others. Before returning to this let us look briefly at how Luke describes the community of goods and the common prayer practiced at Jerusalem.

In regard to community of goods we find these phrases: "held all things in common," "none of them ever claimed anything as his own," "everything was held in common," "sell their property and goods," "sold their property and houses and donated the proceeds," "sharing their food," "dividing everything on the basis of each one's need," "to be distributed to everyone according to his need." In regard to prayer we find: "the prayers," "of one accord in the temple," "praising God," "they were all of one accord at the Portico of Solomon."

The activity of the apostles is described as "teaching," "performing wonders and signs," "witnessing to the Resurrection with great power," again, "performing signs and wonders," healing and casting out unclean spirits, administering the goods of the community (implied in 2:45 and 4:35).

All of this reality is placed in a context of sacred awe by Luke's use of the word "fear" *(phobos)*, "there was fear in every soul," (2:43—there are a whole series of variants for this verse that speak of "a fear generated through the apostles which was great and upon all," "great fear came on the whole church and on all who heard of it"). In the Lucan writings this term occurs twelve times and in every instance it is the reaction of the people to a manifestation of the divine presence and power. Luke seems then to be using this word here in order to sustain the impression of an experience pervading the whole community as the result of a special action of God. This atmosphere is reflected also in the location of the summary statements. The first is the conclusion of the Pentecost event. The second is found between two series of events: Peter's healing of the lame man, the subsequent persecution of Peter and John, the prayer of the community that resulted in "the whole place shaking and everyone being filled with the Holy Spirit and proclaiming the word of God with boldness," and, the incidents of Barnabas, Ananias, and Sapphira. The third links together these last two incidents and the second persecution by the Jerusalem authorities. The other emotion described by Luke is that of "joy and simplicity of heart" (2:46) and he is also careful to note the respect in which the early community was held by all (2:47, 5:13, cf. also 4:33).

It might be possible to sum up our findings so far under the four headings given by Luke in 2:42. There he refers to the "teaching of the apostles," which could be expanded to include their power and miraculous witnessing to the Resurrection. The next term he uses there is *"koinōnia"* and we could interpret this to imply a sharing of goods as well as a sharing of life and common praise of

God. The next term, "the breaking of bread," has exercised commentators for centuries. It is, admittedly, a common phrase for the Eucharist. Most probably it has that meaning here while not excluding the total meal-context in which the Eucharist took place. The last term, "the prayers," refers to the meetings of the early Christians at the temple, but also to meetings for prayer such as described in 4:23–31. The only factor in our analysis that is not explicitly included in Luke's fourfold description is that of reverent awe and the term "believer."

Before passing on to a consideration of the larger context out of which Luke is drawing his information and terminology it might be well to pause briefly to locate some of the above key ideas within the rest of the Lucan writings and the New Testament. The two basic themes, as we have said, are that of "communion" and "Resurrection." The theme of communion is expressed in words linked to the root *koinos*, in a description of the sharing of goods and unity at prayer. The theme of Resurrection is touched upon in the words "witness," "wonders and signs," "great power," "fear," "believers," and in the description of healing.

Dom Jacques Dupont, in an article on "The Union Among Christians in Acts,"[3] has treated most of the unity themes to which reference has just been made. Basing ourselves on his study, on the wealth of material devoted to the term *koinōnia*,[4] as well as on the recent attention given to the notion of the Church as communion,[5] we may note by way of example the following aspects of unity evoked by Luke's description in the summary statements. First, we should observe that within the Lucan corpus, the theme of unity is not restricted to the summary statements in Acts. We find besides the insistence on resolving "disputes" through humility, which is constantly reiterated in the third Gospel (cf. Lk 9:46ff, 22:24ff, 12:37, and so on), the theme of repairing the division at Babel worked through the Pentecost event. We also find expressions such as: "together they devoted themselves to constant prayer" (Acts 1:14), "and when the day of Pentecost came it found them gathered in one place" (Acts 2:1), "all were filled with the Holy Spirit" (Acts 2:4, cf. 4:31), and so on. The Pauline preoccupation with unity and his teaching that the oneness of the Church derives from the oneness of God is well known. This is also reflected in Matthew's explicit teaching regarding the unity necessary among the disciples before their prayer can be heard (cf. Mt 5:23, 6:14, 18:19–20, 35, and so on).

---

3 D. J. Dupont, "L'union entre les premiers chrétiens dans les Actes des Apôtres," *Nouvelle Revue Théologique* 91 (1969): 897–915.

4 J. Y. Campbell, "*Koinonia* and its Cognates in the New Testament" in *Three New Testament Studies* (Leiden: Brill, 1965), 1–28. See also the article on *koinonia* in *Theological Dictionary of the New Testament*, vol. 3 (Grand Rapids, MI: Eerdmans, 1968), 789–809.

5 J. Hamer, *L'Eglise est une Communion* (Paris: Cerf 1962); Y. Congar, "Conscience ecclésiologique en Orient et en Occident," *Istina* 6 (1959): 187–236; M. J. Guillou, "Eglise et 'Communion.' Essai d'ecclésiologie comparée," *Istina* 6 (1959): 33–82. This is, of course, one of the key themes in the thought of John Paul II.

Luke's use of *omothumadon* reflects the Pauline use of such phrases as "think the same thing" (cf. Phil 4:2; 2 Cor 13:11; Rom 12:16, 15:5) and is summed up in Philippians 2:2, "Fill up my joy by thinking the same thing *(to auto phronēte)*, having the same love, being of one soul *(synpsychoi)*, thinking as one *(to en phronountes)*." This latter exhortation is followed by Paul's use of a liturgical hymn to put forth the humility of Christ as the model and condition for Christian unity.

Dom Dupont has already noted that Luke's *epi to auto* is used forty-five times in the Bible to translate adverbs made from the root *yahad* ("one"). The phrase in Acts 2:47, "day by day the Lord joined together *(prosetithei . . . epi to auto)* those who were being saved," finds its echo in the Qumran phrase "join the community" *('asp leyahad;* cf. 1 QS 5:7, 8:19, and so on). We will return to this later when studying the background of the summary statements.

The only instance of *koinōnia* and the two occurrences of *koinos* in Acts are found in the summary statements. The use of this root in the context of sharing material goods is found in many places in the New Testament. There are, for instance, the four passages in the Pauline letters where Paul is discussing the collection to be taken up for the "poor" (Gal 2:10, perhaps also Rom 15:26) or "the saints" (Rom 15:25–26; 1 Cor 16:1; 2 Cor 8:4, 9:1, 12) at Jerusalem. In three instances this *koinōnia* or sharing is linked to the word *diakonia* (Rom 15:25–26; 2 Cor 8:4, 9:12–13). Another text where *koinōnia* bears the meaning "the sharing of goods" and has liturgical overtones is in Hebrews 13:16: "Do not neglect good deeds and *koinōnia*. God is pleased with such sacrifices." In Acts 11:29 we find the collection taken up as a result of the prophecy of Agabus described as a *diakonia*. In Romans 15:27 Paul describes the collection as an exchange of *sarkika* (literally "fleshly") for the *pneumatika* ("the spiritual") conferred by the mother church. He uses the same image in describing the sharing *(koinein)* by which the Philippians gave him something for what they had received (Phil 4:15; see also Gal 6:6).

All of these references throw light on the Lucan use of *koinōnia* and its cognates in the summary statements but they do not exhaust its resonances. There is first of all the ideal of common life alluded to in some of the descriptions of the disciples gathered around Jesus. They held a common purse (Jn 12:6, 13:29); traveled together and were helped by some women of the company (see Lk 8:3); the disciples looked upon themselves as gathered around Jesus, their Rabbi. Besides the Lucan insistence upon leaving all to follow Jesus (Lk 5:11, 28–29, 18:28), there is the characteristic Lucan phrase in 14:33: "None of you can be my disciple if he does not renounce all his possessions" (see also 12:33a). However, as is well known, the deeper aspects of communion of which the sharing of material goods is an external expression are described by Paul in terms of sharing the sufferings of Christ (Phil 3:10), sharing in the body and blood of Christ (1 Cor 10:16), the *koinōnia* of the Holy Spirit (2 Cor 13:13; Phil 2:1). These are echoed in the phrases in the First Letter of John in which *koinōnia* describes a communion with Christ (1 Jn 1:6), "with the Father and the Son" (1 Jn 1:3), and "with each other" (1 Jn 1:3, 7). All of these overtones are exploited when in the early monastic writings reference is made to the "holy and true *koinonia* whose founder, after the apostles is the Apa Pachomius." It is difficult to imagine that Luke is unaware of these overtones himself when he uses the term *koinōnia* to describe the early Christian community.

We should observe in passing that the first use of the term *ekklēsia* in Acts occurs in 5:11, which, whether or not it is considered part of the summary statement, is consciously used in parallel with the other terms denoting the group of believers, *koinōnia, plēthos, epi to auto,* and so on, found in the first two summary statements.

The closest parallel to the Lucan use of the term "signs and wonders" in the summary statements and his description of the healing miracles is found on the so-called longer ending to the Marcan gospel: "Signs like these will accompany those who have professed their faith" *(pisteusasin)*. "They will use my name to expel demons. They will speak new tongues, they will be able to handle serpents, they will be able to drink deadly poison without harm and the sick upon whom they lay their hands will recover" (Mk 16:17). Then, there are undoubted resurrection overtones in the letter of James, which speaks of the presbyters praying over a sick man "anointing him with oil in the Name. This prayer of faith *(pisteōs)* will save *(sōsei)* the sick man and the Lord will raise him up *(egerei)*" (Jas 5:15).

The use of *dynamis* to describe the apostolic preaching is a commonplace in Paul (cf 1 Thes 1:5; 2 Cor 2:4–5; and so on). As is well known, this same term has resurrection overtones throughout the Pauline letters (Rom 1:4; 2 Cor 12:12, 9; and so on). The presence in the summary statements of the terms "signs," "wonders," "power," as well as the word "fear," reflect the whole atmosphere created by Paul's description of himself in 2 Corinthians. "Indeed I have performed among you with great patience the signs that show the apostle, signs and wonders and deeds of power" (2 Cor 12:12).

To sum up then, the summary statements in Acts present three tableaux in which the early community at Jerusalem is described as experiencing the presence of the risen Christ in a reverential awe begotten of faith and witnessed to by the signs and power and the apostolic witness, as well as by their experience of union with one another—a union strengthened and expressed by their common prayer and the pleasing sacrifice of their material sharing.

The Larger Context of the Lucan Description

Historians are quick to point out that the *vita communis* described in Acts could not have been a complete communism: There would have been no need to describe Barnabas's act of generosity in Acts 4:36–37 if such a gesture were necessary for entrance into the community, and at least some of the disciples in Jerusalem must have still owned homes, which they placed at the disposal of the community (Acts 12:12). Then, too, the common life of Jesus and the early disciples does not seem to have excluded the fact that well into the apostolic ministry the disciples still had access to boats and that the beloved disciple had some wherewithal to take care of Mary, the Mother of Jesus (see Jn 19:27).

When we ask the question as to the elements at work in forming the community life at Jerusalem, we are confronted with two facts: the undoubted presence of Qumran influences in the terminology and structure of the community, and the careful Lucan use of words that depict the Christian Church as the fulfillment of the Greek ideal of friendship.

The excellent studies by Fitzmyer and Johnson[6] in regard to the relation between Qumran and Acts leave no doubt that the early Christians were conscious of the spirituality and practices of the Qumran community. Not only does the phrase *epi to auto* reflect the root *yahad*, as we have seen, but the word *koinōnia* itself seems related to the Qumran description of itself as a community. Both groups describe themselves as "the Way" (Acts 9:2, 19:9, 23, 22:4, and so on, 1 QS 9:17–18, 10:21, and so on). The term *plēthos* in Acts 4:32 should be translated as "full assembly" or "congregation," as also in Acts 6:5, 15:30, and possibly 15:12. At Qumran, the term *harabbím*, "the Many," has the same connotation (cf. 1 QS 61:7–9, CD 13:7; and so on). The term refers to a plenary meeting of the group in order to decide important matters (cf. Acts 6:2).[7]

The Qumran practice of sharing wealth is well known. It seems certain that for full membership, at least in the group governed by the *Manual of Discipline*, complete renunciation of property was strictly required and infractions or fraud were severely punished. Near the very beginning of the *Manual of Discipline* we read these lines: "All those who freely devote themselves to his truth shall bring all their knowledge, powers, and possessions into the Community of God, that they may purify their knowledge in the truth of God's precepts and order their powers according to his ways of perfection and all their possessions according to his righteous counsel" (1 QS 1:11–13). In practice this meant first of all some solemn expression of desire to enter the Community. This was followed by a year of waiting during which the novice took no part in the official functions of the Community and retained the possession of his own goods. During this time his "spirit and deeds were examined" (1 QS 6:14–17). "Then, when he had completed one year within the Community, the Congregation shall deliberate his case with regard to his understanding and observance of the Law." If he is accepted, he enters into the life of the Community, though he does not as yet take part in their

---

[6] J. Fitzmyer, "Jewish Christianity in Acts in Light of the Qumran Scrolls" in *Studies in Luke–Acts*, ed. L. Keck and J. Martyn (New York: Sigler Press, 1966), 233–57; S. Johnson, "The Dead Sea Manual of Discipline and Jerusalem Church of Acts" in *The Scrolls and the New Testament*, ed. K. Stendahl (New York: Herder & Herder, 1957), 129–42.

[7] See H. Huppenbauer, "*rbym, rwh, rb* in der Sektenregel," *Theologische Zeitschrift* 13 (1957): 136–37. There is also an excellent discussion in H. Ringgren, *The Faith of Qumran* (Philadelphia: Fortress, 1963): 211ff.

sacred meals and his goods are in the care of the "supervisor," *(mᵉbaqqer)* who, however, "shall not spend it for the Congregation" (1 QS 6, 18–20). After a second full year, "he shall be examined," and if he is accepted, "he shall be inscribed among his brethren in the order of his rank for the Law, and for justice, and for the pure Meal; *his property shall be merged* and he shall offer his counsel and judgment to the Community" (1 QS 6, 21–23, *italics added*).

It is difficult to determine exactly to what extent the community of Qumran was poor. The fact of shared wealth is not synonymous with communal poverty. Pliny the Elder in his *Historia Naturalis* (5:17) describes the Essenes as "without women, without love, without money," but he is probably going on hearsay. The community often designated itself as "poor" *('anî)* or "needy" *('ebyôn)*, but this terminology derives as much from the vocabulary of the Old Testament, especially the Psalter, as it does from any self-conscious desire to be poor. There are, however, enough textual and archaeological indications to warrant the conclusion that the community at Qumran was not wealthy and did not seek wealth. The sectarians did not seek "the wealth of violence" (1 QS 10:19) and were convinced that "no riches equal your Truth" (1 QH 15:22).

We have seen how the summary statements in Acts specifically mention that the community of goods saw to it that "none was needy among them" (Acts 4:34). There are provisions among these connected with Qumran for the same type of aid. Philo explicitly mentions the care the Essenes took of the sick and the aged, and Josephus, in his famous description of the Essenes in his *Wars of the Jews* (II, 8) praises their care for one another and their hospitality. In the *Damascus Rule* we read the following provisions:

> This is the rule for the Congregation by which it shall provide for all its needs: They shall place the earnings of at least two days out of every month into the hands of the Supervisor *(mᵉbaqqer)* and the Judges, and from it they give to the fatherless, and from it they shall succor the poor and the needy, the aged sick and the homeless, the captive taken by a foreign people, the virgin with no near kin, and the maid for whom no man cares, the orphaned children, and every one of the brethren whose house in one way or another is threatened with danger (CD 14:11–17).

These stipulations reflect perhaps the condition of those who did not live at Qumran. They married and retained their property while accepting the spirituality and outlook of the congregation. It is about these that the *Damascus Rule* speaks in 7:6–8: "And if they live in Camps according to the order of the earth (as it was from ancient times) marrying (according to the custom of the Law) and begetting children, they shall walk according to the Law and according to the statute concerning binding vows. . . ." The word "Camps" seems to refer in the documents to gatherings of the sect, how well organized we do not know, who lived outside the main Community in the desert. Some of the prescriptions of the *Damascus Rule*, and perhaps even of the *Manual of Discipline*, and other documents seem to be principally concerned with them: regarding groups of ten (1 QS 1:8–10), contributions for the poor (CD 18:13–17), and so on. Now, if we add to this the descriptions given by Philo and Josephus of the Essenes living in the towns of Palestine and numbering in all about 4,000, we have a picture of a sect scattered throughout the country who were easily recognized by their strict and characteristic observance of the Law and by their connection with a communal, frugal, and celibate ideal that they practiced in varying degrees.[8]

We have seen above how the Qumran community described itself as "poor," reflecting there an Old Testament ideal more than a financial condition. This same outlook is echoed in regard to the Jerusalem community by Paul who, as we have seen, refers to the Christians in Jerusalem as "the poor" or "the saints." When we combine this with the reverential way in which Paul speaks of the Jerusalem church as the "church of God" for whom he took up a collection, we can see that the originator of that special place in the Christian imagination held by the Jerusalem community because of its fervent life of poverty and unity was Paul himself (cf. 1 Thess 2:14; 1 Cor 15:9; Gal 1:13; 1 Cor 10:32, 11:16).

In his treatise on friendship in the *Nicomachean Ethics* (8:8–11), Aristotle quotes the proverbs *Koina ta philōn*, "Between friends all things are in common," and *en koinōnia ē philia*, "Friendship is in sharing." There were also current expressions such as *philōn ouden idion*, "Among friends nothing is private." These phrases echoed frequently in the neo-Pythagorean theories about communal ownership and friendship. These philosophers often quoted Plato in the *Republic*.[9] In the first century B.C., Philostratus in his life of Apollonius of Tyana is also engaged in a similar effort to portray an ideal human life. There seem to be echoes of some of these phrases in the well-known description of the Essenes given by Josephus and Philo. The presence within Hellenistic culture of these ideas and terminology can hardly be ignored when we read in Acts that the early Christians held "everything in common" *([ta] panta koina)*, and also that "no one called anything private" *(idion)*. We will see Cassian link Greek theories about friendship with the text in Acts 4:32. In so doing, he undoubtedly is faithful to Luke's intention in describing the common life at Jerusalem whose structures and shared wealth may have come more consciously from Qumran, but whose life in the Resurrected Lord fulfilled the aspirations of Greek culture.

---

8 For a supple analysis of the celibate ideal at Qumran, see H. Hübner, "Zölibat in Qumran?" *New Testament Studies* 17 (1971): 153–67.

9 For references see the article by Dupont (n. 4) and the article *Koinonia* (n. 5). There is an interesting article on *koinonia* and friendship by Sister A. Maris, "*Koinonia*: Its Biblical Meaning and Use in Monastic Life," *American Benedictine Review* 18 (1967): 189–212.

The Use of the Summary Statements
in Acts in Early Christian Literature

In assessing the influence of the summary statements in Acts upon the early communities throughout the Christian world, we must take two factors into account. One is the Hellenistic and Judaeo-Christian influence at work in these communities, and the other is the description in Acts of how these influences coalesced to produce the ideal community at Jerusalem. It is impossible to determine exactly in most instances which came first, but one thing is certain, there sprung up very early within the bosom of the local churches small groups of ascetics who spontaneously bound themselves together without losing their communion with the larger context in which they found themselves, and who, independently of one another, began to lead a life that we would term today "premonastic." The existence of such groups has been verified in Syria by Voobus who finds such communities at Odessa and Osrhoene as early as the year one hundred.[10]

These communities and their spirituality had an influence upon Eustathius of Sebaste and Basil of Cappadocia, and indirectly influenced some dimensions of the same type of life in Egypt.[11]

In Syria we find a strong ascetic ideal that ultimately resulted in the Messalian heresy, but whose early beginnings should not be viewed as dimly as does Voobus. There are many indications that the spirituality of Qumran influenced these early ascetics. They called themselves the "Sons/daughters of the Covenant" *(qyama)*, which Beck describes as a "confraternity" and which he maintains designates an ecclesiastical state: *un ordre d'ascetes celibataires vivant dans les conditions d'un etat ecclesiastique.*[12] The term *qyama* is often the equivalent of the Hebrew *berit,* and there is an undoubted reference to the desert ideal in this phrase. DeVaux and others[13] have already spoken of the desert ideal of the Qumran community who described themselves in such terms as a "community of eternal covenant" (I QS 5:4), and also speak of a "covenant of eternal community" (II QS 3:II) and of those who "enter a new covenant" (CD 6:19). Black undoubtedly goes too far when he reduces the celibate ideals of Syria to the Holy War concepts of Qumran, but he is probably correct in linking some aspects of celibacy to the concept of priestly holiness reflected in the Scrolls.[14] It

---

[10] A. Voobus, *History of Asceticism in the Syrian Orient* (Louvain: Secrétariat du Corpus SCO, 1958, 1960).

[11] See J. Gribomont, "Le Monachisme au Sein de l'Eglise en Syrie et en Cappadoce," *Studia Monastica* 7 (1965): 7–24.

[12] E. Beck "Ascetisme et Monachisme chez Saint Ephrem," *L'Orient Syrien* 3 (1958): 280–81.

[13] R. deVaux, *Les institutions de l'Ancien Testament* (Paris: Cerf, 1958), 1, 30ff.

[14] M. Black, "The Tradition of Hasidaean-Essene Asceticism: Its Origins and Influence," *Aspects du Judéo-Christianisme. Colloque de Strasbourg, 1964* (Paris: Presses Universitaires France, 1965): 19–32.

is significant in this regard that the Gospel of Thomas uses the word *monachos* in four logia (4, 16, 49, 75), in one of which the expected *parthenoi* of Matthew 25:10 is replaced by *monachi*. This, according to Quispel, reflects the same type of Judaeo-Christian influence that we find in the Syriac use of the word *ibidaja*, also deriving from the root meaning "one" or "alone."[15]

The ever-present mystery of the *therapeutae* described by Philo (*Vita cont.* 21–90) in Egypt is another instance of Judaeo-Christian influence, but again it is difficult to assess what historical part they played in the development of community life in Egypt despite the assertions of Eusebius in his *Ecclesiastical History* (2:5). Milik describes the way of life of the *therapeutae* as being "analogous to that of the Essenes" and concludes:

> So from its modest beginnings in the second century B.C. the Essene movement spread widely throughout the Jewish world. At least four different branches are known to us, the celibates of Qumran (solitaries and cenobites), the married Essenes living in isolated Jewish villages of southern Syria, the Palestinian "Tertiaries," and the Therapeutae, Egyptian Jewish hermits.[16]

Research in the area of actual historical connection between Essenian piety and Christian asceticism has only begun, while the relation to other forms of Jewish spirituality, such as that characterized by the Hasidim and others, is still too uncertain to be relied upon. We must restrict our study here to the communal dimension of that type of life that appealed to the summary statements in Acts for its model. Studies by Gribomont, Veilleux, Beck, Leloir,[17] and others have established the fact that there was a pre- or protomonastic stage to be found in the *communities* of Christians who formed themselves within the structure of the local church, who dedicated themselves to a life of asceticism and service, who in some places were closely associated with the local clergy, and who governed themselves by a variety of simple and supple arrangements. Rather than attempt here to summarize the work of the above-mentioned scholars, I refer the reader to the excellent summary to be found in the early

[15] G. Quispel, "L'Evangile selon Thomas et les origins de l'ascèse chretienne," *Aspects du Judéo-Christianisme,* 34–52. Some aspects of logia 49 and 75 have been studied by Marguerite Harl, "A propos des logia de Jesus: Le sens du mot *monachos*," *Revue des Etudes Grecques* 78 (1960): 464–74.

[16] J. Milik, *Ten Years of Discovery in the Wilderness of Judaea,* trans. J. Strugnell, Studies in Biblical Theology 26 (London: SCM Press, 1959): 92.

[17] Gribomont, "Le Monachisme au Sein," n. 11. Beck "Ascetisme et Monachisme," n. 3. See L. Leloir, "Saint Ephrem, moine et Pasteur," *Theologie de la Vie Monastique, Theologie* 49 (Paris: Aubier, 1961), 85–97. The two works of Armand Veilleux that are pertinent here are "La Liturgie dans le Cénobitisme Pachômien au Quatrième Siècle," *Studia Anselmiana* 57 (Rome, 1968), and "The Abbatial Office in Cenobitic Life," *Monastic Studies* 6 (1968): 3–45.

part of the article by Veilleux,[18] certain aspects of which should be mentioned here because of their relevance to the theme of this chapter.

1. There were two currents within early Christian asceticism. "The one stemmed from Judaeo-Christian encratism and led to the first communities of ascetics, whether of the urban or desert type, the other led from the urban schools of spiritual training to the school of the desert" (6).

2. The Judaeo-Christian type of community asceticism made its influence felt, not only in those churches of similar linguistic and cultural orientation, such as in Syria, but also was responsible for the movements associated with Eustathius of Sebaste, Basil in Cappadocia, and Pachomius in Egypt (7).

3. Obedience in this type of community can be described in these words that Dom Gribomont uses in regard to the Basilian communities: "Obedience is defined as perfect conformity to the commandments of God as revealed in Scripture; this is incumbent upon all and does not imply any necessary reference to an abbot. It finds its norm, when one is called for, in the needs and opinions of others, and favors the advice of those who have a particular charism for discerning the will of God" (10, translation by Veilleux).

What characterized the premonastic movement of Judaeo-Christian origin was, among other things, that they formed *communities* of people who were drawn together by a common desire to carry out their baptismal promises to the full. In this they differed from those groups who, along the lines of the catechetical schools (especially Alexandria), gathered around a master. This distinction cannot be maintained as ironclad. Many communities undoubtedly began around some charismatic leader, and indeed, for whatever influence it might have had, the Qumran community itself was, if not founded, then at least strengthened by the coming of the Teacher of Righteousness. Still, there is a very great difference between a school, even a school of spirituality, and a community. The former embodies an ecclesiastical function and contains an important aspect of the Church; the latter in its being is a realization of Church.

Some Early Texts

If we turn from an attempt to establish historical connections between Jewish and Hellenistic piety and Christian community life to consider textual allusions to the summary statements in Acts, we find that some areas of the early Church seem to have been much more attuned to the apostolic ideal of communal life than others.

---

[18] Veilleux, "The Abbatial Office."

I. The Didache

No matter how we assess the Jewish background of the first six chapters of the *Didache*, it is obvious that the doctrine stems from those currents of thought in which interaction between Judaism and Hellenism had already taken place. We read in *Didache* 4:8: "Do not turn away *(apostrepho)* the one who is in need. Rather you should share *(sugkoinōneseis)* everything with your brother and not call anything your own *(idia)*. For if you are sharers *(koinōnoi)* in what is immortal how much more in that which is mortal." There are terminological correspondences in the phrase to Matthew 5:42 *(apostrepho)*, Hebrews 13:16, and Acts 4:32. The basic presupposition of this instruction is a life in common. Audet links this atmosphere to the same context as *adelphotes* of 1 Peter 5:9.[19]

Because of its relationship to the *Didache* we will list here the passage from the *Letter of Barnabas*: "You should share *(koinōneseis)* in everything with your neighbour and not call anything your own *(idia)*. For if you are sharers *(koinonoi)* in what is uncorruptible how much more in that which is corruptible."[20]

2. St. Ephrem

The *Didache* may reflect, if we accept its Syrian origins, an earlier expression of the same spirituality we find in Ephrem. The most overt communal overtones evident in the spirituality of Syria are to be found in the use of phrases like "sons/daughters of the Covenant." In hymns whose authenticity may be questioned, but whose antiquity is well established, we find that the apostolic life is conceived mostly in terms of asceticism without the same emphasis on communal life we will find in Egypt. In a hymn in honor of Abraham Kidunaia we find this description:

> With the eyes of your soul you gazed on the Apostles and Prophets, and etched them in your members. Whoever looked on you saw them in you. Their chastity was depicted in you, their uprightness was shown forth in you; you clothed yourself with their ascetic life, clothing your body with their fasts, and from your mouth their prayers burst forth.[21]

An interesting interpretation of the "apostles and prophets" of Ephesians 2:20 is found in this hymn in honor of Julianus Sabba:

> He carried the Beatitudes in all his faculties, and in his members he bore their power. He gazed on the Prophets and Apostles; his two eyes loved the two beauties, and his two ears listened to the unity of the two Covenants.[22]

---

[19] J. P. Audet, *La Didachè. Instructions des Apôtres* (Paris: Gabalda, 1958), 333.

[20] For an assessment of the *Letter of Barnabas*, see E. Robillard, "L'epître de Barnabé: trois époques, trois théologies, trois rédacteurs," *Revue biblique* 69 (1971): 184–209.

[21] T. J. Lamy, *Sanct Ephraemi Syri hymni et sermones* (Malines, 1899–1902), 3:758.

[22] Ibid., 3:870.

3. Egypt

The Egyptian origins of what is now termed "monasticism" are still shrouded in mystery. It is difficult for the modern historian to assess exactly the role of Anthony and Pachomius, those two giants around who have been clustered the attributes of many of their predecessors. The intuitive genius of Pachomius is only beginning to be appreciated in our own day and he appears to have been not the organizer-soldier of a pre-existing movement so much as the true father of the *koinōnoi*. It is in the literature emanating from Pachomius and his immediate disciples that we find the most explicit developments of the theology contained in the summary statement of Acts. But before we analyze this literature it is worth noting the interesting reference to Acts 4:32ff found in St. Athanasius's account of Anthony's conversion: "As he was walking along, he collected his thoughts and reflected how the Apostles left everything and followed the Savior, also how the people in Acts sold what they had and laid it at the feet of the Apostles for distribution among the needy, and what great hope is laid up in heaven for such as these" (*Vita Ant.* C2).[23]

We learn from the life of Pachomius that an angel told him: "It is the will of God that you serve men in order to call them to him."[24] In the same life of Pachomius we read that as the first brethren started to gather around him he gave each one his appointed task and took care of whatever money they possessed or earned. They trusted him because they knew him to be "an honest man and because, after God, he was their father." This arrangement that he had established with them could be adjusted in keeping with their weakness, as the apostle says: 'I became weak with the weak in order to gain the weak' (1 Cor 9:22) . . . he proceeded in this way because he saw that they were not ready yet to bind themselves together in that perfect community as it is described in the Acts in regard to the believers: 'They were of one heart and one soul and all goods were in common and no one said of the things that belonged to him this is mine.' " (Another manuscript of the same life of Pachomius adds at this point the text from Heb 13:16: "Do not neglect good works and *koinōnoi*. Sacrifices of this kind are pleasing to God.")[25]

In the Bohairic life of Pachomius, we read of three men who came to Pachomius and,

---

[23] Translation of the *Vita Antonii* is basically that of R. Meyer, *The Life of St. Anthony,* Ancient Christian Writers 10 (Westminster, MD: Newman, 1950). The use of Mt 19:21 in early monastic literature is extensive. See, for example, *Liber Orsiesii* 27; Cassian, *Institutions* 7:16, 27; *Conferences* 3:4, 7; 8:3; St. Basil, *Longer Rule* 8, 9; *Shorter Rule* 101, 205. St. Augustine was meditating on this incident in the life of Anthony when he had his own dramatic conversion based on Rom 13:13–14 (*Confessions* 8:12), and Mt 19:21 figures in the account of St. Francis's vocation. (See the *Vita* by St. Bonaventure, ch. 3.)

[24] For a discussion of this text, cf. Veilleux, *La Liturgie* 169, n. 9.

[25] L. T. Lefort, *Les Vies coptes de Saint Pachome et de ses premiers successeurs* (Louvain; Bureaux du Musém, 1943), S (1) p. 3, 12–32; S(3) p. 65, 31–33.

Having entered the holy *koinōnia*, they were exercised in many ascetic practices. They saw him working alone in all the departments of the monastery, cultivating the vegetables, preparing food, answering the door when someone knocked; and if someone were sick, he used to take care of him. For he used to say in his heart, of the three who lived with him, "They are neophytes and they have not arrived yet at that maturity by which they can serve others." In fact, he used to exempt them from all duties saying "That to which you are called, strive to achieve." (1 Tim 6:12; 1 Cor 9:24).[26]

This notion of mutual service as being the mature fruit of the apostolic life in the "holy and true *koinōnoi*" is the most characteristic aspect of Pachomian spirituality. Pachomius had been told to serve men and in the service he offered to those who lived near him and were in need or to those who came to him and needed his patience as he waited for them to mature, he honored "the agreement he had made with God."[27]

This lesson was not lost on the disciples of Pachomius. In the famous *Third Catechesis of Theodore* we read: "We are the children of the holy vocation of the *koinōnoi*."[28] We find applied to Pachomius phrases such as "Our father by whom the life of cenobites was founded,"[29] and "Our father, who first established coenobia."[30] Finally, we have this text, again in the *Third Catechesis of Theodore*: "We thank God, the Father of Our Lord Jesus Christ, for having made us able to forget our pains and distresses (cf. 1Cor 1:2–4) by the sweet fragrance of the submission and solidity in faith of the law of the holy and true *koinōnoi* whose author, after the apostles, is Apa Pachomius."[31]

Perhaps the one text in Pachomian literature that embodies nearly all of the resonances set up by the word *koinōnoi* in this early period is found in the *Liber Orsiesii*:

That this coming together of ours and our communion (lat. *Communio*, prob. *koinōnoi*) by which we are joined together is of God the apostle teaches us when he says: "Do not forget good works and sharing; God is pleased by sacrifices of that kind (Heb 13:16). And then we read in the Acts of the Apostles: "The multitude of believers was of one heart and soul, and no one called anything his own; rather they held everything in common.

---

[26] L. T. Lefort, *Oeuvres de s. Pachome et de ses disciples,* Corpus scriptorum christianorum orientallium 107 (Louvain: L. Durbecq, 1936), 15, 9–25.

[27] Lefort, *Les vies coptes,* S(1) pp. 4, 6–7.

[28] *Liber Orsiesii* in *Pachomiana Latina* by A. Boon, 23. L. T. Lefort, *Oeuvres,* 125, 9–11.

[29] A. Boon, "Letter of Theodore" in *Pachomiana Latina* (Louvain: Bureau de la Revue, 1932), 105.

[30] Liber Orsiesii in *Pachomiana Latina,* by A. Boon, 116.

[31] Lefort, *Oeuvres,* 41, 20–24.

The apostles gave witness to the Resurrection of the Lord Jesus with great power" (Acts 4:32–33). The Psalmist agrees to these words when he says: "Behold how good and pleasant it is for brothers to dwell as one" (Ps 132:1). So those of us who live in coenobia and are joined to one another by mutual love, should be zealous for discovering how, in this life, we may have fellowship with the holy Fathers so that in the future life we may share in their lot; knowing that the Cross is the source of our doctrine, and that we must suffer along with Christ (Rom 8:17) and experience the fact that without tribulations and sufferings no one attains the victory.[32]

The theme of the *koinōnoi* extending to all those who have preceded them is a commonplace in Pachomian literature and explains why all the Old Testament and New Testament images used of the Church are applied with such facility to the *koinōnoi*.[33]

It also helps us to understand how the Old Testament saints were looked upon not only as models but as sharers in this same holy and true *koinonia* and as unique realizations of that same charism of the Holy Spirit that moved in Egypt and throughout the Church. This same type of spirituality is reflected in this passage from Athanasius's *Letter to Dracontium* (4):[34]

It is necessary for us to walk by the standard of the saints and the fathers and imitate them, knowing that, if we depart from them, we become aliens from their communion *(koinōnoi)*.

We read in Colossians 1:24, "Now I rejoice in my sufferings for you. . . ." This dimension of the apostolic life is also a realization of that sharing by which the *koinōnoi* is established. "Carry the burdens of one another and thus you will fulfill the law of Christ" (Gal 6:2). Alluding once again to Acts 4:32 we find these words in the *Third Catechesis of Theodore*:

Being all of one heart, suffering one for another, practicing fraternal love, mercy and humility according to the injunction of the Apostle Peter (1 Pet 3:8), following one and the same voice and putting into practice its words in all our acts with the conviction of faith knowing that in thus listening we make ourselves servants for Jesus about whom we have heard in the Gospels the voice of the Father declare "This is my beloved Son in whom I take delight. Listen to him."[35]

---

[32] Liber Orsiesii in *Pachomiana Latina*, by A. Boon, 50 (142, 14–29).

[33] See P. Tamburrino, "Les Saints de l'Ancien Testament dans le ier Catéchèse de saint Pachôme," *Melto* 4 (1968): 33–44.

[34] Quoted in Stephen Benko, *The Meaning of Sanctorum Communio*, ed. S. L. Greenslade, *Studies in Historical Theology* 3 (Naperville, IL: Allenson, 1964).

[35] Lefort, *Oeuvres,* 51–52.

4. St. Basil

Basil's preferences for cenobitic life over the eremitic life are well attested. In the two "Rules of St. Basil," the first two summary statements of Acts are cited twelve times.[36]

It is interesting to note that few of these make any explicit reference to the theme that the *koinōnoi* of these urban groups of ascetics was a continuation of the church at Jerusalem. The witness is perhaps all the stronger in that a relationship is presupposed between the two communities, and regulations for Christians in Cappadocia can be derived from descriptions of Christians at Jerusalem. Also, Basil's view of these communities is very similar to the institution in the Syrian church, which, as we have seen bears the name "sons/daughters of the Covenant."

In Basil's *Eighth Homily on the Famine* he refers to the generosity of the "three thousand" who right after Pentecost shared all their goods. He then goes on to point to the example of the common life of some pagans who hold nothing as private and whose nobility makes the avariciousness of many Christians all the more deplorable.[37]

5. St. Augustine

Augustine's preoccupation with common life began in earnest after his appointment as Bishop of Hippo. The most fascinating part of the summary statements in Acts for him was the phrase "one heart and one soul," but he does not ignore the economic aspect of life in common. Father Melchior Verheijen has consecrated an article to the study of Augustine's use of Acts 4:32–35.[38] There are least fifty occurrences in the writings of St. Augustine where this text is theologically operative. It will suffice to quote but a few here:

(i) He who wishes to make a place for the Lord should rejoice, not in private joy, but in the joy of all *(gaudio communi)*.[39]

(ii) If, as they drew near to God, those many souls became, in the power of love, but one soul and these many hearts but one heart, what must the very source of love effect between the Father and the Son? Is not the Trinity for even greater reasons, but one God? . . . If the love of God poured forth in our hearts by the Holy Spirit, who is given to us, is able to make of many souls but one soul and of many hearts but

---

[36] Relying on the index in L. Lèbe, Saint Basile. *Les Regles Monastiques: Introduction et Traduction* (Editions de Maredsous, 1969).

[37] Cited by Giet in *Les Idées et l'Action Sociales de Saint Basile* (Paris: Gabalda, 1941), 112–13.

[38] *Théologie de la Vie Monastique, Theologie* 49 (Paris: Aubier, 1961), 201–12.

[39] In Ps 131, *Patrologia Latina* 37:1718.

one heart, how much more are the Father and the Son and Holy Spirit but one God, one Light, one Principle?[40]

(iii) First of all, because you are gathered together in one that you might live harmoniously *(unanimes)* and that there be one soul and one heart toward God, you should not call anything your own.[41]

(iv) And you should not call anything your own but let all things be common to you and distributed to each one of you according to need.[42]

6. Cassian

In the writings of Cassian we encounter for the first time a conscious and reflexive use of the summary statements in Acts put at the service of theological and ecclesiastical presuppositions. Dom de Vogüe has pointed out the two "versions" of the account of the church at Jerusalem that Cassian presses into service.[43] Cassian is under pressure and is trying to solidify and reform monasticism in Gaul. He appeals to Egyptian monasticism as the authentic and authoritative source of all monastic tradition. His problem then is to justify this authority by linking it to apostolic tradition.

In the *Institutiones* (2:5) we find the tradition of the twelve psalms to be said at the morning and evening Office. Cassian, wishing to establish the authority of this practice, attributes it not only to angelic intervention but also to the earliest centuries of the Church in Alexandria. There is no doubt that Cassian is depending here upon Pachomian sources, notably the "Rule of the Angel," but he is unable to so much as mention Pachomius because of his need to justify the tradition by direct linear descent from the apostles. The story runs this way: The disciples of St. Mark at Alexandria were living like true monks, withdrawn from the city, and engaged in a life of severe asceticism. Their Synaxis consisted of fifty or sixty psalms. In order to temper their zeal and enable their followers to keep up, an angel appeared and prescribed twelve psalms for the morning and evening prayer. Cassian then goes on to note that not only did the Christians of Alexandria exceed those of Jerusalem by the fervor and length of their prayers, but they also added to the community of goods described in Acts an asceticism that was heroic. So much for what Dom de Vogüe calls the "Alexandrian version" of Cassian's use of Acts.

In the *Collationes* (18:5–8), in the conference of Abbas Piamun, we have what Dom de Vogüe calls the "Jerusalem version." Cassian creates here a sort of "historical romance" by linking Acts 4:32–35 with the account in Acts 15 of the meeting at Jerusalem. After the compromising made necessary by the influx

---

[40] In Joann. 39:5, CC 36:347f.

[41] Rule of St. Augustine, *Patrologia Latina* 32:13, 77.

[42] Ibid., 79.

[43] "Monachisme et Eglise dans la Pensée de Cassien" in *Théologie de la Vie Monastique*, 213–40.

of many gentiles and witnessed to by the text in Acts 15, some of the early Community, anxious to maintain their first fervor, set off for the desert where they practiced community of goods and celibacy. "This was the only kind of monk and the oldest: first not only in time but also in grace, and which preserved itself inviolate to the time of the Abbas Paul and Anthony, and whose traces we can see today in fervent coenobia."

There is also in the *Collationes* (16) a conference by Abba Joseph on friendship. There, as we have noted above, Cassian is probably consciously drawing upon the Hellenistic ideals of friendship and describes how this is fulfilled in Christian community:

> How can he who has set out on the way we have described ever break with his friend? For he has radically cut out the first cause of arguments, which usually arise because of small material things of no real value, by calling nothing his own. He is observing with all his might that which we read in the Acts of the Apostles about the unity of the believers: "The multitude of believers was of one heart and soul and no one called anything his own; but everything was held in common" (*Coll.* 16:6).

Conclusion

We have seen in the early Christian texts a use of the summary statements in Acts that runs the gamut from literal application within a similar historical context *(Didache)* to historical romance (Cassian). Midway between these we find a typological use of the text as in the Pachomian literature. Though Pachomius is described as being the founder of the *koinonia* "after the apostles," there is no attempt to make a historical link between him and them except insofar as Pachomius was baptized into the same faith and Church.

If we consider Cassian's use of Acts to be a particular application, and if we consider the *Didache* and the *Letter of Barnabas* to be inspired by the same historical context as Acts, we see that we are left with the Pachomian (and perhaps Syrian), the Augustinian and the Basilian uses of Acts. How could we characterize this use of the text that shares with Luke an attempt to give verbal consistency to a charismatic moment in the history of the Church by describing it in terms of its ultimate ideal?

Figura[44]

Before returning to consider Luke's procedures we could perhaps pause briefly and consider the typological or figural[45] function of Scripture itself, especially in its relationship to monastic life. Monasticism is a way of life, or better perhaps,

---

[44] For a discussion of this term, see the next chapter.
[45] For the sake of this discussion I will treat these words as interchangeable.

it is a way of living. It is the expression of some deep intuition within the human spirit that seeks to concretize man's nostalgia for God and make of this yearning the mainspring of the way a person lives on this globe. It is often as baffling for the one who seeks to live this way as it is for those who behold them, and yet to both there is an inner truth being said that requires for its saying not only the mouth of a man, but the whole of his being. In its mature state, this way of life, as is the case with any mature thing, harmonizes and resolves the conflicts that are inherent in it. But such maturity is rare, and so there are studies such as this present one in which we attempt with our minds to chart a course for our lives that will lead to that knowledge of God that gives substance to the things we hope for. We should remember that God's revelation of himself to man, and God's revelation of man to himself, specifies and gives consistency to the vague intuitions and longings that all men carry in the center of their being as a certain fringe of conscious participation in the reality as the image of God.

It was the essential vocation of the Hebrew people, forced on them by the initiative and the insistence of God, that they should formulate and suffer the true meaning of man's experience of incompleteness. "God" is not the culminating experience of an intricate balance between self-abnegation and self-acceptance, between understanding of this world and willingness to go beyond it. God, the living God, is the incomprehensible Master and Lover who enters into the details of human life with a meticulous jealousy, only to seem to subvert by revelation what he has expressly commanded; who barges into life uninvited, forcing his people on by promises already believed because of his trustworthiness. He saves his people from the effects of their own evil even while punishing them. He speaks, thundering and whispering, things that make the heart of man reel with their secret and yet cry out in a new awareness of being lonely. He is a God of mystery, beyond holiness yet present, always the same yet always unexpected. "Yes, you are a hidden God, the God of Israel, the Savior" (Is 45:15).

Every act of God, by the greatness of the potential it announces, and by the disillusionment of man's small capacity to realize it, is an act that points to the future. God stirred up such a vision of what could be, that this vision tore off the protective and cautious covering over man's heart and forced him to look into the abyss of what he truly longs for. Because God chose to act this way with this people, the salt of the haunting knowledge of God has stopped the world from settling into corruption. Man is challenged out of a resentful caution that seeks to wrest from a god of his own making a security even man suspects it cannot give. The price paid for this salt is high. In the moving words of Gerhard von Rad: "[T]his people had not been destined to find rest in a single revelation of its God."[46] We, of the New Covenant, also yearn for a completion of what has been given to us.

---

[46] G. von Rad, *Old Testament Theology*, trans. D. M. G. Stalker, vol. 2, *The Theology of Israel's Prophetic Traditions* (New York: Harper and Row, 1965).

Radically, it is this awareness of incompleteness that has made man not only dissatisfied with himself, but dissatisfied with the acts of God that have yet to yield all their promise. Thus, in the Bible, the beauty and incompleteness of God's acts (including the creation of man) form the basis of that continual process by which successive events are called by the name of a previous event. Accompanying this there is a transposition of name and function whose new realization partially fulfills the expectation aroused before while at the same time opening up new vistas of possibility. So we see, nearly four centuries after David, Ezekiel still presenting God as nostalgic for what never was:

> YHWH says this: I am going to call the shepherds to account. I am going to take my flock back from them and I shall not allow them to feed my flock. . . . I mean to raise up one shepherd, my servant David, and to put him in charge of them and he will pasture them; he will pasture them and be their shepherd. I, YHWH, will be their God, and my servant David shall be their ruler. I, YHWH, have spoken. (Ez 34:10, 23)

In the same vein, the sufferings of Jeremiah, through which the anguish of God was incarnate for his people, is promised a redemptive meaning in the suffering of the Servant who "justifies many" (Is 53:11). For as we see the Servant, "like a lamb that is led to the slaughter-house, like a sheep that is dumb before its shearers never opening its mouth," we recall the prayer of Jeremiah: "Yet I was like a trusting lamb being led to the slaughter-house not knowing the schemes they were plotting against me" (Is 53:7 and Jer 11:19).

This transposition of themes, events, and symbols from one level of history to another has much in common with that activity by which the human mind strives to make sense of the welter of experience by relating it to some one concrete thing. It is the basis of much poetic imagery, and it is the dynamic underlying what we call the "analogical function."[47] By this I mean the application to a new or expected concrete act of God, of expressions already symbolizing (making present) a previous concrete act of God. This function is based on the two most constant aspects of God's ways with men, namely the essential future orientation of God's personal initiative, and his consistency. Because God is always the same, always thinking "thoughts of peace" (Jer 29:11), there is a continuity to the way he acts despite the baffling inconsistency he seems to evince. This continuity is discerned amidst the pain of incompleteness and incomprehension and it is asserted on the basis of common "structure-factors" whose biblical name is "the memory of God."[48] There are many studies made of this facet of revelation that concentrate on the successive layers of editing in the biblical texts, or on the

---

[47] I will treat this at greater length in chapter 11.

[48] See B. S. Childs, *Memory and Tradition in Israel*, Studies in Biblical Theology 37 (London: SCM, 1962), esp. ch. 3, "God Remembers."

dynamics of this function itself, either within the Old Testament or in relating the Old and New Testaments.[49] There are also some studies that highlight the typological function of the Liturgy,[50] and others still that note the way that, within the New Testament itself, words and phrases now uniquely applicable to Christ are used of the vocation of the disciples and of the history of the Church.[51] Then, of course, there is the abundant wealth of patristic figural thinking.[52]

Monastic Typology

This rather long discussion has been necessary in order to trace, even briefly, a history of the reception of the Summaries in the Book of Acts. This enables us to situate and understand what the early fathers are telling us about themselves and about their communities. First of all, their way of life finds a precedent and an echo in the hearts and ways of life of many men of the most varied views about God, existence, and the cosmos. Second, as they are conscious of themselves, they are simply responding to the Word of God as they have heard it preached in the Church. Third, the biblical images they use show that they are aware of having inherited an acute sense of the incompleteness still present in God's plan even as this has been brought to perfection in Christ. They know too that this vocation, which was always within the life of God's people, is now distilled in the life of Jesus and continued in the Church.

With regard to the first of these affirmations concerning the common human substratum of the monastic way of life, we should bear in mind that, as Father Hausherr has put it: "Nothing strictly spiritual is proper to the monk as such."[53]

We are discussing *a way of life* whose inspiration lies deep in the human heart, and it is not surprising that the *anima naturaliter Christiana* of humankind should express itself this way. The radicalizing and purifying of this drive began with God's call of Abraham (itself a theme dear to monasticism—Cassian, *Conferences* 3). This distilling purification continued throughout that process

---

[49] For a study of this point, see Jean-Paul Michaud, "Des quatre sens de l'Écriture. Histoire, théorie, théologie, herméneutique," *Église et Théologie* 30 (1999): 165–97.

[50] J. Danielou, *From Shadows to Reality* (Westminster, MD: Newman Press, 1960); idem, *The Bible and the Liturgy* (Notre Dame, IN: University of Notre Dame Press, 1956).

[51] Fr. D. M. Stanley has a fine article on "The Theme of the Servant of Yahweh in Primitive Christian Soteriology and its Transposition by St. Paul," *Catholic Biblical Quarterly* 16 (1954): 385–425; and, though the word "typology" is not used, there is the study by T. W. Manson showing the application to the Church of the terminology and events proper to the Son of Man: *The Servant Messiah* (Cambridge: Cambridge University Press, 1961), ch. 5. "The Messianic Ministry: The Passion of the Son of Man."

[52] For a modest beginning in this vast subject, see G. Lampe and K. Woollcombe, *Essays on Typology*, Studies in Biblical Theology 22 (London: Alec R. Allenson, 1957); H. de Lubac, *Exegese Medievale*, 4 vols (Paris: Cerf, 1959, 1961).

[53] Cited this way in the *Bulletin of Monastic Spirituality*, 1968, n. 126; *Cistercian Studies* 3 (1968): 73.

described above, by which God's people were forced to go beyond their hopes by the renewed acts of God. The positing of causal dependence on the basis of material similarity is a hazardous undertaking,[54] and the various causal assignments made by scholars serve rather to prove the universality of this human aspiration rather than reduce all expressions of it to one clearly isolated phenomenon.

In the light of this, what can we say that Luke is doing in the way he describes the early community at Jerusalem? How did the early fathers understand him? These questions require a reunderstanding of the faith-sophistication of the early Church. Our differentiated consciousness makes it necessary for us to take apart the various dimensions of Luke's reporting. We must separate history and symbol, and must attempt to understand symbol in a new way, if we are to join them again for the healing of our minds and to gain an intuitive grasp of what is being said to us regarding early community life. Differentiation is an advance of the human mind but it is only a complete process when what was distinguished is placed back in a simpler more intuitive context. Understanding this process, it seems to me, is the hermeneutical problem confronting our modern "return to the sources." There are two ways of approaching this: (1) We may by scholarly effort recreate the thought-context that gave rise to our documents and then attempt to transpose that into our modern mindsets; (2) we may by a living experience of community understand what is being described and thus arrive at an intuitive sympathy with the charismatic moment embodied in the Word of God. Actually, of course, we need both approaches if we are to understand and express ourselves in terms of revelation.[55] Let us restrict ourselves here to a few lines about the use Luke is making of his summary statements in the early chapters of Acts.

The Summary Statements

Luke, in reworking the material he uses in his summaries, is purposely distilling out of the situation a certain ideal that was realized in a more diffused fashion within the historical life of the early community. This distillation or abstraction to a pure state never existed as such, neither in the early Jerusalem community nor in any subsequent attempt. The disciples of "one heart and one soul" of chapter 4 are those who in chapter 6 are having a dispute over precisely that sharing of goods for which they are praised.

I have called Luke's procedure an artificial distillation of a reality that never exists in its pure state but only in combination with other factors, which, while

---

[54] Cf. *The History of Religions, Essays in Methodology,* ed. M. Eliade and J. Kitagawa (Chicago: University of Chicago Press, 1961), esp. the articles by J. Danielou and M. Eliade. I have touched on some aspects of this problem of comparing constellations of life-factors in "Cistercian Monasticism and Modern Adaptations," *Cistercian Studies* 3 (1968): 287–90.

[55] See chapter 11, this volume.

they may be considered "dross," are the human fabric without which the ideal could never be given historic consistency. The early texts that quote these summaries were instinctively aware of Luke's theological procedure and easily appealed to it for justification and explanation of their own attempts to embody that charismatic moment of the early Church in an alloy composed of their charism and their time.

We often speak of the summaries as an idealization, implying often that Luke is not describing the actual historical situation. Perhaps it would be better to call Luke's description a "type" or "figure."[56] These terms have been applied to the relationship between the Old and New Testament beginning with the New Testament itself, but perhaps there was some wisdom in the way tradition continued to see in the life of the Church recurrent realizations of the types found in the Scriptures. Thus, when Luke says that "no one was in need *(endeēs)*" (Acts 4:34), he is pointing to the early community as being the realization of what was in his day understood to be a promise of the eschatological era: The Septuagint version of Deuteronomy 15:4 promises "there will not be among you any one in need *(endeēs)* because the Lord your God will surely bless you in the land which the Lord your God is giving to you."

We are living in the period of partially realized eschatology. Whenever the sacred space of true communion is created, we know that that reality described in Acts is being realized once again among us and that this Church-event is itself a type, a further realization of the anagogic sense of the summary statements in Acts. There is the past, present, and future of true typology, and the blending of event and symbol. In a true gathering in the Name of Christ there is experienced a foretaste of that presence promised us forever. We seek to find words that mediate our experience of this moment, which shares in that act by which the Church was created and which leads to that moment when Church will be completed. We find that the words of the sacred text sum up, preserve, and intensify that experience: "The assembly of the believers was of one heart and soul and no one called anything his own; rather, everything was shared among them."

---

56 See Erich Auerbach, "Figura," in *Scenes from the Drama of European Literature* (Gloucester, MA: Peter Smith, 1973), 11–76.

5 Reading the Story of the Centurion's Boy "In the Spirit in Which It Was Written"

THIS STUDY is an example of what the ancients called *lectio divina*, sacred reading. The healing action of Jesus mediated to us in the texts of the two (or three) Gospels that contain it is still alive now in the risen humanity of Christ, and it is available to us if we read in faith. By showing the unexpressed theological and literary principles that underlie a faith reading of the text, this chapter means to show the way to an integration of the ancient mystical understanding and modern biblical study.

• • •

IN a famous phrase, analyzed by Fr. Ignace de la Potterie,[1] the Dogmatic Constitution *Dei Verbum* (12) summed up a millennial tradition when, after having outlined the need for a careful literary and historical study of the text, it went on to state that "sacred Scripture must be read and interpreted in the same Spirit in which it was written."[2] Reading the Scripture in the same Spirit in which it was written is a formulaic manner of expressing what the whole of Tradition meant by the "spiritual meaning" of Scripture. The Council text itself refers us to a text of St. Jerome:

> Even if he does not stray from the Church, anyone who . . . understands
> Scripture otherwise than in the sense demanded by the Holy Spirit in

---

This chapter is an adapted version of a previously published article, "St. Matthew's Spiritual Understanding of the Healing of the Centurion's Boy," *Communio* 25 (1998): 161–77.

[1] Fr. Ignace de la Potterie, "Interpretation of Holy Scripture in the Spirit in Which It Was Written," in *Vatican II: Assessment and Perspectives I,* ed. René Latourelle (New York: Paulist, 1988), 220–66.

[2] I will study this text closely in Chapter 11.

whom it was written can be called a heretic; his choice belongs to the works of the flesh, for he has chosen the worst.[3]

In this reflection on the text of Matthew 8:5–13, an attempt will be made to read the text in the Spirit in which it was written. Then the Spirit who abides in the text and in the Church, and in us as we receive this text, may bring us into contact with Our Lord Jesus Christ who, at this moment is living in that glorious and transformed humanity that is still marked with all that transpired during "the days of his flesh" (Heb 5:7). In order to do this we will first reflect on the nature of Matthew's Gospel itself as an instance of a very particular form of history writing, one that reveals to us the true meaning of all history. We will then read the Gospel text closely and try to follow the dynamic movement of the Holy Spirit who desires to join us to Christ in this mystery.

Gospel History

The Gospels were not written to defend, promote, or perpetuate the memory of a dead master, but to put us in touch with the living Lord. As such, they are a sacrament: They contain what they signify. In order to understand this we must reflect briefly on the prophetic, that is, God-given and normative, vision of history they present to us. It is in the Gospels that the biblical understanding of history attains it fullest expression because they narrate for us the events of Christ's life in a manner that enables us to see them in their completed state in the glorified humanity of Jesus. Let us first speak of history and then of narrative.

No historical event is fully intelligible unless and until it is seen in its final outworking. This means that, ultimately, history will be totally intelligible only when it is completed. There is, however, the history of one man who has arrived at that point already, and he is at once its Lord and its goal. Just as the life of every human being continues to be part of the person even after death, so the earthly life of Jesus Christ is part of his existence even now. There are two differences, however, and these form, implicitly or explicitly, the foundation of the way the Gospels are written. The first of these differences is the fact that Jesus is risen from the dead, and all that he said and did has risen with him and continues to be part of his glorious humanity even now: "And I saw in the midst of the throne and the four living beings, and in the midst of the elders, *a lamb standing as having been slain* having seven horns and seven eyes which are the seven spirits of God sent into all the earth" (Rev 5:6). Jesus, the lamb still bearing the marks of his slaughter, is now endowed with divine power and knowledge.

---

[3] *On Galatians 5:19–21* (*Patrologia Latina* 26, 445A–B). Translation from de la Potterie, "Interpretation of Holy Scripture," 229. For an ample collection of similar patristic expressions consult the same article, as well as Ignace de la Potterie, "The Spiritual Sense of Scripture," *Communio* 23 (4; 1996): 738–56.

These earthly experiences have made of his humanity a multifaceted source of grace for those who turn to him in faith.

That which Jesus lived through, what tradition calls the "mysteries of the life of Christ," are, each in their own way, a source of particular blessing and grace for those who touch them.[4] This theological view is already present in the Letter to the Hebrews, which tells us: "We do not have a high priest unable to share by experience our weaknesses, (but one) having been tested in all ways, because he is like us, (however) without sin." The verb "having been tested" is, in Greek, a perfect passive participle whose meaning is expressed by Zerwick-Grosvenor as "having triumphantly passed the test Jesus is forever tried and tested."[5] It is precisely because he is fixed in that act of love in which he died, and "is forever tried and tested" that the exhortation is given to us: "Let us approach, then, with assurance the throne of grace that we might receive mercy and find grace at the right time of need" (Heb 4:15–16). Not only will we receive a compassionate reception, but Jesus, having learned obedience from what he suffered, has become "*the source* of eternal salvation for those who obey him" (Heb 5:9). The High Priest we are urged to approach has not only shared our temptations and overcome them, he still bears his wounds, he forever retains the effects of his passage among us, and in his now glorious humanity, he is the source or cause of our salvation: Power goes out from him (see Lk 6:19, 8:46).

The new situation of Christ, which is a transformation rather than a rejection of the former state of his humanity, is the reason the various events of his life are life-giving to those who come in faith contact with his humanity through the sacraments, the Scriptures, and intimate prayer. The reason, however, the sacred humanity of Christ is the source of divine life is because it is joined to the divinity of the Word. This is the second difference between Jesus Christ and any other human being in this world or the next. St. Thomas Aquinas speaks of the efficient causality of the resurrected Christ: "[I]n so far as the humanity of Christ, according to which he rose, is in a certain sense the instrument of his divinity and operates by its power."[6] The transformed humanity of Christ—his mind, will, emotions, memory, as well as his body—is now apt to be the instrument of his divinity in conferring a special grace on the believer in keeping with the event of his earthly life that the Church, or each person, turns to. This is the basis, not only of the "mysteries" of the Rosary, but in a more profound sense of the Liturgical Year itself. To recall a text of St. Leo:

---

[4] The reader interested in following up on this theme will find this article helpful: A. Solignac, "In his *Mystère*," in *Dictionnaire de Spiritualitè X.* (Paris: Beauchesne, 1980), 1861–74.

[5] Max Zerwick and Mary Grovesnor, *A Grammatical Analysis of the New Testament* (Rome: Biblical Institute Press, 1979), 662.

[6] *Summa theologiae,* 3, 56, 1 ad 3. The reader who wishes to pursue this question can consult with profit the study by Stanislaus Lyonnet, "La valeur sotériologique de la résurrection du Christ selon saint Paul," *Gregorianum* 39 (1958): 295–318.

All those things which the Son of God both did and taught for the reconciliation of the world, we not only know in the account of things now
past, but we also experience in the power of works which are present.[7]

It is important to realize that this intuition of the early Church and the
medieval theological tradition is but a continuation of the view set forth in such
texts as those from the Book of Revelation and the Letter to the Hebrews we have
just considered. It is also already contained in the Gospel accounts of the events,
the mysteries, of the life of Christ. While this prophetic interpretation of reality is
based on a vision of the glorified humanity of Jesus, which is the humanity of the
Word of God, it is also based on an understanding of history opened up for us by
the Incarnation itself, as being the ultimate realization of God's presence to history. This understanding is implicit and most probably inarticulate in the Gospel
accounts, but it is there. Before approaching the text of Matthew's Gospel we
should reflect briefly on what may be called the "interiority of history," which is
the ground for the interiority of the text, both of which are mediated by the
Spirit by which the text was written and who is present in the text.

The Interiority of History[8]

We have already seen that no event is completely intelligible until all the potential of that event has been realized. Thus, it will take centuries at least to grasp
the full significance of that act in which Gandhi picked up a pinch of salt and in
so doing challenged the British presence in India, or of Martin Luther King's
gesture in sitting at a lunch counter in Alabama. These moments gathered
around themselves, through the conscious activity of the protagonists, a world of
forces and consequences that can never be understood by a mere surface analysis
of the factors that went into the events, and much more by an ignorance of the
chain of consequences that flowed from them. The same may be said about the
words and gestures of Jesus. These are only understandable by a prophetic pene-
tration into what really took place. This is achieved in part at least by an experience of the power of that event as it touches the life of the Church now. This
mysterious dimension of an event may be called its "interiority."[9]

Perhaps a simple example will help. Suppose that you and I are at a social
gathering and we both see Jones walk across the room and shake hands with
Smith, who responds by taking Jones's hand in both of his own and smiles at
him. I may see nothing remarkable in the occurrence, but then you turn and
explain to me that Jones and Smith have been enemies for twelve years. You

---

[7] *On the Passion,* 12 (*Sources Chrétiennes* 74, 82).

[8] The theme of the interiority of history is a leitmotiv of this volume, and will form the
basis of the final chapter.

[9] For a discussion of interiority and the Spirit-dimension of history the reader is referred
once again to the study by de la Potterie, "The Spiritual Sense."

reveal to me part of the interior dimension of this event, and thus allow me to share in your appreciation of what really took place. Now suppose that we were both present at the crucifixion of Jesus, and you turned to me and said: "There is the salvation of the world." You would be correct: Faith had given you a capacity to grasp what is really and objectively happening.

Now let us suppose that you are going to narrate for the Church that gesture of Jesus by which he healed the Centurion's boy; that is, let us suppose that you are St. Matthew. How would you compose your narration of an act of Jesus whose interior dimension is lost in the depths of his divine personhood, an event, moreover, that is now past but which lives on in the transformed humanity of Jesus Christ, and which has the power to affect those who contemplate this mystery in faith? Perhaps the best way to answer that question is to read very carefully the actual text of Matthew 8:5–13.

The Matthean Narrative

The Text of the Gospel

This is the event as St. Matthew presents it in his text, given here in a very literal translation:

> As he entered Capernaum, there came to him a centurion entreating him and saying: Lord, my boy is lying in the house paralyzed, suffering terribly.
>
> And he said to him: I will come and cure him.
>
> And making answer the Centurion said: Lord, I am not fit that you should come under my roof. But only say the word and my boy will be healed. For actually, I am a man under authority myself, having soldiers under me; and I say to this one go, and he goes; and to another come, and he comes; and to my servant do this and he does it.
>
> Jesus, hearing, marveled, and said to those following: Amen, I say to you, with no one in Israel have I found such faith. I say to you many will come from the east and the west and they will recline with Abraham and Isaac and Jacob in the Kingdom of Heaven, but the children of the kingdom will be cast out into the darkness which is outside where there will be weeping and gnashing of teeth
>
> And Jesus said to the Centurion: Go back, as you believed, let it be done for you.
>
> And the boy was healed in that very hour.

Some Principles of Narratology

Some of the results of modern literary and historical studies can be of help in understanding how Matthew proceeds in his narrative to mediate the interiority of this event. There is first of all the nature of narrative itself, and then there are the peculiar characteristics of a literary anecdote, or, better, to use the terminology of André Jolles, a *memorabile*.[10] We will treat briefly each of these in turn.

Narrative may be defined as the literary presentation of a complete action. The words "complete action" are intended first of all to distinguish narrative from lyric, description, chronicle, and so on, but they also serve to indicate that, in one way or another, the action must be presented as ending. The expression, "literary presentation" refers to the fact that narrative imitates an action, that is, it reproduces the action itself on another plane of existence in such a way that the action is present in the narrative, on another level of being: Event becomes word. In the narrative under consideration, one could "report" the action by saying, "Jesus healed a centurion's boy at the latter's request even while the boy was still at a distance from him." This report, however, is not a narrative. The action is described but not presented. One of the most prominent theoreticians of narrative expresses the nature of plot, which is the "soul" of narrative, this way:

> The minimal complete plot consists in the passage from one equilibrium to another. An "ideal" narrative begins with a stable situation which is disturbed by some power or force. There results a state of disequilibrium; by the action of a force directed in the opposite direction, the equilibrium is re-established; the second equilibrium is similar to the first, but the two are never identical.[11]

For our purposes here it suffices to note that the action, which can be "reported," is given a potential literary existence when it is made into a plot. The action exists as such on a literary level when it is imitated by the verbal texture of language. It is at this point that we must advert to the second of the aspects mentioned above, namely the characteristics of a short narrative.

From a stylistic point of view, the Gospel narratives have much in common with short stories told about rabbis and other prominent Jewish sages in the literature of Judaism. There is this difference, however: The Jewish stories are never told to exalt a particular rabbi, but usually to illustrate an exegetical or ethical point, and this makes them different from the stories about Jesus, "whose entire purpose is to accentuate his might and power."[12] If we attend to the *literary function* of the Gospel narratives, we see, however, they are more like the Hellenistic "memoires" (*apomnēmoneuma* or Latin, *memorabile*) in that they seek to present one concrete event in such a way that, while retaining its uniqueness, serves as a commentary or even a paradigm for many aspects of

---

[10] André Jolles, *Einfache Formen*, 2nd ed. (Tübingen: Max Niemeyer, 1958), 200–218.

[11] Tzvetan Todorov, *The Poetics of Prose*, trans. Richard Howard (Ithaca, NY: Cornell University Press, 1977), 111.

[12] Ephraim E. Urbach, *The Sages: Their Concepts and Beliefs*, trans. Israel Abrahams, 2 vols. (Jerusalem: Magnes Press, 1975), 116–17.

human life. André Jolles gives the modern example of a well-written account of a suicide in the daily newspaper.[13]

In a *memorabile* (and Matthew's account of the Centurion's boy approximates this form), all the details of the event are bound together by a higher factuality than that of the event itself. Aspects are mentioned that are not directly related to each other nor even necessarily to the event itself, but which have an interconnectness on a higher level where they carry and mediate the meaning of the event on a broader plane. To mention, for instance, in the account of a woman's suicide, that her husband was out bowling at the time, is to adduce a fact that has no particular relevance to the event; but it serves nevertheless to raise the event to the level where it reveals, even if so slightly, something of its own interior dimension and serves as a reflection of modern life. In a genuine narrative of this type, there are many details that are ordered to one another and to a higher order in a significant relationship even when they do not have a direct relation to the event itself. Let us move on now to read our text very carefully in order to discover the ways in which Matthew places this event within the context of a higher order. In so doing we will begin to understand how to read it in the Spirit in which it was written.

The Four Levels of Reading a Biblical Text

Somewhere in the middle of the twelfth century, Guigo, the second man to bear that name and the ninth prior of the Grande Chartreuse, composed a little treatise titled *Scala Claustralium,* or "A Ladder for Monks," which sums up the monastic tradition regarding the practice of *Lectio Divina,* or "Sacred Reading."[14] In this treatise Guigo outlines four steps, or perhaps moments or aspects, of reading the Sacred Text "in the same Spirit in which it was written." He lists them as: reading *(lectio)*, meditation *(meditatio)*, prayer *(oratio)*, and contemplation *(contemplatio)*. We will consider each briefly and then apply them to our text.

Reading is the process by which we come in contact with the text and allow it to make an impact on us. Guigo says it is like eating a grape, the experience of its sweetness stirs us on to that purity of heart that leads to understanding:

> So wishing to have a fuller understanding of this, the soul begins to bite and chew upon this grape, as though putting it in a wine press, while it stirs up its power of reasoning to ask what this precious purity may be and how it may be had.[15]

---

[13] Jolles, *Einfache Formen,* 200ff. In this article, I am dependent upon Jolles's analysis of this aspect of narrative.

[14] The most convenient access to Guigo's text is found in Guigo II, "The Ladder of Monks," in *The Ladder of Monks and Twelve Meditations* (Kalamazoo, MI: Cistercian Publications, 1978), 6–26.

[15] Ibid., IV, 69.

Meditation is concerned with the reality mediated by the text; it seeks to come into contact with that reality.

> When meditation busily applies itself to this work, it does not remain on the outside, is not detained by unimportant things, climbs higher, goes to the heart of the matter, examines each point thoroughly.[16]
>
> Prayer is born of the desire to understand, to be touched and enlightened by the light of God.
>
> So the soul, seeing that it cannot attain by itself to that sweetness of knowing and feeling for which it longs, and the more the heart abases itself, the more God is exalted, humbles itself and betakes itself to prayer. . . . Nor do I ask this, Lord, because of my own merits, but because of your mercy.[17]

Finally, the soul, now alive with desire for the Lord, and engaged in intimate conversation with him, making known its state and calling out to the Lord, is visited by the Lord himself.

> But the Lord, whose eyes are upon the just and whose ears can catch not only the words, but the very meaning of the prayers, does not wait until the longing soul has had all its say, but breaks in upon the middle of its prayer, runs to meet it in all haste, sprinkled with sweet heavenly dew, anointed with the most precious perfumes, and He restores the weary soul, He slakes its thirst, He feeds its hunger.[18]

The Sacred Reading of the Matthean Text

When we moderns read a text such as that of Guigo, we tend to think of the four "steps" of the ladder as four stages in a methodology that is applied to a text that lies before us and that requires a "technique" in order to get it to yield its meaning. Guigo and his contemporaries, because of the biblically informed world in which they lived and because of their liturgically based life of prayer, did not have this modern understanding of a text. In order to overcome our modern handicap, we must realize that a text is not an inert object but an instance of intersubjective communication: Matthew, through his text, is speaking to us, and we must listen to him in order to be borne by his teaching into the presence of Christ.[19] For that

---

[16] Ibid., V, 70.

[17] Ibid., VI, 72–73.

[18] Ibid., VII, 73–74.

[19] In speaking of "Matthew" here I do not intend to ignore the questions of redaction but rather to insist that there is no such thing as an "authorless" text. See Jorge J. E. Gracia, "Can There Be Texts Without Historical Authors?" *American Philosophical Quarterly* 31 (3; 1994): 245–53.

reason we will concentrate in our reading and meditation on following the movement that Matthew has conferred upon his text.

Reading the Text

Notice first of all the rhythm of the action. All converges on Jesus and all flows from him. The three moments of "equilibrium—disequilibrium—new equilibrium" all center around Jesus and his decisive action. This is the most common rhythm of narratives about Jesus in the Gospels, and it is the rhythm of prayer. In this case, Jesus enters Capernaum, and immediately the "equilibrium" of this situation is confronted by a "disequilibrium," the meeting with the Centurion.

All the action takes place in conversation: in the interaction between Jesus and the Centurion, and in the final authoritative word, "Go back. As you believed, let it be done for you." In between the initial meeting and the authoritative word there are two short speeches. First, the speech of the Centurion (the longest address of anyone in the Gospels except for Jesus), and then Jesus' words to "those following." Both of these sections are concerned with faith. We may note as well the atmosphere of intimacy and direct conversation in the interaction. The needy Centurion (with whom we can identify) comes to tell Jesus of his boy's plight (compare, by contrast, Luke's long preliminary description and the presence of intermediaries in Lk 7:1–3). Jesus responds to the Centurion directly. This is typical of the intimacy Matthew describes between Jesus and the believer in many of his narratives. Thus, in contrast to Mark and Luke, Jesus notices and heals Peter's mother-in-law without anyone speaking to him about her, and she, once healed, gets up and serves *him*, as opposed to *them*. (Mt 8:15/Mk 1:31/Lk 4:39).[20]

It would be helpful if at this point the reader were to go back and "read" the text of Matthew. That is, in following the narrative line established by Matthew allow the Holy Spirit to awaken in one's heart a desire to penetrate this mystery in the life of Christ; a mystery of faith, intimacy, and healing power. As Guigo put it: "[T]he soul begins to bite and chew upon this grape, as though putting it in a wine press, while it stirs up its power of reasoning."

Meditation Upon the Matthean Text

While reading the text concentrates on the text itself as our first access to the event, meditation looks to the deed or word of Jesus mediated by the text, and follows the lead of the Evangelist as he opens up for us the true depth of what transpired. This takes place in two settings. There is first and foremost the reading of the text at the Liturgy where, we are told, Christ "is present in His word,

---

[20] Instances of this type of procedure abound. Thus, only in Matthew does Jesus say that he looks forward to sharing the wine of the Kingdom "with you" and later asks the disciples to stay and watch "with me" (Mt 26:29, 38).

since it is He Himself who speaks when the holy scriptures are read in the Church."[21] The speaking of the Lord, and the breaking of the bread in the homily are ways in which the Gospel text is meditated upon together. Together, we follow the lead of the sacred author and "use our reason" to reflect upon and come into contact with the gesture of Jesus. This is the first way that sacred reading is an actualization of the text.

The second way, one which we can engage upon here, and one which flows from and prepares for the Liturgy, is that of seeing how Matthew makes of this event a paradigm, a summation of the whole mystery of Christ.

Using and adapting what was said above about a literary *memorabile*, we can follow Matthew's teaching art as he leads us to meditate upon this act of Jesus. The event is made a paradigm of intimate faith. As we have already seen, Matthew, in narrating the way he does, makes this event another example of direct and intimate relating between Jesus and another, a model of a believer. He thus links this event with many others in his Gospel that deal with faith. We should note as well Jesus' remarks in praise of the Centurion's faith and in prophecy of those who will be with him and the Patriarchs in the Kingdom. Note first of all that these remarks are addressed to "those following." While not completely awkward, this designation is stylistically odd enough to alert us to their true audience (compare Luke's "the crowd following him" [Lk 7:9]). These remarks are addressed *to us*, who follow Jesus: His words have an effective history, Jesus is still proclaiming his Gospel.

We may note as well the prophecy concerning those who will recline with Abraham and Isaac and Jacob. The tradition had preserved these words, but their original context is not known. Matthew uses them here, while Luke reserves them for a discourse addressed to those who presumed on a superficial contact with Jesus (Lk 13:22–30). As Jesus uttered it, the saying was a prophecy of the entrance of the Gentiles into the eschatological banquet of the Kingdom and a menacing prediction that those for whom it was first destined will be rejected. The prophecy reflected earlier prophecies already recorded in the sacred tradition (Is 45:6; 49:12; 59:19; Zech 14:9, 16; and so on), while the threat declared that what had been prophesied was now in the process of realization with consequences for Jesus' contemporaries. Matthew applies the same principle to Christians who, by making light of the promise through a half-hearted faith, risk being found unfit for the Kingdom. He is careful to tell us that Jesus says that the "children of the Kingdom" will be cast out into the darkness. The only other instance of this expression in the First Gospel is in Matthew 13:38 where it clearly designates Christians. This is probably one more subtle warning to the Christians themselves that there is nothing guaranteed about their position in the Kingdom if they do not continue in faith to adhere to all that Jesus commanded (see Mt

---

[21] *Constitution on the Sacred Liturgy,* §7.

28:20).[22] We may observe as well how Matthew, by using words reminiscent of Jesus' words to the two blind men (Mt 9:29) and the Canaanite woman (Mt 15:28), links this event to others in a higher order where we see the efficacy of the faith he stirs up in us: "Go back, as you believed, let it be done for you."

As we meditate, under Matthew's inspired direction, on this healing of the Centurion's boy, we are aware that Jesus is calling us to faith, to a trusting belief in him that recognizes his authority both to help and heal us now and to give us commandments that direct us to life with him in the future Kingdom. Matthew has, through the subtle use of language, used apparently unrelated details to firmly establish this action of Jesus as one more instance in his Gospel of the call to discipleship. It is here, obviously, that we must accept the invitation to a direct and intimate relationship with Jesus and begin to pray.

Praying with Matthew's Text

Reading brings us into familiarity with the text, meditation brings us into contact with the action of Jesus in which, under the author's guidance we see and hear him. Prayer prolongs that contact, makes it more personal, and adds the note of desire. This prayer can take place in the context of the Liturgy when together we have had the word broken open for us, or it can take place when we are alone or with others in a non-liturgical context. In any event, prayer is authentic to the degree that it is personal, though personal does not mean individualistic. The work of the Holy Spirit within us makes us more interior, but in a transparent way that is at the other extreme from introspection.

Precisely because prayer is personal it is difficult to write about. Yet, something may be said about the kind of prayer worked in us by this text. First and foremost, we must recognize that we have been brought into an atmosphere in which a trusting faith is praised, and ultimately receives its goal. On the other hand, we who follow Jesus are warned against a complacent and routine faith. In short, we are being led to see how much we need to speak to Jesus, to enter into that intimate and personal relation with him in which we both experience and ask for a deeper faith. We knock, we seek, we ask, and we come to know for ourselves the hidden joy of speaking with Jesus. At this point we reach the fourth aspect of sacred reading.

Contemplation

Contemplation is the intimate awareness of the presence of the Lord. This is not a purely human act, rather, the human activity that has preceded this point

---

[22] This type of procedure is found elsewhere in Matthew. Compare, for instance, the warning addressed in Luke to those who will claim that they ate and drank with Jesus and that he taught in their streets (Lk 13:26). Matthew applies these words to these charismatics of his community who do not do the will of the Father (Mt 7:22–23).

is analogous and is already the work of the Holy Spirit. Just as a fire is preparing green wood all along so that it finally takes on the quality of the fire and bursts into flame, so the Holy Spirit unobtrusively prepares the person for the fire of this intimate knowledge of Jesus, and then confers the gift. As Guigo has put it: "But the Lord . . . does not wait . . . , but . . . runs to meet (the soul) in all haste."

The most perfect realization of this rhythm is found in the Liturgy when, after making the Centurion's words our own, "O Lord, I am not worthy," the Lord comes to us himself, to transform us into himself: Awareness of what is taking place at this moment is the summit of contemplation, and the repeated actualizing of this text.

In our own personal reading as well the Word comes to visit us: He knocks, and if we open, he comes to sup with us (see Rev 3:20). In the case of the narrative we have just reflected upon, the gesture of Jesus was made present and interpreted for us by the sacred author. We are brought into contact with, and are sustained by the grace of, this act of Jesus, which is forever a part of his glorified existence. We become aware of the Lord telling us: "I am the First and the Last and the One who lives. Once I was dead but now I live—forever and ever" (Rev 1:17–18). The action of Jesus that day in Capernaum has opened up for us and we are aware of being intimately close to him as he applies the power of his healing word to our lives. We also learn the power of intercessory prayer; we learn to go to Jesus for the sake of others and trust him to act. We have followed the advice of Rupert, the monk of Deutz, who, commenting on this event as John relates it, urges us: "What he did then, let us listen to now, and in his external action let us make out the mystery."[23]

---

[23] *Corpus Christianorum Latinorum,* Series Medievalis, 9, 231.

6 Israel as the Spouse of YHWH

IN ORDER TO UNDERSTAND the depth and power of the analogical image we are studying here, we must first grasp the nature of imagery and the evocative power of language, particularly the Hebrew language. It is next very helpful, by way of preparation for an analysis of the first three chapters of Hosea, to look briefly at the terms in Hebrew for "infidelity," "profligacy," "treachery," and so on. A close reading of the Hosea text mediates to us the unfathomable mystery of God's love, his spousal fidelity and jealousy, and, finally, his merciful love. We are then in a position to see how this love of God was embodied in Christ who has espoused his Church in a covenant of blood.

• • •

THERE are in the Old Testament three basic metaphors, drawn from the realm of personal relations, which occur with remarkable frequency in designating the relationship between YHWH and his people. The first of these is that of the relation between a king and his people, the second is that between a father and his son, and the third is that between husband and wife. The first two of these occur in more passages than the third, but the metaphor of marriage receives a more extended development.[1] In this study I will restrict myself to the manner in which the Old Testament mediates a knowledge of God and his covenant relationship to us through the metaphorical analogy of the relation between husband and wife, and most specifically how this understanding became an active part of the biblical tradition through the prophetic activity of Hosea.

This chapter was originally published as "Israel as the Bride of YHWH," *Anthropotes* 9 (2000): 129–54.

[1] I owe this observation to the very helpful study by Elaine June Adler, "The Background for the Metaphor of Covenant as Marriage in the Hebrew Bible" (Ph.D. Dissertation, University of California, 1990).

There will be three parts to the discussion. I will first treat the principal elements of covenant thinking that contributed to the powerful theological use of the metaphor by the prophet Hosea. In the second section I will consider the first three chapters of Hosea and their development of the analogy, writings of Hosea and of those who followed and developed his insight. Third, I will reflect on Hosea's teaching on the manner in which the marriage covenant and the Sinai covenant are analogically related and what this has to say about the metaphysics of relationality.

Part One: Marriage Elements in the Covenant Thinking of Israel

In the search for antecedents to the fully formed use of the marriage metaphor by Hosea, who wrote sometime in the latter half of the eighth century B.C., scholars tend to look in two directions. There is first the prevalent overlap of terminology in speech, about the covenant on the one hand and marriage on the other, some of which undoubtedly preceded Hosea. There is also the sexual nature of the pagan cults that existed side by side with the worship of YHWH and that were always a snare to Israel. I will concentrate on the first of these.

The Covenant Itself

It is important to bear in mind that the very existence of the covenant with YHWH contained elements that rendered almost instinctive the overlap just mentioned. First and foremost, Israel was unique in having a covenant with its God. There is no evidence that any other people ever expressed its relationship to its gods in these terms. No other god demanded absolute and exclusive fidelity: He was but one in a large panoply of forces. No other god chose a people for his own as did Israel's God: "You shall be to me a special possession of all the peoples—for all the earth is mine" (Ex 19:5, see Am 3:2; Dt 4:19–20). The obligation of exclusive fidelity on the part of Israel, and the promise of protection and care on the part of YHWH found its closest human counterpart in the marriage relation between man and woman. Thus, it is not surprising that terms that were originally applied to one of these relationships were easily transposed to apply to the other. I say "easily" because there is in the nature of the Hebrew language, especially as it became the vehicle of revelation, an innate capacity to form metaphors and analogies. It suffices, for instance to consider the semantic field of the root *'hb*, which can be translated as "to love" but which can be found operative in fields as diverse as romantic love and political alliance.[2] The capacity to use language in this way is well described by W. Norris Clarke:

---

[2] One may consult, for instance, Luis Alonso Schökel, *Diccionario Biblico Hebreo-Español* (Madrid: Trotta, 1994), and for a special accent on the political overtones, William Moran,

There is an indispensable role played in our thought and language by those systematically vague and elastic terms that alone can catch the similarities and affinities running all up and down and across the universe, especially between the realms of matter and spirit, cosmos and psyche. This is the secret life of the mind nourishing all metaphor, poetry, and art: the insight into authentic similarities and affinities across the universe.[3]

I wish now to look at some of the "systematically vague and elastic terms" linking human marriage and the covenant with YHWH. Rather than attempt the almost impossible task of dating this material, I will merely present some examples of this linguistic phenomenon that shows that the prophet Hosea found already "held in solution" as it were many components of what he succeeded in crystallizing into a powerful image analogy of the nature of God's relation to his people.

The Interrelatedness of Marriage and Covenant Terms

1. Adultery (n'p)

The clear meaning of this verb is stressed in Leviticus 20:10–21 where the crime is sexual intercourse between a married woman and any man not her husband. The primary offended party is the husband whose wife must reserve herself exclusively for him in order to insure that the man's children are the legatee heirs of his name and possessions. A man, married or not, who has intercourse with an unmarried woman may or may not be guilty of some offense, but it is never called adultery.[4] In both accounts of the "ten words," the nuclear expression of the covenant requirements, we read "you shall not commit adultery" (Ex 20:14 = Dt 5:18). What is clear is that adultery was a crime against God; that it was an offense against the covenant; and that, in its regard, we read exhortations calling adultery an "abomination" (Ez 22:11), making both parties ritually impure (Lev 18:20; Num 5:13; and so on), and statements to the effect that adultery is one of the sexual crimes causing the land to "vomit out its inhabitants" (Lev 18:24–25).[5]

"The Ancient Near Eastern Background of the Love of God in Deuteronomy," *Catholic Biblical Quarterly* 25 (1; 1963): 77–87.

[3] William Norris Clarke, *The Philosophical Approach to God: A Neo-Thomist Perspective,* The Fourth James Montgomery Hester Seminar (Winston-Salem, NC: Wake Forest University, 1979), 52.

[4] It is instructive in this regard to compare Mark 10:11, "Whoever sends away his wife and marries another commits adultery *against her.*" (Mt 19:9 says the substantially the same thing.)

[5] For a more ample treatment of this subject, to which I am indebted here, see Elaine Adler Goodfriend, "Adultery," in the *Anchor Bible Dictionary* (New York and London: Doubleday, 1992), 1:82–87. It is in this connection that the "ordeal rite" prescribed in the case of a wife suspected of adultery, but not caught in *flagrante delicto,* should be

The pre-exilic prophetic tradition is deeply dependent upon the covenant and the legal and narrative traditions, which articulated the practical demands of the covenant.[6] In regard to marriage, we see this in the number of times the sin of adultery is referred to in the prophetic oracles against the nation. In what may well be an allusion to the ten "words" of Exodus 20:1–17 and Deuteronomy 5:6–21, Hosea declares, "There is no fidelity, no mercy, no knowledge of God in the land. False swearing, lying, murder, stealing and adultery; in their lawlessness bloodshed follows upon bloodshed" (Hos 4:1–2).[7] The seriousness of the sin of adultery is evidenced by fact that it is classified with murder (Job 24:14), treachery (Jer 9:2), misuse of God's name (Jer 29:23), and oppression of the widow (Mal 5:5), and that the law required that it be punished by death. In the wisdom material, the adulterous woman is described as "strange" or "foreign" (see, for example, Pr 2:16). These terms refer to her relation to the adulterer, but cannot help but evoke the memory of the exhortations to have no "strange" or "foreign" gods besides YHWH (Dt 32:16; Jer 5:19; and so on). Infidelity and promiscuous contact with another's wife not only breaks the terms of the covenant with YHWH, it is itself a preparation for and a symbol of a deeper infidelity: It is tantamount to giving oneself to a foreign god. Thus it is not a large step to apply the root *n'p* directly to Israel's infidelity to the covenant with YHWH. This is especially notable in Hosea (3:1, 7:4), Jeremiah (3:8–9, 5:7, 9:2, 23:10, 14), and Ezekiel (16:32, 38; 23:37, 45).[8] The basis for this designation, as has been said, is the fact that Israel, unlike any other people in regard to their god, was obliged to be dedicated exclusively to YHWH.

2. "The Great Sin" (ḥăṭâ gĕdolâ)

Known in both Egyptian and Ugaritic literature as a designation for adultery,[9] this expression is also found in its literal sense in Genesis 20:9 where Abimelek

---

considered. Here again the preoccupation is with the legitimacy of her children. See Michael Fishbane, "Accusations of Adultery: A Study of Law and Scribal Practice in Numbers 5:11–31," *Hebrew Union College Annual* 45 (1974): 24–45.

6 An impressive list of the covenant blessings and curses found in the Pentateuch, esp. the Book of Deuteronomy, which figure in the prophetic preaching is presented by John D. W. Watts, ed., *Word Biblical Commentary*, vol. 31, *Hosea-Jonah*, by Douglas Stuart (Waco, TX: Nelson Reference & Electronic Publishing, 1987), xxxiii–xliii.

7 For other texts linking a catalogue of covenant violations with adultery, see D. N. Freedman and B. E. Willoughby, "N'P," in *Theological Dictionary of the Old Testament, IX*, ed. Helmer Ringgren, G. Johannes Botterweck, and Heinz-Josef Fabry (Grand Rapids, MI: Eerdmans, 1998), 113–18, at 116.

8 Several of the texts in Ezekiel speak of the rite of sacrificing children to gods as adultery; see also Isaiah 57:1–6.

9 J. J. Rabinowitz, "The Great Sin in Ancient Egyptian Marriage Contracts," *Journal of Near Eastern Studies* 18 (1959): 73; William Moran, "The Scandal of the 'Great Sin' at Ugarit," *Journal of Near Eastern Studies* 18 (1959): 280–81.

confronts Abraham with his lie about Sarah that nearly "brought upon me and upon my kingdom a great sin."[10] Unique to the biblical tradition, however, are the four occurrences of the phrase to describe the worship of the Golden Calf at Sinai (Ex 32:21, 30–31) and at Dan and Bethel (2 Kgs 17:21) accompanied both times by the cry: "Behold Israel your God (or gods) who brought you up from Egypt" (Ex 32:8; 1 Kgs 12:28). It is not clear why just this form of idolatry merits this epithet, but it is obvious that the sacred authors consider the attribution to some other god of the act by which YHWH brought Israel out from Egypt to be a particularly heinous example of Israel's lack of exclusive adherence to him.

3. To Be Faithless (bgd)

The verb, which occurs some 49 times in the Old Testament, means "to act contrary to the duty required by law or established by a relationship of loyalty into which the parties have entered." It refers to an "objectively measurable offensive behavior."[11] As such, it is operative in contexts as diverse as: marriage, political relations, the cult, social relations, and relations with YHWH. In Jeremiah 3:6–10 we find *bgd* used in connection with most of the words that exploit the metaphor of marital infidelity: "Faithless Judah" is compared to "apostate" Israel who "played the harlot," "committed adultery," and yet did not return to YHWH. This is reiterated in Jeremiah 3:20: "Surely, as a faithless wife leaves her husband, so have you been faithless to me, O house of Israel, says the Lord' " (see also Jer 5:11; Hos 5:7, 6:7).

4. To Be Disloyal (m'l)

The word refers to "the legally definable relationship of trust that exists between two persons."[12] Very often failure in the relationship consists in depriving someone of something that is rightfully theirs. A very high proportion of the 44 instances where the root is found describe an act of infidelity to YHWH, often with the overtones of failure to observe his rights and holiness, or to fail to fulfill a sacred duty such as an oath. In one instance *m'l* refers to marital infidelity. It is a case in which the act is "hidden from the eyes of her husband" thus accenting the overtones of treachery that are often connected with the term: "If a man's wife goes astray and is disloyal committing disloyalty against him and a man lies with her . . ." (Num 5:12–13).

---

[10] See, as well, Genesis 39:9 where Joseph describes the proposal of Pharaoh's wife as a "great evil *(ra'â)*."

[11] M. A. Klopfenstein, "BGD," in *Theological Lexicon of the Old Testament*, ed. Ernst Jenni and Claus Westerman (Peabody, MA: Hendrickson, 1997), 198–200, at 199. This paragraph is indebted to Klopfenstein's article.

[12] R. Knierim, "M'L," in *Theological Lexicon of the Old Testament*, 680–82, at 681.

5. To Be Profligate (znh)

This is the term most frequently used to describe Israel's truck with foreign gods and nations. Its basic meaning is to have irregular sexual relations. Thus, a prostitute is called a *zônâ*, and various nouns formed from the root refer to licentious and obscene behavior. Though the word can refer to prostitution in the literal sense (*ex. gr.* Gen 38:15; Jgs 15:1; 1 Kgs 3:16–28), the majority of its occurrences refer to Israel's lustful and profligate unfaithfulness to YHWH. The is most often used with the preposition "after" and may be translated "to whore after." Here are some examples:

> Exodus 34:12–16: Take heed to yourself, lest you make a covenant with the inhabitants of the land whither you go, lest it become a snare in the midst of you. You shall tear down their altars, and break their pillars, and cut down their Asherim (for you shall worship no other god, for the Lord, whose name is Jealous, is a jealous God), lest you make a covenant with the inhabitants of the land, and when they whore after their gods and sacrifice to their gods and one invites you, you eat of his sacrifice, and you take of their daughters for your sons, and their daughters whore after their gods and make your sons whore after their gods.

This text is significant for several reasons. First, YHWH is said to have the name "Jealous" *(qanna')*, another term that pertains to the overlap between marriage and the covenant, as we will see below. Second, the inhabitants of the land are said to "whore after" their own gods. This is the sole instance of the use of the expression in connection with *pagans* performing their own rites. It is either said in anticipation of the result that is that the Israelites, in infidelity to their covenant with YHWH, "whore after" the pagan gods, or it is an allusion to the sexual rites that accompany some of the pagan ceremonies. Though Adler has, correctly in my opinion, pointed to the exaggerations in the theory of sacred prostitution,[13] the evidence of some sort of sexual dimension in the cult of Baal seems undeniable. For this reason I opt for the second opinion though it does not exclude the fact that the "whoring after" done by the pagans can finally result in their imitation by Israel.

> *Judges 2:16–17:* Then the Lord raised up judges, who saved them out of the power of those who plundered them. And yet they did not listen to their judges; for they whored after other gods and bowed down to them; they soon turned aside from the way in which their fathers had walked, who had obeyed the commandments of the Lord, and they did not do so.

This is part of the editorial introduction to the Book of Judges in which the writer is accenting the rhythm: faithlessness—oppression—cry to YHWH—

---

13 Adler, "The Background" 323–26; 164–295a.

raise up a "judge" who saves—repetition of faithlessness. The editor of Judges is generally considered to be a representative of the Deuteronomistic school and to be dependent upon the line of thought initiated by Hosea. The evidence however is not conclusive.

> *Judges 8:27:* And Gideon made an ephod of it [the gold from his conquest] and put it in his city, in Ophrah; and all Israel whored after it there, and it became a snare to Gideon and to his family.

While it is impossible to tell exactly what the "ephod" was, it was clearly a religious object considered a personal possession that finally became some sort of idol. This use of *znh* with a material object that somehow is related to a god is found as well in Ezekiel 6:9 ("and I was grieved at their whoring heart that they turned away from me and at their eyes that whored after idols")[14] and Ezekiel 20:30, 23:30 ("whoring after the *nations* and defiling yourself with their idols"), and elsewhere.

We may ask why there is such a marked preference for this root when speaking of the worship and attention Israel gives to other gods and to other nations and their gods. The answer seems to be that it serves to accentuate that this form of adultery is one characterized by unrestrained lust for contacts other than YHWH: It is a profligate, repeated, indiscriminate, and incessant adultery.

6. Other Expressions

Among the many "systematically vague and elastic terms" that could be considered here, I will select only three. First there is the notion of "jealousy." Not only is YHWH's name "Jealous," as we saw above (Ex 34:14), but very often the term is used in connection with YHWH's intolerance of any rival. Thus we read in the Decalogue in the prohibition of the making and worshipping of idols: "[Y]ou shall not bow down to them or serve them; for I YHWH your God am a jealous God, visiting the iniquity of the fathers upon the children to the third and the fourth generation of those who hate me [prefer another to me] . . ." (Ex 20:5; Dt 5:9). This is echoed in Deuteronomy 4:24, "For YHWH your God is a devouring fire, a jealous God" (see also Dt 6:15; Jos 24:19).[15]

Corresponding to this jealousy is the fact of YHWH's love for his people. While the term has an even broader semantic field than does our word "love," there are instances where it clearly evokes the affection between husband and wife. Thus, we read in Deuteronomy 10:15, ". . . yet the Lord set his heart in love upon your fathers and chose their descendants after them, you above all

---

[14] Ibid., 330.

[15] For a more extended treatment of this notion, see *Theological Lexicon of the Old Testament,* 3, 1145–47.

peoples, as at this day." YHWH chooses Israel to have a special relation to him, he does this because he "set his heart" upon her and "loved" her. The first of these expressions, *ḥšq*, refers to an attraction that results in "a reasoned and unconditional decision."[16] The second verb, therefore, describes a love that is preferential and productive of a selective choice.

Another use of the root *'hb* (love) that is evocative of the metaphor of marriage between YHWH and his people can be found in the manner in which Israel's foreign covenant partners, and the gods they serve, are called "lovers." It is characteristic of the elasticity of Hebrew that the term can mean merely a friend or ally (1 Kgs 5:15 [political relation]; 2 Sm 19:7 [David's soldiers]; Jer 20:4, 6 [friends/allies]), as well as an illicit lover. In this latter sense Jerusalem is said to mourn the absence of her "lovers" who have betrayed her, to whom she calls out to no avail (Lam 1:2, 19), while in Jeremiah YHWH calls out to Jerusalem pointing out that all "your lovers" (partners in the alliance against Babylonia) are "destroyed" and "on the way to captivity" (Jer 22:20, 22).[17]

Conclusion

The remarkable interpenetration of images evoked by the vocabulary we have just studied points to an intuition, deep in the heart and soul of Israel, that could discern an analogy between the relation of YHWH and his people and that of a husband and wife. Both were based on a choice; both demanded exclusive fidelity on the part of the one chosen; "love," as covenant fidelity and as deep affection, characterizes the relation; and finally, infidelity is "faithlessness," "treachery," "adultery," and "profligacy." It is impossible for us to determine when and how this image-analogy first took root in Israel. It was based on a metaphysical intuition that arose as a metaphor and was developed by many users of the Hebrew language, some of whom are represented in the sacred text. In literary terms we are dealing with an "expansive" or "sunken image," that is, an image that is latent and not explicitly articulated even while it is operative and determines the line of thought.[18] Though it is impossible at this point to assess how explicit the terminological overlap had made the image, it is clear the prophesying of Hosea brought this form of discourse to a

---

[16] Wallis in *Theological Dictionary of the Old Testament*, V:263.

[17] It is interesting to observe that, despite the use in Hebrew of the notion of "whoring" to apply to alliances with foreign nations that involved worship of their gods (Ez 23:3 and so on), there does not seem to be any use of this metaphorical language outside Israel. The proposal of E. Weidner to read *a-na-ku* as "commit adultery" in one Hittite non-aggression treaty has not met with general acceptance *Politische Dokumente aus Kleinasien, Bogasköi-studien* (Leipzig: 1923), 104, lines 58–59.

[18] Still valuable for a discussion of the various functions of image is the study by René Wellek and Austin Warren, *Theory of Literature* (New York: Harcourt, Brace and Company, 1948), especially ch. 15.

critical mass and made of it a privileged symbol of YHWH's covenant choice and Israel's covenant responsibility.

Part Two: The Use of Marriage Symbolism in the First Three Chapters of Hosea

There were approximately 230 years from the beginning of "classical" prophecy with Hosea and Amos to the exile of the Southern Kingdom (750–521 B.C.). The canon of Scripture contains the works of nine prophets from this period. As has already been mentioned, the books of Hosea, Jeremiah, and Ezekiel contain fully developed passages utilizing the theme of Israel as the bride of Yahweh that are in a line of dependence and development. There are four other passages from this period that may or may not have been influenced by Hosea, but there is no real development of the analogical symbol in these texts.[19]

Hosea is responsible for the intensification and development of two of three images mentioned at the beginning of this essay (King, Father, Spouse). In chapter 11 we are presented with YHWH as a father offended by his ungrateful son for whom he had done everything. Despite all logic he does not destroy this people. Here, as in the spousal image, we are confronted with the transcendent mystery of love: "[M]y own heart turns against me, within me my pity is aflame. I will not return to ruin Ephraim, for I am God, not man; the Holy One in the midst of you" (Hos 11:8–9). We can see in this passage the same intensification of love that served as the catalyst bringing together and sublating the inchoate use of matrimonial images to portray the covenant between YHWH and his people that we will now consider.[20] I will begin with a presentation of the text of Hosea 1–3.

The Introduction

1. The word of YHWH, which came to Hosea son of Beeri in the days of Uzziah, Jotham, Ahaz, and Hezekiah kings of Judah and in the days of Jeroboam the son of Joash king of Israel.

---

[19] The four passages are, first, Isaiah 1:21–23 and 23:15–17 (these passages apply to Jerusalem and Tyre, respectively, and seem to use the epithet "harlot" to refer to a profligate attitude and easy trafficking with commercial partners), then Mi 1:6–7, which seems to refer to idolatry, and Nahum 3:4–5, which seems to combine the aspects of easy trafficking and idolatry.

[20] Hosea's procedure, both in its advance beyond his predecessors and in his dependence upon them, is aptly portrayed in this description of sublation given by Bernard Lonergan: "What sublates goes beyond what is sublated, introduces something new and distinct, yet so far from interfering with the sublated or destroying it, on the contrary needs it, includes it, preserves all its proper features and properties, and carries them forward to a fuller realization within a richer context." *Method in Theology,* (New York: Herder & Herder, 1972), 241.

The Relationship Destroyed

2. The beginning of YHWH's speaking to Hosea:

YHWH said to Hosea:

> Go, take for yourself a harlot wife
> and harlot children.
> For the land goes off a-whoring
> away from YHWH.

3. And he went and he took Gomer, daughter of Diblaim, and she conceived and bore him a son.

4. And YHWH said to him:

> Call his name Jezreel
> for in a little while
> I will seek the blood at Jezreel
> from the house of Jehu
> and I will bring an end to the kingdom of Israel.

5. And it will be on that day
that I will splinter the bow of Israel
in the Valley of Jezreel.

6. And she conceived again and bore a daughter, and He said to him:

> Call her name Not-pitied
> for I will not pity again
> the house of Israel;
> No, I will surely hold it against them.

7. I will pity the house of Judah
and save them by YHWH their God.
I will not save them by bow or by sword,
by war or by horses and horsemen.

8. And she weaned Not-pitied,
and she conceived and bore a son.

And He said:

> Call his name Not-My-People
> For you are not my people
> and I am no more there for you.

1. The number of the children of Israel
will be like the sands of the sea;
neither measured nor numbered.
And it will be in that place
where it was said to them:

"You are not my people."
It will be said to them,
"Sons of the living God."

2. They will be assembled
   the sons of Judah
   and the sons of Israel
   all together
   And they shall set up for themselves
   one head
   and they shall go up from the Land.
   How great is the day of Jezreel!

3. Say to your brother,
   "My People"
   and to your sister,
   "The Pitied One."

The Jealousy and Love of YHWH

4. Declare against your mother,
   Declare!
   For she is not my wife,
   and I am not her husband.
   Let her put aside her whoring,
   from her gaze,
   and her adultery
   from between her breasts.

5. Lest I strip her bare
   and leave her like the day she was born,
   and make her like a desert
   set her like a withered land,
   and kill her with thirst.

6. Upon her children I will have not pity,
   for they are the offspring of whoring;

7. for their mother is a harlot
   she who bore them plays with shame.
   She says:

   > I will go after my lovers,
   > who give me my bread and my water,
   > my wool and my flax,
   > my oil and my drink.

8. Therefore, behold me
   hedging in her way with thorns;
   I will put up a fence
   and fence her,
   and her tracks she will not find.

9. She will pursue her lovers
   but she will not catch them;
   she will seek them
   and not find them.

   And then she will say:

   I will go and return to my first man;
   for it was better with me
   then than now.

10. And she does not know
    that it was I
    who gave her the grain
    and the wine and the oil
    and the silver I increased for her
    and the gold they used for Baal.

11. Therefore I will go and take back
    my grain in its time;
    and my wine in its season.
    I will snatch away my wool and my flax,
    she used to cover her shame,

12. and now I will lay bare her nakedness
    in the eyes of her lovers
    and no man will save her from my hand.

13. I will put an end to her joy,
    feast, new moon, Sabbath and festival.

14. I will ruin her vine and her fig tree
    of which says
    these are to me my hire
    which my lovers have given me;
    I will make them a jungle
    and the beasts shall devour them.

15. And I will visit upon her
    the days of the Baals
    when she burned incense to them
    and decked herself in nose ring and necklace

and went after her lovers,
and me
she forgot completely.
An oracle of YHWH.

16. Therefore, behold
I am alluring her
and I will lead her in the desert
and I will speak upon her heart.

17. I will give to her vineyards there
the valley of Akor will be the gate of hope
And she will respond there
as in the days of her youth
on the day of her coming up
from the land of Egypt.

18. And it shall be on that day—the oracle of YHWH—
You will call me "my husband"
no longer will you call me
"my Baal."

19. I will take the names of the Baals from her mouth,
no longer will those names be remembered.

20. I will make a covenant for them
on that day,
with the beasts of the field
and the birds of the heavens
and the things that move on the ground.
The bow and the sword, and war
I will break off from the land,
and I will lay them down to sleep all trusting.

21. I will plight my troth with you forever
I will betroth you to myself
in justice, in right, in love, and tender pity.

22. I will betroth you to myself
in faithfulness
and you will know YHWH.

23. And it shall be on that day
I will respond—the oracle of YHWH—
I will respond to the heavens,
and they will respond to the earth,

24. and the earth will respond to the grain,
    to the wine, and to the oil,
    and they will respond to Jezreel.

25. I will sow her for myself on the land
    I will pity Not-pitied
    and I will say to Not-My-People
    You are my people
    and he will say
    my God.

The Spouses are Reunited: Sign and Reality

1. And YHWH said to me again:

     Go, love a woman
     who loves a paramour and is adulterous.
     For YHWH loves
     the sons of Israel
     though they turn to stranger gods
     and love their raisin cakes.

2. So I bought her for myself
   For fifteen shekels of silver
   And a homer and a half of barley.

3. And I said to her:

     Many days you must wait for me
     You must not act the harlot
     You will belong to no man
     And even I will not come near you.

4. Yes, for many days the sons of Israel must wait.
   No king nor prince,
   no sacrifice or pillar,
   no ephod or teraphim.

5. Afterwards they will return,
   the sons of Israel,
   and they will seek
   YHWH their God
   and David their king.
   They will tremble in awe at YHWH
   and his beauty.
   At the end of days.

The Basic Movement and Message of the Text

Presuming that the problems connected with this text and the plethora of solutions proposed in regard to these problems is well enough known, I will simply propose my understanding of the text as we have it. These problems and their proposed solutions do not affect my goal here, which is to understand how Hosea, and his editor, portray the relation between YHWH and Israel in terms of a marriage covenant and the significance of that for biblical theology.

Hosea, as I have mentioned, is responsible for the transformation of what was, until his time, a "sunken image" into a vibrant symbolic analogy. At the heart of this process was a transforming experience of the love of YHWH. Hosea's love for Gomer, which defied all that reason and culture would expect of him, and which was the source of his suffering, his anger, and his desire for reunion, provided him with his living experience of the unfathomable mystery of YHWH's love for his people.

The Rhythm of the Text

The first three chapters of Hosea form a unity. They are narrative written in a poetic prose as contrasted with the oracular utterances of the rest of the book (chapters 4 through14). There are many first person references and these are divided between the "I" of God and the "I" of Hosea, which are sometimes difficult to differentiate. There are three movements to the text. There is, first, an account of the destruction of the marriage (1:2–8) with a passage that proleptically points to the resolution of the drama (2:1–3). This is followed by a soliloquy in which the protagonist(s) express anger, unrequited love, plans for bringing about reconciliation, and finally a prophecy of restoration (2:4–25). The final section describes the reconciliation of Hosea and Gomer, which is then seen as an anticipation of the complete reconciliation effected by YHWH "at the end of days" (3:1–5).

In a way not unlike the book of Job, the author takes a basic plot, in this case the story of the destruction and restoration of a marriage relation (sections one and three above), and inserts into it a long section in which the dynamic of the process is traced in all its turbulent oscillation. The movement of the text thus realizes the nature of narrative that can be defined as the literary presentation of a completed action, or in the words of Tzvetan Todorov already considered:

> The minimal complete plot consists in the passage from one equilibrium to another. An "ideal" narrative begins with a stable situation which is disturbed by some power or force. There results a state of disequilibrium; by the action of a force directed in the opposite direction, the equilibrium is re-established; the second equilibrium is similar to the first, but the two are never identical.[21]

---

[21] Tzvetan Todoroz, *The Poetics of Prose,* trans. Richard Howard (Ithaca: Cornell University Press, 1977), 111.

The three stages outlined by Todorov are set forth in the threefold rhythm of our text with the central section, characterized by the action of two forces, being the place where the deep inner mystery of the restored equilibrium is revealed. At this distance judgments regarding responsibility for the present form and structure of the passage can only be approximations. The deep insight born of an intense experience and the words that articulate this are from Hosea. The basic plot reflects his life experience. It is presented here as his "prophetic credentials" in much the same way as the inaugural experience and commissioning of Isaiah (Is 6:1–13). Jeremiah (Jer 1:4–10), Ezekiel (1–3), and in another way Amos (Am 7:1–6) served as their authenticating credentials. Hosea's marriage, the suffering that it caused him, and the final restoration of that marriage constituted, under the word of YHWH, his prophetic call, his experience of God, and the credentials that he presents. For every prophet the encounter with God and the subsequent commission become both the matrix and the informing principle of his message. So too, and in a unique manner, Hosea's marriage and his mystical experience of the love of God found in and through his love for his unfaithful wife are the prism through which he understands and proclaims the greatness of Israel's sin, the justice of the punishment, and the promise of unmerited restoration.

The First Section: Hosea 1:1–2:3

Strictly speaking, in the first part of this section (1:2–8), we are only told, in the third person, of Hosea's marriage and of the names YHWH tells him to give to his children. The description of Gomer as a "harlot wife" applies to her first and foremost because she is a member of a people who go "a-whoring away from YHWH." We are lead to infer, and this will become clearer later on, that Gomer, in her own life, has broken the covenant with YHWH by breaking her covenant with Hosea. While the three Old Testament texts that explicitly call marriage a covenant (*běrît*: Prov 2:17; Ez 16:8; Mal 2:14) postdate Hosea, the notion underlies much of the overlapping terminology we have previously considered.[22]

The names of the children are ominous.[23] The first-born son is called Jezreel because YHWH "will seek the blood at Jezreel from the house of Jehu." Though the general sense is clear, the exact reference is hard to determine.[24] The girl child is called "Not-pitied," signaling an end to the demonstration of compassion YHWH has had for his people and is probably an allusive prophecy

---

[22] For a complete, if occasionally exaggerated, study of marriage as covenant, see Gordon Paul Hugenberger, *Marriage As a Covenant: A Study of Biblical Law and Ethics Governing Marriage Developed From the Perspective of Malachi, Supplements to Vetus Testamentum* 52 (Leiden: Brill, 1994).

[23] Compare Isaiah 7:7; 8:8:1–4, 18.

[24] For a comprehensive discussion, see Francis I. Andersen and David Noel Freedman, "Hosea," in *The Anchor Bible* (New York: Doubleday and Co., 1980).

of the northern exile. It is likely that v. 7 is a scribal addition, perhaps of an oracle delivered by Hosea, distinguishing between Israel and Judah and preparing
for the prophecy of reunification in 2:2. The third child, a boy, is called "Not-
My-People," by far the worst sign of all. In legal terminology God breaks the
covenant with his people. The phrase *lō' 'ammî* undoes the covenant vow
implied in the oft-repeated phrase "my people" *('ammi)*[25] in the same way as
the divorce formula "not my wife" *(lo' 'išti)* dissolves the marriage commitment
"my wife" *'išti).*[26] The next line is a probable allusion to the alternative expression of the name of YHWH in Exodus 3:14, where God describes his name as
'ehyeh ("I will be [there for you]") By these last two statements the covenant is
annulled and Israel becomes, in effect, but one more among the people of the
earth without a special relation to YHWH.

The first three verses of chapter 2 (in the Hebrew enumeration) contain two
oracles of restoration reversing the names given to the children in chapter 1. They
are so closely linked to what precedes that they may be considered as Hosean oracles and probably part of this original section. There are some important features
in these passages. Thus in 2:1, there is first an allusion to the promise made to
Abraham, thus indicating that it is YHWH's prior choice that grounds his mercy,
and this is followed by a renewal of covenant formula where "Not-My-People"
becomes "Sons of the living God." The second passage (2:2–3) contains the
prophetic assurance that a day will come when there will be one "head" ("king")
over both the north and the south, and Jezreel will be the site of the restoration of
the covenant with the whole people. These two passages have been placed here by
the inspired editor to anticipate what will take place after the tumultuous inner
conflict described in the following section.[27]

The Second Section: Hosea 2:4–25

It is interesting to observe that Hosea 11:5–9 has many of the same features as
our passage. YHWH begins the soliloquy there by reflecting on the tender care he
had for his people, his son, as he called them out of Egypt (11:1–4). He then
calls to mind their infidelity and the punishment this evokes (11:5–7). Overcome by love ("my own heart turns against me"), he promises to come again in
mercy to his people and thus show them at a still deeper level the secret of his
very nature: "For I am God, not man, the Holy One in the midst of you."

---

[25] See Exodus 6:7: "I will take you to me to be a people, and I will be to you a God"; also,
Leviticus 26:12; Deuteronomy 27:9. For the same illocutionary formula regarding the
special adoption of the king, see 2 Sm 7:14.

[26] For a treatment of the atmosphere of these illocutionary statements, see Roland de Vaux,
Ancient Israel, vol. 1, *Social Institutions* (New York: McGraw Hill, 1965), 32–36.

[27] I have treated this "checkerboard" manner of redacting Old Testament texts in Francis
Martin, *Narrative Parallels to the New Testament, SBL Resources for Biblical Study* 22
(Atlanta: Scholars Press, 1988); see the Introduction.

In the section under consideration YHWH is the only speaker, though he does quote "her" as she debates within herself, moving first toward her "lovers" and to her "first man." In the first part, vv. 4–15, YHWH (Hosea) thinks of the offense, his disgrace, and the punishment he will inflict. It begins with a covenantal confrontation using specifically legal terms. The people (Hosea's children) are told to "declare" (*rîbû*—a legal term) against their mother Israel (Gomer) that she is "not my wife" and he is "not her husband," thus effecting a divorce. And then comes the threat of being stripped: probably a gesture by which an offended husband disgraces the adulteress and indicates that he will take care of her no longer (see Jer 13:22, 26).[28] The references to "desert," "withered land," and "thirst" clearly move the image to a prophecy of a scorched earth policy to be perpetrated by the coming invader.

The second part of chapter 2, verse 7 is the first of the "quotes" that YHWH attributes to his people. The "lovers" here are, as we have seen, the Baals who were considered to be bestowers of fertility. YHWH's reaction is introduced by the first of three "therefores" (vv. 8, 11, 16), a phrase, which, as H. W. Wolff points out, normally "marks the transition from the proof of guilt to the threat of punishment."[29] In Hosea, the expression is found only here and at 13:3. The manner in which Hosea uses the term points to a logic unique to God himself. Here, in v. 8, the punishment now is one destined to bring Israel back: YHWH will make it impossible for Israel to worship the Baals and then she will decide to return to her "first man," even though "she does not know" that YHWH has been the source of all her blessings.[30] The second "therefore" introduces a change (vv. 11–15). The offended Spouse returns to think of punishment. He will strip the land of its pro-

---

[28] Early legislation regarding adultery envisaged only the death of the man, while the woman may have been stripped in order to indicate, as has been said, that her husband no longer had care of her, and as a humiliation. Later enactments, particularly those in the Deuteronomic code, treated the woman as a responsible agent and proscribed the death penalty for her as well: "If a man is caught lying with the wife of another man, both of them shall die, the man who lay with the woman as well as the woman. So you shall purge the evil from Israel" (Dt 22:22; also Lv 20:10). It was not until a later time in the postexilic period that the death penalty ceased to be applied to adultery and was restricted only to murder, with adultery punished by exclusion from the community (see Prov 5:9–14). This point is developed by Anthony Phillips, *Ancient Israel's Criminal Law: A New Approach to the Decalogue* (Oxford/New York: Schocken 1970), 28ff. For a treatment of how the Deuteronomic code evinces a developed sense of individual dignity, see Louis Stulman, "Sex and Familial Crimes in the D Code: A Witness to Mores in Transition," *Journal for the Study of the Old Testament* 53 (1992): 47–63.

[29] Hans Walter Wolff, *Hosea: A Commentary on the Book of the Prophet Hosea*, trans. Gary Stansell (Philadelphia: Fortress, 1974), 36. Wolf points to some 77 occurrences of the phrase in the prophetic writings.

[30] It is sometimes objected that this notion of winning Israel back is faulty given the fact that legislation (Dt 24:1–4) proscribed the taking back of a woman who had been divorced. This overlooks the fact that the case envisaged is one in which the woman *has*

duce, deprive the people of the festivals in which they celebrate the bounty of the Baals, and make the land a jungle, visiting on her "all the days of the Baals" when "she decked herself out in nose ring and necklace and went after her lovers." What is worse, "me, she forgot completely." Biblically "to forget" means to so hold YHWH's saving acts in contempt that they no longer have any effect on the life and consciousness of the people and the individual.

With verse 16, we see how the heart of YHWH "turns against him." Israel's return to YHWH will take place because YHWH will take the initiative. This third "therefore" introduces an action that can follow upon nothing in the text. The consequence of Israel's forgetting YHWH is that he will "allure" her—the word implies seduction (Ex 22:15), enticement (Jer 20:7), or even deception (Jer 20:10). He will "lead her into the desert," the idyllic place of their first meeting (Jer 2:1–3: "I remember the faithfulness of your youth, your bridal love; you followed me in the desert. . . .") He will "speak upon her heart"—an expression that signifies love, infatuated desire to be together (Gen 34:3), intimacy (Ru 2:13), comfort (Is 40:2), and even the act of winning back an errant wife (Jgs 19:3). The result will be, YHWH says, that "she respond there as in the days of her youth, on the day of her coming up from the land of Egypt."

Then, in 2:18–22, YHWH seems to break out of his soliloquy and address Israel directly, foretelling the moment when the covenant vows will be renewed: "You will call me, 'my husband.'" Never again will YHWH be called Baal.[31] The oracle continues, now in the third person (vv. 19–20), promising a covenant that will extend to the land and its fertility. He then turns to his spouse: "I will plight my troth with you forever, I will betroth you to myself. . . ." All the words that speak of a perfect covenant relationship are then invoked and the promise concludes: "And you will know YHWH." The daring use of the term "know" (yd') in this betrothal context brings all its other connotations into a new and hitherto unsuspected and intimate key.

The notion of "the knowledge of God" is a central one in Hosea.[32] The root yd' occurs seventeen times in the book with various nuances, some of which develop the linguistic potential of the term as he inherited it; this can be seen in subsequent use, especially in Jeremiah. The English word that captures most of

---

married another man, and then wishes to come back. In any case according to Jeremiah 3:1–5, YHWH is quite prepared to dispense himself from this prescription.

[31] The use (rather infrequent) of *baal* in Israelite theophoric names dates back to a time when the term signified "lord" and its connection with the Canaanite fertility god was not so powerful. Because of these later connotations the term *baal* is frequently replaced by *boshet* ("shame") in the Hebrew Bible: see 2 Sam 4:4; 9:3–13; 21:8–9; and so on. For a discussion of this see *Harper's Bible Dictionary*, ed. Paul Achtemeier (San Francisco: Harper and Row, 1985), 626–27. For the position that the reference in our text is to syncretism, see Wolff, *Hosea*, 38–39.

[32] See the fine article by Hans Walter Wolff, "'Wissen um Gott' bei Hosea als Urform von Theologie," *Evangelische Theologie* 12 (1952–53): 533–54.

the developed semantic field is "recognize," which can mean both "perceive" and "acknowledge." "Perceive" extends to include not only "discern" but also "experience" and, in this sense, "know intimately." "Acknowledge," on the other hand, implies a movement of the will, a choice of someone or an acceptance of their authority. "To know God," therefore, means to discern his presence and action, to experience him and be in communion with him, but it also means to choose him and obey him.[33] Thus, the famous expression "knowledge of God," found in Hosea 4:1 and 6:6, refers to this lack of perceptual obedience caused by spiritual and bodily profligacy, and the same can be said of 5:4 ("they know not YHWH"). Israel's acknowledgment of YHWH as her only God is prescribed in Hosea 13:4,[34] while the following verse evokes more the sense of "choice" on the part of YHWH ("I knew you in the wilderness").[35] There are two texts in which the fullness of what it means to "know YHWH" are indicated: our present text (2:22) and 6:3, and both are in the context of a renewed covenant.

Jeremiah well understood the significance of Hosea's teaching. In a denunciation of Jehoiakim's extravagant building program, and its concomitant manipulation of the poor, Jeremiah invokes the example of Jehoiakim's father, Josiah: "Because he dispensed justice to the weak and the poor, it went well with him. Is this not knowledge of me?—An oracle of YHWH" (Jer 22:16). More important still is Jeremiah's prophecy of a new covenant, "not like the covenant I made with their fathers." Because of the action of YHWH placing the principle of response in the hearts of his people, "all will know me from the least to the greatest." This prophecy, which forms the basis of the First Letter of John,[36] is obviously dependent upon Hosea's prophecy of restoration in 2:22: "You will know YHWH," you will discern and experience him, you will have an intimacy with him of which marital intimacy can be but an icon, you will delight to obey him, acknowledging what he has done for you and your gratitude to him. Perhaps the best way to sum up the full meaning of this prophecy of Hosea and Jeremiah (and Ezekiel 36:24–28) is to read Origen's definition of what "to know" means in the Bible: "Scripture says of those who are joined and at one with something, that they know that to which they are joined and in communion."[37]

---

[33] It is interesting to observe how closely this understanding of knowledge is approximated by modern anthropology, which sees choice and reason as being the surface expressions of the spirit of man in which intuition (*intellectus*) and freedom are reciprocally active.

[34] Hypocrisy in this matter is condemned in Hosea 8:2 (compare 1 Jn 2:4: "The one who claims: 'I have come to know him,' while not keeping his commandments, is a liar."), while acknowledgment is forced on Israel by the "days of punishment" mentioned in Hosea 9:7.

[35] Compare Amos 3:2, "You only have I known of all the families of the earth . . . ," while the notion of acquiescence or acknowledgment is found in Hosea 8:4 ("They set up princes with my knowledge.").

[36] See the discussion of this Letter in Chapter 7.

[37] *In Joan.*, 19 (*Patrologia Graeca* 14, 529).

In the final three verses of this section, the "soliloquy" turns outward and the alternation between second and third person is sustained. YHWH continues to think of his future plans, but now he is announcing them to the world. The covenant with the land announced in vv. 19–20 is now expanded: The heavens and the earth will join in and thus, by YHWH's covenantal action, and not by that of the Baals, Jezreel will have "grain, wine, and oil." In the final lines the promise is complete: Not-pitied will be once again the object of YHWH's merciful and particular care, and the covenant vows are pronounced: "my people—my God."

The Final Section: Hosea 3:1–5, The Spouses are Reunited: Sign and Reality

The opening line of this section makes explicit reference to the first section by describing YHWH as speaking "again." The command is now to "Go, love a woman," thus putting the accent on love as the mysterious source of the reunion. Hosea avoids the technical term "take"(1:2) that designates a stage of the marriage process, thus indicating that this is not a new marriage but the renewal of a destroyed marriage.[38] Gomer "loves" as well: She loves a paramour and is adulterous. We see here how the whole foundation of Hosea's experience lies in "loving" Gomer and not repudiating her completely but rather renewing the marriage covenant: His life is the prophetic sign of what YHWH plans to do. For "YHWH *loves* the sons of Israel" even though they are adulterous: "[T]hey turn to stranger gods and *love* their raisin cakes."[39]

In order to effect the return of Gomer Hosea must pay a price, and then stay aloof (vv. 2–3). The significance of the expression "fifteen shekels of silver and a homer and a half of barley" is probably so bound to its cultural context as to be devoid of specific significance for us.[40] All we know is that it cost Hosea something to recover his wife. He then tells her that she is to wait many days for him, not playing the harlot, belonging to no man, and that he himself will not come near her. This imposed period of continence is also an enacted prophecy of the future of Israel, as the following two verses (vv. 4–5) explain. Verse 4 describes the time of deprivation and waiting. The sons of Israel must wait, like Gomer, "many days" without the fixed points of their religious culture that directed them to YHWH's presence and signified his care. Finally, "they will return"—the notion here is conversion, a coming back to YHWH. This

---

[38] For a discussion of the technical terminology covering the various stages of the marriage commitment, see Angelo Tosato, *Il Matrimonio Israelitico, Analecta Biblica* 100 (Rome: Biblical Institute Press, 1982), especially ch. 5.

[39] These cakes are associated with the pagan cult. They may evoke for the audience something similar to the dough-cakes for the "Queen of Heaven" condemned in Jeremiah 7:18. See Andersen/Freedman, *Hosea*, 298.

[40] For the expression "half (a homer) or barley," the LXX reads "a jug of wine." But this does not enlighten us as to the significance of the price or why it is mentioned here.

return will be characterized by "seeking YHWH their God and David their king." The prediction of a united kingdom picks up the theme from 2:2, while the mention of YHWH as "their God" echoes "my husband" (2:18) and "my God" (2:25). The term "seek" implies a movement of trust and obedience (Zech 8:22; Zeph 2:3; Mal 3:1), and is further specified by a movement of trembling "in awe at YHWH and at his beauty."[41]

This will take place "at the end of days." The expression, which occurs about twelve times in the Old Testament, refers in varying ways to the significant ending of one period of time and the beginning of another even more significant. "Days" as they are now known will end because of an act on the part of YHWH and they will give place to new days and new realities: "It shall come to pass at the end of days that the mountain of the house of the Lord shall be established as the highest of the mountains, and shall be raised above the hills; and all the nations shall flow to it" (Is 2:2; Mi 4:1). When YHWH acts to make a new marriage covenant with his people, a new era will begin. It will happen when "these days" are over.

Part Three: Hosea's Share in YHWH's Unrequited Love

Edward Schillebeecx once acutely remarked:

> Revealing his covenant through the medium of human marriage, God simultaneously revealed to men a meaning of marriage which they had not hitherto suspected.[42]

It is important, at the end of this study, to seek to penetrate the "meaning of marriage" in the light of the covenant between YHWH and his people. This can serve a twofold purpose. First, it can allow us to understand Hosea's metaphysics of relationality. The inchoate insight expressed in the "vague and elastic terms" linking the marriage covenant with the Sinai covenant, which we considered in Part One, is brought to a new depth in Hosea's experiential share in God's covenant love for Israel. Second, though this aspect is beyond the scope of the present study, such a reflection can establish the objective analogy, based on a participation in being, that exists between YHWH's covenant relation and its fulfillment as this is described in Ephesians 5:31–32:

> For this reason, a man will leave his father and mother and be joined to his wife and the two will become one flesh. This Mystery is great: for my part, I am speaking in reference to Christ and the Church.

---

[41] I read *ṭôbô* rather then MT *ṭûbô* though either is acceptable, and I see here an allusion to YHWH's promise to Moses that he would see "all my beauty" (Ex 33:19).

[42] Edward Schillebeeckx, *Marriage: Human Reality and Saving Mystery* (London: Sheed and Ward, 1984), 33.

Reflections on the Use of the Marriage Analogy

In *Fides et Ratio*, Pope John Paul II accented the importance of time, that is, history in the Christian dispensation:

> God's Revelation is therefore immersed in time and history. Jesus Christ took flesh in the "fullness of time" (Gal 4:4); and two thousand years later, I feel bound to restate forcefully that "in Christianity time has a fundamental importance."[43] It is within time that the whole work of creation and salvation comes to light; and it emerges clearly above all that, with the Incarnation of the Son of God, our life is even now a foretaste of the fulfillment of time which is to come (cf. Heb 1:2). (Par. 11)

No theologian, however, after having made use of the historical disciplines in order to render the text more intelligible, can avoid the further question: "Now that we can report on what the text is saying, how can we understand what the text is talking about?" As I stated above, Hosea's predication concerning God's covenant love for Israel is based upon his experience that his love for Gomer is a participation in YHWH's love. We have seen that Israel's possession of a covenantal relation to YHWH and its subsequent use of spousal terms to mediate a dimension of that relation are unique in the whole of the history of religion. This must be taken seriously. The covenant relation is itself based upon and expressive of acts of God in time, in history, and these events participate in a proleptic manner in the mystery of the Incarnation, and in its own highpoint in time: the death and resurrection of Jesus. There is thus a mysterious participation in which all God's acts in human history are related to the supreme act, the cross, which realizes and is completely the action of God, and is the exemplar and instrumental efficient cause of all the other acts.[44] It is for this reason that, already within the Old Testament itself, there is a relating of successive acts of God as realizations of the same plan even as Israel "looked for a new David, a new Exodus, a new covenant, a new city of God: the old had thus become a type of the new and important as pointing forward to it."[45]

This type of participation includes, however, not only event, but also relation. The new covenant in the blood of Christ confers an infinite and eternal concreteness, so to speak, upon the reality of relation and grounds what may be called a metaphysics of relation. All relations in the plan of salvation, especially all covenant relations such as marriage, share in the reality of God's love for his people and are, as it were, its sacrament. This is why the author of the Letter to

---

[43] Apostolic Letter *Tertio Millennio Adveniente* (10 November 1994), 10: *Acta Apostolicae Sedis* 87 (1995): 11.

[44] Some of this is treated by Hans Urs von Balthasar in *A Theology of History* (San Francisco: Ignatius, reprint, 1994).

[45] Gerhard von Rad, *Old Testament Theology*, trans. D. M. G. Stalker, vol. 2, *The Theology of Israel's Prophetic Traditions* (New York: Harper and Row, 1965), 323.

the Ephesians can see the reality of Christ and his marriage to the Church already present, as exemplar and instrumental efficient cause at creation itself.

The power of Hosea's understanding, born of suffering, sustained and instructed Israel and its prophets for centuries because he was able to experience his love for Gomer not as sharing in YHWH's love in a predicamental way but in an ontological way. This love was an anticipation of the mystical understanding of love articulated by St. Augustine who had experienced it in Christ: "Love your neighbor, then look within yourself at the source of this love. There you will see, as far as you are able, God."[46] In another place he explains why this is so: "Let him love his brother, and he will love the same love. For he knows the love with which he loves, more than the brother whom he loves. So now he can know God more than he knows his brother: clearly known more, because more present; known more, because more within him; known more, because more certain."[47]

This understanding of what is hidden in every relationship as a possibility is the deepest meaning of what is expressed by saying that Israel is the bride of YHWH.

---

[46] "Dilige . . . proximum: et intuere in te unde diligis proximum. Ibi videbis, ut poteris, Deum." (Tract. in Joan. 17, 8 [Patroligia Latina 35,1532]). It is for this reason that I understand 1 John 4:19–20 as enunciating a metaphysical principle and rather than a moral exhortation: "We love because he first loves us. If someone says: 'I love God' and hates his brother, he is a liar. The one who does not love his brother whom he has seen, God, whom he has not seen, he cannot love."

[47] De Trinitate VIII, 8, 12 (Patrologia Latina 42, 957). Translation from Alexander Roberts and James Donaldson, Nicene and Post-Nicene Fathers, First Series: Volume III, (Oak Harbor, WA: Logos Research Systems, Inc.), 1997. The references to Augustine are from the introduction to Aurelius Augustine, Commentaire de la Première Épître de S. Jean, ed. J. Daniélou, H. de Lubac, et al., trans. Paul Agaësse, Sources Chrétiennes 75 (Paris: Cerf, 1984), 49.

7 The Integrity of Christian Moral Activity: The First Letter of John and *Veritatis Splendor*

THIS CHAPTER LOOKS at the encyclical *Veritatis Splendor* with the eyes of Johannne theology, particularly the understanding, implicit in the First Letter of John, concerning the source of Christian action. Given the particular Johannine understanding of "truth" and the encyclical's insistence on the intrinsic relation between freedom and truth, this study looks at the Johannine understanding of how the knowledge of God is the place where freedom and truth meet.

• • •

THERE is an interesting debate in Catholic circles concerning whether or not *Veritatis Splendor* is "biblical." Some mean by this term "in keeping with the results of historical criticism," while others seem to look for a series of passages in the encyclical that could serve as "proof text" for positions otherwise already established. Perhaps a better approach to the question is to determine whether or not the encyclical views reality in the light of faith and has recourse to a biblical, prophetic interpretation of reality in making its case. While admitting that some biblical texts are used more as allusive illustrations than as direct sources of doctrine, this article will maintain that the encyclical is biblical in that it looks upon reality and discourses about it in categories that are part of the biblical tradition. In order to establish this point, a comparison will be made between the encyclical and the First Letter of John in regard to truth as a source of moral activity.

One of *Veritatis Splendor*'s major themes is that of the intimate relation between freedom and truth. Reactions to this theme show that it is possible to consider it, and indeed the whole encyclical, from one of two perspectives, which

This chapter was originally published as "The Integrity of Christian Moral Activity. The First Letter of John and *Veritatis Splendor*," *Communio* 21 (1994): 265–85.

we may call "ethical" and "theological." The theme of freedom and truth can, for instance, be studied in the context of conscience. In such a context, confusion over the universal truth about the good inevitably results in each individual independently "determining the criteria of good and evil and then acting accordingly" (§32,2).[1] This leads ultimately, as the encyclical points out, to a loss of freedom itself. We may call this perspective on the problem of freedom and truth an "ethical" perspective. The integrity of a human act is seen as the correspondence between the judgment of conscience, based on the truth, and the objective act performed in conformity with and expressive of the truth.

The other perspective on this question is one that I am calling "theological" because it takes the word of God to be the truth informing the conscience. In this perspective truth is not merely a norm for action, it is the source of action itself.

There are many ways in which one might compare the ethical and theological perspectives. One would be to say that they can be roughly compared to promise and fulfillment: that is, there is both continuity and transcending discontinuity. An example of the continuity between the two perspectives can be found in the manner in which Thomas Aquinas can say of both the "natural law" and the light of faith that they are "imprints of the divine light."[2] The transcendent discontinuity lies in the fact that the light of revelation or faith is twofold: There is the light of *what* is revealed (*fides quae*) and the light *by which* it is perceived (*fides qua*).

God's revelatory action includes both lights, as can be illustrated by this text from 2 Corinthians 4:6: "The God who said, 'Out of darkness light shall shine,' is the one who has caused his light to shine in our hearts, for the enlightenment which consists in the knowledge of the glory of God on the face of Jesus Christ." The light of God moves our hearts to assent to the true and objective reality of Jesus Christ. In and through this assent comes a genuine knowledge. It is by the light that comes from God that one is able to grasp the light of God on the face of Jesus Christ. The efficacy of the word of God, its quality of being "living and active" (Heb 4:12) is ultimately linked to the fact that it derives from the divine light revealed in and through Jesus Christ.

Based on the conviction that the encyclical embodies a theological perspective and treats ethical questions within this perspective, this article will proceed in two steps. First, there will be a brief consideration of the enabling power of the word of God as this is alluded to in the encyclical and taught in the New

---

[1] Numbers in parentheses refer to section numbers in the encyclical followed by the paragraph in the section. Thus, §32,2 refers to section 32, the second paragraph.

[2] In regard to natural law, the encyclical cites *Summa theologiae* 1–2, 91, 2 (footnotes 76 and 82); see also 1, 12, 11 ad 3. In regard to *sacra doctrina*, see *Summa theologiae* 1, 1, 3ad 2. This latter text speaks of *sacra doctrina* as an imprint of the "divine knowledge." There is a nuance of difference between "light" and "knowledge" in these texts, but it does not affect my argument.

Testament, especially in the First Letter of John. Second, there will be a study of 1 John 1:6–2:11, much of which is quoted in the encyclical (§89). This text will be illuminated by investigating the anthropology implicit in 1 John. It is hoped that in this way we will be able to appreciate the biblical foundation for the encyclical's teaching on the integrity of a human act as it is informed and empowered by the truth.

Revelation: The Power of the Word

It is not my intention here to treat this subject in all its amplitude, but rather to signal the fact that the encyclical's perspective on human activity is "theological" in the sense defined above. This theological perspective can reveal in a clearer light the structure of the ethical dimension of human activity because the acts of the human faculties, and their relation to their objects, are not changed by being divinized through grace; rather, they are brought to their fulfillment. Grace reveals to us the true reality of nature, a reality obfuscated by sin, and enables discourse about nature to be grounded in revealed truth without distorting nature. This principle explains as well the ease with which the encyclical speaks of "natural law" and "fulfillment" in the same breath, as it were.

The notion that revelation is enabling and not merely informing is found as a leitmotif throughout the encyclical. In §8,2 *Redemptor Hominis* is cited to the effect that "A person must 'appropriate' and assimilate the whole of the reality of the incarnation and redemption in order to find himself." In several texts we have the theme that fulfillment of the law can only come about by grace, in imitation of Christ,[3] and this is further developed by calling the Gospel "the source of all saving truth and moral teaching" (§28,2, citing *Dei Verbum*, 7). The famous passage in Jeremiah 31:31–34 to which we will return in a moment is cited in §45,1 when calling the Holy Spirit the new law. The concept of moral judgment through connaturality is linked to Paul's exhortation to a renewal of the mind (Rom 12:2),[4] while still another text speaks of that activity by which the Church draws its educative power "in constantly looking to the Lord Jesus."[5] Finally, there are two passages that are particularly illustrative of this theological perspective on human acts and for this reason I will quote them.

> Communion with the crucified and risen Lord is the never ending source from which the Church draws unceasingly in order to live in freedom, to give of herself and serve (§87,2).

---

3 §§11,2; 15,2; 19,2; 22,3; and 24,1. In the last of the texts just enumerated we read concerning the commandment of love, "We are speaking of a possibility opened up to man exclusively by grace, by the gift of God, by his love." The text goes on to cite 1 Jn 4:7–8, 11. The further theme of conformity to Christ is sounded in §§73,1 and 85,2.

4 §64,1.

5 §85,2.

> Christian faith . . . is not simply a set of propositions to be accepted with intellectual assent. Rather faith is a *lived knowledge of Christ,* a living remembrance of his commandments, and a truth to be lived out. A word, in any event, is not truly received until it passes into action, until it is put into practice [§88,5, emphasis added].

With the explicit use of the term "word" in the last statement we move to a consideration of the general New Testament understanding of the power of the word. The act of God, mediated and received in faith, is effective; it brings about a change. The truth of Jesus Christ as conveyed through preaching is the word of God. As Rudolf Schnackenburg expresses it: "Christian preaching is not merely moral exhortation under a religious aspect, it rather proceeds from God's effective saving activity *(heilsvollem Handeln)* in regard to human beings."[6]

This conviction is manifest not only in the manner in which the New Testament uses the term *logos* and *logos tou Theou,*[7] but in the fact that this word is active in the believers. In writing his first letter to the Thessalonians Paul expresses his gratitude to God, "because, having received the word of God preached by us, you accepted it not as a human word but as it truly is, *the word of God which is at work in you the believers*" (2:13). From among many such expressions, we may note: "the word of the cross . . . is the power of God" (1 Cor 1:18); ". . . the word of truth, the gospel . . . is bearing fruit and growing . . ." (Col 1:5–6); "you have been born anew not from a perishable seed but from an imperishable one, the living and abiding word of God . . . this is the word that has been proclaimed to you" (1 Pet 1:23–25; see also Js 1:18). This notion is found as well in the synoptic explanation of the parable of the seed sown and producing various quantities of fruit: "[T]he seed is the word of God" (Lk 8:11; see also Mt 13:18–23; Mk 4:13–20).

The Empowerment Promised in the New Covenant

Perhaps the clearest expression of the New Testament teaching in regard to the power of the word is found in the First Letter of John and its relation to the Old Testament promise of a New Covenant. In an article written 45 years ago, Marie-Émile Boismard opened the way for much of the understanding of the First Letter of John by pointing to the hidden link in the Letter between the prophecy in Jeremiah 31:31–34 and John's teaching about the knowledge of

---

[6] Rudolf Schnackenburg, *Die Johannesbriefe,* Herders theologischer Kommentar zum Neuen Testament, XIII/3 (Freiburg: Herder, 1984), 163.

[7] See, among other studies, the article on *legō* and so on, in the *Theological Dictionary of the New Testament,* Vol. IV, ed. G. Kittel, trans. G. W. Bromiley (Grand Rapids, MI: Eerdmans, 1967), esp. 114–36.

God and his indwelling.[8] The Jeremiah passage, one of the most studied passages in the Old Testament, is a meditation and a promise. It is generally agreed that the ideas if not the actual composition derive from Jeremiah.[9] The text runs as follows:

> Behold days are coming, a word of YHWH, and I will make a covenant with the house of Israel and the house of Judah, a new covenant. Not like the covenant which I made with their fathers on the day when I took them by their hand to lead them out from the land of Egypt; they broke my covenant, and I made myself husband to them, a word of YHWH. For this is the covenant I will make with the house of Israel after those days, a word of YHWH; I will put my Torah within them, and on their hearts I will write it, and I will be God to them and they will be to me a people. And no one will teach his neighbor any more, or anyone his brother saying "Know YHWH!" For they will all know me from their least to their greatest, a word of YHWH, for I will forgive their iniquities and their sins I will remember no longer.

As a meditation, this text reflects on the fact that the first covenant was inadequate because the people were incapable of responding to YHWH: They broke the covenant. As a promise, this text points to a time when God himself will provide the interior principle of response: He will put his Torah within them and write it on their heart. When that time comes no one need teach another saying "Know YHWH!" To know God means two things: to experience his reality and to acknowledge his authority.[10] This will happen because God will forgive his people and forget their sins. The interior principle of response, as the encyclical teaches, is the Holy Spirit (see §45,1). This is in keeping with the whole of tradition, as expressed in Thomas Aquinas whose text the Pope quotes. What is particularly important in the teaching of 1 John is that this action of the Holy Spirit is linked to the word of God. *Believers will not sin = means God will write the covenant in our heart. No one to teach = cov. arrived.*

Revelation as an "Oil of Anointing" and as a "Seed"

Before studying part of the Johannine passage quoted at length in §89,1, it will be helpful to consider two other expressions in 1 John that shed light on the notion that the word of God is rendered effective in the believer and becomes

---

8 M.–E. Boismard, "La connaissance dans l'Alliance Nouvelle d'après la Première Lettre de Saint Jean," *Revue Biblique* 56 (1949): 366–91.

9 For a study of the present state of research in regard to this passage, see Barbara A. Bozak, *Life 'Anew': A Literary–Theological Study of Jer. 30–31,* Analecta Biblica 122 (Rome: Pontifical Biblical Institute, 1991).

10 For a brief consideration of this expression, particularly as it is used by Jeremiah, see Francis Martin, "The Humanity of Christian Mysticism," *Cross Currents* (1974): 233–47, and the literature cited there.

the very energy by which he or she acts through the activity of the Holy Spirit. These expressions are the "oil of anointing" and the "seed of God."[11]

"The oil of anointing" is found in 1 John 2:20, 27 in a passage that is treating the eschatological actuality of the conflict between the false teaching of those who have left the community and the teaching the believers received "from the beginning" (2:24); the whole passage covers 2:18–28. John is writing to point out to his readers that they "all are in possession of knowledge" *(oidate pantes)*.[12] The reason for this is that "you have an oil of anointing *(chrisma)* from the Holy One" (2:20). He writes to them not because they do not know the truth, but to tell them that they know it (2:21). In order to understand this passage we must understand that for John truth is the revelation of the Father, embodied and made manifest in the words and deeds of Jesus Christ his Son, most especially his act of love on the cross. This revelation becomes the principle of activity within the Church and within each believer by the action of the "Spirit of Truth" (Jn 14:17, 15:26, 16:13; 1 Jn 4:6), who, for this reason, may himself be called "the Truth" (1 Jn 5:6). The oil of anointing, then, is the baptismal catechesis heard "from the beginning," that is, the time of conversion. This word of revelation, grasped in the light of faith, is the dynamic source of interior teaching.

The second occurrence of *chrisma* in this passage confirms this. We read in 2:27: "And as for you, the oil of anointing which you received from him abides in you and you have no need that anyone should teach you. . . ." We may notice first of all the allusion to the eschatological promise in Jeremiah 31:34: "And no one will teach his neighbor any more, or anyone his brother saying, "Know YHWH!"[13]

They do have people to teach them (Jer 31.31)

[11] An understanding of both expressions has been greatly clarified by the work of Ignace de la Potterie. The results of previous studies are summed up in *La Vérité dans Saint Jean*, Analecta Biblica 73/74 (Rome: Pontifical Biblical Institute, 1977). Since the pagination is consecutive through the two volumes, I will cite the title, *Vérité*, and the page number.

[12] For a complete study of this text, see Ignace de la Potterie, "L'onction du chrétien par la foi," *Biblica* 40 (1959): 12–69. I will refer to the author as "John" throughout without prejudice to such vexed questions as the authorship of the Fourth Gospel, the Letters, and the Book of Revelation, and their mutual relationship. Certainly, there is an intimate link between the Gospel of John and the First Letter. The letter is defending and expounding teaching found in the present Gospel, but it is impossible to determine whether the Gospel was actually made public by the time the Letters were written. In regard to authorship, neither the Gospel of John nor the Letters of John name their author, though in the Second and Third Letters the author describes himself as "the elder" *(o presbyteros)*. In contrast, the author of the Book of Revelation, a work that has some relation to the other four works just mentioned, does name himself "John" (Rev 1:1, 4, 9; 22:8). No other name than John has ever been associated with these writings, but neither antiquity nor modern scholarship has been consistent in identifying exactly who is meant by this "John." For more information, see Martin Hengel, *The Johannine Question*, trans. John Bowden (London/Philadelphia: SCM/Trinity Press International, 1989).

[13] This theme is also present in Jn 6:45 which cites Is 54:13 ("and they will all be taught by God"), a text that manifestly depends upon the Jeremian text.

To know the hard + to experience god - that's what the con. gives.

Again, in regard to the *chrisma*, it is clear that the source of the believers' knowledge and certitude is the word of revelation as it is rendered fruitful by the action of the Holy Spirit and is thus a bearer of the truth, the living knowledge of the Father. All those who have received this oil of anointing know God as Jeremiah promised, and they know his plan of salvation realized in Jesus Christ.

We have just seen the manner in which the First Letter of John considers the message heard at baptism to be an oil of anointing, provided it is interiorized and allowed to produce its effect in the believer. The same can be said in a more marked manner of the "seed of God," which abides in the believer. This expression is found in the following text:

freedom from and incapacity to sin. - eschatological promise.

> All who are born of God do not commit sin, because his seed abides in them and they cannot sin because they are born of God. (1 Jn 3:9)

gia e anchora!

It is simply impossible to understand this statement unless we allow that for John this seed is some God-given energy that bears along those who yield to it. This has been a constant understanding of tradition. Ignace de la Potterie sums up the Greek patristic interpretation of these words by saying: "The seed of God is an interior force through whose action the soul ceases to be in harmony with sin; in letting itself be led by the dynamism that is in it, the soul becomes in truth incapable of choosing what it is evil." As representative of this tradition, he cites the words of the tenth-century Greek Bishop and exegete Oecumenius: "When someone who is born of God gives himself over to the indwelling Christ who is in him by the grace of adoption, he remains beyond the attacks of sin."[14] *Unless we is an eschat. promise. "canot sin" = last days have arrived.*

What John asserts here is once again the fulfillment of a prophecy; it expresses the expectation of God's people. We read in a postexilic text, for instance, a development of the promise in Jeremiah 31:31–34 as this was deepened by Ezekiel 36:25–26: "Your people, all of them righteous, will possess the land forever" (Is 60:21).[15] The wisdom tradition sees this freedom from sin as due to the believer's appropriation of God's teaching: "The one who obeys me will not be put to shame, those who work with me will never fail" (Sir 24:22; see Prov 9:6; Is 55:3).[16] Sirach's identification of wisdom with the law (Sir 24:23) finds an echo in the manner in which Psalm 37:31 speaks of the just man: "The law of his God

---

14 "L'impeccabilité du Chrétien d'après I Joh. 3,6–9," in *L'Évangile de Jean. Études et Problèmes*, Recherches Bibliques, 3 (Desclée de Brouwer, 1958): 161–78, at 162. Oecumenius's text is found in his *Commentary on First John*, 7 (*Patrologia Graeca* 119, 684).

15 This same theme is picked up in 4 Ezra 9:31: "For behold I sow my law in you and you shall be glorified through it forever." Translation by Bruce M. Metzger in *The Old Testament Pseudoepigrapha*, vol 1., *Apocalyptic Literature and Testaments*, ed. James H. Charlesworth (New York: Doubleday, 1983), 545.

16 For a discussion of this text, see Alexander di Lella, *The Wisdom of Ben Sira*, Anchor Bible 39 (New York: Doubleday, 1987), 336.

Victory over sin is yielding to revelation of the Father, yield to light of the gospel. This makes sin impossible. God's word is a principle of light.

is in his heart, and his steps do not falter," and Psalm 119:11 declares: "In my heart I have hidden your promise, so that I do not sin against you."

The notion that the Gospel revelation fulfills in a transcendent way the role formerly expected of wisdom or of the law is expressed in texts that speak of "being purified by obedience to the truth" (1 Pet 1:21), or of being cleansed "because of the word I have spoken to you" (Jn 15:3). The role is attributed to the Holy Spirit: "Walk by the Spirit and you will not realize the desire of the flesh" (Gal 5:16). However, it is with the text in 1 John 3:8 that we arrive at the most developed understanding of how the word of the Lord, the Gospel, made active by the Holy Spirit, becomes the actual source of energy by which the believer gives historical expression to the truth. The baptismal catechesis is guarded by the believer by "abiding in the word," a process that maintains the reality of the death and resurrection present within consciousness. This reality, however, is never inert: It is the act of love in which Jesus died. As the believer yields to this, the love of Christ becomes the power by which that which was once proclaimed retains its life–giving power. This is why the believer "cannot sin." As de la Potterie expresses it: "From the side of human beings, the only condition laid down to obtain victory over sin is entire docility and submission to the teaching and the direction of the Holy Spirit."[17]

Such an understanding of Christian moral activity means that only a theological approach to the question of the integrity of human acts can provide the right perspective. This is precisely the perspective of the encyclical.

Prepared with this background, I would like now to consider sections 88 and 89 of *Veritatis Splendor*, which bear the title "Walking in the Light," alluding to 1 John 1:7. The sections address the dichotomy between faith and morality, an intensification of the divorce between freedom and truth (§88,1). The principal aim of these sections is to point to the integrity of Christian moral activity, which flows from the light of God and reveals it. In this connection, John Paul II cites 1 John 1:5–6, 2:3–6, which links abiding in God with the kind of moral activity that imitates the life of Christ by sharing in it.[18]

> As St. John writes, "God is light and in him is no darkness at all. If we say we have fellowship with him while we walk in darkness, we lie and do not live according to the truth. . . . And by this we may be sure that we know him, if we keep his commandments. He who says "I know him" but disobeys his commandments is a liar, and the truth is not in him; but whoever keeps his word, in him truly love for God is perfected. By this we may be sure that we are in him: he who says he abides in him ought to walk in the same way in which he walked. (1 Jn 1:5–6; 2:3–6) (§89)

---

[17] Ibid.,167.

[18] Actually, there are several references to the First Letter of John in *Veritatis Splendor*. One may consult the following sections for some examples: 14,3; 24,1.3; 26,1.

The Three Levels of Christian Existence

In order to approach the Johannine text correctly, it will be helpful to draw attention to the manner in which John describes the levels of the human personality as it is divinized by sharing in God's life. At the deepest part of the person there is the area where we share the divine life. In modern terms we would speak of "grace," meaning the ontological modification of the human being that enables someone to know and love God in the way in which God knows and loves himself. When we say that God imparts his life to us we mean that we have been changed at the deepest point of our existence so that we can enter into a communion of Persons, namely, the Father, the Son, and the Holy Spirit. We share this life in the Son, receiving all from the Father, reflecting him, and breathing back the Spirit of love. We begin this mode of existence even in this life. This is how Thomas Aquinas describes the full maturing of the gift of wisdom in a believer. It is an act by which the Word visits the soul; he is not just any word "but a Word breathing forth love." "Thus, not according to any perfection of the mind whatever is the Son sent, but according to that teaching action *(institutio)* or instruction of the mind by which it bursts forth in an affection of love as it is said in John 6:45, 'All who hear from the Father and learn, come to me'. . . ."[19]

The First Letter of John uses many terms to describe the divine life imparted to us. We may speak of the level at which this takes place within the human being as "interior₁." The realities found at the level of the interior₁ modify the very source of the personality and are all synonyms for sharing the divine life. The terms John uses in this Letter are: "to have" God, the Son, or Life;[20] to have "communion" with God;[21] to be "born of God";[22] to be a "child" *(teknon)* of God;[23] or simply to be "of God";[24] and finally to "abide" mutually, God in the believer and the believer in God,[25] which may be expressed as well by speaking of a reciprocal being "in."[26] It is at the level of interior₁ that we are being remolded into Christ, the firstborn among many brothers and sisters (Rom 8:29). The elevation of our being by God takes place initially in those movements toward him that are the first stirrings of faith, and it is completed at the moment of baptism when faith becomes the God-given act by which we are justified.[27] This is the moment of transformation, when we

---

[19] *Summa theologiae* 1, 43, 5, ad 2.

[20] 2:23; 5:12; see 2 Jn 9; see also 3:14; 5:11–13.

[21] 1:4; 3:3.6.

[22] 2:29; 3:9, 10; 4:7; 5:1, 4, 18.

[23] 3:1, 2, 10; 5:2.

[24] 3:10; 4:4, 6; 5:19 (see 2 Jn 11).

[25] 2:6, 24, 27; 3:4, 24; 4:12, 13, 15, 16.

[26] 2:5; 4:4; 5:20.

[27] "The act of faith itself is the first act of justice which God works in the believer. By the fact that the believer puts his faith in God, the justifier, he subjects himself to God's justification

are divinized and become the dwelling place of the Holy Spirit who will continually act to bring about our conformity to Christ at every level of our being.

In addition to the deepest interior level, that of interior$_1$, there is another interior level which we may call interior$_2$. This is the level of conscious awareness and conscious activity. It may be considered "subjective" in the sense of a personal, appropriated awareness, but not in the Kantian sense of being forged by one's own mind. One of the most characteristic words used for this level of activity is to "know." Experiential knowledge is usually expressed by using the verb *gignōskein*: to know God or a divine reality[28] or to recognize the criterion of a spiritual reality, often expressed in a phrase like "in this we know."[29] The verb *eidenai* is also used, usually with the nuance of "to possess knowledge."[30] This activity of the believer corresponds to God's act of revelation, an act by which he manifests and communicates himself as well as a knowledge of his plan of salvation (see *Dei Verbum* §2 and §6). The interior act of faith, which responds to this revelation, is mentioned in the Letter,[31] as is the exterior act of confessing one's faith (see below). The act of personalizing the realities made known by faith is described in 1:6 as "doing the truth," as we shall see. John describes the act of God, as it exists in the believer, by designating several realities on the level of interior$_2$, the level of conscious awareness. He speaks, for instance, of "the word" or "what you heard from the beginning";[32] of "the truth";[33] again, of "the oil of anointing" (*chrisma*, 2:20, 27); and of "the seed" (3:9). All of these terms, particularly the last two, as we shall see, refer to God's act of self-revelation as it reaches the believer through the action of the Church and takes up residence in the believer's heart. Then, by the action of the Holy Spirit, it becomes a dynamic source of energy enabling the Christian to believe and confess Jesus as the Son of God, even amid difficulties, and to imitate God's love, overcoming sin (3:9) and laying down one's life for the others (3:16). The final reality that exists at this level is that of the witness of the Holy Spirit.[34]

There is, finally, the level of exterior activity, involving the whole body person and thus becoming, in a complete sense, historical activity. It is at this level that we see what the encyclical calls "the lived knowledge of Christ." The First Letter describes this activity by such terms as "walking in the light" (1:7), "con-

---

and so receives its effect." Thomas Aquinas, *Super Epistolam ad Romanos,* Caput 4, Lectio 1, in *Super Epistolas S. Pauli Lectura,* ed. P. Raphaelis Cai (Torino: Marietti, 1954), #331. See also *On Rom* 3:22 (Marietti ed.), #302.

[28] 2:3, 4, 13, 14; 3:1, 6, 16; 4:6, 7, 8, 16; 5:20.

[29] 2:3, 5, 18, 29; 3:19, 24; 4:2, 6, 13; 5:2.

[30] 2:20, 21, 29; 3:2, 5, 14, 15; 5:13, 15, 18, 19, 20.

[31] 4:16; 5:1, 10, 13.

[32] Word: 1:10; 2:5, 7, 14; "what you heard from the beginning": 2:24.

[33] 1:8; 2:4, 21; 3:18, 19; 4:6; 5:6.

[34] 3:24; 4:13.

fess our sins" (1:9), "keep his commandments/word,"[35] "do the will of God" (2:17), "walk as he walked" (2:6), "conquer the evil one/the world,"[36] "confess the Son,"[37] "practice justice,"[38] "purifies himself as he is pure" (3:3), "love each other,"[39] "lay down our lives" (3:16), "love in deed and truth" (3:18).

A Consideration of I John 1:6–2:11:Two Antithetical Developments of the Theme of Light

The opening *Prooemium* of the Letter (1:1–4) insists on the reality of the historical appearance of the Life and the fact that acceptance of this witness creates "communion" *(koinōnia)* between the one announcing the message and those who welcome it. This is followed by a formulation of a basic theme of the whole Letter: "And this is the message which we heard from him and proclaim to you: God is light and there is no darkness in him at all" (1:5). The word "light" here implies a fullness of beauty, wisdom, power, compassion, and holiness. A deeper understanding of what is intended by this word is mediated throughout the course of the Letter, especially with the twice repeated statement that "God is love" (4:8, 16). It should further be observed that in this Letter, as in the New Testament generally, the term God *(Theos)* refers to God the Father.[40]

At this point in the Letter, the author presents a double set of three antithetical statements (1:6–2:2, 2:3–11), portions of which are cited in §89,1 (1:5–6, 2:3–6). I wish now to study these two sets of statements in order to illustrate the anthropological viewpoint already discussed theoretically. This will enable us to appreciate the convergence between the encyclical and biblical teaching on the theological nature of human acts. We will see in the Johannine texts to be studied here that the author presupposes that Christian activity is an integral movement from the divine life in the depths of a believer to bodily, historical activity.

---

[35] 2:3, 5; 3:22, 24; 5:2, 3.

[36] 2:13, 14; 5:4, 5.

[37] 2:23; 3:23 (probably); 4:2, 3, 15.

[38] 2:29; 3:7, 10.

[39] 3:11, 23; 4:7, 11, 12, 21.

[40] It is clear that for the New Testament the term "God" *(Theos)* meant the God and Father of our Lord Jesus Christ. As Raymond Brown observes: "It is quite obvious that in the New Testament the term 'God' is applied with overwhelming frequency to God the Father, i.e., to the God revealed in the Old Testament to whom Jesus prayed" ("Does the New Testament Call Jesus God?," *Theological Studies* 26 [1965]: 545–73; at 548). In fact, the three certain (Jn 1:1; 20:28; Heb 1:8–9), and five very probable (2 Thes 1:12; Tit 2:13; 1 Jn 5:20; Rom 9:5; 2 Pt 1:1) instances where *Theos* is extended to include Jesus are examples of the whole New Testament strategy of bringing terms (such as *Kyrios*), gestures (such as "worship"), and statements (such as "I and the Father are one" [Jn 10:30]) into relation with Jesus to mediate what the later tradition would appositely call his divinity.

So integral is this relationship that one is able to declare the presence or absence of a reality at the two interior levels on the basis of activity.

1 John 1:6–2:2

The first of the threefold antithetical statements treats the theme of communion with God and the activity that manifests either its presence or absence in one who claims to possess this communion.

> 6a   *If we say* that we have communion with him
> 6b   and we walk in the darkness,
> 6c   we are lying and we are not doing the truth.
> 7a   If, however, we walk in the light,
> 7b   as he is in the light,
> 7c   we have communion with one another,
> 7d   and the blood of Jesus his Son cleanses us from every sin.
>
> 8a   *If we say* that we do not have sin,
> 8b   we are misleading ourselves
> 8c   and the truth is not in us.
> 9a   If we acknowledge our sins,
> 9b   he is faithful and just so that he forgives us (our) sins
> 9c   and cleanses us from every iniquity.
>
> 10a   *If we say* that we have not sinned,
> 10b   we make him a liar
> 10c   and his word is not in us.
>
> 2:1a   My little children,
> 1b   I am writing these things to you so that you do not sin.
> 1c   And if anyone does sin, we have a Paraclete with the Father,
> 1d   Jesus Christ, the one who is just;
> 2a   and he is the atonement for our sins;
> 2b   not for ours alone,
> 2c   but also for the whole world.

The passage is structured by the threefold repetition of "If we say" (6a, 8a, 10a), followed in the first two instances by another "If" (7a, 9a), and in the third instance by an exhortation based on the universal efficacy of the death of Christ. The initial statement in each case (6a, 8a, 10a) is characterized as a lack of truth: 6c, 8c, 10c. It is difficult to imagine that John has in mind only those who have left the community and who deny certain basic aspects of Christian teaching such as the physical and historical reality of Christ and his divine sonship. It is more likely that, while he has these people in mind, the author is not engaging in polemics at this point. When he wants to refer explicitly to such people, he does not speak of "us" but of "them."[41] A contrast is established between "walking in the darkness"/"walking in the light" (6b/7a); and between saying that "we do not have sin"/"acknowledge our sins" (8a/9a). The result of walking in the light and acknowledging our sins is, respectively, having communion with each other and being cleansed by the blood of Jesus. This is further specified as being forgiven our sins and being purified from every iniquity. In the last antithesis refusal to admit sin makes God a liar, since he has sent his Son precisely as the Lamb who takes away the sin of the world (Jn 1:29). The exhortation speaks of Jesus as "Paraclete," exploiting the forensic notion of the term and linking it with an intercessory role.[42] It also describes him as the "just one" in a probable allusion to Isaiah 53:11, speaks of his death as an atonement *(hilasmos)*, and extends the expiatory power of this atoning sacrifice to include the whole world. This last statement clearly indicates the universal vision of the author and removes him from the category of "sectarian" sometimes applied to him.[43]

The first of the antitheses (vv. 6–7) is an illustration of the anthropological teaching outlined above. Verse 6 speaks of a reality at the level of interior$_1$, namely "communion with him." If we claim to possess divine life but walk in darkness, that is, we do not keep God's commandments, especially that of love for each other (2:3, 3:10, and so on), then the exterior level of our existence proves that there is no such divine life within us. It is important to understand the direction of this argument. John is not saying that out of our own resources we can produce moral activity that proves we are somehow in communion with God. He is saying rather that the divine life within us is the source of all genuinely Christian activity. If that activity is present, then the divine life is being "sacramentalized," made manifest, in and through our actions on the level of historical existence.[44] The argument moves, as it were, from the presence of a

---

41 See, for instance, 1:19–20, 26; 4:1–6.

42 On the contrary, the four applications of the term to the Spirit (Jn 14:16, 26, 15:26, 16:7) develop the revelatory and teaching action of the Spirit in the context of coming to the aid of someone in a situation of forensic contestation. See F. Porsch, "paraklētos," in *Exegetical Dictionary of the New Testament*, vol. 3, ed. Horst Balz and Gerhard Schneider (Grand Rapids, MI: Eerdmans, 1993), 28–29.

43 There is no doubt that the immediate audience of 1 John is a restricted group that has experienced some defections. I am convinced, however, that it is impossible at this stage to reconstruct the history of the group and then impose that history as the heuristic structure within which to interpret the Letter. Very often those who attempt this speak of the Johannine group as a "sect." Besides being anachronistic, this terminology ignores the universal aspects of the text itself and fact that the Church at large easily recognized in the Letter an expression of the "rule of faith." The most consistent attempt to interpret 1 John within the framework of a reconstructed history is that of Raymond E. Brown, *The Epistles of John,* Anchor Bible, 30 (New York: Doubleday, 1982).

44 The notion of the sacramentality of human acts is developed in John Paul II's catechesis on the theology of the body. For the relationship between "mystery" and "sacrament" in this

plant back to the existence of a seed: If someone is walking in the light, we may conclude that there is divine life in him or her.[45]

It is important to notice the terms that John uses to describe the state of one who claims to possess this divine life and yet walks in the darkness: Such a one is lying and not "doing the truth." These words express more than a simple lack of coherence between saying and doing. In this very first antithetical expression of Christian life we find a particular Johannine teaching based on the notion of truth.[46] It is with this understanding of truth in mind that we must interpret the expressions "lying" and "doing the truth." We will begin with the latter.

"Do the truth" is a biblical phrase, which, as applied to God (Neh 9:33) or human beings (2 Chr 31:20), means to act with fidelity and uprightness.[47] The expression underwent a semantic change in the intertestamental period. "Truth" became more identified with the law, and thus "doing the truth" designated a human activity by which one lived in accord with the will of God as expressed in the law.[48] In the two Johannine passages that use the phrase (Jn 3:21; 1 Jn 1:6), the light of God himself, as this is revealed in Jesus, replaces the law and thus the accent is rather on the revelation of the Father.

In v. 6c, "walking in the darkness" is the opposite of yielding to God's revelation and interiorizing it so that the revealed reality becomes itself the force by which one gives exterior expression to the divine life. Thus, communion with God is both effected by God's work of faith in the believer, as the believer yields to this work, and also grows through faith as the believer gives over more and more of his or her being to the action of God. "Doing the truth" is a *mediating* function on the level of $interior_2$: By according oneself in faith to God's act of revelation the person is enabled to act in a way that is consonant with the divine life present at the level of $interior_1$.

That is why, according to v. 7, "walking in the light" manifests and augments two realities found at the level of $interior_1$. There is, first, communion with each other based on our common life in the Trinity (1:3); and second, flowing from this participation in the common life of the Church, "the blood of Jesus his Son

---

catechesis, see *The Theology of Marriage and Celibacy: Catechesis on Marriage and Celibacy in the Light of the Resurrection of the Body* (Boston: St. Paul Editions, 1986), 215–23.

[45] If someone were to object that it might be possible to produce actions that derive from human resources but which *seem* to come from the divine life, John would respond that there are criteria for judging the genuine quality of the "plant." Among these criteria are public confession that Jesus is the Son of God (2:23; 4:2, 3, 15), and a love that lays down one's life (3:16, 18).

[46] For the analysis that follows I am indebted to the relevant pages of *Verité*.

[47] The two instances in the Hebrew Bible are augmented in the Septuagint, for example: Gen 32:10, 47:29; Is 26:10; Tob 4:6, 13:6; Sir 27:9.

[48] For examples, see the *Testaments of the Patriarchs* (*T. Benj.* 10,3; *T. Gad* 3,1–2; *T. Aser* 2,8, and so on) and the Qumran Literature (1 QpHab 7,10–11; 1 QS 8,1–2). *Verité*, 480–83.

cleanses us from every sin." Our communion with each other provides the place where the outpoured life of Jesus Christ still has the power to "purify our conscience from dead works to serve the living God" (Heb 9:14). This awareness of the ongoing actuality and availability of the act of love in which Christ died is a characteristic of the teaching of the Letter, particularly in 5:6–8.

1 John 2:3–11: An Analysis of Three Claims

The citation in the encyclical moves from 1 John 1:6 to the second of the threefold series in this part of the Letter in which three claims are considered (2:3–11). The first of the antitheses is more important than the others. For that reason I will treat it at length and then proceed to a more rapid consideration of the other two.

The First Antithesis: 1 John 2:3–5

> 3a And in this we know that we have come to know him:
> 3b if we keep his commandments.
> 4a *The one who claims:* "I have come to know him,"
> 4b while not keeping his commandments,
> 4c is a liar,
> 4d and the truth is not in that one.
> 5a But whoever keeps his word,
> 5b truly in that one the love of God has been made perfect.
> 5c In this we know that we are in him.

Once again, a principle is enunciated: "And in this we know that we have come to know him: if we keep his commandments." Throughout the Letter various criteria are introduced by the use of the formula: "in this we know."[49] These criteria, usually some exterior reality (3:24 and 4:13 are exceptions), witness to the existence of an interior reality, at either level. The argument is always from the existence of the plant to the existence of the seed, or from the existence of the river to the existence of its source. In this text, the fact that we keep the commandments of God allows us to argue back to the authenticity of our knowledge of God: Genuine knowledge produces the fruit of obedience.

On this basis the claim "I have come to know him" is analyzed. The one who makes this claim and does not keep God's commandments "is a liar, and the truth is not in that one." Once again, as in 1:6, the notions of "lie" and truth" are introduced. In the previous instance, communion with God (interior$_1$) is linked to exterior conduct: walking in the light. Here a reality at the level of interior$_2$ (knowledge of God) is linked to exterior obedience. It should be observed that the notion of "lie" here means more than merely claiming

---

[49] In addition to 2:3, see 2:5; 3:19, 24; 4:(2), 6; 5:2.

exteriorly something that one does not possess. Such a lie flows from the lack of truth, that is, the lack of God's revelation within one.[50] Just as it is impossible to keep God's commandments without that personalized revelation of God that brings about and flows from God's life within us, so a claim to possess that revelation without showing it in action is a lie and demonstrates that such knowledge does not exist within the person. This line of reasoning governs the text in 1:6, as we have seen, as well as that in 4:20: "If someone says, 'I love God' and hates his brother, he is a liar.'"

To the inconcinnity of the false claim is contrasted the integrity of faith activity: "But whoever keeps his word, truly in that one the love of God has been made perfect. In this we know that we are in him." In contrast to the use of the verb *tērein* (keep) with "commandments," which is a rather common New Testament expression,[51] the use of *tērein* with *logos* (word) is a Johannine turn of phrase.[52] It adds a note of interiority to the expression "keep the commandments."[53] To "keep" the word of God thus designates an intense and interior activity (interior$_2$), initiated and sustained by the Holy Spirit, by which the revelation of God, a knowledge of himself, and his plan of salvation, is appropriated to become the source of action. The exterior activity of the believer realizes and manifests God's plan: He or she "keeps" God's commandments.

Though the notions of "truth" and "word" are very closely related in Johannine theology,[54] there seems to be a slight difference. "Truth" refers to the revealed knowledge of the Father as this comes about in Jesus, while "word" is more generic and speaks of this same revelation as it is directive of activity.

It is said of the one who keeps God's word, "truly in that one the love of God is made perfect." We should first note that the word "of" in the phrase "the love of God" serves to link the two realities "God" and "love" together without restricting the meaning to either the subjective genitive (God's love for us) or the objective genitive (our love for God). By using what grammarians call a "general" genitive,[55] John refers at once to God's love for us as the source of our love for God. This love is made perfect in objective historical acts. The purpose of the love of God in us is to conform us to Christ, and this conformity reaches its full stature when we act like Christ acts, that is when we "walk as he walked" (2:6) and lay down our lives for our brothers and sisters (3:16–17).

---

[50] Such an indictment is very strong. In Jn 8:44 the same thing is said of the devil.

[51] Mt 19:17; Jn 14:15, 21; 15:10; 1 Cor 7:19; 1 Tm 6:14; 1 Jn 2:3, 4; 3:22, 24; 5:3; Rev 12:17; 14:12.

[52] Jn 8:51, 52, 55; 14:23, 24; 15:20; 17:6; 1 Jn 2:5 (Rev 1:3; 3:8, 10; 22:7, 9).

[53] "*Logos* is also a broader concept than *entolai* [commandments] in that it includes the word of revelation received in faith. . . ." Schnackenburg, *Die Johannesbriefe,* 103, n.1.

[54] Note "truth" in 1:6c, 8c parallel with "word" in 1:10c, and the same parallel in 2:4 and 5.

[55] See Maximilian Zerwick, *Biblical Greek Illustrated by Examples,* ed. and trans. Joseph Smith, Scripta Pontificii Instituti Biblici, 114 (Rome: Pontifical Biblical Institute, 1963) §§36–41.

The notion that the mutual love between God and ourselves, a love that exists in us because of God's previous historical acts (4:9–10), reaches its goal in our historical acts of love, is confirmed by 4:12 and the passage in 4:17–18.[56] The first of these texts reads: "God, no one has ever seen. If we love each other God abides in us and his love, in us, is brought to perfection." Here, as in 2:4–5, we find linked the notions of the perfecting of love and the indwelling of God. It is obvious that the love for each other spoken of in 4:12 consists of total human acts that proceed from God's love for us and finally characterize the whole personality, thus witnessing to the fact that God abides in us. As St. Leo said: "Let the faithful scrutinize their souls, and submit the intimate movements of their heart to an authentic examination; and if they find reposing in their conscience any fruits of love, then let them not doubt that God is within them. And now, in order to become more capable of receiving such a guest, let them open up even wider by works of perduring mercy."[57]

The context of 4:17–18 is one of eschatology anticipated:

> In this has love been perfected with us, so that we might have confidence on the day of judgment; because just as he is, so also are we in this world. Fear is not in love, but perfect love casts fear out, because fear has to do with punishment; the one who fears has not been perfected in love.

Verse 17 states that God has brought love to perfection with us *(meth hēmōn)*, that is, his love has finally become the principle activity in the whole of our personality, so that we may have now a witness and an anticipation of the confidence that we will have on judgment day, because we can see that, by his work, "just as he is, so also are we in this world." Verse 18 contrasts fear and perfect(ed) love. The fear spoken of here describes the state of conscience of a believer who knows that the love of God dwells in him or her but is also conscious that there are areas of the personality that are not purified and submitted to this movement of God. Perfect love, love that has reached its goal in activity that participates in God's love for all humankind, casts out this fear. The fruit, then of yielding to the action of God within us is that we are perfected in love and possess this witness to God's eternal purpose for our lives. We are already called his children and the full development of what that means will only be apparent when he appears (3:2–3).

The first antithesis ends with another criterion: "In this we know that we are in him" (2:5). In this case the criterion points backward to what has just been said.[58] We know that we are in him (interior$_1$) because, by the action of

---

[56] For this discussion one should consult Edward Malatesta, *Interiority and Covenant*, Analecta Biblica 69 (Rome: Pontifical Biblical Institute, 1978), 128–32.

[57] *Sermons for Lent* 10, 3 (*Sources Chrétiennes* 49, 77–78).

[58] The "this" of these phrases can point to either what has been said (as in 2:5; 3:19; 4:6) or what is going to be said (2:3; 3:16; 4:2; 5:2).

the Holy Spirit, we keep his word (interior$_2$) and because in us the love of God has been made perfect (exterior): Our exterior acts of love possess the integrity of flowing from and witnessing to the divine life in us, and these acts are mediated by the conscious appropriation of God's revelation and his will.

A Summarizing Reflection on I Jn 2:3–5

It is easy to see how profoundly this passage has formed the thinking of the author of First John. To point out only the most salient aspects, there is the positing of an interior principle of life (interior$_1$); the accent on the knowing of God (see the list given previously) both as experience and as obedience; the fact that this knowledge is the possession of every believer (2:20–21, 27); and the connection between this knowledge and the doing away with sin,[59] alluded to in 1:7, 2:2, 3:8, 16; and especially 4:8–10 and 5:20. Though the Letter never cites this text (no Old Testament text is cited in 1 John), it is obvious that the new covenant of intimacy, shared life, living, and effective knowledge of God and his will, is the heart of its message. The very incompatibility between a claimed knowledge of God and failure to keep his commandments is established on the basis of Jeremiah's use of the Old Testament expression "knowledge of God." Boismard sums up the teaching of First John in regard to this expression in the following manner:

> Now we can define the "knowledge of God," comparing it with our divine birth and the presence of God: if the expression "to be born of God" indicates that we have received in us a principle of life causing us to act like God because this principle emanates from God; if the expression "we abide in God and God abides in us" describes the presence of God in our soul, a presence implied by his activity in us, the expression "to know God" denotes the subjective coming to awareness of this divine presence brought about by his action in our soul. But we should note carefully: the presence of God is not "known" except in so far as it is the principle of activity; but this activity of God is first of all his love. God is love, and God loves in us, and God gives us the capacity to love by his own love. To know God is then to know the Love, it is to become aware of God Love [Theos-Agape] radiating love in our soul.[60]

The Second and Third Antitheses: 2:6–8 and 2:9–11

The two further antitheses read as follows:

---

[59] This connection is already established by the words instituting the Eucharist in Mt 26:28; Mk 14:24; Lk 22:20; 1 Cor 11:25.

[60] Boismard, "La connaissance," 388.

6a   *The one who claims* to abide in him,
6b   ought, just as he walked,
6c   to walk that way himself.
7a   Beloved, it is no new commandment I write you,
7b   but an old commandment which you had from the
     beginning.
7c   The old commandment is the word which you heard.
8a   Again, I do write to you a new commandment,
8b   which is made true in him and in you,
8c   because the darkness is passing away
8d   and the true light is already shining.

9a   *The one who claims* to be in the light,
9b   while hating his brother,
9c   is in the darkness even now.
10a The one who loves his brother abides in the light,
10b and there is nothing in him to cause a fall.
11a But the one who hates his brother is in the darkness,
11b and he walks in the darkness,
11c and he does not know where he is going
11d because the darkness has blinded his eyes.

The second antithesis picks up from the first the theme of being "in him" to examine another claim: "The one who claims to abide in him ought, just as he walked, to walk that way himself." The first pronoun ("him") refers to God the Father, the second to Christ: The claim to abide in God must be authenticated by living as Jesus lived. The text goes on to explain in what that consists, namely obedience to the commandment of love.

In verse 7 this commandment is called "old" because it was heard "from the beginning." In fact it is the "word which you heard." Here and in 2:24 the "beginning" *(archē)* refers to the beginning of a person's Christian life, and the "word" or "commandment" heard from the beginning refers to the baptismal catechesis. While there might be some doubt as to what is meant by the "old commandment," this is dispelled by what follows immediately: "Again, I do write you a new commandment which is made true in him and in you" (2:8). There is no doubt now that the commandment is that of mutual love (see Jn 13:34, 15:12–17). It is described as *alēthes*, which should be translated "made true."[61] The new commandment is established as solid both in and through Jesus and in and through the disciples. The promise of the new covenant, with its inner and dynamic law is "made true," that is, fulfilled in the love of Jesus for his Father and for the disciples, and in the disciples' love for Jesus, for the Father, and for each other. Because the prophecy is being fulfilled, we know

---

[61] For a discussion of this term, see Brown, *The Epistles of John,* Anchor Bible, 267.

that the eschatological age has dawned, "the darkness is passing away and the true light is shining."

The third antithesis takes up the theme of light and darkness and links it to love, thus returning to the statement at the beginning of this section (1:5) and specifying more clearly the relation between light and love. This forms a bridge to the second statement about *Theos,* namely that he is *agapē* (4:8, 16). The mode of argument is the same. A claim to be in the light means a claim to share God's life, since he is Light. This is completely negated by hatred since, once again, God is Love.

As we conclude this examination of two sets of antitheses we can more readily appreciate the biblical roots of the statement in the encyclical that "faith is a lived knowledge of Christ." This knowledge is lived first in the sense that it is appropriated and interiorized in the life of the believer through the action of the Holy Spirit. It is also lived because it thus becomes the wellspring of that exterior activity by which God conforms the whole of our personality to Jesus. Knowledge is born of transformation and grows in conformity. Didymus the Blind, when commenting on how Adam is made according to the image of God, who is Christ, speaks of the act of revelation by which we come to know Christ in and through sharing in the reality of Christ: "Paul understood this well when he said, 'until Christ be formed in you' (Gal 4:19), thus teaching that the true understanding of who Christ is, when it enters the soul, leaves there the imprint of Christ and makes of the soul an image in accord with Christ."[62]

Conclusion

In the preface to his work *The Acting Person,* John Paul II clearly takes a stand whose affinity with the outlook of the First Letter of John should now be apparent:

> Since Descartes, knowledge about man and his world has been identified with the cognitive function—as if, only in cognition, and especially through knowledge of himself, could man manifest his nature and his prerogative. . . . In fact, it is in reversing the post-Cartesian attitude toward man that we undertake our study; by approaching him through action.[63]

The citations from the encyclical given earlier and others that could be adduced, especially from the discussion on the morality of a human act deriving from a consideration of its object (e.g., §§78–79), show that the Pope is consistent in his viewpoint, which is in fact that of traditional Christian moral thinking. I have tried in this article to show that from a theological perspective

---

62 *On Genesis* §58 (*Sources Chrétiennes* 233,147).

63 Karol Wojtyla, *The Acting Person,* trans. Andrzej Potocki and Anna-Teresa Tymieniecka, Analecta Husserliana 10 (Dodrecht/Boston: Reidel, 1979), vii-viii.

the teaching of 1 John is a particularly profound focusing of the New Testament understanding of the power of the Gospel to be an effective force in the performance of human acts. Through the alchemy of a faith-sustained yielding to the divine truth revealed in the cross of Christ, what seems to be a merely cognitive reality becomes, in actuality, a source of energy, the enabling power of Christian activity.

This revealed word can be termed an "oil of anointing," or a "seed," "the word," or "the truth." It is the effective mediating point between the divine life within the interior depths of a person, the ability to share in the Trinitarian life, and the historical action that manifests it. Because of this appropriated reality it is possible to speak of a "faith made effective through love" (*pistis di' agapēs energoumenē*, Gal 5:6). The divine reality perceived becomes the source of Christian activity. It is in becoming aware of the divine source of this activity that we know God. This is admirably expressed by Augustine who is speaking about 1 John 4:7 in the context of his *Commentary on the Gospel of John*: "Love your neighbor, then look inside yourself to see whence comes this love; and there you will see, as far as you are able, God."[64]

Veritatis Splendor argues for the integrity of human acts. Ethically considered, this integrity is based upon the fact that human intention expresses itself through human bodily, and therefore historical, acts. Theologically considered, the integrity of Christian activity is based upon the mediation effected through the action of the Holy Spirit who empowers the believer to give human existence to the shared life of Christ conferred at baptism. It is for this reason that the clear confession of faith in the reality of Jesus as Son of God and the generous laying down of one's life out of love are the criteria by which it is possible to assert the authenticity of the life within us, the knowledge that we claim to have of God, and the reality of our own participation in the historical activity of Jesus, come in flesh, by whose act of love on the cross we have been saved and the Father's love has been revealed. To quote §87,2 once again:

> Communion with the crucified and risen Lord is the never ending source from which the Church draws unceasingly in order to live in freedom, to give of herself and serve.

---

[64] *Tracts on John* 17, 8 (*Patrologia Latina* 35,1532).

8 The Holiness of the Church: *Communio Sanctorum* and the Splendor of Truth

THIS SECOND STUDY of *Veritatis Splendor* approaches the encyclical not from the perspective of a biblical writing but from that of a biblical theme, that of holiness and its relation to communion within the People of God. Such an approach has some of the characteristics of what was once known as "biblical theology," that is, the attempt to analyze and then transpose to other intellectual categories some aspect of biblical teaching. This can be done if it be borne in mind that the second set of categories, while they can help render some biblically mediated reality more intelligible, are not exhaustive of that reality and always serve the biblical revelation.

• • •

Introduction

In an ancient baptismal rite practiced in Syria, Egypt, and Africa, the bishop begins by asking the candidate, "*Credis in Deum . . . in Jesum Christum . . . ?*" and continues with: *Credis in Spiritum sanctum in sancta Ecclesia?*"[1] The final three words of this last question most probably refer back to the previous two questions as well, thus implying that the Trinity is manifested in the life, worship, and teaching of the Church. It may be, however, that Irenaeus had a different understanding of the relation between the Holy Spirit and the holy Church in his famous phrase, "*Ubi enim Ecclesia, ibi et Spiritus Dei, et ubi Spiritus Dei, illic Ecclesia et omnis gratia.*"[2] In any event, certain realities mediated in these ancient expressions must be grasped if we are to move closer to a common

---

This article first appeared in *Nova et Vetera*, 2(2):367–92 .

[1] For a discussion of this text, see Henri de Lubac, *The Christian Faith: An Essay on the Structure of the Apostles' Creed*, trans. Richard Arnandez (San Francisco: Ignatius Press, 1986).

[2] *Adversus Haereses* 3,24 (*Patrologia Graeca* 7, 966B). Cited in ibid., 204, n.4.

understanding today of what it means to say that the Church is holy and that it is and bears within itself the *communio sanctorum*. The first of these realities is the oneness of the Church. Our belief takes place "in the holy Church," not in the churches. Second, the oneness of the Church may be seen as the work of the Holy Spirit or of the whole Trinity.[3] Third, the holiness of the Church lies in the fact that it has been made so by the one God: Father, Son, and Holy Spirit. Thus holiness and oneness are two integral aspects of the Church's being.

In this brief chapter, I wish to reflect on the mystery of the one holy Church and seek to present an understanding of this mystery in such a way that we can appreciate the intimate connection between the splendor of truth and the radiance of this splendor as it appears in the *Communio Sanctorum*. As the encyclical itself expresses it:

> The natural law "is nothing other than the light of understanding infused in us by God, whereby we understand what must be done and what must be avoided. God gave this light and this law to man at creation." He also did so *in the history of Israel,* particularly in the "ten words," the *commandments of Sinai,* whereby he brought into existence the people of the Covenant (cf. Ex 24) and called them to be his "own possession among all peoples," "a holy nation" (Ex 19:5–6), which would radiate his holiness to all peoples (cf. Wis 18:4; Ez 20:41).[4]

In this study, I wish to explore the intimate connection established by the encyclical between sharing in the holiness of God and the radiation of that holiness. To this end, I will proceed in two steps. I will first consider the biblical teaching on the mystery of God who is holy and the relation between this holiness and the holiness of his people. In this part of the study, I will enlist some philosophical and theological insights that can render more intelligible especially the New Testament teaching about our relation to God and his holiness. Then, in the second part, I will reflect on some modern discussions of the unity and holiness of the Church. In this I will present some characteristic Catholic understandings of the expressions: *sancta ecclesia* and *communio sanctorum*.

Part One: The Holiness of God and of His People

Old Testament Teaching

A Sense of the Holy
It is a fact that we find in the Old Testament some vocabulary and attitudes in regard to the numinous well described by Hans Urs von Balthasar:

---

[3] Thus Cyprian describes the Church as *"de unitate Patris and Filii and Spiritus Sancti plebs adunata"* (*De orat. dom.* 23; See Vatican II, *Lumen Gentium* 4).

[4] *Veritatis Splendor* §12. The text quoted in the encyclical is from Thomas Aquinas, *In Duo Praecepta Caritatis et in Decem Legis Praecepta. Prologus.*

Along with the creature's primal intuitive knowledge concerning the abyss in being between a relative and an absolute, between the world of men and that of the gods, there also comes a primal concept of holiness: everything within the world that belongs to the realm of the divine or the god is radically "set aside" or "separated" from the world . . . and it is therefore dangerous for mortals to approach it.[5]

We see this natural intuition is caught up into an understanding of God conferred upon Israel through revelation. Two things emerge as a result of this revelation. First, the notion of "holy" is first and foremost a *personal* attribute of YHWH and not a vague, numinous force that permeates the world of gods and men.[6] Holiness, therefore, is the inner mystery of God's unique being. Second, this personal God is creator, and that means he is unique:

> The object of creation is without exception something outside the divine. The action of God as creator is directed exclusively to the world. God is outside creation; to be created means to be not-god.[7]

Glory is the outer manifestation of that mystery, and Name is the expression of his being that he shares with us as gift. Because of his generosity we are enabled to know something of God and indeed are taught to imitate him. I wish to give here a brief survey of some of the ways in which Israel thus understood and spoke of God and the mystery of his being.[8]

How Israel Understood the Holy[9]

The presence of God means the presence of the Holy. Places where God reveals himself are thus sometimes called holy. Moses is told, "Do not come near; put off your shoes from your feet, for the place on which you are standing is holy ground" (Ex 3:5; see Jos 5:15). In another place Moses says to God: "The people cannot come up to Mount Sinai; for you yourself charged us, saying, 'Set bounds about the mountain, and consecrate it (*qiddsto*—"make it holy").'" At

---

5 Hans Urs von Balthasar, *The Glory of the Lord: A Theological Aesthetics,* ed. John Riches, trans. CRV, Erasmo Leiva-Merikakis and Brian McNeil, *Vol. VI: Theology: The Old Testament* (San Francisco: Ignatius Press, 1991), 61.

6 This is brought out well by Walther Eichrodt, *Theology of the Old Testament,* trans. J. A. Baker, vol. 1, *The Old Testament Library* (London: SCM Press Ltd., 1961), 270–82.

7 Claude Westermann, *Genesis,* vol. I/1, *Bibl. Kommentar Altes Testament* (Neukirchen-Vluyn, 1974), 26.

8 I have left aside many other expressions wherein the "primal intuitive knowledge" shared by all human beings is also voiced. These are well treated by H. P. Müller, "QDS," in *Theological Lexicon of the Old Testament,* ed. Claus Westermann and Ernst Jenni (Peabody, MA: Hendrickson, 1997), 1103–18.

9 With a few exceptions the quotations from the Bible in this paper have been slightly adapted by the author from the RSV. Those from other published translations are noted.

the same Sinai incident, Moses is commanded to "consecrate (qdš)" the people to prepare them for the coming of YHWH on the mountain (Ex 19:10), a command he also gives to the people to prepare them for the manifestation of YHWH in providing food for them (Num 11:18). The abiding of YHWH in the midst of his people perpetuates this sanctifying presence:

> There I will meet with the people of Israel, and it (the tent of meeting) shall be sanctified by my glory [manifestation of my holiness]; I will consecrate the tent of meeting and the altar; Aaron also and his sons I will consecrate, to serve me as priests. (Ex 29:42–44)

This notion underlies the expression "holy assembly" (*miqr'* [from the root *qr'* "to call"] *qdš*),[10] which occurs some nineteen times in the Old Testament, usually in connection with the phrase "appointed feast *(mw'd)* of/for YHWH." God's people are most themselves, they are in a particular way "holy" when they are assembled to worship and praise YHWH and know his presence in their midst. Thus, in the introduction to the list of appointed feasts (within which we find the expression "holy assembly" eleven times), we read: "Say to the people of Israel, The appointed feasts of YHWH which you shall proclaim as holy assemblies, my appointed feasts, are these" (Lev 23:2). Having been called by YHWH, the people belong to him and thus are holy: "For you are a people holy to YHWH your God; YHWH your God has chosen you to be a people for his own possession, out of all the peoples that are on the face of the earth" (Dt 7:6).

We see that YHWH will call himself Holy in order to indicate that he is "utterly other": "I will not unleash my anger, I will not return to ruin Ephraim for I am God, not man. In the midst of you, the Holy One: I do not come to destroy" (Hos 11:9). And this truth is proclaimed in Israel's life of praise: "There is none holy like YHWH, there is none besides you; there is no rock like our God" (1 Sam 2:2). "Who is like you, O YHWH, among the gods? Who is like you, majestic in holiness, terrible in glorious deeds, doing wonders?" (Ex 15:11). The notion that YHWH reveals or manifests his holiness by his "glorious deeds" is a central theme in the prophet Ezekiel.

> As a pleasing odor I will accept you, when I bring you out from the peoples, and gather you out of the countries where you have been scattered; and I will manifest my holiness among you in the sight of the nations (Ez 20:41).
>
> Sidon, I am against you and I shall show my glory in your midst. People will know that I am YHWH when I execute judgment on her and show my holiness in her. (Ez 28:22, NEB)

---

[10] It is important to note here that the Septuagint employs a neologism in order to translate *miqr' qdš*, namely, *klētē agia*. This forms the basis for many Pauline turns of phrase, as we will see. For more on this, see Lucien Cerfaux, *The Church in the Theology of St. Paul*, trans. Adrian Walker and Geoffrey Webb (New York: Herder & Herder, 1963), 118–20.

The Lord YHWH says: When I gather the Israelites from the peoples among whom they are dispersed, I shall show my holiness in them for all the nations to see. (Ez 28:25, NEB)

I shall hallow my great name, which you have profaned among those nations. When they see that I reveal my holiness through you, they will know that I am YHWH, says the Lord YHWH. (Ez 36:23, NEB)

It is not only that God's actions reveal his holiness, the mystery of his being, but human actions reveal his holiness as well as reveal man to himself. As the encyclical expresses it:

> *What man is and what he must do becomes clear as soon as God reveals himself.* The Decalogue is based on these words: "I am the Lord your God, who brought you out of the land of Egypt, out of the house of bondage" (Ex 20:2–3). In the "ten words" of the Covenant with Israel, and in the whole Law, God makes himself known and acknowledged as the One who "alone is good"; the One who despite man's sin remains the "model" for moral action, in accordance with his command, "You shall be holy; for I the Lord your God am holy" (Lev 19:2); as the One who, faithful to his love for man, gives him his Law (cf. Ex 19:9–24 and 20:18–21) in order to restore man's original and peaceful harmony with the Creator and with all creation, and, what is more, to draw him into his divine love: "I will walk among you, and will be your God, and you shall be my people" (Lev 26:12). (*VS* §10)

Negatively, our failure to obey obscures the holiness of God. Moses is told that he will die before entering the Promised Land, just as Aaron has already died: "[B]ecause both of you broke faith with me in the midst of the people of Israel at the waters of Meri-bath-kadesh, in the wilderness of Zin; you did not manifest my holiness in the midst of the people of Israel" (Dt 32:51; see Num 27:14).[11] The notion that by responding to YHWH's offer of a covenant the people become, "to me a kingdom of priests and a holy nation" (Ex 19:6) means that they are meant to manifest God's holiness by keeping faith with him. This extends to each individual Israelite who is told, "You shall be holy for I, YHWH, your God, am holy" (Lev 19:2 *et passim*), which is to say, the Israelite by his actions becomes more and more like God. The significance of this refrain is well expressed by John Hartley whose words can serve as a summary of our consideration:

> Israel is to be *qdš*, "holy" because Yahweh, her God, is *qdš*, "holy." . . . Holiness is the quintessential quality of YHWH. In the entire universe, he

---

[11] It is probable that Moses' sin on this occasion was to arrogate to himself the saving power, the holiness of YHWH. He is told in Num 20:12: "Because you did not believe/trust me so as to manifest my holiness in the sight of the Israelites, you will not lead this community into the land I am giving them."

alone is intrinsically holy. The nominal sentence, YHWH is holy, points in this direction. That God is holy means that he is exalted, awesome in power, glorious in appearance, pure in character. God's holiness is contagious. Wherever his presence is, that place becomes holy. Since Israel's holiness is learned and is derived from YHWH, the command for Israel to become holy is expressed in a verbal sentence; the use of the verb *yhy* "be, become," captures the maturing dimension of holiness on the human plane. Being YHWH's representative on earth, Israel is to evidence in her community characteristics that are similar to God's.[12]

Holiness in the New Testament

The fact of Christ, one Person in two natures, literally a hypostatic union, creates a new category and thus gives new understanding to all of the Old Testament. In the light of Christ risen from the dead the entire understanding of holiness acquired in the Prior Testament is enshrined, deepened, and carried to a higher plane. The Incarnation is not merely a piece of new information to be placed in preexisting categories. Rather, knowledge of this reality changes all that we previously knew. When Helen Keller, blind, deaf, and apparently dumb, first perceived the relation between words and things, as her teacher, Anne Sullivan, traced the letters "water" on her hand as water was flowing over it, a new dimension of being was disclosed to her, not just as new thing.[13] The Incarnation is a disclosure of an even greater magnitude.

It was already perceived, for instance, that the unity of God's people derived, not only from the fact of a common revelation and a common worship, but also more profoundly from the fact that "God is one." In the light of Christ it was further understood that the oneness of the Church is caused by the fact that it shares in a mysterious way in the very unity of God himself. The holiness of God, the mystery of his triune being, is the reason for the holiness, and thus the unity of the Church.[14] We have seen that the people are never more holy as a people than when they are gathered together to worship and praise God and know his presence. Now that Christ is among us we understand that holiness is realized in that act in which God's people, in the Holy Spirit, gather and celebrate in sacrament that communion of persons that shares in the very communion of the Trinity.

Since the being of God only exists in three hypostases, we must understand God to be relational in his essence: The eternal, freely willed, relationality of

---

[12] John E. Hartley, *Leviticus,* ed. David A. Hubbard, *Word Biblical Commentary* 4 (Dallas: Word Books, 1992), 312.

[13] I owe this clarifying example to Robert Sokolowski, *Eucharistic Presence: A Study in the Theology of Disclosure* (Washington, DC: Catholic University of America Press, 1993), 201.

[14] For a development of this theme, as well as Jewish and Hellenistic expressions of divine unity, see Francis Martin, "Pauline Trinitarian Formulas and Christian Unity," *Catholic Biblical Quarterly* 30 (1968): 199–219.

the Father is the personal source of the Son and the Spirit who are equal to him in an infinite movement of freedom and love. Holiness, the mystery of God's inner being, is therefore, a mystery of communion.

In the following section, I will look briefly at the ways in which the New Testament predicates holiness of the Father, the Son, and especially the *Holy Spirit*. I will then look at the ways in which the endowment of "holy" is predicated of the Church. We will then finally be in a position to reflect theologically on the mystery of the Church as holy.

The Holy God in the New Testament

The New Testament does not apply the term "holy" with great frequency to the Father or to Jesus his Son, and some of these New Testament usages clearly cite or reflect the Old Testament. In order to understand these latter, we must bear in mind the entirely new dimension of reality opened up to the New Testament community by the resurrection of Christ. In this new dimension not only the teaching of the Old Testament, but even the words of Jesus himself now reveal their true inner meaning. Before this event, who could have ever imagined the true identity of the Father and the depth of intimacy to which he calls us with himself? Who could have understood the meaning of Jesus' use of the word Abba before Jesus' glorious resurrection and the outpouring of the Holy Spirit? Or again, who could have understood the meaning of the exhortation expressed in the words of Leviticus 11:44 (19:2, and so on), "Be holy as I am holy" (1 Pet 1:16)? We must surely hear this exhortation within the entirely new context of those who were ransomed by the precious blood of Christ, who was known before the foundation of the world but revealed in the final time (see 1 Pet 1:17–21). We will return to this.

God the Father is called "holy" *(agios)* in the lines immediately preceding those just cited from the First Letter of Peter: "[B]ut as he who called you is holy, be holy yourselves in all your conduct . . ." (1 Pet 1:15). Mary sings that "his name is holy" (Lk 1:49), Jesus addresses him as "holy Father" (Jn 17:11), and the Book of Revelation tells us of " the four living creatures, each of them with six wings, are full of eyes all round and within, and day and night who never cease to sing, Holy, holy, holy, is the Lord God Almighty, who was and is and is to come!" (Rev 4:8, see also 6:10).

Then we see how Jesus is addressed in Peter's act of faith: "and we have believed, and have come to know, that you are the Holy One of God" (Jn 6:69). John surely intends this in its most solemn sense, as opposed to the demons quoted in Mark 1:24 and Luke 4:34.[15] The angel tells Mary that the Holy Spirit will come upon her and "the child to be born will be holy, he will be called the Son of God" (Lk 1:35). Jesus himself is "filled with the Holy

---

[15] I say "as opposed to the demons" reported in the Synoptic tradition. What the Evangelists, at level three of the tradition, intended is more likely to be ironic: What the demons confessed was true in a way they could not suspect.

Spirit" (Lk 4:1), anointed by the Holy Spirit at his baptism (Acts 10:38; Lk 3:22) in such a way that his works manifest his unique holiness. Peter, like Isaiah, when confronted with such a manifestation of holiness is brought to confess his sinfulness (Lk 5:8; Is 6:5). Peter tells the inhabitants of Jerusalem, "you denied the Holy and Righteous One" (Acts 3:14), a title whose full meaning is now revealed since Jesus has been "instituted Son of God in power according to the spirit of holiness due to resurrection from the dead" (Rom 1:4). Thus, John receives instruction: "And to the angel of the church in Philadelphia write: 'The words of the holy one, the true one, who has the key of David, who opens and no one shall shut, who shuts and no one opens" (Rev 3:7). Finally, believers are told, "But you have an oil of anointing from the Holy One, and you all have knowledge" (1 Jn 2:20).[16]

It is significant that the Spirit of the Father and the Son is called the *Holy* Spirit, using an expression already present in the Old Testament.[17] Jesus is conceived by the action of the Holy Spirit (Lk 1:35), in his ministry is anointed by God with this same Spirit (Acts 10:37–38; Mt 3:16, par.), and now raised to the right hand of the Father, "he received the promised Holy Spirit from the Father and has poured him out" (Acts 2:33). The Spirit is mentioned with the Father and the Son in two texts that accent the unity of the Church (1 Cor 12:4–6; Eph 4:4–6); it is in their threefold name that the baptismal mandate is given (Mt 28:19); and it is through Christ, in one Spirit, that we both (Jew and Gentile) have access to the Father (Eph 2:18). Indeed "in one Spirit we were all baptized into one Body . . . and we all drank of one Spirit" (1 Cor 12:12–13). It is the one Spirit of the Father and the Son who gives access to the mystery of their being and thus makes the Church both one and holy. We will see how prominent is the unifying and sanctifying action of the Holy Spirit as we now discuss how the Church is holy.

One Holy People

I have already pointed out that the Septuagint by coining a new phrase, *klētē agia*, to translate the Hebrew expression "holy assembly," provided Paul with vocabulary

---

16 Some commentators would see the title "Holy One" as being applied here to the Father, but the context and general tone of the passage favor seeing the risen Jesus as the "Holy One." See Rudolf Schnackenburg, *The Johannine Epistles: A Commentary*, trans. Reginald and Ilse Fuller (New York: Crossroad, 1992), 142–43.

17 "Paul's experience of God as Spirit, as mysterious vivifying and inspiring power, was of a piece with the experience of *ruach* attested by Moses (2 Cor. 3:16) and the prophets before him. That experience could be more clearly defined and recognized by reference to Christ, as the Spirit of Christ. But it was not another Spirit which was so designated, only the Spirit of God, the Spirit given by God. If the character of Christ had now defined the character of the Spirit, it was the Spirit of God which was so defined." Quoted from James D. G. Dunn, *The Theology of Paul the Apostle* (Grand Rapids, MI: Eerdmans, 1998), 717.

to express part of his understanding of the church. In writing to the Corinthians, he first calls himself a "called apostle *(klētos apostolos)* of Jesus Christ," and then describes them as the "Church (assembly/*ekklēsia*) of God at Corinth, made holy in Christ Jesus, 'holy called ones' *(klētois agiois)*" (1 Cor 1:2). Much of the same vocabulary is found in the opening lines of the Letter to the Romans, and in the Letter to the Colossians.[18] The influence of the Septuagint phrase as adapted by Paul is certainly one of the sources of his ability to call Christians "holy/*agioi*" (Rom 8:27–28, 16:2; 1 Cor 6:1–2; Eph 1:1; and so on).

If we strive to grasp more deeply what is implied in the call of God, we will be able to more adequately understand the New Testament teaching regarding the holiness of the Church. This call, in effect, is made up of two realities: the sanctifying work of Christ on the cross and the action of the Holy Spirit in bringing people into touch with this work. This rhythm of the work of God is well expressed in the teaching of the First Letter of John (5:6): Jesus Christ *came*, that is, he accomplished the work of redemption, and the Spirit *bears witness*, that is, he brings people to know and be transformed by that work. Or again in the words of the Letter to the Hebrews (9:13–14): "For if the blood of goats and bulls and the ashes of a heifer sprinkled on those defiled sanctifies for the purification of the flesh, how much more the blood of Christ who by the eternal Spirit offered himself unblemished to God, will purify your conscience from dead works for the worshipping of the living God?" Christ offered himself by the "eternal Spirit" who in this sacrifice accomplished what the "eternal fire" did in the old sacrificial system.[19] The transforming fire of the Spirit who moved Jesus to die in an act of love is the one who animates those who, "baptized into his death," now walk in newness of life/Spirit (Rom 6:3–4, 7:6).

The New Testament expresses in several different ways the fact that, by his death out of love, Jesus has reconciled us to God and sanctified us. There is first of all the rhythm of "love—give himself over" that we find in Galatians 2:20: "The life I now live in the flesh, I live in faith, faith in the Son of God who loved me and gave himself over for me." This is repeated in Ephesians 5:2 and applied to the obligation of husbands to their wives in Ephesians 5:25. We read in John 14:31 that Jesus goes to his passion in obedience to the Father and to show the world his love for the Father: "But that the world might know that I love the Father; and as the Father commanded me, so I do . . . rise up, let us go from here." Jesus' self-gift to the Father merited his exaltation that consisted in rendering his humanity apt to reveal his divine Personality: "And therefore God exalted

---

18 In Romans, *klētos apostolos*, which is then specified as "set apart for the Gospel of God" (1:1), *klētoi Iēsou Christou* (1:6), *agapētois Theou, klētois agiois* (1:7). In Colossians 3:12, "Put on then as the *eklektoi tou Theou, agioi kai ēgapēmenoi* . . ." (elect of God). For a complete treatment of this theme, see Lucien Cerfaux, *The Church in the Theology of St. Paul*, trans. Geoffrey Webb and Adrian Walker (New York: Herder & Herder, 1959).

19 See Albert Vanhoye, "Esprit éternel et feu du sacrifice en He 9,14," *Biblica* 64 (1983): 263–74.

him and gave him the Name that is above all names, so that at the name of Jesus every knee should bow . . . and every tongue confess to the glory of God the Father that Jesus Christ is Lord" (Phil 2:9–11, cf. Is 45:22–25). This act of love, accomplished in the fire of the Holy Spirit, makes Christ's blood capable of purifying our conscience from dead works in order to serve the living God. Because he possesses a body, Christ is able to give human, historical existence to the will of God: "In this will, we have been sanctified through the offering of the body of Jesus Christ once for all" (Heb 10:10). For this reason Paul tells us: "The body is not for immorality but for the Lord, and the Lord is for the body. . . .You have been purchased at a price, therefore glorify God in your body" (1 Cor 6:14, 20). We are holy, we belong to God, we are the people he has acquired (Eph 1:14) and we join those in heaven who sing: "Worthy are you to receive the scroll, and to open its seals because you were slain and purchased for God with your blood from every tribe and tongue and people and nation; and made them for our God, a kingdom and priests, and they will reign upon the earth" (Rev 5:9).

This action of God in Christ changes us. Our holiness is not that of an external adherence to God's people at worship, rather "we are the true circumcision, who worship by the Spirit of God, who boast in Christ Jesus, and put no confidence in the flesh" (Phil 3:3). Christ dwells in us by faith and the Spirit of God is in our inner being (Eph 3:16–17; see Rom 8:10–11). This means that we have been called into "participation in his Son" (1 Cor 1:9) and we have "participation in the Holy Spirit" (2 Cor 13:13; see Phil 2:1).[20] This participation extends to sharing in the sufferings and resurrection of Christ: "that I may know him and the power of his resurrection, and participate in his sufferings, becoming like him in his death, that if possible I may attain the resurrection from the dead" (Phil 3:10–11; see Rom 8:15), which means that Paul's wounds are "the brand marks of Jesus" (Gal 6:17),[21] and that we are "always carrying in the body the death of Jesus, so that the life of Jesus may also be manifested in our bodies" (2 Cor 4:10).

The Church's union with Christ is set forth even more powerfully with the use of the analogies of vine and branches, temple, and most important, body. In this last predication, which is Pauline, it is revealed to us that we are physically joined to the Holy One (Jn 6:69; 1 Jn 2:20; Rev 3:7, 16:5) and make one reality with him. This fact is the basis for Christian chastity (1 Cor 6:12–20), it

---

[20] For an ample treatment of these texts and a justification of the above translation of *koinōnia*, see J. Y. Campbell, "Κοινωνια and Its Cognates in the New Testament," in *Three New Testament Studies* (Leiden: Brill, 1965), and the discussion in Dunn, *The Theology of Paul the Apostle*, 561–62, 616–17.

[21] "Already it is evident that the body of man, the focus of suffering in this world, was viewed by Paul as the sphere where Christ's rule becomes visibly evident." Robert Jewett, *Paul's Anthropological Terms: A Study of Their Use in Conflict Settings.* Vol. 10, *Arbeiten zur Geschichte des antiken Judentums und des Urchristentums* (Leiden: Brill, 1971). [commenting on this text.]

is the source and reason for Christian *agapē*, and for good order in the community (1 Cor 12–14), it is the context within which we offer our whole selves *(sōmata)* to God as a "living sacrifice, holy and pleasing to God," and practice mutual love and concern (Rom 12:1–2 + 3–8 + 9–21). Not only have we received from his fullness (Jn 1:16), but this fullness from him who is the Head "from whom the whole body, joined and knit together by every joint with which it is supplied, when each part is working properly, makes bodily growth and upbuilds itself in love" (Eph 4:15). We are thus parts of him and parts of each other (1 Cor 12:12–31). This union is not only spiritual, it is human, that is, it involves the physical dimension of our personality as well as the spiritual (see Heb 2:14–16). Failure to recognize this, failure to "discern the Body," has resulted in "many of you being ill and infirm, and a considerable number are dying" (1 Cor 11:29–30).

Marriage, Communion, and the Splendor of Truth

It is particularly in the spousal mystery that the relation between holiness and communion shows us the perfective nature of truth: Truth desired and received becomes a value, and as a value it becomes a force, a power:

> In a particular way, it *is in the Crucified Christ* that *the Church finds the answer* to the question troubling so many people today: how can obedience to universal and unchanging moral norms respect the uniqueness and individuality of the person, and not represent a threat to his freedom and dignity? The Church makes her own the Apostle Paul's awareness of the mission he had received: "Christ . . . sent me . . . to preach the Gospel, and not with eloquent wisdom, lest the cross of Christ be emptied of its power. . . . We preach Christ crucified, a stumbling block to Jews and folly to Gentiles, but to those who are called, both Jews and Greeks, Christ the power of God and the wisdom of God" (1 Cor 1:17,23–24). *The Crucified Christ reveals the authentic meaning of freedom, he lives it fully, in the total gift of himself* and calls his disciples to share in his freedom. (*VS* §85)

The mystery of the physical union of Christ and his Body is important for our understanding of the holiness of the Church. We will reflect fully on the most mature expression of that union as set forth in the Letter to the Ephesians 5:21–33 in chapter 10. Here it suffices to note how the holiness of the Church is directly attributed to the act of love in which Christ died, a theme we touched upon above:

> Husbands, love your wives just as Christ loved the Church and gave himself over for her that he might make her holy, purifying her in the washing of water, with a word, that he might present to himself the Church resplendent, not having spot or wrinkle or anything of the sort, but that she be holy and without fault. (Eph 5:25–27)

This is an eschatological vision of the completed work of Christ: the Church, his bride "holy and without fault" thus realizing the eternal plan of the Father (see Eph 1:4). This plan is being worked out even now, and that is why the Church is incipiently holy: The believers are called "holy" nine times in this Letter alone,[22] and their corporate reality is called a "holy temple" (Eph 2:21).[23] They are God's new creation, the Christ (see 1 Cor 12:12; 1:13[?]).[24] The great mystery, therefore, is in the *fact* of Christ's physical union with the Church, a union effected by the Holy Spirit. This is the deepest source of the Church's holiness.

That all of the great work of Christ actually exists now in an actual and historical dimension is due to the action of the Holy Spirit. At baptism believers receive the Holy Spirit in their hearts: "[H]e has put his seal upon us and given us his Spirit in our hearts as a guarantee" (1 Cor 1:11; Eph 1:13; see Rom 5:5); "God has sent the Spirit of his Son into our hearts" so that we can, with all truth pray and relate to the Father as Jesus did and does. Because the same Spirit dwells within us, the Church is one and holy:

> The Father and the Son wanted us to enter into communion with each other and with them through what is common to them and wanted to join us together as one through that Gift that they both possess together, namely the Holy Spirit, God, and Gift of God. It is in him that we are reconciled with the Deity and that we enjoy the Deity.[25]

The Spirit co-institutes the Church as Christ institutes it, that is, because of the Spirit, the Church brought into existence and made one and holy by Christ, actually lives its existence authentically: It is actually one and holy.[26] Just as it is because of the action of the Holy Spirit that Christ, in his human nature exists, so it is because of the same Holy Spirit that the Church, in its

---

[22] Eph 1:1, 15,18; 2:19; 3:8,18; 4:12; 5:3; 6:18.

[23] The reader is referred to chapter 10 for a complete discussion of this theme.

[24] Gordon Fee, one of the few commentators to comment on 1 Cor 12:12, says that the phrase "so it is with the Christ" is a form of metonymy: "Thus, 'Christ' means the church as a shortened form of the 'body of Christ.'" This is true as far as it goes, but what could Paul possibly mean by employing such a shortened form at all? See Gordon D. Fee, *The First Epistle to the Corinthians,* ed. F. F. Bruce, *The New International Commentary on the New Testament* (Grand Rapids, MI: Eerdmans, 1987), 603.

[25] St. Augustine, *Sermon 71,12,18* (*Patrologia Latina* 38,454), cited in Yves Congar, "The Holy Spirit Makes the Church One," in *I Believe in the Holy Spirit* (New York: Seabury, 1983), 23.

[26] The term "co-institute" is found in Yves Congar, "The Church is Made by the Spirit," in *I Believe in the Holy Spirit.* For a development of this notion using the term "constitute," see John D. Zizioulas, *Being As Communion, Contemporary Greek Theologians* 4 (Crestwood, NY: St. Vladimir's Seminary Press, 1985).

actual human and historical nature, exists. This mystery of the action of the second and third Persons of the Trinity characterizes all their activity outside the Godhead in both creation and redemption. The Spirit hovers over creation and over the people (Gen 1:2; Ex 19:4; Dt 32:11) and thus the word addressed by God has its effect: There is light, there is a people made one by being addressed as one.[27]

It is in this light that we can understand the New Testament teaching in regard to the Holy Spirit and the Church. Having been baptized in one Spirit into one Body (1 Cor 12:13) we have "participation in the Spirit" (2 Cor 13:13; Phil 2:1; see above), and "he who cleaves to the Lord is one Spirit with him" and becomes a temple of the Holy Spirit within him whom he has from God (1 Cor 6:17,19). It is by the "ministry of the Spirit" that God's people are formed (2 Cor 3:4–11). They are justified and sanctified "in the name of the Lord Jesus Christ and in the Spirit of our God" (1 Cor 6:11). Indeed, "when the goodness and loving kindness of God our Savior appeared, he saved us . . . in virtue of his own mercy, by the washing of regeneration and *renewal in the Holy Spirit*, which he poured out upon us richly *through Jesus Christ our Savior*" (Tit 3:4–7).[28] I will end this all too brief section with a quote from *Lumen Gentium* (§8), which may serve to sum up a Catholic understanding of the Spirit and the Church.

> Just as the assumed nature inseparably united to the divine Word serves him as a living instrument of salvation, so, in a similar way, does the communal structure of the Church serve Christ's Spirit who vivifies it by way of building up the body (cf. Eph 4:16). This is the unique Church of Christ, which in the Creed we avow to be one, holy, catholic and apostolic. After his resurrection our Savior handed her over to Peter to be shepherded. (Jn 21:17)

Part Two: Communion of Persons and *Communio Sanctorum*

In this part, I wish to reflect briefly on three aspects of holiness and unity as they are relevant to our understanding of the holiness of the Church. First, I will discuss the priority of ontology over morality in a consideration of personal holiness, I will then place the discussion within the context of the relational character of the human person: the Body of Christ as holy. Finally, I will look at what the traditional understanding of *communio sanctorum* can add to a more profound grasp on the note of "holy" as applied to the Church.

---

[27] For a study of this rhythm in the theology of Saint John. see Ignace de la Potterie, "Parole et Esprit dans S. Jean," in *L'Évangile de Jean. Sources, Rédaction, Théologie*, ed. M. de Jong, *Bibliotheca Ephemeridum Theologicarum Lovaniensium* 44 (Gembloux: Duculot, 1977).

[28] These last two texts are illustrative of the rhythm "institute–constitute" mentioned earlier.

Moral Actions and Ontological Change

It is simply a matter of common wisdom that a person becomes virtuous or vicious as a result of a consistent series of repeated decisions. Unfortunately, this wisdom was not sufficiently operative in the course of the last few hundred years of Christian moral thinking, which contented itself with the question, "What is the law?" rather than the ancient and much more profound question, "What must I do in order to arrive at the goal of my life and find happiness?"[29] As Joseph Pieper once expressed this basic law of moral action: "Human activity has two basic forms: doing *(agere)* and making *(facere)*. Artifacts, technical and artistic, are the 'works' of making. We ourselves are the 'works' of our doing."[30] The consequence of recent law-based moralism (as opposed to morality) has been that we read the New Testament exhortations to a holy life as having little to do with the objective state of our being. Yet, what the New Testament teaches us is really that our actions are meant to flow from our ontological union with Christ and to increase our participation in his life by yielding to the activity of the Holy Spirit moving us to acts of love.[31] If holiness is a share in the mystery of God's being, then, in our own case as well, it is an ontological reality. I believe that this is the intent of the famous statement in 2 Peter 1:3–4:

> His divine power has bestowed on us everything that makes for life and godliness, through the knowledge of him who called us to his own glory and excellence, by means of which he has bestowed on us his precious and magnificent promises, that through them you may become sharers *(koinōnoi)* of the divine nature having escaped from the corruption that is in the world as a result of desire.

The phrase "sharers of the divine nature" while it borrows its terminology from Jewish-Hellenistic mysticism is referring to the common New Testament theme that we have become children of God, animated by his Spirit (Rom 8:5; 14–17; Gal 4:6), that we have fellowship *(koinōnia)* with the Father and with his Son Jesus Christ (1 Jn 1:3); that a Christian is a sharer *(koinōnos)* in the glory to be revealed (1 Pet 5:1). With such parallel expressions available (see also Col 2:9 *plērōma—peplērōmenoi)*, it is exaggerated reductionism to restrict

---

[29] For a history of this situation and an analysis of its causes and remedies, see Servais Pinckaers, *The Sources of Christian Ethics,* trans. Mary Thomas Noble (Washington, DC: The Catholic University of America Press, 1995).

[30] Josef Pieper, *The Four Cardinal Virtues,* trans. Lawrence E. Lynch Richard, Clara Winston, and Daniel Coogan (South Bend, IN: University of Notre Dame Press, 1966), 29. Consider this remark by Karol Wojtyla: "The self constitutes itself precisely through the acts proper to man as a person." Karol (Pope John Paul II) Wojtyla, "The Person: Subject and Community," *Review of Metaphysics* 33 (2; 1979/80): 273–308.

[31] For a development of this point, see chapter 3.

this text to similar expressions elsewhere in extra-biblical literature when the precise point is to show that now in Christ these aspirations have been fulfilled.

Peter teaches us that our holiness comes from knowledge of the One who has called us to his own glory and excellence and that our immortality is fundamentally a share in his own. The text goes on immediately to urge us to supplement our faith with virtue, our virtue with knowledge, and finally our godliness with brotherly affection and our affection with love (see 2 Pet 1:5–7). Our acts therefore are changing us and bringing us into a deeper participation in the divine nature. I recognize that most modern commentators tend to avoid this line of thinking, being content to point out the relation in Jewish-Hellenistic mysticism between immortality and sharing in the divine nature. I think, however, that the massive patristic tradition cannot be ignored here. As J. N. D. Kelly puts it:

> His [the author's] tentative ideas, however, were destined to provide a firm scriptural foundation for the vast theology of redemption by the divinization of human nature which, beginning with Clement of Alexandria, was to dominate the patristic centuries and remains immensely influential in large sections of the Church down to the present day.[32]

While the text from 2 Peter is helpful it is not necessary in order to establish the point that holiness for the Church and for all the persons who make up the Church is an ontological quality and not merely a moral quality. Before passing on to consider the intrinsically relational quality of moral action we should add two reflections. We should first observe that human activity is always historical, that is, it is the activity of a being who is both spiritual and material, whose spirituality pervades his materiality and gives it a properly human dimension. Spirituality for a human being is not immateriality, and, as we shall see, it is not individual but shared. Holiness is a complete fulfillment of the human person because it realizes the transcendent orientation of the whole human being and results in a transformation that is perfected in that act in which the Trinity gives himself unreservedly to the whole spiritual-material being in an embrace of love that is eternal life.

Second, genuine holiness realizes and sublates the autoteleological drives of human nature, bringing them to a transcendent fulfillment.[33] Thus, to quote Karol Wojtyla:

---

[32] J. N. D. Kelly, *A Commentary on the Epistles of Peter and Jude, Thornapple Commentaries* (Grand Rapids, MI: Baker, 1981 reprint), 304.

[33] The process I am referring to is aptly portrayed in this description of sublation given by Bernard Lonergan: "What sublates goes beyond what is sublated, introduces something new and distinct, yet so far from interfering with the sublated or destroying it, on the contrary needs it, includes it, preserves all its proper features and properties, and carries them forward to a fuller realization within a richer context." Bernard Lonergan, *Method in Theology* (New York: Herder & Herder, 1972), 241.

Man fulfills himself, he realizes the autoteleology of his personal self through the transcendent dimension of his action. The transcendence of truth and good has a decisive influence on forming the personal subject as is evident in the analysis of conscience and morality. The same analysis allows one to penetrate more profoundly the contingency of man, elucidating how essential is his striving for self fulfillment, how in this striving he is constantly torn between good and evil, between self-fulfillment and nonfulfillment. . . .[34]

The Human Person as Essentially Relational

In his recovery of the thinking of the Cappadocians in regard to personhood, John Zizioulas has managed to forge a link between the enormous reversal effected by these saints within classical Greek thought and the modern move from the "turn to the subject" to the "turn to the person."[35] I wish, in just a few lines, to show how this understanding of the human person renders intelligible the twofold holiness of the Church, individual and corporate.

The understanding that, within the Trinity, the Father is the very source of the Divinity for the Son and Spirit helps us to understand that Person is not added to substance, as though with the Trinity there were a neutral substance equally divided among the Persons. It is rather that the Father, as essentially Father, hypostasizes the Divinity in a relational manner eternally and freely begetting the Son and giving rise to the Spirit who is, as it were, the subsisting "we" between the Father and the Son. Having arrived at this insight, it is easier to see that the human person is also essentially relational, and that, in a created manner, which does not identify substance and relation, it is still possible to understand that a human person hypostasizes his or her substance, drawing it up into the very relational nature of personality. This means that community, when it is genuine, is not added to personhood but belongs to it essentially, though only in such a way that the selfhood of each person is enhanced and not diminished.

The classical definition of person, given by Boethius (and modified somewhat in the course of history) asserted basically that a person is "an individual substance of a rational nature."[36] Modern philosophical and theological thought

---

34 "The Person: Subject and Community," 287. For a discussion of how these philosophical principles are elaborated in terms of nature and saving grace, see Gerard Beigel, *Faith and Social Justice in the Teaching of Pope John Paul II*, American University Studies, Series VII, Theology and Religion 191 (New York: Peter Lang, 1997), ch. 3, "Man Within the Sphere of Redemption."

35 Zizioulas, *Being As Communion*. That this mode of thought is also part of western theological thought, see Yves Congar, "The Father, the Absolute Source of Divinity," in *I Believe in the Holy Spirit*.

36 For a discussion of this definition and its history, see Max Müller et al., "Person," in *Sacramentum Mundi: An Encyclopedia of Theology*, ed. Karl Rahner (New York: Herder & Herder, 1969), 404–19.

has advanced the understanding of person and thus would understand these terms in a more existential manner than that in which they were formerly understood. When "substance" is seen in the light of creation, it becomes obvious that it is what it is by its relation to God, that it subsists as what it is, and that it expresses what it is by relation to other beings. Thus, W. Norris Clarke proposes a triadic structure of being: "being *from* another, being *in* oneself, and being *toward* others."[37] Given the dynamic structure of all being it is true to say that the *individuum*, the *concretum*, seen in the light of its reality as created, is constituted by relation: to God, to itself and to other beings. This last relation, that to other beings, is what Maritain calls "the basic generosity of existence,"[38] in which every being at its own level does impart something of itself: *bonum est diffusivum sui.*

Similarly, when we reflect on what "rational" means, we see that the unique and incommunicable reality of a person is also constituted by relation, it is *from* God, it relates in itself and to itself, and it is a being *toward* others. Because in regard to person we are concerned with a spiritual reality that is one who possesses itself and can reflect upon itself, we are in the presence of the mystery of freedom. From this point of view we can see that what is unique in the instance of person is that this threefold relation is actualized in the personal activity of freedom by which the relation, accepted and lived in love, becomes *relationship*. Thus, the particular property of a "rational" substance is that it is constituted by relation in such a way that this is given properly human existence in the free acts by which the person realizes him or her self. This philosophical elaboration is expressed biblically by saying that man is the image of God, and can find himself only in a relationship of mutual self-giving love.

> For Adam, the first man, was a figure of Him Who was to come, (20) namely Christ the Lord. Christ, the final Adam, by the revelation of the mystery of the Father and His love, fully reveals man to man himself and makes his supreme calling clear. . . . Indeed, the Lord Jesus, when He prayed to the Father, "that all may be one . . . as we are one" (John 17:21–22) opened up vistas closed to human reason, for He implied a certain likeness between the union of the divine Persons, and the unity of God's sons in truth and charity. This likeness reveals that man, who is the only creature on earth which God willed for itself, *cannot fully find himself except through a sincere gift of himself* (*Gaudium et Spes*, §§22,24 emphasis added).

The mention of the Trinity in the above text points once again to the fact that *communio* in the Church is an icon of the Trinity, a realization on the human level of the mystery and fulfillment of person through love. This communion is a

---

[37] Walter Norris Clarke, "A Response to David Schindler's Comments." *Communio* 20 3 (3; 1993), 596.

[38] Jacques Maritain, *Existence and the Existent* (New York: Doubleday, 1957), 90.

communion of *persons*. On the created level of the Church it can increase or decrease according to the degree of love with which the created and graced persons actually give themselves to each other in love: Their actions affect their being and the being of the whole Church. These actions cannot be, of their nature, purely spiritual. They must be human actions and thus the holiness of the Church has a physical dimension: It is realized by body-persons. I will return to this in discussing *communio sanctorum*.

The final point to be realized here in the discussion of *communio personarum* is that the Catholic view understands the nature of these relationships to be stronger than death since they are centered on the relationship to the risen Christ whose Body we are. It is for this reason that the "communion of saints" includes the Church triumphant, the Church suffering, and the Church militant, and that the celebration of the heavenly banquet gathers all of the Church together. I will give here some expressions of this faith from Vatican II.[39]

> Until the Lord shall come in His majesty, and all the angels with Him and death being destroyed, all things are subject to Him. Some of His disciples are exiles on earth, some having died are purified, and others are in glory beholding "clearly God Himself triune and one, as He is"; but all in various ways and degrees are in communion in the same charity of God and neighbor and all sing the same hymn of glory to our God. For all who are in Christ, having His Spirit, form one Church and cleave together in Him. Therefore the union of the wayfarers with the brethren who have gone to sleep in the peace of Christ is not in the least weakened or interrupted, but on the contrary, according to the perpetual faith of the Church, is strengthened by communication of spiritual goods.
>
> For by reason of the fact that those in heaven are more closely united with Christ, they establish the whole Church more firmly in holiness, lend nobility to the worship which the Church offers to God here on earth and in many ways contribute to its greater edification. For after they have been received into their heavenly home and are present to the Lord, through Him and with Him and in Him they do not cease to intercede with the Father for us, showing forth the merits which they won on earth through the one Mediator between God and man, serving God in all things and filling up in their flesh those things which are lacking of the sufferings of Christ for His Body which is the Church. Thus by their brotherly interest our weakness is greatly strengthened. (*Lumen Gentium*, §49)

---

[39] See Christoph Schönborn, "The 'Communion of Saints' as Three States of the Church: pilgrimage, purification and glory," *Communio* 15 (1988): 169–81. For an even stronger expression, see Zizioulas, *Being as Communion*, ch. 4, "Eucharist and Catholicity." One might also consult the study by Paul McPartlan, *The Eucharist Makes the Church: Henri de Lubac and John Zizoulas in dialogue* (Edinburgh: T&T Clark, 1993).

Communio Sanctorum

The origins of this expression and its precise original understanding are shrouded in the mists of history.[40] This much is clear: From a very early date the phrase referred to two different but interconnected realities, namely, participation in holy things, specifically Baptism and Eucharist, and communion among those sanctified by the Holy Spirit. I will give here two quotes from Catholic authors to give an idea of how the phrase actually functions in Catholic thought and practice. The first is from the *Commentary on the Apostles Creed* by St. Thomas Aquinas:

> Just as in a physical body the operation of one member conduces to the good of the whole body, so it is in a spiritual body such as the Church. And since all the faithful are one body, the good of one member is communicated to another: *every one*, as the Apostle says, (Rom. xii, 5) *members, one of another*. Wherefore among points of faith handed down by the Apostles, is that there is a community of goods in the Church, and this is expressed in the words *Communion of saints*. Now of all the members of the Church Christ is the principal, for He is the head: *He . . . hath made him head over all the Church which is his body* (Eph. i, 22). Accordingly Christ's good is communicated to all Christians, even as the power in the head is shared by all the members.
>
> This communication is effected by the sacraments of the Church, wherein the power of Christ's passion operates, the effect of which is the bestowal of grace unto the remission of sins. . . .[41]

The second text is by Hans Urs von Balthasar who reflects a typically Catholic sense of interconnection between the saints on earth and between those in heaven and those on earth. After speaking of the vertical dimension of unity and holiness effected by the Holy Spirit, von Balthasar goes on to speak of the "horizontal element," which equally owes its existence to the same Spirit.

> The extent to which the "saints"—those who attempt to take seriously their sanctification by the holy triune God and to respond to it—are able in their community to be, to live, to work, and to suffer for one another can only begin to be realized when one has grasped the principle which welds them

---

[40] For a study of these origins one may consult Stephen Benko, *The Meaning of Sanctorum Communio*, ed. S. L. Greenslade, Studies in Historical Theology 3 (Naperville, IL: Allenson, 1964). J. N. D. Kelly, *Early Christian Creeds,* 3rd ed. (London: Longman, 1972), "The Communion of Saints," 388–97.

[41] Thomas Aquinas, "Exposition of the Apostles' Creed," in *The Three Greatest Prayers: Commentaries on the Our Father, the Hail Mary and the Apostles's Creed* (Westminster, MD: Newman Press, 1956), 80.

together into the unity of the community of the Church: the unity of the triune God manifested in the self-giving of Christ and poured out in the Holy Spirit. For this unity is nothing other than pure being-for-another. . . .

It is here that the biblical concept of fruitfulness is introduced. This supersedes (but without destroying their limited meaning) the concepts of works and rewards, which at first, as images taken from the world of human labor, presuppose a system of individuals distinct from one another in order to be able to stress the effective "being-for" of the "saint" (that is to say of the truly believing, hoping, loving man). . . .

There is perhaps no more comforting truth about the Church than that in it there is a community, a communism of saints. For, on the one hand, this means that there is a continually overflowing richness on which all the poor may draw; it is called the treasure of the Church. It is precisely the same as the incalculable fruitfulness of those who offer themselves and all they have to God to dispose of for the sake of the brotherhood.[42]

Conclusion

In the Catholic tradition the expressions *sancta ecclesia* and *communio sanctorum* have come to designate two aspects of the one mystery of the holiness of the Church. The first puts the accent on the aspect of person, and of how the "subsisting altruism" of the Trinity is shared in and manifested in the human dimension. The second places the accent on *what* is shared, namely the life of Christ as he shares himself in the Eucharist. One of the contributions of the encyclical *Veritatis Splendor* is, as we have seen, to set forth the rhythm between holiness received and holiness manifested. Let this text from the encyclical sum up this teaching in the context precisely of the Eucharist:

The lives of the saints, as a reflection of the goodness of God—the One who "alone is good"—constitute not only a genuine profession of faith and an incentive for sharing it with others, but also a glorification of God and his infinite holiness. The life of holiness thus brings to full expression and effectiveness the threefold and unitary *munus propheticum, sacerdotale et regale* which every Christian receives as a gift by being born again "of water and the Spirit" (Jn 3:5) in Baptism. His moral life has the value of a "spiritual worship" (Rom 12:1; cf. Phil 3:3), flowing from and nourished by that inexhaustible source of holiness and glorification of God which is found in the Sacraments, especially in the Eucharist: by sharing in the sacrifice of the Cross, the Christian partakes of Christ's self-giving love and is equipped and committed to live this same charity in all his thoughts and

---

[42] Hans Urs von Balthasar, *Elucidations,* trans. John Riches. (London: S.P.C.K., 1975), 58–59, 62.

deeds. In the moral life the Christian's royal service is also made evident and effective: with the help of grace, the more one obeys the new law of the Holy Spirit, the more one grows in the freedom to which he or she is called by the service of truth, charity and justice. (*Veritatis Splendor* §106)

9 The Paradox of the Beatitudes: Between Eschatology and History

THIS STUDY is an attempt to render more intelligible the teaching of Jesus encapsulated in the Beatitudes of Matthew and Luke. The first part of the study isolates the Beatitudes held in common by both Synoptics and then proceeds to contextualize them within the biblical tradition in order to describe and thus understand their meaning. The second part reflects theologically on their significance both in this world and in the world of fulfillment.

• • •

THE Beatitudes mark the frontier between history and eschatology. They accent the biblical vision of *peripateia* or "reversal." They are Jesus' description and promise of that reversal between what seems to be and what really is and will be, thus between what seems to be good in our blunted vision of reality and what is good now already and will be eternally: "Indeed, each of the Beatitudes promises, from a particular viewpoint, that very 'good' which opens man up to eternal life, and indeed is eternal life" (*Veritatis Splendor* §16). In this brief study I wish to reflect on the Beatitudes as expressing the Christian life in all its paradoxical practicality. After a few brief words on paradox, I will first consider the text of the four beatitudes held in common by Matthew and Luke. Then, will consider the theology of these beatitudes and conclude with some remarks on their paradoxical nature.

Henri de Lubac once wrote: "Paradox is the reverse of what, properly perceived, would be synthesis. . . . Paradox is the search or wait for synthesis."[1] The Greek word *paradoxos* can evoke the notion of something strange, wonderful, or

This article first appeared in *Anthropetes* 17 (2001):225–38.

[1] Henri de Lubac, *Paradoxes of Faith,* trans. Sadie Kreilkamp, Paul Simon, and Ernest Beaumont, 2nd ed. (San Francisco: Ignatius Press, 1987 reprint).

remarkable (*ex. gr.* Lk 5:26). One dictionary gives the following definitions: "A statement contrary to common belief. A statement that seems contradictory, unbelievable or absurd but that may actually be true in fact. Something inconsistent with common experience or having contradictory qualities."[2] To call the Beatitudes paradoxical is to say that they are strange and wonderful, that they seem unbelievable or absurd, even contradictory, but are actually true. They invite us to rise to a plane of life and understanding where we can experience their synthesis.

In this brief essay I will present the historical and literary evidence for the position that the four beatitudes common to Matthew and Luke represent a tradition common to them both, one that has its origins in Jesus himself. I will prescind from the question of how that common tradition reached them, that is, I will not enter into the discussion of hypothetical Q, its proposed variations in Q^{mt} and Q^{lk} and will content myself with the common core of material that can be studied both in its own right and within the canonical contexts of the two Gospels.[3] After this preliminary work, I will look at the vocabulary in the Beatitudes, its origins in Second Isaiah and elsewhere, and its meaning in the preaching of Jesus. Finally, I will consider this teaching in its paradoxical reality as it sustains and guides the Church through its pilgrimage to the place where the paradox is fulfilled without being destroyed.

Part One: The Text of the Beatitudes

The phrases that have merited the title "the Beatitudes" are found in two accounts of a discourse given by Jesus. In Matthew 5:1–12 they form the overture to a large tightly structured collection of Jesus' teaching which he is reported to have delivered after having ascended "the" mountain: thus, "The Sermon on the Mount." In Luke the beatitudes and woes are the opening phrases of a shorter discourse delivered by Jesus after choosing the apostles and coming down to a level place: thus "The Sermon on the Plain." The following schema presents the two texts in a linear synopsis. In this very literal translation the Matthean text is kept in upper case when it parallels Luke and is in smaller print when it is unique to itself. The Lucan text is in ordinary type for the parallels with Matthew and in smaller print when it is unique. The four beatitudes that are common to both Gospels are numbered.

The Beatitudes in Matthew 5:2–12 and Luke 6:20–26

1. **M.** Blessed the poor in spirit, for theirs is the kingdom of the heavens.
   L. Blessed the poor, for yours is the kingdom of God.

---

[2] *Webster's New Universal Unabridged Dictionary* (New York: Simon and Schuster, 1983).

[3] For a good assessment of the career of "Q" and other synoptic problems I refer the reader to David Laird Dungan, *A History of the Synoptic Problem. The Canon, the Text, the Composition, and the Interpretation of the Gospels*, The Anchor Bible Reference Library (New York: Doubleday, 1999).

2. **M.** Blessed those mourning, for they shall be consoled.
   L. Blessed those weeping now, for you will laugh.

   M. Blessed the meek, for they will inherit the land

3. **M.** Blessed those hungering and thirsting for righteousness
   L. Blessed those hungering now
   M. for they shall be satisfied.
   L. for you will be satisfied.

   M. Blessed the merciful, for they will find mercy
   M. Blessed the pure of heart, for they will see God
   M. Blessed the peacemakers, for they will be called sons
       of God
   M. Blessed those persecuted for the sake of righteousness,
       for theirs in the kingdom of heaven.

4. **M.** Blessed are you when they revile you
   L. Blessed are you when men hate you and exclude you
       and revile
   M. and persecute and speak all evil against you because of me.
   L. and cast out your name as evil because of the Son of Man.

   M. Rejoice and be glad because your reward is great in heaven
   L. Rejoice on that day and leap for joy for behold, your
       reward is great in heaven
   M. for thus did they persecute the prophets before you.
   L. for in the same way their fathers treated the prophets.

   L. But woe to you the rich, for you have received your
       consolation
   L. Woe to you who are filled now, for you will be hungry
   L. Woe to those laughing now, for you will mourn and weep
   L. Woe when all men speak well of you, for in the same way
       their fathers treated the false prophets.

Certain features of the above text meet the eye immediately. Both Matthew and Luke have material that is not in the other Gospel. In Luke, there are some verbal variations in the four beatitudes held in common, but the most notable difference is the presence of four "woes" corresponding to the four beatitudes. In Matthew, on the other hand, there are five beatitudes not found in Luke at this point. The best explanation for this is most probably that they are additions to a shorter text. Matthew or his predecessor added them based on the teaching of Jesus expressed in the form of beatitudes or in some other form. This can be seen for instance in the case of the beatitude concerning the "meek" *(praeis)*, the second part of whose wording is identical to LXX Psalm 36:11 ("The meek shall inherit the land"), while the adjective *praus* is found only three other times in the New Testament, twice in Matthew with regard to Jesus (Mt 11:29, 21:5) and in 1Peter 3:4. The actual word "merciful" *(eleēmōn)* occurs only in Matthew's beatitude and in Hebrews 2:17, but the notion, often connected with Jesus' teaching, is attested abundantly.[4] "Purity of heart" is an Old Testament ideal frequently expressed in the Psalms (LXX Ps 23:3–6,[5] 50:20, 72:1,13; see also Jer 24:7; Ez 36:25–27; Prov 22:11). It is found equivalently in Jesus' teaching about complete interior integrity, especially in Matthew (Mt 5:28, 15:18–20, 23:25–28). The ideal of "peacemaker," while having some Old Testament roots (Prov 10:10) reflects an early rabbinic ideal of one who actively risks in order to bring peace to a situation of conflict.[6] Finally, the term "persecution" in Matthew's eighth beatitude is present in the last common beatitude as well. Matthew probably added this beatitude and linked it to "justice" in order to conclude a second block of four beatitudes in a way that echoed the concluding phrase in the first block ("hunger and thirst for justice"). The promise of inheriting the kingdom of heaven then forms an inclusion with the first beatitude.

The additional material in Luke consists of the four "woes" as can be seen above. The interjection *ouai* is found 45 times in the New Testament where it signifies, particularly in the mouth of Jesus (29 times), an exclamation of grief over a lamentable situation. Nearly all commentators attribute the presence of these four statements to the activity of Luke or a predecessor in the line of the tradition that he inherited.

The Text of the Four Beatitudes Common to Matthew and Luke

In beatitude "1" above, there are three differences between Matthew and Luke: Matthew has "in spirit" as a qualifier to those called blessed; his address is in the third person as opposed to Luke's second person; and the kingdom is designated as "of the heavens" (Mt) or "of God" (Lk). The third of these differences

---

[4] See M. Dumais, "Sermon sur la Montagne," in *Dictionnaire de la Bible Supplément. Tome Douzième*, ed. Édouard Cothenet Jacques Briend (Paris: Letouzey & Ané, 1996). For a discussion of this matter, see pp. 808–9.

[5] This passage is probably the immediate background for the wording of Mt 5:8 since the psalm is responding to the question "who can ascend the mountain of the Lord?"—a formula quite close to the liturgical notion of "seeing God," while v. 6 speaks of those who are "seeking the face of the God of Jacob."

[6] For a treatment of this notion, see Jacques Dupont, *Les Béatitudes. Tome III, Les Évangélistes, vol. III, Études Bibliques* (Paris: Gabalda, 1973), 640–64. The promise that they will be called "sons of God" refers to the fact of their future adoption by God because they were willing to risk out of love in order to bring the good of peace to others. This is close to the theme of "paradox" or "reversal" characteristic of the beatitudes common to Matthew and Luke.

is stylistic and will characterize numbers "2" and "3," the second probably represents a reworking by Luke or his source while the first is an important theological modification on the part of Matthew that we will treat in Part Two. In number "2" above there are four differences: the address; those blessed are differently described (mourning/weeping), Luke adds "now," while the blessed will "laugh" in the future (Lk) or "be consoled" (Mt). In regard to number "3," we may note the same difference of address and the presence in Matthew of the words "and thirsting for righteousness" not found in Luke.

Number "4" above is first of all very different from the other three with their aphoristic style. This blessing is long and detailed and while both Evangelists agree to put the address in the second person, there are many differences in vocabulary between them. Given the fact that the Gospels are at the end of a line of oral and written transmission that has already developed different interpretative traditions in handing on the words and deeds of Jesus, it is not possible to reconstruct an "original" text.[7] We may however, be attentive to the stylistic characteristics of the Evangelists and return tentatively to an earlier stage of the transmission. While not sharing Jacques Dupont's optimism about the accuracy of his reconstruction or his confidence in "Q," we may offer the following as a valid approximation of what underlay the material available to Matthew and Luke when they came to compose their Gospels: "Blessed will you be when men hate you and exclude you and bring out an evil name against [="accuse"] you because of the Son of Man. Rejoice and be glad because your reward is great in heaven; for thus did they persecute the prophets before you."[8]

One final word about the two texts is in order before examining the paradoxical theology of the four common beatitudes. In the first three beatitudes (the poor, the mourning, the hungering), Matthew has retained more explicit allusions to the Septuagint wording of passages in Second Isaiah that promise consolation to those suffering in exile:[9]

> The Spirit of the Lord is upon me, for this reason he has anointed me. He
> has sent me to preach the good news to the poor *(ptōchois)* . . . to console
> all the mourning *(parakalesai pantas tous penthountes).* . . . You shall be

---

[7] For a good account of the influence of oral tradition, see Paul Achtemeier, "*Omne verbum sonat:* The New Testament and the Oral Environment of Late Western Antiquity," *Journal of Biblical Literature* 109 (1990): 3–27. The result of many years of historical work in the origin of the Gospels is well summed up in *Dei Verbum §19* and expressed again in the Catechism #126, which describes the three stages in the formation of the Gospels: "The life and teaching of Jesus," "the oral tradition," "the written Gospels."

[8] Jacques Dupont, *Les Béatitudes. Tome I. Le problème littéraire—Les deux versions de Sermon sur la montagne et les Béatitudes* (Louvain: Nauwelaerts, 1958).

[9] For a complete discussion of "the message of consolation" including the theme at Qumran, see Jacques Dupont, *Les Béatitudes. Tome II. La Bonne Nouvelle,* 2nd ed. (Paris: Gabalda, 1969), 92–99.

called priests of the Lord, ministers of God, you shall eat the wealth of the nations (Is 61:1–2,6).[10]

They will not hunger or thirst *(ou peinasousin oude dipsēsousin)* . . . but he who has mercy on them will console *(parakalesei)* them. (Is 49:10; see also 55:1–3, 65:13.)

Despite the fact that we cannot be sure of Jesus' exact words, it is most likely that he too alluded to Second Isaiah in pronouncing these beatitudes. The fourth beatitude, that concerning the persecuted, was probably uttered at another time, perhaps later in his ministry, when he began to prepare his disciples to be the successors to Israel's prophets.

Part Two: The Message of the Core Beatitudes

Blessed are the poor (in spirit), for theirs (yours) is the kingdom of heaven (God)

The three key words—"blessed," "poor," and "kingdom"—make of this beatitude "the first in order and as it were the parent and generation of the virtues."[11] We will dedicate the largest proportion of our consideration to this beatitude since the questions raised and answered here will apply to the other beatitudes, especially those concerning the mourning/weeping, and the hungry.

Blessed

A culture reveals much of itself in what it calls "blessed" or "happy." *Makarios* is a Greek word that reflects both its native context within ancient Greek and more recent Hellenistic culture, and its transposed context within Hellenistic Judaism whose own roots are in the religious tradition and sacred literature of Israel. As is the case with so many words in the New Testament we must attend carefully to the manner in which cultural insights and ideals of the Greek world have been subtly or overtly transformed within the biblical tradition that preceded the New Testament, and then transposed again in the light of the incarnation and the resurrection.

In the Greek tradition the words *makarios* and *olbios* are often synonymous and the earliest instances of them speak of the happiness of those who have been initiated into the divine mysteries and are thus prepared to join the gods after death.[12] The word became more common and more ordinary by the time

---

[10] Luke, as is well known, uses this passage in his programmatic scene in Lk 4:16–30.

[11] Ambrose *On Luke* 5,51 cited in Hans Dieter Betz, *The Sermon on the Mount*, ed. Harold W. Attridge et al., Helmut Koester, *Hermeneia* (Minneapolis: Fortress, 1995), 111, n.134.

[12] For a complete discussion of this point with copious examples, see Betz, ibid., 93–119. I fault Betz, however, for not appreciating the enormous change that takes place within a monotheistic and ethical culture in the consideration of what makes for blessedness or happiness.

of Aristotle, being employed less by poets than by philosophers as they praised the simple unencumbered life often in the form of an aphoristic phrase followed by a reason, a literary form probably inherited from Egypt. Thus, the poverty of Socrates is described and praised by Plato and Xenophon and the blessing of poverty is the subject of a prayer at the end of the *Phaedrus*.[13] It should be noted, however, that the blessedness of a poor life consists in the fact that the philosopher, like the gods, is without needs.

In the Septuagint nearly all the instances of *makarios* represent the root *'šr*, a term which appears late in Jewish literature and is most often found in the "philosophical" tradition of the wisdom literature.[14] Here too the influence of Egyptian literature is apparent both in form and in content yet, as with all wisdom borrowing from Egypt, what is seemingly a simple borrowing is really a "sublation" of the material into the context of the covenant.[15] To understand the real intent of the interjection *'ašre* we should realize that the accent is more on the notion of "congratulations" rather than that of "blessing." The felicitation can be directed in two ways. They are congratulated who have received some blessing from the Lord: "Blessed the man whose sin is forgiven" (Ps 32:1); "Blessed the people to whom such blessings fall! Blessed the people whose God is YHWH!" (Ps 144:15); "Blessed is he whose help is the God of Jacob" (Ps 146:5).

On the other hand, and these blessings constitute the majority of the sayings, congratulations are offered to those who pursue a course of action that is in keeping with the will of God since this constitutes both a present and future blessing: "Blessed is the man who does not walk in the counsel of the wicked . . . the way of the wicked will perish" (Ps 1:1,6); "Blessed is the man who fears the Lord always; but he who hardens his heart will fall into calamity" (Prov 28:14); "Blessed is he who considers the poor! The Lord delivers him in the day of trouble, the Lord protects him and keeps him alive; he is called blessed in the land; you do not give him up to the will of his enemies " (Ps 41:1–2; note the "reason" given for the blessedness as in the Gospel beatitudes). Finally, there are a number of beatitudes pronounced on those who trust in God: "Blessed are all who take refuge in him" (Ps 2:12); "Blessed are the men whose strength is in you, in whose heart are the highways to Zion. . . . O Lord of hosts, blessed is the man who trusts in you!" (Ps 84:6, 13); "He who gives heed to the word will prosper, and blessed is he who trusts in the Lord" (Prov 16:20).

---

[13] Texts in Betz, ibid., 116–17.

[14] For a study of this word, see Henri Cazelles, "ashrê," in *Theological Dictionary of the Old Testament* (Grand Rapids, MI: Eerdmans, 1974), 445–48.

[15] The process I am referring to is aptly portrayed in this description of sublation given by Bernard Lonergan: "What sublates goes beyond what is sublated, introduces something new and distinct, yet so far from interfering with the sublated or destroying it, on the contrary needs it, includes it, preserves all its proper features and properties, and carries them forward to a fuller realization within a richer context." Bernard Lonergan, *Method in Theology* (New York: Herder & Herder, 1972), 241.

The Poor

If we ask ourselves, who are the poor who are pronounced "blessed," we see that in a way, neither of the above Old Testament categories is adequate. The blessing is given to the poor as a grace, while at the same time, some action on the part of the poor is implied, since the fundamental allusion is to those poor who were suffering in the exile because of their fidelity to YHWH and to whom the anointed messenger is promised. Deep fidelity to God has sociological consequences especially in a situation of persecution and oppression.

We may see the same principle at work in regard to another class of people who are classified as those "who tremble at the word of YHWH." In the same Second Isaiah we read, Thus says the Lord: "Heaven is my throne and the earth is my footstool; what is the house which you would build for me, and what is the place of my rest? All these things my hand has made, and so all these things are mine, says the Lord. But this is the man to whom I will look, he that is humble and contrite in spirit, and trembles at my word" (Is 66:1–2; see 66:5). This oracle is addressed to those who wanted a temple to YHWH more as a statement of their own restoration rather than as a gesture of gratitude for return from the exile. They are reminded of those who, because of their unswerving fidelity to YHWH, are "humble and contrite in spirit" and not among the powerful and influential. We see this same group referred to in the Book of Ezra: "Then all who trembled at the words of the God of Israel, because of the faithlessness of the returned exiles, gathered round me while I sat appalled until the evening sacrifice" (Ezra 9:4; see also 10:3).[16]

In the same way, being poor is a sociological reality. Those who eschew the unjust exercise of power and who do not compromise the will of God are not likely to be among the rich and powerful. This is all the more true in times of persecution as can be seen in any modern country that makes life difficult for Christians. In proclaiming the poor blessed, Jesus at one and the same time made a messianic claim for himself—he is the anointed servant sent to the poor foretold in Isaiah 61—and he asserts that the underprivileged are now the privileged. Luke, by simply mentioning the "poor" accents the sociological condition of those so addressed, making no distinction between those whose lot is to be poor and those whose faith decisions have made them poor. God, in sending Jesus, has made a preferential option for the poor, but they are free to accept or reject his offer. Matthew places the accent on the internalizing of what makes the poor privileged, namely a broken heart. The expression "poor in spirit" *('anwê ruah)* is found twice at Qumran, though in both cases the text is isolated by lacunae.[17]

---

16 " 'All who trembled at the words of the God of Israel' is shown to be by 10:3, Isa 66:2 and 5 to be a stereotyped expression in the post-exilic community for strict observers of the law." H. G. M. Williamson, *Ezra, Nehemiah,* ed. John D. W. Watts David Hubbard, vol. 16, Word Biblical Commentary (Waco: Word Books, 1985), 133.

17 The first text is in the Hymn Scroll (1 QH 14.3), and the second is in the War Scroll (1 QM 14.7).

Ulrich Luz sees in these texts, especially the second, a combination of nuances, "despairing, without help" and "humble."[18] In any case, just as Luke implies some openness on the part of the poor to receive the blessing, so Matthew does not so internalize physical poverty as to ignore the fact that humility and being without resources can exercise a mutual and sociological causality.

The Kingdom of Heaven/God

Just as "poor" contains within itself the notions of "mourning" and "hungry," so too does "the kingdom of God" contain within itself all the other promises.[19] Without a doubt the proclamation of the breaking into history of the Kingdom and Reign of God, its presence and its future consummation is the very core of Jesus' preaching as it is recorded for us in the Synoptics.

> As announced by Jesus, the reign of God is not an awareness of God's sovereign power over the universe or of God's kingship over Israel, long established and still enduring, though both these concepts are presupposed. It is the announcement of God's kingship in its full realization, fully active, eschatologically irrevocable.[20]

God has begun, in the preaching, life, death, and resurrection of his Son, Jesus Christ, to inaugurate his kingdom. This kingdom is the realm where all that God ever promised his people is transcendentally fulfilled. The poor are those who know the truth of the kingdom in "icon," that is, they experience the kingdom but in a mode of existence not proper to the kingdom itself. Just as the Eucharist is the heavenly banquet of the kingdom present in icon, so the limitations and suffering of the poor who receive the kingdom are the sacrament of its power and the promise of its fulfillment. Blessedness, congratulations, are pronounced by Jesus upon those who perpetuate the interior and exterior state of the poor, mourning, and hungry exiles who awaited the good news to be proclaimed by the messenger, "Your God has begun to reign!" (Is 52:7). They are now blessed because the one anointed to bring good news to the poor is here, present, still in our midst, and it has not yet appeared what they shall be.

Blessed those mourning (weeping now), for they shall be consoled/you will laugh.

As we have seen, the consolation of the mourners is already part of the mission of the servant to come. In this sense the beatitude simply transposes into another

---

18 Ulrich Luz, *Matthew 1–7. A Commentary*, trans. Wilhem C. Linss (Minneapolis: Augsburg, 1989), 233.

19 That for Matthew the expression "the kingdom of the heavens" is a circumlocution for and the equivalent of "the kingdom of God" can be seen in Mt 19:23–24 where the two expressions are in parallel. See also Mt 13:28; 21:31, 43.

20 Rudolf Schnackenburg, *God's Rule and Kingdom*, trans. John Murray (Freiburg: Herder, 1963), 82.

key the message of the first beatitude and proclaims once again the fulfillment of that prophecy. Luke, who retains the term "mourn" in his woes, changes it here to accent once again that the weeping now will be turned into laughter then. Just as, at the initial fulfillment of the prophecy of restoration from exile, "Our mouth was filled with laughter, and our tongue with rejoicing" (Ps 126:2), so at the eschatological fulfillment of the promise there will be laughter and song. This is a striking expression of the paradox of Jesus' proclamation.

Why do the blessed ones mourn? It is already stated in the Isaiah text that the servant will bring to those who are experiencing the reality of sin in their solidarity with a sinful people now suffering from the unjust oppression of others, "a diadem in place of ashes, oil of gladness in place of mourning" (Is 61:3). Mourning is the reaction to sin, our sin, which is a part of the sin of the world. Just as Jesus mourned over Jerusalem, in mysterious solidarity with his sinful people, just as Jeremiah, identified with God, expresses his desire that "my head were a spring of water, my eyes a fountain of tears, that I might weep day and night over the slain of the daughter of my people" (Jer 8:23), so too those in the kingdom still mourn for the state in which they find themselves as part of God's people.[21] But they already know consolation and are sure of what awaits them when God will wipe away every tear from their eyes (Rev 7:17).

Blessed those hungering (now) (and thirsting for righteousness), for they (you) will be satisfied.

If a just man is hungry, his very hunger pains are the sacrament of his desire for justice, and if a man hungers and thirsts for the justice of God, he will know physical hunger in solidarity with his brother. For a hungry man experiences in his body the inequities and sin of the world, and a man who desires that the justice of God be realized in this world, must finally feel in himself the deprivation caused by injustice.[22] Once again we see Luke accenting the sociological reality and Matthew interiorizing it without "evaporating" it.

It is legitimate to ask what the nature of the *dikaiosunē* for which the blessed ones long. The early Church understood it to be a striving for rectitude or righteousness, while the Reformers took it to mean a desire for *justitia imputata*. Ulrich Luz comes down firmly in favor of the early understanding and excludes any attempt to see both an "active" and a "passive" relation to *dikaiosunē*.[23]

---

[21] For a profound study of the notion of "mourning" in Christian spirituality, see Irénée Hausherr, *Penthos. The Doctrine of Compunction in the Christian East,* trans. Anselm Hufstader, Cistercian Studies, 53 (Kalamazoo, MI: Cistercian Publications, 1982).

[22] For an eloquent treatise on hunger and justice, see Paulo Freire, *Pedagogy of the Oppressed,* trans. Myra Bergman Ramos (New York: Herder & Herder, 1970).

[23] Ulrich Luz, *Matthew 1–7. A Commentary,* trans. Wilhem C. Linss (Minneapolis: Augsburg, 1989), 237. This is also the opinion of W. D. Davies and Dale C. Allison, *The*

Righteousness, however, particularly in the Matthean understanding, includes giving food to the hungry, drink to the thirsty, welcome to the stranger, clothing to the naked, companionship to the sick and imprisoned. Those who do not do this "will go off to eternal punishment, but *the righteous* to eternal life" (Mt 25:46). Surely then, human striving for justice or righteousness means that, by human God-enabled activity, the order willed by God takes on a historical and human dimension. It is interesting in this regard to observe that, while in Greece prophetic figures appealed to God to secure justice for the poor and hungry, in Israel it is God himself who is pleading on their behalf.[24]

Blessed are you when they (men hate you and exclude) revile you. . . .
Rejoice (on that day) and be glad (leap for joy) for (behold) your reward
is great in heaven. For thus did they persecute (their fathers treated)
the prophets (before you).

It is probable, as I have stated above, that this felicitation was pronounced by Jesus toward the end of his life. It was included along with those that drew on Isaiah 61 because this beatitude has in common with the preceding three the theme of future manifestation of the whole of the paradox: "[H]e has exalted the lowly, the hungry he has filled with good things" (Lk 1:52–53). By this very fact the three former beatitudes take on an added note. They are not only a declaration of the blessed state of the poor, mourning, and hungry, they are a description of what is expected of disciples and what they can expect. It is probably for this reason that this beatitude is echoed in other places in the New Testament.[25] They are, to respond to Robert Guelich's question, both entrance requirements and eschatological blessings; they describe the paradox that is the inevitable consequence of discipleship.[26] Having said this, we should proceed to discuss the paradoxical nature of these beatitudes.

Gospel According to Saint Matthew, Volume 1, International Critical Commentary (Edinburgh: T&T Clark, 1988). 327.

[24] For a development of this theme, see André Neher, *L'Essence du Prophétisme,* ed. Jean Huppolite, *Épiméthée. Essais philosophiques* (Paris: Presses Universitaires de France, 1955).

[25] "But if you do suffer because of righteousness, (you are) blessed" (1 Pet 3:14); "If you are reviled for the name of Christ, blessed are you, for the Spirit of glory and of God rests upon you" (1 Pet 4:14). Note the two-part aphorism, with an explanation preceded by *oti.* "Blessed is the man who perseveres in trial, for when he has been proven he will receive the crown of life that he promised to those who love him" (Jas 1:2). Again note the aphoristic style and the explanation.

[26] Robert A. Guelich, "The Matthean Beatitudes: 'Entrance Requirements' or Eschatological Blessings?," *Journal of Biblical Literature* 95 (1976): 415–34.

Part Three: The Paradox

Jesus of Nazareth is the living revelation of the paradox, both as history and as eschatology. He was poor, he mourned, he was hungry and persecuted. He is in the kingdom, in fact he is the kingdom, and he is consoled, satisfied, and rejoicing. We may trace out here two levels of the paradox. There is the paradox of reversal, and, mysteriously, there is the paradox of abiding. The first begins now and continues in the fulfilled kingdom, the second is only apparent in fulfillment.

In the essay referred to above, de Lubac goes on to say: "Paradoxes: the word specifies, above all, then, things themselves, not the way of saying them."[27] The paradox we are speaking about here is a change of state, it pertains to "things themselves," and it is due to the same "law of reversal" we find in the Old Testament, in places such as Psalm 107:33–43, the Song of Hannah (1 Sam 2:1–10), and so on. However, now the reversal is foreseen, not for some future "day" when God will change history as we know it, but at a moment when, literally, there will be a new heaven and a new earth. In brief, the reversal is now seen in the light of the resurrection of Jesus and the hope that means for all who are joined to him. Thus, the full meaning of "kingdom," "consoled," "be satisfied" cannot be known except by extrapolating from the icon experience available even now and by gazing on Jesus.

Then there is the level of abiding paradox. At one level the resurrection of Jesus and that awaited by all believers only increases the paradox because, along with the reversal of state there is the perdurance of the former state. The "poor" are still "poor," just as Jesus is still the Lamb who was slain but is now "standing in the midst of the throne and the four living creatures and the elders" (Rev 5:6). The poor are still poor in spirit: This can be seen, for instance, in the case of Mary, the Mother of God. Having lived her life on the border between history and eschatology she illustrates perfectly that human history is not obliterated by the reversal but revealed for what it is: Transformation is not absorption. In regard to human life, an existence in time: What is, always is, but its true nature is only revealed at the eschaton. The angel asked John if he could say who those were who were standing in white robes around the throne of God. He could not, so the angel replied:

> These are they who have come out of the great tribulation; they have washed their robes and made them white in the blood of the Lamb. Therefore are they before the throne of God, and serve him day and night within his temple; and he who sits upon the throne will shelter them with his presence. They shall hunger no more, neither thirst any more; the sun shall not strike them, nor any scorching heat. For the Lamb in the midst of the throne will be their shepherd, and he will guide them to springs of living water; and God will wipe away every tear from their eyes. (Rev 7:14–17)

---

[27] Lubac, *Paradoxes of Faith,* 10.

The paradox is this: Something of time perdures in eternity, yet it is changed. What perdures is a participation in Christ. Whatever of time shares in Christ becomes eternal, while whatever does not share in Christ is, literally, wasted time. In that sense many poor people will be as surprised to hear the invitation to the kingdom, as will be those who fed and clothed and visited them.

We see now that the reason, therefore, that the core beatitudes are in a broader context in the present Gospel text. This broader context either laments the outcome of those who are not poor, sad, hungry or persecuted (Luke), or shows the wider dimension of what makes a heart genuinely poor: single heartedness, mercy, peacemaking, meekness (Matthew). We who have heard these words are not destined to be surprised on that day. We are rather meant to recognize, in its paradoxical perdurance, the poverty, hunger, mourning, and persecution that have been reversed but not destroyed. This is the heart of Jesus' words of congratulation to those who share his life on earth. Yes, the Father "will make all things new," not by starting again but by raising to new life. He promises, "To the thirsty, I will give a gift from the spring of life-giving water." There is a thirst that perdures and even a poverty and a mourning, but these are now the basis for a satisfaction that paradoxically means "there will be no more death or mourning or weeping or pain" (see Rev 21:4–7).

10 The New Feminism: Biblical Foundations and Some Lines of Development

THE FIRST TWO parts of this study are biblical in nature. They are descriptive theology in that they interpret the texts of Genesis and Ephesians with the help of the historical disciplines thus establishing what realities are being mediated by the text and, particularly in the case of Ephesians, comparing this with similar material in the surrounding environment. The final section of the essay makes use of philosophical and theological insights in order to render the realities mediated by the biblical text more intelligible.

• • •

THE term "new feminism" is well enough known not to need explanation.[1] It can be said that it represents a definitive shift from a consideration of women's rights to reflection on the very nature of woman herself. Only from this second vantage point will it be possible to articulate the new humanism required

---

A previous version of this chapter originally appeared in a volume edited by Michele Schumacher. Fr. Francis Martin, "The New Feminism: Biblical Foundations and Some Lines of Development," in *Women in Christ: Toward a New Feminism*, ed. Michele M. Schumacher, (Grand Rapids, MI: Eerdmans Publishing Co., 2003), 141–68. My thanks to the publisher for allowing me to include the work here.

[1] The expression "New Feminism" has achieved notoriety because of the use made of it by Pope John Paul II in his recent writings. The most salient papal text in this regard is found in *Evangelium Vitae* §99: "In transforming culture so that it supports life, women occupy a place, in thought and action, which is unique and decisive. It depends on them to promote a 'new feminism' which rejects the temptation of imitating models of 'male domination,' in order to acknowledge and affirm the true genius of women in every aspect of the life of society, and overcome all discrimination, violence and exploitation." For other expressions of this notion in the writings of John Paul II, see the whole of the paragraph cited; also *Mulieris Dignitatem*, §4, 5, 18, 20, and 30; *Letter to Women* §9; *Laborem Exercens* §19.4; also Paul VI, *Vatican II, Closing Speech,* December 7–8, 1965.

by this change of perspective. By integrating what is true in the efforts of the rights-oriented feminism into the question, "Who is a Woman?," we will arrive at a genuine development of doctrine in the area of Christian anthropology.[2]

Basing ourselves on the reflections of John Paul II regarding the various states of human existence, and expanding them for our purposes here, we can say that humanity knows three fundamental states: that of innocence, or pre-history; that of sinfulness or history as we know it; and that of transformation, when all that is truly human is transformed by the immediate self-gift of the Trinity offered to every human being, and even to material creation itself. The second state itself must be considered in two different historical realizations: the time before Christ when the spark of hope was kept alive in and through Israel, and that after Christ, the state of restored humanity or recapitulation. This last named state is an anticipated realization of the state of transformation, which will be the healing of our present condition of "diminished existence" in and through the sublation of the state of innocence effected by the Cross of Christ.[3]

In studying biblical anthropology, therefore, we must look at the basic teaching on the nature of man as this is presented in the first two chapters of Genesis, and the account of the diminished existence that is ours as a result of sin. But we must also listen to the description of a humanity in the state of recapitulation if we are to understand the reality of man and woman. This study will thus have three parts. Part One will consider the teaching of Genesis, humanity as created by God and its present diminished existence. Part Two will reflect on humanity, man and woman, in the state of restored existence, and this is presented in Ephesians 5:21–33. Part Three will offer some brief philosophical considerations on the new feminism based on the two previous parts.

Part One: Basic Teaching on Man and Woman As Found in Genesis 1–3

It is interesting to observe how often the early chapters of Genesis are invoked in discussions of marriage, man, and woman. The anti-divorce stance of Malachi

---

[2] This study relies upon an earlier work and develops it in several directions. Portions of that earlier work are used here with the permission of the editor. See Francis Martin, "The New Feminism: A New Humanism?" *Josephinum Journal of Theology* 8 (1; 2000): 5–26.

[3] A customary Christian view that divides history into the periods of Israel, the Church, Heaven is summed up in this phrase of St. Ambrose: *"Primum igitur umbra praecessit, secuta est imago, erit veritas. Umbra in lege, imago vero in evangelio, veritas in caelestibus."* On Psalm 43 (*Corpus Scriptorum Ecclesiasticorum Latinorum,* 64, 204). The division I am referring to here is also found and forms one of the basic structures of Karol (John Paul II) Wojtyla, *The Theology of the Body: Human Love in the Divine Plan,* trans. L'Osservatore Romano (Boston: Pauline Books and Media, 1997).

2:11–13 is grounded in this material as is the position of the Qumran covenanters.[4] Jesus himself cites Genesis 1:27 and 2:24 in the debate with the Pharisees on divorce (Mt 19:4–5; Mk 10:6–7). While Paul has recourse to these chapters when discussing some aspects of woman–man relating (1 Cor 11:2–16, 6:12–20), the Letter to the Ephesians uncovers unsuspected depths in Genesis 2:24. It is well-known that Pope John Paul II has dedicated many lines to a consideration of Genesis 1–3.

It is customary to look upon the Book of Genesis as an edited composite made up of an initial text that considers the order and structure of creation and that is joined by way of a preface to a more historical and poetic account. The tradition represented in the first chapter is also represented at key points by the editor, usually considered to belong to the "Priestly" school of thought as he works with written material from another tradition, usually called "Yahwistic."[5] We will begin with the first of these traditions.

The Image of God

There are five passages in the Old Testament that use the term "image" when describing man and his relationship to God. Three are found in the early chapters of Genesis and the other two (Sir 17:3 and Wis 2:23) clearly depend upon the Genesis teaching. I will give here a literal translation of the three Genesis texts, leaving the words *'ādām* and Elohim without a translation.

> And Elohim said: "Let us make *'ādām* in our image, as our likeness, that they may rule over the fish of the sea, and the birds of the heavens, and the tame beasts, and all the earth, and all the creeping things creeping on the earth." And Elohim created the *'ādām* in his image: in the image of Elohim he created him, male and female he created them. (Gen 1:26–27)

The next text is found after the Yahwist account of creation, the sin of the first couple and the murder of Abel. It introduces the second *toledot* or generation

---

[4] For a discussion of this material, see Francis Martin, "Marriage in the New Testament Period," in *Christian Marriage: A Historical Study*, ed. Glenn Olsen (New York: Crossroad Publishing Company, 2001), 50–100. See also Joseph A. Fitzmyer, "The Matthean Divorce Texts and Some New Palestinian Evidence," *Theological Studies* 37 (2; 1976): 197–226.

[5] The designations "Priestly, Yahwistic," and so on, while they are no longer used to refer to separate written traditions joined somewhat mechanically by an editor, are still useful to describe different blocks of material that were edited in their present form sometime in the postexilic period. For a discussion of these issues as they relate to our problem and for more extensive literature, see Francis Martin, "Male and Female He Created Them: A Summary of the Teaching of Genesis Chapter One," *Communio* 20 (1993): 240–65.

section.[6] By once again insisting on the fact that *'ādām* is still the image of God despite all the sin introduced into history, the redactor is making his point that sin cannot completely efface the primary resemblance and relation that *'ādām* has to God.

> This is the list of the generations of *'ādām*: On the day when Elohim created *'ādām* he made him in the image of Elohim; male and female he created them, and he blessed them and called their name *'ādām* on the day they were created. And *'ādām* lived one hundred and thirty years and he begot in his likeness, as his image, and he called his name Seth. (Gen 5:1–3)

The last of the texts that speaks of the image of God follows upon the account of the flood, that ultimate punishment for the universal corruption of mankind. Once again, even after this disaster brought on by human sin, the image quality remains and is the source of the dignity of *'ādām*, still the object of God's special care:

> He who sheds the blood of the *'ādām* by *'ādām* his blood will be shed. For in the image of Elohim he made the *'ādām*. But you, be fruitful, be many, swarm on the earth and be many (or rule) on it. (Gen 9:6–7)

There are two points that emerge from these texts. The first is that only *'ādām* is the image of God, and the second is that *'ādām* is male and female. We will look briefly at these points since they form the basis of the search to articulate the genius of woman.[7]

Paramount in the ancient Near East is the notion that the image makes present the power of what is imaged. This is the reason all images of YHWH are forbidden to Israel: YHWH will be present and reveal himself and his power according to his own good will and pleasure; to try to manipulate this is an

---

6 For a discussion of these ten divisions of the Book of Genesis, see Gordon J. Wenham, *Genesis 1–15,* ed. David A. Hubbard and Glenn W. Barker, Word Biblical Commentary 1 (Waco: Word Books, 1987), xxii.

7 I am summing up here work I developed more at length in "Male and Female He Created Them: A Summary of the Teaching of Genesis Chapter One," *Communio* 20 (1993): 240–65. For more information, see Gordon Wenham, *Genesis 1–15,* and Claude Westermann, *Genesis,* vol. I/1, *Bibl. Kommentar Altes Testament (BKAT)* (Neukirchen-Vluyn: 1974), 147–55, where there are sizeable bibliographies. The most complete survey of recent thinking is found in the balanced study of Gunnlaugur A. Jønsson, *The Image of God: Genesis 1:26–28 in a Century of Old Testament Research,* Coniectanea Biblica, Old Testament Series 26 (Stockholm: Almquist & Wiksell International, 1988). See also Phyllis Bird, "Male and Female He Created Them: Gen 1:27b in the Context of the Account of Creation," *Harvard Theological Review* 74 (1981): 129–59.

abomination.[8] On the contrary, for the pagan world, the multiplication of images of the gods was an exercise of piety. In the same way, a king could multiply his presence and authority, it was thought, by setting up images of himself. The presence of both terms "image" and "likeness" on the statue of a king, set up to assert his authority over a region,[9] confirms the suggestion frequently made that the basic notion mediated by the declaration of the divine intention in Genesis 1:26 is that 'ādām is to be God's vice regent, the embodiment of his authority here on earth.

Against this background it is most likely that the expression of God's intention in the Priestly tradition asserts that 'ādām is the royal representative of God himself, embodying and exercising God's own authority in regard to the earth and all that lives on it. This certainly is the line of thought developed by Psalm 8, which continues the royal terminology in its meditation upon Genesis 1: "You have crowned him with glory and honor, you have made him rule over the works of your hands, you have put everything under his feet" (Ps 8:6–7).[10] However, while the notion of royal representative correctly locates the basic category of thought, or the basic semantic shape of the term, it does not exhaust all the implications of the statement of God's purpose as the Priestly author intends it.

In addition to the fact that Elohim must make 'ādām capable of ruling,[11] he also addresses him directly. The presence of the Sabbath at the end of the Priestly text points to still another facet of 'ādām: his vocation to worship while the mention of God's special care in protecting the blood of 'ādām (Gen 9:6) also points to a unique dignity. In trying to elaborate a biblical understanding of man as the image of God, we must take all three texts into account. The useful survey by Gunnlaugur Jønsson[12] enables us to categorize opinion along a spectrum of five points.[13] At one extreme we find the opinion of Ludwig Köhler (1880–1956) and others who maintain that the image of God is to be found in the fact that

---

[8] This is the original significance of the commandment, "You shall not make an image (pesel) for yourself . . ." (Ex 20:4; Dt 5:8). For an excellent discussion of the denial of images of YHWH to Israel, see Gerhard von Rad, *Old Testament Theology*, vol. 1, trans. D. M. G. Stalker (New York: Harper and Brothers, 1962), 212–19.

[9] A. R. Millard and P. Bordreuil, "A Statue from Syria with Assyrian and Aramaic Inscriptions," *Biblical Archeologist* 45 (1982), 135–41.

[10] For a study of this psalm, see Luis Alonso Schökel, *Treinta Salmos: Poesía y Oración, Estudios de Antiguo Testamento* 2 (Madrid: Ediciones Cristiandad, 1981), 63–78.

[11] By reading the verb form as an indirect volition, the phrase is saying: "Let us make 'ādām . . . that they might rule. . . ." That is, "Let us make them capable of representing us ("in our image") so that they may rule." Had the author wished to express the notion that being the image of God consisted totally in having rule, he could have used another grammatical form (a "converted perfect"): "and then they will rule. . . ." We will return to this point.

[12] Jønsson, *The Image of God*.

[13] Ibid., 155.

humans have an upright bodily posture and can gaze at what is above.[14] At the other extreme we have the venerable position of Philo and most of the Church Fathers and theologians that the image of God is to be found exclusively in the spiritual dimension of a human being. This seems to be the understanding of Sirach 17:3 and Wisdom 2:23, the only other places in the Old Testament where the term "image" occurs in relation to man. While this position rightly grounds the reality of image in the God-given capacity to represent God and relate to him, it tends to ignore the physical dimensions of humanity and, in the Christian tradition, seeks to restrict resemblance to the Trinity in the structure of the human soul and its faculties.[15] We will return to this in discussing the manner in which human beings, as persons, are both constituted relationally and must freely enact relationship.

Coming in from these extremes, we find two opinions that seek to express the reality of image in terms that sum up the position in Genesis 1:26–28 and the other Genesis texts. The first of these is what I have been calling "royal representative" and what Jønsson calls the "functional interpretation." With the notable exceptions of Claus Westermann and James Barr, this opinion, with differing nuances, is held by nearly all Old Testament scholars.[16] The second opinion, whose most strenuous proponent was Karl Barth, and which is sustained by Westermann and others, is that the image of God is to be found in the divinely conferred capacity to relate to God.[17] It is possible to integrate these latter two by considering what in humankind makes it apt to be God's representative and how the other image statements develop the relational dimension of image while retaining the basic semantic field of *ṣelem* (image). We will return to this.

Male and Female

By using the Hebrew terms *zākār* and *nĕqēbah*, which accent the physical characteristics of male and female, the author of Genesis 1 is telling us two things: First, that physicality enters into the imaging of God (bodily, therefore historical, existence is the sphere in which God is imaged, that is made present); and, second, that this is accomplished by *ʾādām* as male and female. This is particularly clear if we pay close attention to the wording of the first two texts given above: "And Elohim created the *ʾādām* in his image: in the image of Elohim he created him, male and female he created them" (Gen 1:26–27); and, "On the

---

[14] Jønsson, *The Image of God,* 107–12.

[15] For a good study of the importance of this theology, see Jaroslav Pelikan, "Imago Dei. An Explication of *Summa Theologiae,* Part I Question 93," *Calgary Aquinas Studies,* ed. Anthony Parel (Toronto: Pontifical Institute of Mediaeval Studies, 1978), 27–48.

[16] See the summary of opinions in Jønsson, *The Image of God,* 219–25.

[17] For an account of this opinion and its relation to the "point of contact" dispute with E. Brunner, see Jønsson, *The Image of God,* 65–76.

day when Elohim created *'ādām* he made him in the image of Elohim; male and female he created them, and he blessed them and called their name *'ādām* on the day they were created" (Gen 5:1–2).

The key to understanding these texts lies in an appreciation of what is conveyed in the term *'ādām.* Of the 47 instances of the word *'ādām* in the book of Genesis, 46 occur in the "world history" found in the first eleven chapters of Genesis and even there they are concentrated around the decisive events of world history: creation, sin, the flood, and the tower of Babel.[18] In the first three chapters, where humanity is considered in its constitution and its state of diminished existence, *'ādām* covers a semantic field that includes "humanity," "humankind," and an individual person most often referred to as "the man," though the word is beginning to take on the characteristics of a personal name (Gen 4:25). None of the above English equivalents mediate exactly what the Hebrew term conveys. In the translation of the two principal texts above we can see an oscillation between the singular: "he created him, male and female he created them" (Gen 1:26–27); "he made him in the image of Elohim; male and female he created them . . . blessed them . . . called their name *'ādām* . . . they were created" (Gen 5:1–2).[19] This oscillation and the insistence that male and female are made in the image of God and *together* receive the name *'ādām* forces us to say that the sacred text is teaching that *'ādām* as the image of God exists as male and female. That is, male and female are different realizations of the one reality of image as royal representative capable of being addressed by God, and of imitating and worshipping him. Furthermore, part of this image reality is realized in obedience to the command: "Be fruitful, be many, fill the earth and subjugate it." This contradicts, as we shall see, the notion that gender is irrelevant in considering the essence of human nature. The traditional understanding of a human being as the image of God accents his resemblance to the Word of God Incarnate and/or his spiritual endowments has actually been deepened and opened from within itself from the modern sensitivity to the fact that *'ādām* as male and female shows us the constitutively relational nature of the human person.

One Flesh: Chapters Two and Three of Genesis

The teaching on man and woman in the second and third chapters of Genesis may, for our purposes here, be gathered around three points. First, the relation between God and *'ādām*; second, the relation between man and woman; and third, the damaged state of those relations in our present diminished existence.

---

[18] For a complete study of this term, see Claus Westermann, "Adam," in *Theological Lexicon of the Old Testament 1,* ed. Ernst Jenni and Claus Westermann (Peabody, MA: Hendrickson, 1997), 31–42.

[19] This second text is framed by two uses of *'ādām*, which refer to an individual, though viewed as joined to his posterity. See the study by Jean de Fraine, *Adam and the Family of Man,* trans. Daniel Raible, CPPS (New York: Alba House, 1965).

God and Adam

After the "structural" presentation of creation in Genesis 1, we are immediately placed in the historical perspective of Genesis 2 and 3 with the remark in Genesis 2:5 that the reason there was as yet neither green plant nor field shrub is because "YHWH God had not sent any rain on the earth and there was no 'ādām to cultivate the soil ('ādāmâ)" Culture depends upon both divine and human activity. Then "YHWH God fashioned the 'ādām with dust from the soil ('ādāmâ) and breathed into his nostrils the breath of life and the 'ādām became a soul alive." This text states three things. First, that man is formed directly by God; second, that he is a mysterious unity of matter and breath; and third, that in common with other creatures he is a "soul alive" and yet achieves this status in a unique way: being endowed with the very breath of God.[20] Thus, the more humanistic tradition with which we are dealing here, rather than have recourse to the abstract notion of "image," portrays 'ādām as endowed with the vital quality of God, his breath.

But there is more. The 'ādām who is taken by YHWH Elohim and settled in the garden, as Israel was taken and settled in the land, is given a command, a sort of covenant. He is invited to a higher level of relation with God: that of trust and obedience. That is, he is offered a covenant, a command from God through which he may express his response to all that God has done for him and can move from a self-contained existence to one that is more profoundly relational.

A Helper Matching Him

Despite the fact that he can somehow share the life of God and relate to him in personal trust, YHWH God sees that 'ādām's being alone is "not good." (A daring statement considering the use of the word "good" in the previous account.) It is at this point that God deliberates with himself, "let me make," and describes the object of his intention as being "a helper matching him." Grammatically the words do not reveal the gender of this "helper" but they evoke the notion that

---

[20] Note that being a "soul alive" is not what distinguishes 'ādām from the rest of creation; the same is said in 2:19 of all the animals named by the man, and is used in Genesis 9:9; 1:20, 21, 24 of various living things. What makes the man unique is that he has been given life-breath directly by God; there is something of God in him. There are places in the Book of Job that reflect the same notion of being formed from earth and possessing the spirit/breath of God. Thus Elihu says to Job: "For the spirit (rûah) of God has made me, the breath of the Almighty (nišmat šadday) gives me life. . . . Behold I am like yourself with respect to God, I too, have been pinched from clay" (Job 33:4, 6; see also 34:14–15). In the same vein, the Book of Wisdom describes the miserable lot of the potter who makes clay gods: "His heart is ashes, his hope meaner than dirt, and his life more ignoble than clay, because he knew not the one who fashioned him and infused him with an active soul and breathed into him a vital spirit" (Wis 15:10–11). The translation is taken from David Winston, *The Wisdom of Solomon,* Anchor Bible 43 (New York: Doubleday, 1979), 285.

the helper (the word is most often used of God as helper)[21] is destined to over-come the solitude of *'ādām* by "matching" him. YHWH God has a mysterious "sleep" come upon *'ādām* as upon Abraham at the moment of the covenant-promise (Gen 15:12) and taking a rib, extracts from *'ādām* something hidden within him, as it were, and builds it up "into a woman." Then, like the friend of the bridegroom he leads her to *'ādām*.[22] For the first time *'ādām* speaks:

> This one, at last
> is bone from my bone and flesh from my flesh;
> this one shall be called woman,
> for from man was
> this one taken.

The helper is someone who matches *'ādām* but is not a replica. She is woman *(iššâ)* because she is taken from, yet differs from, man *(îš)*. Communion is between likes who are yet unlike. In naming her, *'ādām* himself assumes a new name: Her presence "matching him" is a revelation of who both of them are in relationship. The poetic and theological genius who articulates this deep reality in regard to humanity sees its paradigmatic realization in the marriage relation-ship, which he portrays in terms of a covenant. The words "bone" and "flesh" allude to the conditions presupposed or effected by a covenant proposed in these terms. To cite but one example: When the tribes of Israel approach David at Hebron to ask him to accept the kingship, they describe themselves as "your bone and your flesh" (2 Sam 5:1; see also 19:13). It is precisely because of this unique covenant that "a man leaves his father and his mother and cleaves to his wife and they become one flesh." The degree of alienation from our own physi-cality that we modern westerners experience makes it almost impossible to understand the "one flesh" relationship spoken of here. By marrying, a man assumes as his primary relationship that which he has to his wife with whom he makes one new family (one of the meanings of "flesh" in Hebrew). In that covenant relationship—sealed, fostered, and deepened through spiritual, psy-chic, emotional, and physical intercourse—the two human beings create a third

---

[21] Nineteen of the twenty-one instances of the noun refer to divine help. See Jean-Louis Ska, " 'Je vais lui fair un allié qui soit son homologue' (Gen 2,18). A propos du terme *'ezer*-'aide,' " *Biblica* 65 (1984): 233–38. Marie de Merode, " 'Une aide qui lui corre-sponde.' L'exégèse de Gen 2,18–24 dans les récits de l'Ancien Testament, du judaïsme et du Nouveau Testament," *Revue Théologique de Louvain* 8 (1977): 329–52.

[22] Rabbi Abin, commenting on this verse, said: "Happy the citizen for whom the king acts as the bridegroom's friend," *Genesis Rabbah*, 18,3. The question of whether to translate the phrase here as "to *'ādām*" or "to the *'ādām*" involves a discussion of whether one con-siders the massoretic interpreters to be treating the word as a proper or common noun. I will treat some of the theological implications of this question later. For the philological aspect, see Cassuto, *A Commentary*, 166–67.

reality: a communion of persons that has as its fruit new human life.[23] The expression of this free and unveiled communication is found in the concluding line of Genesis, chapter 2: "They were both naked, the man and his wife, and they felt no shame with one another."

Diminished Existence

The disobedience of '*ādām* ("Is it that you have eaten of the tree which *I* told *you* not to eat?") brings in its train the two most primal effects of sin: shame—they knew they were naked; and fear—they heard his voice and hid (Gen 3:7–8, 11). Then, in the only instance in the Bible in which God himself directly adjudicates punishment, the serpent, the woman, and the man are addressed. The serpent is cursed and, in a mysterious passage, victory is promised to the seed of *the woman*.[24] The woman is promised "labor" in bringing forth children—her glory becomes also her pain—and then the new conditions of the relationship between herself and the man are described: "Your urge will be towards your husband and he will dominate you." The two sides of this now warped and adversarial relationship are described in terms of domination and connivance in domination. In the man/woman relationship (the paradigm of all human relating) we are shown the depth of the wound inflicted by sin. The lie of power and the lie of helplessness feed off each other and have produced such a situation that even two millennia of Christianity have made little more than a beginning in unmasking and overcoming the bondage brought by sin into the history of human relating.

Not only is the relation man/woman, husband/wife, paradigmatic of all human relating, but its degree of integrity or disintegration affects all of human life and human society. This is true not only because the relation of parents to each other has a preponderant effect on the humanity of their children, but also because the interior poise or lack of it that derives from this fundamental relationship of man and woman has its repercussions in all of a person's ability to realize the goal of human life in reciprocal relations of generosity and receptivity. The wound caused in us by the disruption of our relation to God has resulted, as Genesis teaches, in shame, fear, and death. These three produce an adversarial relation between man and woman who cannot be human without each other, but who strive for self-realization and self-protection by domination on the part of the man and by the woman's self-denying acceptance of this in her willingness to trade freedom for security. The following text from *Mulieris Dignitatem* §10 expresses the effects, particularly upon the woman, of this disruption:

---

[23] For a more complete discussion of this issue, see N. P. Bratsiotis, "Basar," in *Theological Dictionary of the Old Testament II*, ed. G. J. Botterweck and Helmer Ringgren (Grand Rapids, MI: Eerdmans, 1975) and the discussion later in this article.

[24] This is one of six texts in the Old Testament which attribute seed to a woman: Gen 3:15, 4:25, 16:10, 24:60; Lev 22:13; Isa 54:3. Additional texts which merit attention are Num 5:28; 1 Sam 2:20; Ruth 4:12; Gen 19:32, 34, 38:9.

Therefore when we read in the biblical description the words addressed to the woman: "Your desire shall be for your husband, and he shall rule over you" (Gen 3:16), we discover a break and a constant threat precisely in regard to this "unity of the two" which corresponds to the dignity of the image and likeness of God in both of them. But this threat is more serious for the woman, since domination takes the place of "being a sincere gift" and therefore living "for" the other: "he shall rule over you." This "domination" indicates the disturbance and loss of the stability of that fundamental equality which the man and the woman possess in the "unity of the two": and this is especially to the disadvantage of the woman, whereas only the equality resulting from their dignity as persons can give to their mutual relationship the character of an authentic "communio personarum." While the violation of this equality, which is both a gift and a right deriving from God the Creator, involves an element to the disadvantage of the woman, at the same time it also diminishes the true dignity of the man.

The man is not cursed, but through him the universe ("the ground") is cursed and becomes recalcitrant. The man's efforts to implement the commission given to him by God now become "labor." And finally, there is death—the place where there is no praise of God. Death means being cut off from shared life. Having been formed from dust and endowed with the very breath of God, 'ādām must now live under the weight of an illusory need to dominate and with the threat of being cut off from Life, passing his days in futility.

Much more could be said in regard to the depth of the rupture that has taken place in human relations. The daily tale of the Kosovos, the Northern Irelands, the suicide bombings, the enforced sterilizations, the battered women, and homeless men all confirm it. Specifically in regard to man/woman relations, we should consider the ways in which woman has been particularly victimized in the relation of domination and dominated. There is, however, a wounding of the man in this twisted relationship that has not been sufficiently appreciated. By forcing a sort of alienation to exist between himself and woman, man has returned to a state, not of productive solitude, but of frustrated fear and loneliness: "It is not good for man to be alone." By seeking to extort what can only be given freely, man condemns himself to the counterfeit of the only thing that can give meaning to his life. In the struggle for existence in this world, the man exerts a kind of dominative power not only in regard to the material universe but also in his relations. This too leads to frustration since, as John Paul II often says, joining two principles: "A human being, whether male or female, is a person, and therefore, 'the only creature on earth which God willed for its own sake'; and at the same time this unique and unrepeatable creature 'cannot fully find himself except through a sincere gift of self.' "[25]

---

[25] *Mulieris Dignitatem*, §10, citing *Gaudium et Spes*, §24.

In this sense, fatherhood, in the full sense of the term is more difficult to achieve than motherhood because it involves an imitation of God the Father that can only take place through identification with Jesus. To quote "Adam," the character in Karol Wojtyla's play, *The Radiation of Fatherhood*: "After a long time I came to understand that you do not want me to be a father unless I become a child. That is why your Son came into the world. He is entirely Yours."[26] The inability to surrender and thus become a source of life is the deepest wound in the man, and that is why, though the woman is the more oppressed, the man is often weaker.[27] The very tangible and human fact of the disruption of human relating is the measure of the power of the redemption brought to humanity by Jesus Christ.

Part Two: The Letter to the Ephesians

Though there are many other texts that could be studied in order to arrive at a more complete Old Testament anthropology, it is generally agreed that the most complete expression of that anthropology is to be found in the first three chapters of Genesis, which we have just considered. It is significant to realize how unique this anthropology is in its historical milieu. In the contiguous material that has come down to us there is no comparable understanding of *'ādām* as male and female, or the importance of that relationship.[28] As Gerhard von Rad expresses it:

> The two presentations [J and P] are alike in that they have as their chief end, though doing it in different ways, the creation of man, that is, mankind as male and female—with the result that the rest of the world is ordered round them as the chief work of Jahweh in Creation. . . . The world and its fullness do not find their unity and inner coherence in a cosmological first principle such as the Ionian natural philosophers tried to discover, but in the completely personal will of Jahweh their creator.[29]

In a similar way the passage found in Ephesians 5:21–33 is unique in its theological stance and, in its development of the Genesis material, represents a high point in New Testament anthropology. We will consider that text now in some detail.

---

[26] Karol Wojtyla, "The Radiation of Fatherhood," in *The Collected Plays and Writings on Theatre* (Berkeley: University of California Press, 1987), 335–64, at 339.

[27] See Walter Ong, *Fighting For Life* (Amherst: University of Massachussetts Press, 1981).

[28] I say this in spite of the evidence adduced by B. Batto who does point out that marriage, or at least sexuality, is important in the Atrahasis myth. See Bernard F. Batto, "The Institution of Marriage in Genesis and in *Atrahasis*," *Catholic Biblical Quarterly* 62 (4; 2000): 621–31.

[29] Gerhard von Rad, *Old Testament Theology*, trans. D. M. G. Stalker, vol. 1, *The Theology of Israel's Historical Traditions* (New York: Harper & Brothers, 1962), 141.

A Domestic Code?

It has become a commonplace that Ephesians 5:21–6:9 is one of a number of early Christian texts, both biblical and extra-biblical, that can be classified as a particular variation of a well-known Hellenistic *topos* variously labeled "on household management," "domestic code," or "on household order." The problem with this approach is its assumption that every discussion of this topic that employs these categories must also share the philosophical presuppositions of its predecessors. This would mean that the appearance in the New Testament literature of households represents a "loss of nerve," a capitulation from an initial egalitarianism to the patriarchialism of the pagan world around it.[30] It is alleged that the early Christians began to speak this way for one of two reasons: either to avoid persecution, since groups allowing too much freedom to women (by not accepting the traditional household) were often considered subversive by the Roman officials, or as a reaction against those fellow Christians who mistakenly opposed the intrinsic patriarchal bias of traditional society. The history of this classification and the differing appeals to one or another background as explicative of the early domestic codes are well enough known. A clear account of recent thinking on this topic is provided by David Balch, though, as will become apparent, I do not agree with his account of the origin or nature of the material usually isolated in the New Testament and early Christian literature and labeled "domestic code" or something similar.[31]

First of all, the term *topos* is not really defined, but a description can be gleaned from the way in which the various commentators use it. The Domestic Code *topos* is a literary form that presented itself to the mind of the ancient pagan authors whenever they discussed life in a household. Most often structured according to the Aristotelian threefold pair model,[32] it embodies the basic presuppositions of antiquity regarding the locus of authority in the male head of the house. The New Testament Domestic Codes are just one instance of the ancient *topos*; they share with the world around them the same literary conventions and presuppositions as the other treatises on household living.

---

[30] Dunn's response to this view is expressed by the remark: "The emergence of a structured teaching regarding the threefold relationships of a typical household should therefore occasion no surprise or require any special or unexpected stimulus; it was simply bound to happen." Dunn, "Household Rules," 56.

[31] David Balch, "Household Codes," in *Greco-Roman Literature and the New Testament: Selected Forms and Genres*, ed. David E. Aune (Atlanta: Scholars Press, 1988). The following texts are usually given as "household order" texts: 1 Pet 2:17–3:9; Col 3:18–4:1l; Eph 5:21–6:9; 1 Tim 2:8–15; 6:1–10; Tit 2:1–10; Didache 4:9–11; Letter of Barnabas 19:5–7; 1 Clement 21:6–9; Polycarp to the Philippians 4:2–6:3.

[32] That is, husband/wife, master/slave, father/children.

This account of *topos* presents two problems. First, the term *topos* is misapplied. It is confusing at best, and misleading at worst.[33] For Aristotle and his contemporaries, "the *topoi* were devices enabling the speaker to find those arguments that would be most persuasive in a given situation."[34] Though this understanding may have been expanded somewhat by ancient writers, there was never a *topos* in regard to Domestic Codes, certainly not in the sense of a literary form with a specific vocabulary and structure that imposed itself whenever the topic was discussed.[35] Second, the varied nature of the extant texts, reflected in the early Christian literature and the New Testament itself, belies such an identification.[36] Most texts in this latter category do not even possess the threefold pair structure considered by David Balch and others to be a hallmark of *topoi*. L. Hartman has shown the weakness of such a classification method, and is followed in this by James D. G. Dunn.[37] References to the components of a household do not imply the existence of a Domestic Code *topos* whose structure imposes itself on successive texts. To describe the whole, it is necessary to discuss parts: In describing a household, an author would certainly allude to its components. Aristotle, with his usual practical acumen, simply identified the components of the household; no author could avoid discussing them altogether.

The countervailing argument, that the New Testament texts have not been subjected to a Domestic Code *topos*, is persuasive. First, New Testament authors were free to discuss the topic and to avail themselves of relevant material in the popular philosophy without accepting either the literary form or the philosophical presuppositions of some its proponents. It is important to observe that the address to husbands and wives (Eph 5:21–33) contains not one significant

---

[33] For a discussion of the ineptitude of the term, see John C. Brunt, "More on the Topos as a Literary Form," *Journal of Biblical Literature* 104 (1985): 495–500. For a complete criticism of the deficiencies of the mode of argument used by modern proponents of the view I have just described, see L. Hartman, "Some Unorthodox Thoughts on the 'Household-Code Form,'" in *The Social World of Formative Christianity and Judaism: Essays in Tribute to Howard Clark Kee*, ed. Jacob Neusner, Peder Borgen, et al. (Philadelphia: Fortress, 1988), 219–32.

[34] Edward P. J. Corbett, "The Topoi Revisited," in *Rhetoric and Praxis*, ed. Jean Dietz Moss (Washington: CUA Press, 1986), 43–57, at 45.

[35] I say this despite the apparent use of the term to denote a discussion of household living in the Stoic author Bryson. See David Balch, *Let Wives Be Submissive: The Domestic Code in 1 Peter*, ed. James Crenshaw, Society of Biblical Literature Monograph Series 26 (Chico, CA: Scholars Press, 1981), 56.

[36] James D. G. Dunn gives a schematic presentation of the threefold pair structure as it is present in the early Christian texts usually designated as Household Order Texts in "The Household Rules in the New Testament," *The Family in Theological Perspective,* ed. Stephen Barton (Edinburgh: T&T Clark,1996), 44–46.

[37] In the article and texts cited above.

word, except "husband" and "wife" in common with the Hellenistic discussions of household management.[38] There is not a word about the man's natural superiority and greater ability to make decisions, nor is there here any mention of the wife obeying her husband, a constant refrain in such literature. In fact, with the exception of the description of Sarah who "obeyed Abraham, calling him lord" (1 Pet 3:6), the term "obey" is never used of wives in regard to their husbands in the whole of the New Testament. This is more than a coincidence as a study of the word that is used exclusively in the New Testament to describe the wife's relationship to her husband can establish.

Second, the attribution of a fall from pristine egalitarianism to pagan patriarchialism employs an historical heuristic structure that forces certain key New Testament texts, which argue for a very different model of Christian origins, to be ignored.[39] Third, and most important, such a structure falsely presupposes that subsequent discussions are dependent upon, and must adopt the world view of, the earlier ones. This same mistake was made in a more drastic manner by the early proponents of a "divine man" concept existing in the surrounding culture and then taken over by Jewish and then Christian propagandists.[40] This mode of thought composes a complex concept on the basis of scattered evidence and then retrojects the reconstructed concept back onto any text that happens to include any of the "features" of the concept thus reconstructed. Such an understanding also ignores the "sublating" process effected by many New Testament texts when using pre-existing material, and the analogical thinking that inspires this process. One may apply here the notion of "sublation" mentioned frequently in these pages. We may conclude this part of the discussion concerning the possible influences upon the author of the text we are considering, particularly Ephesians 5:21–33, by citing the judgment of Rudolf Schnackenburg:

> In his [the author's] enrichment of the existent exhortation for husband and wife in their marriage by the ecclesiastical motif, and his inclusion of Christian spouses in the relationship between Christ and the Church, he has created an instruction on Christian marriage which, in spite of possible

---

[38] This is even true of the word *agapan*, which occurs sometimes as advice to the wife but, not, as far as I can tell, in connection with the husband. For examples of the verb used to describe the attitude of wives, see David Balch, "Neopythagorean Moralists and the New Testament Household Codes," in *Aufstieg und Niedergang der römischen Welt. Teil II, Band 26*, ed. H. Temporini and W. Haase (Berlin and New York: de Gruyter, 1982–88), 397–98.

[39] I have discussed this more at length in *The Feminist Question*, chap. 3, "Christian Origins and the Roles of Women."

[40] See the discussion in Aage Pilgaard, "The Hellenistic *Theios Aner*—A Model for Early Christian Christology?" in *The New Testament and Hellenistic Judaism*, ed. Peder Borgen and Søren Giversen (Peabody, MA: Hendrickson, 1997).

external influences, must be regarded as his own work and consequently must first be declared to be such and appreciated as such.[41]

A Brief Commentary on Ephesians 5:21–33

For the convenience of the reader I will present a literal translation of the verses as they are discussed. Not every aspect of this rich passage will be treated here. Rather, I will restrict my remarks to those aspects that can elucidate our concern here with a Christian anthropology.

Verse 21

Subordinating yourselves to one another in the fear of Christ;

Verse 21 acts as a sort of "hinge" verse, concluding a list of five participles with imperatival force that make more precise what it means to be "filled with the Spirit" (Eph 5:18), pointing out aspects of community life in the Spirit.[42] This last recommendation then leads to a particular aspect of community life, namely life in a Christian family. It calls for mutual self-subordination in the fear of Christ. Since both of the key terms will figure largely in the rest of the passage, and because they are part of a very specific anthropology, we will discuss them briefly.

The participle, *ypotassomenoi,* is a middle form of the verb *ypotassein,* and has the notion of "to subordinate oneself." It is found in four of the six New Testament passages that contain domestic codes.[43] Even within the New Testament the middle form of the verb has a rather large range of meanings, but they can be reduced to a general sense of voluntary self-subordination to the divine order whether this be that of the providential order of the state (Rom 13:1–10; 1 Pet 2:13–17), that of the human institution of slavery (1 Pet 2:18–20; Tit 2:9), that of young people to their elders (1 Pet 5:5), the community to its leaders (1 Cor 16:16), and perhaps that of women to the established order in the community (1 Cor 11:3[?], 14:34[?]). It is also used of Jesus' relation to his parents (Lk 2:51) and of this self-subordination to the Father after the last enemy (death) has been destroyed (1 Cor 15:28).

---

[41] *Ephesians: A Commentary,* trans. Helen Heron (Edinburgh: T&T Clark, 1991), 244.

[42] Ephesians 5:21 as found in the context of the preceding verses: "And do not get drunk with wine—that is dissolute—rather be filled with (the) Spirit, *addressing* one another with spiritual psalms and hymns and songs; *singing* and *praising* with your heart to the Lord; *giving thanks* always in the name of our Lord Jesus Christ to our God and Father; *subordinating* yourselves to one another in the fear of Christ" (Eph 5:18–21).

[43] It is found in Eph 5:21, 24; Col 3:18; Tit 2:5; 1 Pet 3:1. The other two texts alleged as domestic codes, 1 Tim 2:8–15 and 6:1–10, do not contain any specific verbs describing the relation between husbands and wives and, in any case, are not "codes" in any usual sense of the term.

Given the fact that *ypotassesthai* is, with the one exception of *phobêtai* in Ephesians 5:33, the only verb used in the New Testament exhortations to wives, and that this verb, with two exceptions,[44] is *never* found in extant Graeco-Roman and Hellenistic-Jewish literature that discusses wife/husband relationship, we are entitled to see in the New Testament usage evidence of a conscious Christian choice to find a suitable word and fill it with a content proper to Christian marriage. Such a procedure is found in regard to other words such as *agapē, ekklēsia, kerygma, synedēsis,* and many others.

In fact, all of Christian theological predication can be judged as true or false only by taking the words in their total context, in the sentence, and even more broadly, in the context of the New Testament. Thus for instance, the statement, "Christ is alive now," is true when the transposed or analogical meaning of the word "alive" is understood. But this can only be achieved in the light of faith.[45] The exhortation to mutual self-subordination, of which the wife's self-subordination to her husband is a particular instance, is part of a much larger Christian teaching on the role of humility and love in all relationships.[46] Mutual relationships are so described, among other places, in Philippians 2:1–4:

> So if there is any encouragement in Christ, any incentive of love, any participation in the Spirit, any affection and sympathy, complete my joy by being of the same mind, having the same love, being in full accord and of one mind. Do nothing from selfishness or conceit, but in humility count others better than yourselves. Let each of you look not only to his own interests, but also to the interests of others.

Jesus' teaching regarding those who have responsibility in the community is equally important in this regard. Again there are many texts of which the following is an example.

> And Jesus called them to him and said to them, "You know that those who are supposed to rule over the Gentiles lord it over them, and their great men exercise authority over them. But it shall not be so among you; but whoever would be great among you must be your servant, and whoever would be first among you must be slave of all. For the Son of man

---

[44] These are Plutarch, *Moralia,* 142E, and Ps-Callisthenes, *Life of Alexander the Great* I, 22, 4. (Alexander tells his mother who has been offended by Philip: "It is fitting [*trepon*] for a wife to subordinate herself to her husband.")

[45] I owe this remark to Msgr. Robert Sokolowski, in a private communication.

[46] "The findings as a whole suggest that the term *ypotassesthai* played a general catechetical-type role in primitive Christian exhortation." Gerhard Delling, "Tassō, and so on," in *Theological Dictionary of the New Testament VIII,* ed. Gerhard Kittel and Gerhard Friedrich (Grand Rapids, MI: Eerdmans, 1972), 45.

also came not to be served but to serve, and to give his life as a ransom for many." (Mk 10:42–45)

In the light of the overall context, commentators define the meaning of *ypotassomenoi* here and in similar New Testament passages as "a voluntary attitude of giving in, of cooperating, assuming responsibility and carrying a burden."[47] And note that, "The implication is that *the one 'subjecting himself' does so through an act of his sovereign will and that he could equally elect to have done otherwise.*"[48] It should be noted once again that verse 21 with its call to *mutual* self-subordination sets the tone for the rest of the exhortation to follow.

The second phrase that merits some attention is "the fear of Christ." This is echoed in the last line of this section (v. 33) to form an inclusion: "as for the wife, let her fear her husband." The notion is that our mutual subordination and our communion with each other are supernatural realities effected by the death of Christ. Just as "fear of the Lord" is the beginning and perfection of wisdom—the very soul of the reverence, obedience, trust, and awe within a covenant relation with God—so is "fear of Christ" the specification of all these faith attitudes now directed to Christ who has become the source of the new covenant. It is noteworthy that a similar use of the term "fear" occurs in the First Letter of Peter, where as Leonhard Goppelt points out, the term refers to an attitude of reverence before God in the living out of human relations, "in responsibility before God and in view of God's judgment."[49] The final exhortation to wives that they "fear" their husbands must be seen in the same light and reflects a similar combination of affection and responsibility before God as can already be found in Leviticus 19:3, "Let a man fear his mother and father" (note the word order).[50]

---

[47] Markus Barth, *Ephesians 4–6, Anchor Bible* 34A (New York: Doubleday, 1974), 710.

[48] J. W. Bowman, "The Gospel and the Christian Family: An Exposition of Ephesians 5:22 to 6:9," *Interpretation* 1 (1947): 436–49.

[49] Leonhard Goppelt, *A Commentary on 1 Peter*, ed. Ferdinand Hahn, trans. John E. Alsup (Grand Rapids, MI: Eerdmans, 1993), 244. "Likewise, women subordinate yourselves to your husbands so that, even if some are disobedient to the word, through the behaviour of their wives, without a word, they may be won over, as they see your pure behaviour (conducted) in fear" (1 Pet 3:1–2). "Do not be afraid of them and do not be troubled, rather, sanctify the Lord in your hearts, ready at all times to give account to anyone who asks you to answer for the hope that is in you. (Do this) however, with gentleness and fear as those who have a good conscience, so that in regard to that for which you are slandered they will be shamed-those who discredit your good manner of life in Christ. For it is better that—if God so wills it—you suffer as those who conduct themselves rightly and not as those who do evil" (1 Pet 3:14–17). See also 1 Peter 1:17; 2:18.

[50] The Old Testament background sets the context here for the meaning of the term "fear" both in 1 Peter and Ephesians and elsewhere in the New Testament (*ex. gr.* Phil 2:12). The fact that the term is occasionally found in some neo-pythagorean texts, which lack the monotheistic orientation toward God, does not mean that the meaning is the same,

Verses 22–23

22a   *wives to your husbands*
22b   *as to the Lord*
23a   *because a husband is head of his wife*
23b   *just as Christ is Head of the Church:*
23c   *he is the savior of the Body.*

With these verses, the advice to the community is applied to the household. There seems to be a subtle softening even of the Christian use of *ypotassesthai* in v. 22a since the verb is not repeated from v. 21. This also serves to indicate that what is being said here is part of the mutual self-subordination of v. 21. The self-subordination of wives to their husbands is given its proper context with the phrase "as to the Lord" (v. 22b). It will require the rest of the context to give us a more exact understanding of the full meaning of these words, but the general sense is clear. The foundation of the woman's attitude is found in her faith: Her acts of love and self-giving are such that they look to the Lord and terminate in him.[51]

The description of the husband as the "head" of his wife in v. 23a is contextualized by giving the relation between Christ and the Church ("just as"/*ôs kai*) as the exemplar of the husband/wife relationship. That is, the headship of the husband participates in the headship of Christ precisely under this aspect: Christ is "the savior of the Body." The significance of this phrase will be apparent in the consideration of verse 25. The fact that the term "head" is applied to the husband and not to the wife, and that the verb "to subordinate oneself" is applied to the wife and not to the husband leads to the legitimate question as to whether there does not still linger in this text a remnant of the Hellenistic notion of the superiority of the man. I will touch on this in Part III, but it might be remarked here that there is an equal possibility that we moderns, after more than two centuries of cultivating dominative power, may perhaps read into this text our own lingering pagan notion that human relations are determined by the structures of domination and coercion.

Verse 24

24a   *But just as the Church subordinates itself to Christ,*
24b   *so, too, wives to their husbands in everything.*

---

pace David Balch, "Neopythagorean Moralists and the New Testament Household Codes" in *Aufstieg und Niedergang der römischen Welt,* 397.

[51] Note, for instance, how slaves are urged to serve with an attitude of faith, knowing the one they are serving and who it is who will reward them. They are told to obey "as to Christ . . . serving with your inner intention with good will as to the Lord, not to men . . ." (Eph 6:5–8; see also Col 3:23). The point of convergence in using the expression in regard to wives is not that they are the same as slaves, but that their faith vision of their very different place in the Church and in their marriage is equally governed by the reality and accessibility of Christ.

With the exception of v. 33c, these are the last words addressed to the wives. The remaining seventy-five percent of the text is addressed to husbands. Just as Christ's self-giving act of love ("he is the savior of the Body") is held up as the way in which the husband is to be "head" of his wife, so now the loving self-subordination of the Church to Christ is held up to the wife as the exemplar of her relation to her husband "as to the Lord." We should note that once again that the verb *ypotassesthai* is not present in the second part of the sentence, with the result that the noun "wife" is never the direct subject of this verb in the whole passage. Just as the first omission places the wife's self-subordination within the context of the life of the eschatological community, so this omission serves to place her relation to her husband within the context of the Church's relation to Christ, which thus serves as model and source of her relation to her husband. Thus, the expression "in everything" *(en panti)* is not a juridical norm but is measured by the confidence the husband inspires in her by the quality of his love. Thus the relation is not command/obedience, but generosity/receptivity. The rest of the passage seeks to portray the extent of the generosity to which the husband is *obliged* (see v. 28a below).

Verse 25

> 25a *Husbands, love your wives*
> 25b *just as Christ loved the Church*
> 25c *and gave himself over for her*

Just as *ypotassesthai* characterizes the attitude of the wife in most of the exhortations to Christian households (Col 3:18; 1 Pet 3:1; 1 Tim 2:11; Tit 2:4), so *agapan* explicitly (Col 3:19) or equivalently (1 Pet 3:7; Tit 2:6) describes the virtue most needed in the husband. The Ephesians passage, however, goes much further in making explicit what is left implicit in the other texts, namely that this verb must be given its full Christian significance and be a genuine share in the love that God has shown to us in Christ. The specifically Christian love enjoined upon the husband is expressed not only in the characteristic verb *agapan*, but also in the analogical appeal to the act of Christ expressed in the rhythm "loved . . . gave himself over," which takes up the fundamental principal of Christian activity in Ephesians 5:2 (echoing Galatians 2:20) in which Paul tells us that he lives now by faith in the Son of God: "who loved me and gave himself over for me." The term *paradidonai*, "give/hand over," had become by this time a means of evoking the whole passion process.[52] The husband, therefore, is called to love his wife in the power of the act of love in which Christ died

---

[52] See for instance Romans 4:23–25: "It was not written for his sake alone that it was reckoned to him, but also for our sake to whom it is going to be [also] reckoned, we who believe in him who raised Jesus our Lord from the dead, who was handed over for our transgressions and raised for our justification."

and lives forever. The Ephesian text thus initiates a genuine *imitatio Christi* whose basic principle is one of participation in the present reality and activity of Christ.[53] This principle, that *agapan* always involves some share in the cross of Christ, is the source of that restoration, that recapitulation, by which we are enabled to complete our understanding of a revealed anthropology.

Verses 26–27

26a   *that he might make her holy,*
26b   *purifying her in the washing of water,*
26c   *with a word,*
27a   *that he might present to himself*
27b   *the Church resplendent,*
27c   *not having spot or wrinkle or anything of the sort,*
27d   *but that she be holy and without fault.*

Having mentioned Christ's self-giving act on the cross, which the husband is called to imitate, the author lists three reasons for Christ's action *(ina)*; these follow one another as consequences. Strictly speaking, what follows is not part of the analogy, nor part of the anthropological teaching, but a theology of the passion of Christ viewed in the light of its effects.

In mentioning the first of Christ's motives for his act of love, the author chooses to return to a theme already present in the opening hymn (Eph 1:14), namely baptism, but he does so here by investing baptism with the characteristics of the bride's prenuptial bath, a custom known in Judaism and in many ancient cultures.[54] Along with allusions to this practice the author seems to have combined the scene in Ezekiel 16:8–14 in which YHWH returns to the girl child he had previously rescued at her birth. The second goal of Christ's act on the cross is to obtain a beautiful bride, continuing the allusion to Ezekiel 16:8–14. Here, as in Ezekiel, there is no "go between" or "best man," rather Christ presents his bride to himself. The Church has been made holy, consecrated completely to Christ, and purified by the sacramental imparting of that act on the cross by which he created a body, a spouse for himself. Christ's third goal is to ensure that the consecrated, purified, and beautiful bride be "holy and without blemish" *(agia kai amômos)*, thus realizing the Father's plan as already described in the opening hymn: "that we be holy and without blemish in his sight, in love" (Eph 1:4; see Col 1:22).

These lines, which mediate a sense of Jesus Christ's immense love and powerful affection for the Church, are difficult to translate. They show us, in a way similar to the opening hymn, the roots in eternity of the plan by which he gave

---

[53] I have discussed this New Testament notion in "Historical Criticism and New Testament Teaching on the Imitation of Christ," *Anthropotes* 6 (1990): 261–87.

[54] For the literature, see Barth, *Ephesians* 2, 693, n. 340.

us redemption in his blood, and continue by outlining the past act of Christ, his present activity on behalf of the Church, and the ultimate goal of that activity, when there will be a "new Jerusalem, coming down from heaven from God, prepared as a bride adorned for her husband . . . gleaming with the splendor of God" (See Rev 21:2–11). While, therefore, there is no direct relationship between what Christ, the Savior of the Body, has done for his bride and what the husband can do for his wife, there is a comparison offered by showing us what the *agapē* of Christ is really like. This prepares us for the next admonition to the husband, which in turn prepares us to understand the multiple ways in which the author sees Christ and the Church as "one flesh."

Verses 28–30

> 28a *Even so husbands are obliged to love their own wives*
> 28b *as their own bodies.*
> 28c *He who loves his own wife loves himself.*
> 29a *No one ever hated his own flesh;*
> 29b *rather, he provides and cares for it*
> 29c *just as Christ [does] for the Church,*
> 30   *because we are members of his Body.*

A new dimension of the instruction, linking it with the previous presentation of Christ's love ("even so"), begins with the first and only mention of obligation in the whole passage: Husbands are "obliged" *(opheilousin)* to love their own wives as their own bodies. This obligation is rooted in God's love for us manifested in Christ, as 1 John 4:11 expresses it: "Beloved, if God so loved us, we ought *(opheilomen)* to love one another." Also 1 John 3:16: "In this we have come to know love: he laid down his life for us. And we ought *(opheilomen)* to lay down our lives for the brothers." And the same foundation is found in the command in Ephesians 5:1–2, which always lies in the background of this discussion: "Be, then, imitators of God, as beloved children, and walk in love just as Christ loved us, and gave himself over for us, an offering and sacrifice to God unto a fragrant odor." Another way of expressing the debt or obligation incumbent on all Christians is found in Romans 13:8: "Owe *[opheilete]* nothing to anyone, except to love one another; for the one who loves has fulfilled the law [i.e., has more than satisfied all his obligations]."

We may ask why the norm for this love of husband for wife is given not only as that of the love of Christ for the Church, but is also presented as "love for their own *[eautôn]* bodies." I believe that behind these lines stands an Old Testament anthropology that looked upon unity between human beings as grounded on the fact that they share "flesh" *(basar)*. The concept moved in concentric circles. Humanity as a whole can be called "all flesh," and this outer circle becomes progressively denser until the immediate family is considered to be sharing the same flesh. Thus, the laws against incest in Leviticus 18 begin with the enigmatic phrase (literally): "No one shall approach any flesh of his body/flesh *(basar)* to uncover nakedness [i.e., have sexual relations]. I am YHWH." This is further specified by specific instances of what "flesh of his body/flesh" may mean. For example, "You shall not uncover the nakedness of your father, that is, the nakedness of your mother; she is your mother, you shall not uncover her nakedness" (18:6). "You shall not uncover the nakedness of the wife of your father, she is your father's nakedness" (18:7). "You shall not uncover the nakedness of your mother's sister because she is your mother's flesh" (18:13). It is clear from this that there are degrees of what we would call consanguinity, which the Hebrews considered as "con-fleshness." The source of this is marriage. That is why when a man marries a woman they become "one flesh." From their total union there arises a "new flesh" and those born to them are one flesh with them and with each other. In this sense a man's wife is his flesh: Their commitment has given rise to a new entity. The notion that a wife is the "flesh" of her husband is found in the first century *Life of Adam and Eve,* 3: In response to Eve's plea that Adam kill her in order to placate God, Adam says, "How is it possible that I should let loose my hand against my flesh?"[55] We also read in Sirach 25:26: "If she [an erring wife] walks not by your side, cut her away from your flesh with a bill of divorce."[56] In addition, members of the same family are described as being "flesh" of each other. Judah dissuaded his brothers from killing Joseph "for he is our flesh," and Isaiah 58:7, after urging kindness in general to those in need adds, "and do not turn you back on your own flesh."

A development of this notion is found in the phrase (literally) "bone of my bone and flesh of my flesh" and similar expressions, which, as we have seen, indicate the familial bonds, either very close or at least among Israelites, which form the basis for a covenant.[57] Both expressions—"one flesh" and "bone of my bones and flesh of my flesh"—occur in Genesis 2:23–24, texts alluded to in the Ephesians passage we are considering. When we add to this the fact that there is no current word for "body" in Hebrew, we realize that the substitution in Greek of the word *sôma* (body) where *sarx* (flesh) might be expected would occasion no surprise. Paul, in fact, when he loosely cites Genesis 2:24 in 1 Corinthians 6:16 speaks of "one body": "Do you not know that anyone who joins himself to a prostitute becomes one body [with her]? For it says, 'the two will become one flesh.'"

---

[55] James H. Charlesworth, ed., *The Old Testament Pseudepigrapha, Volume 2* (New York: Doubleday, 1985), 258.

[56] For this verse, see Patrick W. Skehan and Alexlander A. Di Lella, *The Wisdom of Ben Sira, Anchor Bible* 39 (New York: Doubleday, 1987) in loc.

[57] For a complete treatment of this point, see Maurice Gilbert, " 'Une Seule Chair' (Gen 2, 24)," *Nouvelle Revue Théologique* 100 (1978): 66–89.

The lines in the passage that we are studying now are based on just this type of thinking and reflect, I think, the fundamental source of Paul's description of the Church as the Body of Christ. All our author has done here is render more explicit the equation Body/Flesh = Bride that Paul had already exploited in 2 Corinthians 11:2–3: "I feel a divine jealousy for you, for I betrothed you to Christ to present you as a pure bride to her one husband. But I am afraid that as the serpent deceived Eve by his cunning, your thoughts will be led astray from a sincere and pure devotion to Christ." Time does not allow us to develop this line of thought here, but it is important to consider some of its anthropological implications for the new feminism.[58]

While it is true that if the wife is the "body" of her husband, the opposite is also true. This second and correlative principle is not developed, I think, because of two reasons. First, the author's perspective is not merely the relation between man and woman, or even that of Adam and Eve, but rather the restored relation between man and woman that is now revealed and made accessible in Christ's relation to the Church. Second, speaking of the woman as the "body" or "flesh" of her husband allows for a greater development of the notion of "head," which does not mean "more elevated" or "superior" but rather "the one who takes the initiative in love." An initiative that does not meet with response is no initiative at all, and thus we are confronted with what I will discuss shortly as "asymmetrical reciprocity." The notion of "body," therefore, evokes the image of intimacy and reciprocity, not that of inferiority or instrument. This latter notion is read into the text from our post-Cartesian mindset. Part of this notion is already caught in the medieval expression that woman is or represents the "humanity" of Christ.[59]

Verses 31–32

31a *For this reason,*
31b *a man will leave his father and mother*
31c *and be joined to his wife*
31d *and the two will become one flesh.*
31c *This Mystery is great:*
32a *for my part, I am speaking*
32b *in reference to Christ and the Church.*

---

[58] For an initial development of what I hope to treat of at greater length in another study, see Paulus Andriessen, "The New Eve, Body of the New Adam," in *The Birth of the Church* (New York: Alba House, 1968).

[59] One could consult the study by Caroline Walker Bynum, ". . . And Woman His Humanity: Female Imagery in the Religious Writing of the Later Middle Ages," in *Gender and Religion: On the Complexity of Symbols*, ed. Caroline Walker Bynum, Stevan Harrel, and Paula Richman (Boston: Beacon Press, 1986).

Without any indication that he is citing a biblical text, probably because he considers it too well-known, the author, with slight variations from our present Septuagint text, begins, "For this reason." The reason in the text is that, as the Lord God *(Kyrios o Theos)* leads the woman to *'ādām, 'ādām* exclaims, "This now is bone of my bones and flesh of my flesh; she shall be called woman because from her man *(andros)* she was taken." In the Ephesians text, the reason referred to is that Christ provides and cares for his own flesh, the Church, because we are members of his body. This is going to be the basis for the comparison.

The Genesis text continues to speak of a man leaving father and mother, which is an aspect ignored by Paul who puts the accent on being joined to his wife so the two become one flesh. The physical union between Christ and the Church is precisely the great Mystery, as the author explicitly says, and it precisely that union that forms the model for husband and wife, and is itself the living source of the love that binds them together. As Pierre Benoit expresses it:

> In this union (between Christ and the Church), which is the model for human marriage, and which is not endowed with any less physical realism, the "mystery" of the Genesis text is fully realized and definitively clarified.[60]

We may ask why the author, after citing the Genesis text with the intention of applying it primarily to the union between Christ and the Church calls it a "mystery." Some commentators point to the fact that *raz* and *sod*, the semitic terms that lie behind the New Testament *mysterion*, can sometimes mean the secret meaning of a text and they apply that meaning here.[61] But the author's point is that the *mysterion* is an aspect of God's plan now revealed. He is insisting on the analogical relation between the union of husband and wife, who become one flesh and the union of Christ and the Church who form one flesh. The "mystery" is not primarily in the text but in the realities it is mediating to us. As Augustine said: *"In ipso facto, non solum in dicto, mysterium requirere debemus."*[62]

With the creation of the New Man by Christ's act on the cross it becomes apparent, as Heinrich Schlier expresses it, that, "In Adam as the original *(ursprünglichen)* man, the creation of God, the future Christ is already hidden, but really present. Christ is the revealed, original man . . . in the creation is already hidden the redemption provided in Christ."[63] Adam, as Paul tells us,

---

[60] "Corps, Tête et Plérôme dans les Épîtres de la Captivité," in *Exégèse et Théologie* 2 (Paris: Cerf, 1960), 107–53; cite at 135.

[61] This is the position of Raymond Brown in his fine study, *The Semitic Background of the Term "Mystery" in the New Testament* (Philadelphia: Fortress, 1968), 65.

[62] *On Psalm 68 (Patrologia Latina* 36, 858). For a number of patristic texts on this same theme see Henri de Lubac, *Catholicism: Christ and the Common Destiny of Man,* trans. Lancelot Sheppard and Sister Elizabeth Englund (San Francisco: Ignatius Press, 1988), 165–70.

[63] *Der Brief an der Epheser. Ein Kommentar* (Düsseldorf: Patmos Verlag, 1958), 278. Translation is basically that of Barth, *Ephesians* 2, 643, n. 141.

was the "type" *(typos)* of the one to come (Rom 5:14), who is the "second man *(anthrôpos)*, the one from heaven" (1 Cor 15:47). While these texts place the accent on Jesus Christ as the individual man who recapitulates the reality of the "first man," our Ephesians text reminds us that, as we now see Christ, the "second man," we understand that creation itself is a prophecy of redemption. This means that in the corporate reality of man and woman, as Genesis describes it, is already present in a proleptic symbol the unity of Christ and the Church. The great mystery, therefore, is in the *fact* of Christ's physical union with the Church. Thus, every union of husband and wife, as they are themselves members of the body of Christ, is a share and a symbol of what is still ineffably mysterious because it is so abundantly real. We will draw consequences from this revelation shortly.

Verse 33

> 33a *But still, let each of you individually*
> 33b *love his own wife as himself,*
> 33c *as for the wife, let her fear her husband.*

The text now returns to conclude the exhortation, mentioning the husband first this time. The initial word, *plên,* may be used, as here, to round off a discussion. A final practical word is offered to each party: The husband should "love" and the wife should "fear." The injunction to the husband is based on Leviticus 19:18 a text, already invoked in rabbinic teaching about marriage. We can read in the Babylonian Talmud the following statement: "Our rabbis taught: Concerning a man who loves his wife as himself, who honors her more than himself . . . Scripture says, 'And you shall know that your tent is in peace.' "[64] But even the Levitical text has been sublated in a way not unlike the Johannine texts, which speak of Jesus telling us to love each other as he loves us (John 15:12, and so on).

We would expect that, just as the key word, *agapan,* used repeatedly in regard to the husband, is echoed in this summary, so too the word *ypotassesthai* would be used in the final address to the wife. Once again, however, as we have seen, the author avoids making the wife the explicit subject of this verb and reverts instead to his general admonition in 5:21, "subordinating yourselves to each other in the fear of Christ." In the Christian life, a fear that is not founded upon love is a monstrosity. The meaning of this phrase must be discovered within the love relation established by Christ among all his members and in a special way between husband and wife. In this sense, we may invoke the famous phrase of Augustine, *"amanti loquor."*

---

[64] bYebamoth 62b.

Part Three: Principles in the Definition of Woman

Having considered the principal biblical texts that mediate to us a revealed anthropology in regard to man and woman, we are ready to institute what will really be a beginning of some philosophical reflections on this revelation in order to render it more intelligible. I will consider only two principles here: Identity and Difference, and Relation of Asymmetrical Reciprocity.

Identity and Difference

The early chapters of Genesis usually employ the term "the man," *hā 'ādām*, with the article, thus blurring the distinction between the word as a personal name and as a common noun. In fact, the Septuagint uses *anthrōpos* to translate *'ādām* throughout chapter one and the first part of chapter two of Genesis, first using *ho adam* (with the article) at Genesis 2:16 and as a personal name at Genesis 2:19 to designate *adam* in the act of naming the animals. This fluidity in the Hebrew text, echoed in its own way by the Greek text, manifests a mentality that sees each human being as the complete embodiment of humanity, realizing humanity and summing it up. This is particularly true of those who are looked upon as the origin of a tribe or a people: Thus, Israel is the name of a person and the name of the people who originated with him. The usual name given to such a perception is "corporate personality," first coined in this sense by H. Wheeler Robinson and subsequently criticized and perfected by others.[65]

This grammatical consideration, however, and the mentality that it manifests, is overshadowed by the manner in which the Priestly tradition, twice as we have seen, explicitly describes *'ādām* as "male and female," using terms that accent their physical differences, and links this with the image of God. Division into male and female, however, cannot mean the creation of two beings, only one of which is fully human. On the other hand, it is not necessary, in fact it is impossible in the light of the biblical texts just considered, to make of gender something that is secondary to being human, something to be assigned along a sliding scale according to predisposition or preference. The philosophical insight that enables us to retain both of these truths is that of "dual unity," which may, perhaps, be better expressed as "identity and difference."[66]

---

[65] See H. Wheeler Robinson, *Corporate Personality in Ancient Israel*, ed. John Reumann, *Facet Books, Biblical Series* 11 (Philadelphia: Fortress, 1964), and his critics, J. R. Porter, "The Legal Aspects of the Concept of 'Corporate Personality' in the Old Testament," *Vetus Testamentu* 15 (1965): 361–80; J. W. Rogerson, "The Hebrew Conception of Corporate Personality: A Re-Examination," *Journal of Theological Studies* 21 (1970): 1–16. For a balanced approach, see Jean de Fraine, *Adam and the Family of Man*, trans. Daniel Raible CPPS. (New York: Alba House, 1965).

[66] I owe this latter phrase to an unpublished study by Angelo Scola, "Il Disegno de Dio sulla Persona, sul Matrimonio e sulla Famiglia. Riflessione Sintetica," conference given at

The term "dual unity" has been made popular through the work of Hans Urs von Balthasar who attributes the term to A. Frank-Duquesne.[67] A dual unity may be defined as "two distinct but inseparable realities, each fulfilling the other and both ordained to an ultimate unity that we cannot as yet imagine . . . two entia in a single *esse*, one existence in two lives, but by no means two different fragments of a whole, to be fitted together like a puzzle. . . ."[68] There are three ways of considering man as a dual unity: body and soul, man and woman, individual and community. It is important to note, however, that man and woman are a unique kind of dual unity since *all* of humanity exists differently in each of them, not merely an aspect, as is the case with soul/body or individual/community. It is for this reason that the expression "identity and difference" is more apt.

In phenomenological terms, man and woman are at one and the same time both "moments" and "pieces."[69] As moments, they are non-independent parts of one reality, "man": They are parts that cannot become a whole. This is their "identity" as *'ādām*. As pieces, they have the quality of being wholes within a larger whole. As moments of the reality "man," they are male and female. Yet, because they are persons, they are also pieces, that is, wholes as parts of a whole. They have another dimension; their maleness and femaleness make up the image of God; they are *'ādām* and not merely another "soul alive," that is merely another animal. Of no other creature can it be said that it is a dual unity in this sense of being made up of both moments and pieces. Angels exhaust their species in their individuality, and animals are not wholes as persons, but only as individuals. This leads us to an important conclusion that will be considered more at length shortly; namely that the fullness of human personhood is found in relationship, and that the prime analogate of this relationship is found fundamentally in the relations between the Divine Persons and proximately in the relation between Christ and the Church.

No one human being exhausts the reality of humanity: There is always the "other" who cannot be reduced to what I am. Man and woman together make up humanity and they are not only "distinct but inseparable realities," they are also ordained to an ultimate unity that is not that of parts going to make up a whole, but rather two modes of existing as human that are irreducible to one another—they are identical and different—as they make a third reality, a com-

---

the Settimana Internazionale di Studio, 22–27 August 1999 (Rome: Pontificio Istituto Giovanni Paolo II per Studi su Matrimonio e Famiglia, forthcoming).

[67] A. Frank-Duquesne, *Création et Procréation* (Paris: Ed. de Minuit, 1951); Hans Urs von Balthasar, *Theo-Drama: Theological Dramatic Theory*, vol. 2, *Dramatis Personae: Man in God* (San Francisco: Ignatius Press, 1992), esp. 365–82.

[68] Duquesne, *Création et Procréation*, 42–46, cited by von Balthasar, *Theo-Drama*, 365–66.

[69] In what follows here I am following the discussion of pieces and moments in Robert Sokolowski, *Introduction to Phenomenology* (New York: Cambridge University Press, 1999), 2–27.

munion of persons. This understanding reverses a way of thinking about human nature that is latent in nearly every cultural expression known to us, namely, that the man is the norm and the woman is the normed. Identity and difference, on the other hand, means that man and woman are reciprocal norms for each other. Being, that is human Being, is not divided: It is asserted as existing in two transcendentally related modes that cannot be reduced to each other.

Relationship: Asymmetrical Reciprocity

As we have seen, the priestly tradition in chapter one of Genesis is a descriptive narrative that presents the structure of creation as it is intended by God. The Yahwist presentation, on the other hand, is an existential poetic narrative that is searching in history for the origins of human existence as we know it. Thus, rather than speak of the image of God, 'ādām is portrayed as the direct object of God's action, formed from the earth and sharing in God's breath, and elevated by an invitation to obedience and trust through a covenant. The woman is taken from 'ādām to match him and be the embodiment of God's help to him. Because of her, 'ādām has someone to "face" him, to be a covenant partner with him, and together they form one flesh in unveiled communication.

Relationship

At this point we must return to our previous consideration of the image of God and enter briefly into a discussion regarding human personhood.[70] The classical definition of person, given by Boethius and modified somewhat in the course of history, asserted basically that a person is "an individual substance of a rational nature."[71] Modern philosophical and theological thought has advanced the understanding of person and thus would understand these terms in a more existential manner than that in which they were formerly understood. When "substance" is seen in the light of creation, it becomes obvious that it is what it is by its relation to God, that it subsists as what it is, and that it expresses what it is by relation to other beings. Thus, W. Norris Clarke proposes a triadic structure of being: "being *from* another, being *in* oneself, and being *toward* others."[72] Given the dynamic structure of all being it is true to say

---

[70] For a more complete account of what I present here schematically, see W. Norris Clarke, "Person, Being, and St. Thomas," *Communio* 19 (1992): 601–18; W. Norris Clarke, *Person and Being* (Milwaukee: Marquette University Press, 1993); David Schindler, "Norris Clarke on Person, Being, and St. Thomas," *Communio* 20, (3; 1993): 580–92; and, W. Norris Clarke, "A Response to David Schindler's Comments," *ibidem* 593–98.

[71] For a discussion of this definition and its history, see Max Müller et al., "Person," in *Sacramentum Mundi: An Encyclopedia of Theology,* ed. Karl Rahner (New York: Herder & Herder, 1969), 404–19.

[72] "Response," 596.

that the *individuum*, the *concretum*, seen in the light of its reality as created, is constituted by relation: to God, to itself, and to other beings. This last relation, that to other beings, is what Maritain calls "the basic generosity of existence,"[73] in which every being at its own level does impart something of itself: *bonum est diffusivum sui*.

Similarly, when we reflect on what "rational" means, we see that the unique and incommunicable reality of a person is also constituted by relation, it is *from* God, it relates *in* itself and to itself, and it is a being *toward* others. What is unique in the instance of person is that this threefold relation is actualized in the personal activity of freedom by which the relation becomes *relationship*. Thus, the particular property of a "rational" substance is that it is constituted by relation in such a way that this is given properly human existence in the free acts by which the person realizes him or her self. In scholastic terms, relation is, in a unique way, an intrinsic mode, or a "proper accident" of the relational substance and this is realized in *act*. In the case of the person, this act is a spiritual act; it is one of freedom. This philosophical elaboration is expressed biblically by saying that 'ādām is the image of God, and can find himself only in a relationship of mutual self-giving love. In order to understand, however, how this relationship transpires between man and woman who are both identical and different, we must look at the foundation of reciprocity, namely generosity and receptivity.

Receptivity[74]

Martin Heidegger has accused Aristotle of having introduced into western thought the identification of *archê* and *aitia*, thus effecting a notion of cause as being always prior and always dominant. This may or not be historically accurate, but the notion is certainly to be found in modernity, which, in this as in many areas has reduced Greek thought to but one aspect of its original abundance. With such a notion of cause, the only correlate can be passivity. Thus, "cause" signifies power and that upon which the cause exercises an influence is patient of that power.

There are two aspects of causality that must be restored to our consideration: These are "generosity" and "person." Both of these are part of the biblical understanding of causality that looks to God as the source and model of what it means to cause. To cause is to communicate actuality in some form. God, the First Cause, communicates being itself to his creatures, not in an act of "domination" but in an act of supreme generosity, and creation is not "passive," it is

---

73 Jacques Maritain, *Existence and the Existent* (New York: Doubleday, 1957), 90.

74 In this section I am indebted to the work of Kenneth Schmitz, especially "Created Receptivity and the Philosophy of the Concrete," *The Thomist* 61 (3; 1997): 339–71; and "Neither With Nor Without Foundations," *Review of Metaphysics* 42 (1988): 3–25. This section also utilizes material found in my study, *The Feminist Question: Feminist Theology in the Light of Christian Tradition* (Grand Rapids, MI: Eerdmans, 1994), especially chapter 6, used with permission of the publisher.

receptive. Created causality shares in its own way the nature of God's causality. This can be seen in the manner in which one being communicates something of itself to another, in the way in which the act of knowing consists in receiving what the known is sharing of itself, and most especially in the interaction of persons. It is important to note that it is proper to spiritual activity that something be shared without loss to the one sharing and that this is received in such a way that there is an increase in being without mutuation.

While there is generosity and receptivity on every level of being, and indeed there is generosity and receptivity in the very act of creation, since God co-creates the receptivity with the creature, it still remains true that what is proper to human interaction is precisely that communication that is being achieved through the mutual causality of freedom: "My argument is that receptivity is a principle of personal being at the concrete level. Far from being a principle that is neither act nor potency, I mean by it an *integral mode* constituted of both act and potency."[75] This will become clearer when we look at the other aspect of human relating, especially that of man/woman relating, namely asymmetry.

Asymmetry

Asymmetry adds the note of difference to the notion of receptivity and the reciprocal "causality" that is realized in the relation of generosity/receptivity. Not only are man and woman, husband and wife, related in such a way that their reciprocal giving and receiving finds its initiative in the man's love and a particular perfection in the woman's love, but their equal contributions are different, they are "asymmetrical."[76] Asymmetry, in our context, refers first and foremost to the fact that "sexual difference, in a significant and immediate way, testifies that the other always remains 'other' for me."[77] When the irreducible "otherness" of the other is taken seriously, then we find a way out of the impasse created by still one more exaggeration of Greek thought. The ancients' self-referential mode of thought was twisted by the Enlightenment so that knowledge of another person is reduced from the abundance and mystery of the other's personal existence to an interior event within the knower. The one aspect of existence for which Kantian epistemology cannot take any account is precisely human interaction, beginning with a simple conversation.

When causality is appreciated in its multiple realizations, and when difference does not automatically imply a relation of "superiority/inferiority," then it is clear that two realities can cause equally though in an asymmetrical manner: soil and seed in the production of a plant, object and knower in the act of knowing. Applied to our consideration here of a new humanism, we can see that human

---

[75] Schmitz, "Created Receptivity," 349.

[76] I am indebted in these few lines to the direction indicated by Angelo Scola, "The Nuptial Mystery at the Heart of the Church," *Communio* 25 (1998): 630–62, esp. 643–49.

[77] Scola, *art. laud.*, 645.

interactive causality, made up of mutual generosity and receptivity, is a unique instance of reciprocal asymmetry. We can see that what has often been lacking in Christian thought, even if at times the lack has been overcome in practice, is an understanding of that mode of being and acting that is irreducibly *personal*. The new feminism, beginning with the Genesis teaching on man and woman, and seeking to elaborate this through the concepts of dual unity, identity and difference, receptivity and asymmetry has begun to form the basis for a genuine development of doctrine, a new humanism that sheds the light of faith on what it means to have an integral humanity expressed in the life of the Church.

The paradigmatic realization of this new humanism is found in the spousal relationship in which, to use the concepts of John Paul II, two subjectivities relating to each other as two unique persons who cannot be reduced to "another self," but who rather form, in a mysterious manner, a "bi-subjectivity."[78] Time does not allow me to develop this concept here. The most striking manifestation of reciprocal asymmetry is to be found in the conception of a child. Not only on the personal level is the conjugal act an asymmetrical realization of love between equals, but the conception itself, as the science of genetics tells us, is an instance of the same equal causality. This biological fact, sublated throughout the whole of the human person, male or female, allows us to move from the medieval notion that in conception the man was *"agens quod inducit formam"* and the woman was *"patiens quod offert materiam,"* to an understanding that in the procreation of a new human life the depth of the mystery of human intersubjectivity finds a human fruit.

This same understanding of procreation shows us that in speaking of the "genius of woman" we are speaking of motherhood, just as in speaking of the "genius of man" we are speaking of fatherhood.

The Cross: The Way to Restored Relationships

The marriage relationship is the most interhuman realization of asymmetrical reciprocity. The husband's role is one of generosity, he is to "communicate actuality" by laying down his life. The wife receives this communication and thus gives it actual existence. A gift not received is not a gift at all. By placing husband and wife in the context of mutual generosity and receptivity, it becomes clear that the only priority in such a relation is the priority of love. In the teaching of Ephesians, as we have seen, the husband is "head" because, in some mysterious way, his loving initiative enables the woman to assume her role as embodying in a particular and preeminent way the vocation of every human being who "cannot find himself except through a sincere gift of self."[79] Com-

---

[78] See, for instance, the Wednesday Audiences of August 25 and September 1, 1982, in Karol (John Paul II) Wojtyla, *The Theology of the Body: Human Love in the Divine Plan,* trans. L'Osservatore Romano (Boston: Pauline Books and Media, 1997), 314–21.

[79] *Gaudium et Spes,* §24.

menting upon the notion of headship, Pope John Paul II states how the principle of "receptivity" is actually realized through the love of the husband.

> That good which he who loves creates, through his love, in the one that is loved, is like a test of that same love and its measure. Giving himself in the most disinterested way, he who loves does so only within the limits of this measure and this control.[80]

When we return once again to the example of Christ as head of his bride the Church, we see that this relationship is initiated by the fact that Jesus Christ is head as "Savior of the Body," and that the husband is to imitate that act by which Christ "loved the Church and gave himself over for her." The answer and healing for the domination, violence, and oppression that are never far from any human relationship are to be found in the act of love in which Jesus Christ died. The Gospels are replete with Jesus' teaching on non-coercive relating.[81] He unmasks the lie of domination and the lie of helplessness by calling us to live out our imaging of God. It is thus that in marriage, the paradigm of all human relating, there is to be realized that form of love that heals and sublates, that is recapitulates, God's original intention by giving it an actual historical existence. That love is a share in Christ's gift of himself on the Cross. It is identical in each person and yet different. It is asymmetrical, being both generous and receptive. In this movement of love, woman has a priority in that, by her very being her receptivity to another involves her in a creative generosity that norms the very meaning of love. This is, to use John Paul II's phrase, the "genius of woman." In the reciprocal relationship between man and wife, the exemplar and source of other relationships, there is one love that restores us to humanity. It is the love within the Trinity as this is breathed out into us by Jesus Christ when he "handed over the Spirit" and the Church was born from his side.

---

[80] General audience of September 1, 1982, in Wojtyla, *The Theology of the Body*, 319.
[81] It is sufficient to read the Beatitudes to see this heart of his teaching.

11 | Some Aspects of Biblical Studies since Vatican II: The Contribution and Challenge of *Dei Verbum*

THIS STUDY begins the process of integrating historical study and theological understanding in exegesis. The first part is a reflection on Chapter 3 of *Dei Verbum*, particularly on the unresolved tension found in paragraph §12. The second part looks at what must be done in order to integrate current exegetical methods within a theological method. The process of integration involves restoring a transcendent dimension to three aspects of human thought intimately involved the critical historiographical study of the Sacred Text: epistemology, history, and language.

• • •

THE final chapter of *Dei Verbum*, titled "Sacred Scripture in the Life of the Church," opens with these words:

The Church has always venerated the divine Scriptures just as she venerates the body of the Lord, since, especially in the sacred liturgy, she unceasingly receives and offers to the faithful the bread of life from the table both of God's word and of Christ's body. . . . For in the sacred books, the Father who is in heaven meets His children with great love and speaks with them; and the force and power in the word of God is so great that it stands as the support and energy of the Church, the strength of faith for her sons, the food of the soul, the pure and everlasting source of spiritual life. Consequently these words are perfectly applicable to Sacred Scripture: "For the word of God is living and active" (Heb 4:12), and "it has power to build you up and give you your heritage among all those who are sanctified" (Acts 20:32; see 1 Thess 2:13).

This study will be published as part of the proceedings of the Theological Symposium convoked by the Sacred Heart Major Seminary of Detroit "The Call to Holiness and Communion: Vatican II on the Church."

I would maintain that only in recovering for our own day access to the mystical bread of the word of God will we be able to bear witness to the world concerning the wonders God has worked for the whole human race. In pursuance of that goal I wish in this study to concentrate on §12 of *Dei Verbum* because we find there, in an unmistakable manner, the challenge issued to theologians of the Bible to avail themselves of all the resources provided by modern critical historiography while at the same time retaining the faith approaches that have nourished the Church for two millennia. Accordingly, my study will have two parts. In the first part, I point to the challenge posed by the document that sets forth the need to use modern historical and literary methods in order to grasp the intention of the human author while at the same time reading and interpreting the Scripture *"eodem Spiritu quo scripta est."*[1] In the second part I will propose some lines of thought that respond to the challenges and lacunae uncovered in the previous analysis.

Part One: The Historical and Literary Task

The title of Chapter 3 of *Dei Verbum* is: "Concerning the Divine Inspiration of Sacred Scripture and its Interpretation." I will look briefly at the first paragraph in this chapter, §11, which speaks of inspiration. Most of our attention, however, will be directed to §12 dedicated expressly to the topic of interpretation. Finally, the last paragraph in the chapter, §13, reflects with Tradition on the condescension of God and concludes with a traditional theme to which we will return.

Inspiration: Paragraph §11

The document wisely eschews discussion of the "mechanics of inspiration" and contents itself with a series of statements that serve to establish a theological space within which to set forth the mystery of the divine authorship of the Sacred Writings, their canonical status, the fact that God employed human authors who freely used their own powers and abilities and are truly authors. At this point there follows a statement whose full import has yet to be realized:

> Therefore, since everything asserted by the inspired authors or sacred writers must be held to be asserted by the Holy Spirit, it follows that the books of Scripture must be acknowledged as teaching solidly, faithfully and without error the truth which God, for the sake of our salvation, wanted put into the sacred writings.

---

[1] "In the same Spirit in which it was written." For a discussion of this phrase, to which I will return, see Ignace de la Potterie, "Interpretation of Holy Scripture in the Spirit in Which It Was Written," in *Vatican II: Assessment and Perspectives. I,* ed. René Latourelle (New York: Paulist Press, 1988), 220–66.

The paragraph concludes with a modified form of the Vulgate's rendering of 2 Timothy 3:16–17: "And thus, all Scripture (is) divinely inspired and useful for teaching, for disputing, for correcting, and for training in justice: that the man of God be fully formed and prepared for every good work."

The Human Authors: The First Theme of § 12

After having asserted that the human authors writing as true authors "consigned to writing everything and only those things which God wanted," and that this activity "transmits without error the truth which God, for the sake of our salvation, wanted put into the sacred writings," the Council Fathers had now to explain how the Sacred Text is to be interpreted. One of the primary purposes of the latter section of §11 had been to rescue the discussion about inerrancy from its previously fruitless debates by introducing the concept of *veritas*, which God, *nostrae salutis causa,* wished to communicate. This eliminates many of the problems of the inerrancy debate and allows a simple acknowledgment of the inaccuracies, historical, textual, and so forth that appear in the Sacred Text.[2] This same notion of the mode of expression now underlies the ensuing discussion of literary genre, culture, and the like, in the attempt to understand the human authors on their own terms.

However, since God speaks in Sacred Scripture through men in human fashion, the interpreter of Sacred Scripture, in order to see clearly what God wanted to communicate to us, should carefully investigate what meaning the sacred writers really intended, and what God wanted to manifest by means of their words.

The opening lines of paragraph §12 place the accent on grasping what "the sacred writers really intended." This introduces a cardinal principle already enunciated by St. Athanasius and quoted in *Divino Afflante Spiritu*:

> Here, as indeed is expedient in all other passages of Sacred Scripture, it should be noted, on what occasion the Apostle spoke; we should carefully and faithfully observe to whom and why he wrote, lest, being ignorant of these points, or confounding one with another, we miss the real meaning of the author.[3]

---

[2] At times there are discrepancies between the present state of our historical knowledge and the statements in the Sacred Text: thus the worldwide "census" under Caesar Augustus in Lk 2:1, the discrepancy in dating between Dan 1:1, and the Chronicle of King Nebuchadnezzar regarding the siege of Jerusalem, and so on. There are also mistaken attributions: Mk 27:9 names Jeremiah while in fact the text adduced in regard to Judas's death is Zech 11:12.

[3] *Contra Arianos* I, 54; *Partrologia Graeca* 26, col. 123 (*Divino Afflante Spiritu* §34). The phrase translated "real meaning" *(alēthinēs dianoias)* also evokes nuances of "real understanding" of the author.

This basic rule governing the interpretation of all texts takes on a particular importance when the interpreter is removed linguistically, culturally, and geographically from the text he or she is studying. There is as well a danger in this manner of expression and it lies in the two dimensions of the verb "to intend." The work of establishing cultural sympathy can result in a reasonably successful attempt to understand the correct tenor of the author's work, what he "intended to say." However the statement is about *something* and that too is what the author intends; his mind intends some reality, some aspect of being and interpreting his text includes participating in the knowledge that the author is communicating. Take for instance the following statement:

> But for men like Kelvin, Crookes and Roentray, whose research dealt with radiation theory or with cathode ray tubes, the emergence of X-rays violated one paradigm as it created another.[4]

Someone in Morocco (or Chicago) could report quite correctly to his audience what Thomas Kuhn intended to say without having any notion of what he is talking about, without, that is, participating in the intention of Kuhn's mind, and grasping the object of his thinking. One telling expression of this truth is found in a phrase of Martin Luther: "The one who does not understand the reality cannot draw the meaning out of the words."[5] The paragraph that describes the historical work of the exegete is well expressed and deserves to be cited in full here:

> To search out the intention of the sacred writers, attention should be given, among other things, to "literary forms." For truth is set forth and expressed differently in texts which are variously historical, prophetic, poetic, or of other forms of discourse. The interpreter must investigate what meaning the sacred writer intended to express and actually expressed in particular circumstances by using contemporary literary forms in accordance with the situation of his own time and culture. For the correct understanding of what the sacred author wanted to assert, due attention must be paid to the customary and characteristic styles of feeling, speaking and narrating which prevailed at the time of the sacred writer, and to the patterns men normally employed at that period in their everyday dealings with one another.[6]

---

4 Thomas S. Kuhn, *The Structure of Scientific Revolutions,* ed. Otto Neurath, *International Encyclopedia of Unified Science* (Chicago: Chicago University Press, 1970), 93.

5 "Qui non intelligit res non postest sensum ex verbis elicere." Tischreden, Weimarer Ausgabe 5, 26, n. 5246.

6 Note the number of times the notion of the intention of the author is invoked here: "Ad *hagiographorum intentionem eruendam,*" attention must be paid to literary forms; the interpreter must investigate what the author *"exprimere intenderit et expresserit;"* finally, due

It is impossible to exaggerate the benefit that has accrued to the study of the Sacred Page and thus to the Church by the correct application of the methods described in this paragraph. We must bear in mind the earlier statement of this document that speaks of the *oeconomia revelationis* taking place *"gestis verbisque intrinsece inter se connexis"* (§2). In this context we may say that in order to participate more fully in the reality mediated by the words—*intentio* understood metaphysically—it is of great importance that we grasp what, in terms of his own context, the author "wants to say"—*intentio* understood psychologically. I will return to this important point later in the discussion.

There are many examples of ways in which historical, literary, and philological research has served to clarify the intention of the author thus illuminating the teaching of the Sacred Text in ways that have led to significant advances in theology. One small example will suffice. Romans 5:12 has always been crucial for an understanding of the relation between Adam's sin and humankind's sin and death. Yet, a key expression in the verse has eluded understanding. The text reads as follows in the *Revised Standard Version*: "Therefore as sin came into the world through one man and death through sin, and so death spread to all men because all men sinned." The last four English words represent the Greek *eph' hō pantes ēmarton,* and these words have received about eleven interpretations.[7] With the electronic capacity to examine the phrase in extant Greek literature the possibilities have been reduced to two: "inasmuch as all have sinned," or, "with the result that all have sinned." In either case, though with different nuances, the teaching of the verse asserts both the causality of Adam in regard to human sin and death and the fact that this causality expresses itself in the sinning of each individual person. This is extremely important in the development of the Church's teaching on original sin.

The Divine Author: The Second Theme of §12

The second section of §12 begins with a long sentence whose opening phrase changes the direction of thought and is followed by statements that point successively to the fact of the canon of Scripture, the Tradition of the Church, and the "analogy of faith." This sentence is then succeeded by remarks regarding the Magisterium and the way in which biblical interpretation both serves this function and is subject to it:

---

attention must be paid to common styles of speech in order to attain a correct understanding of what the sacred author *"scripto asserere voluerit."*

7 See Stanislaus Lyonnet, "Le sens de eph' ho en Rom 5,12 et l'exégèse des Pères grecs," *Biblica* 36 (1955): 436–56.; and especially Joseph Fitzmyer, *Romans. A New Translation with Introduction and Commentary,* ed. William Foxwell Albright and David Noel Freedman, *Anchor Bible 33* (New York: Doubleday, 1992), 413–17.

But, since Holy Scripture must be read and interpreted in the same Spirit in which it was written, in order rightly to draw out the meaning of the sacred texts, no less diligent attention must be devoted to the content and unity of the whole of Scripture, taking into account the living Tradition of the entire Church and the analogy of faith.

It pertains to exegetes to work according to these rules in order to understand and expound more profoundly the meaning of Sacred Scripture so that the judgment of the Church might mature, as it were, by preparatory study. For all of what has been said about the way of interpreting Scripture is subject finally to the judgment of the Church, which carries out the divine commission and ministry of guarding and interpreting the word of God.

Three procedures are listed in this text as part of reading and interpreting Holy Scripture in the same Spirit in which it was written, and these are necessary "in order rightly to draw out the meaning of the sacred texts." There is first, attention "to the content and unity of the whole of Scripture," what may be called "canonical criticism." There is secondly, an account of "the living Tradition of the entire Church." This must refer to the Fathers and liturgies of both east and west as well as the living faith practice of the members of the Church. And finally, there is *"analogia fidei,"* a traditional phrase that emphasizes the fact that not only is the Bible a whole with a multifaceted but consistent message, but also each part of the Sacred Text must be understood as compatible with others in the Canon, indeed as deriving from and contributing to an understanding of the whole.

Reading the Scripture in the Spirit in which it was written means first acknowledging that "no prophecy of scripture is a matter of one's own interpretation, because no prophecy ever came by the impulse of man, but men moved by the Holy Spirit spoke from God" (2 Pet 1:20–21). In a previous chapter we have already seen how Aquinas sums up the rhythm that leads from original revelation to interpretation. The fact that the transmission and reception process is much more complex than the ancients thought does not detract from the solidity of his understanding:

After the level of those who receive revelation directly from God, another level of grace is necessary. Because men receive revelation from God not only for their own time but also for the instruction of all who come after them, it was necessary that the things revealed to them be passed on not only in speech to their contemporaries but also as written down for the instruction of those to come after them. And thus it was also necessary that there be those who could interpret what was written down. This also must be done by divine grace. And so we read in Genesis 40:8, "Does not interpretation come from God?"[8]

---

8 *Summa contra Gentiles* 3, 154.

Aquinas also considers that all the authors of the New Testament were prophetically endowed because they could correctly interpret the Old Testament: "They are also called prophets in the New Testament who expound the prophetic sayings because Sacred Scripture is interpreted in the same Spirit in which it is composed."9

The first consequence, then, of the fact that Scripture is written by the Holy Spirit and must be read and interpreted in the same Spirit is that "no less diligent attention must be devoted to the content and unity of the whole of Scripture." Such a manner of reading and interpreting has been instinctive for most of Christian history. It suffices to look at any patristic writing to experience this: Any part of Scripture may be invoked to shed light on another part. With the advent of historical study and increased attention to the author and the author's intention, the tendency has been to consider a book or part of a book as an isolated entity. Thus, we have the modern phenomenon of studies devoted to "the theology of Jeremiah," or Mark, or Deutero-Isaiah. . . . Such studies are valuable since they allow us to grasp the teaching of individual authors as these are embedded in the concrete consciousness and energy of any one person.10 There are other procedures that are not as useful, and, in fact, are wrong. These consist in trying to determine a more primitive layer of composition, attempting to discern its theological direction, and then attributing to the final and more "orthodox" redaction a different direction. The orientation of most of this work is to consider that the "orthodox" layer was superimposed upon a more primitive and less exclusive view. The multiplicity of opinions resulting from this procedure is evidence enough of its shaky foundation and it often betrays a theological bias on the part the investigator.11

In reaction to an atomizing and pluralizing understanding of the Scriptures there has been a return to the more instinctive manner of considering the totality

---

9 *Ad Romanos* (on Rom 12:8), Marietti ed. §978. For the background of this principle, see Ignace de la Potterie, "Interpretation of Holy Scripture in the Spirit in Which It Was Written." We find in that study this text from Origen describing the responsibility of a bishop or priest: "To learn of God by reading the divine Scriptures and by meditating on them with great frequency, or teach the people. But he must teach what he has learned of God, not from his own heart or any human sense, but what the Spirit teaches" (*In Lev. Hom* 6, 6 [*Sources Chrétiennes* 286, 297], text is on p. 225 of de la Potterie's study.

10 See Kenneth Schmitz, *What Has Clio to Do with Athena? Etienne Gilson: Historian and Philosopher,* vol. 10, The Etienne Gilson Series 10 (Toronto: Pontifical Institute of Medieval Studies, 1987).

11 I have discussed this more at length in my review of *Christology, Controversy and Community: New Testament Essays in Honor of David. R. Catchpole,* ed. David Horrell and Christopher M. Tuckett. Supplements to Novum Testamentum XCIX. (Leiden: Brill, 2000) in *Catholic Biblical Quarterly* 64 (3; 2002): 608–10. For an example of this procedure that finds irreducible diversity in the New Testament, see Carolyn Osiek, "The Family in Early Christianity: 'Family Values' Revisited," *Catholic Biblical Quarterly* 58 (1; 1996): 1–24.

of the text. This return seeks to retain what has been gained through attention to the individual authors and books but to integrate this with "the whole of Scripture." I am, of course, speaking of the approach linked with the name of Brevard Childs which concentrates in a reflective way on the Canon as whole as mediating the divine message by holding all its parts in an overarching unity in diversity.[12] Though the insight is extremely important there remain weaknesses in Childs's approach. Some of these come from a lack of an understanding of Magisterium, some from the sheer vastness of the historical information that has to be integrated, and some from a lack of philosophical insights, for example, analogy, that could help in portraying the transposition process by which the various components of the final text have been formed into a whole.[13] A good description of this process is found in the text by Bernard Lonergan. Lonergan uses the term "sublation," where I prefer "transposition" because of the distance it allows us from Hegel:

> What sublates goes beyond what is sublated, introduces something new and distinct, yet so far from interfering with the sublated or destroying it, on the contrary needs it, includes it, preserves all its proper features and properties, and carries them forward to a fuller realization within a richer context.[14]

The canon is both a work of Tradition and its inspired expression. Surrounding the canon of Scripture and bearing it along is the whole life of the Church, and the exegete must place himself within this movement in order to take "into account the living Tradition of the entire Church." Surprising as it may seem there is hardly any philosophical reflection extant on the nature of what we call tradition.[15] A recent study by Jorge Gracia can serve as an effective beginning.[16] Gracia's main contention is that tradition is action. The action must be voluntary, intentional, repeated by members of social groups, and sig-

---

[12] See Brevard Childs, *The New Testament as Canon: An Introduction* (Philadelphia: Fortress, 1984); Brevard Childs, *Biblical Theology of the Old and New Testaments. Theological Reflection on the Christian Bible* (Minneapolis: Fortress, 1992). See as well C. Theobald, ed., *Le Canon des Écritures. Études historiques, exégétiques et systématiques, Lectio Divina 140* (Paris: Cerf, 1990).

[13] For a treatment of some of these problems, see Paul R. Noble, *The Canonical Approach: A Critical Reconstruction of the Hermeneutics of Brevard S. Childs* (Leiden: Brill, 1995).

[14] Bernard Lonergan, *Method in Theology* (New York: Herder & Herder, 1972), 241.

[15] However, see the study by Kenneth Schmitz, "What Happens to Tradition When History Overtakes it?" *American Catholic Philosophical Quarterly, Supplement* 68 (1994): 59–72.

[16] Jorge J. E. Gracia, *Old Wine in New Skins. The Role of Tradition in Communication, Knowledge and Group Identity, The Aquinas Lecture 2003* (Milwaukee: Marquette University Press, 2003). One should also consult George F. McLean, ed., *Hermeneutics, Tradition and Contemporary Change, Cultural Heritage and Contemporary Change. Series I, Culture and Values Volume 30* (Washington, DC: The Council For Research in Values and Philosophy, 2003).

nificant for their identity. To the observation that, at least in the Roman
Catholic view, Tradition should have verbal content Gracia replies:

> Accordingly, when Roman Catholics talk about beliefs as constituting a
> tradition, for example, they can be taken to be referring to the very actions
> of believing rather than to certain doctrines or to their textual formulation
> . . . what counts in religious faith is the very actions of believing in which
> people engage and, second, ontologically it is such actions that exist—
> doctrines exist only insofar as someone holds them.[17]

The advantage of this statement is that it places liturgy and the whole of
Christian living at the very heart of Tradition. It should be completed by the
nuanced work of Yves Congar, for instance.[18] It should be noted as well that the
notion of Tradition includes the action of the Holy Spirit by which those divine
realities "handed on" are rendered present, accessible, and life giving.[19] I cite Gracia here because his work serves to highlight exactly what can be lacking in modern historical study of the Scriptures, particularly when the action of the Holy
Spirit in the past and in the present is methodologically excluded. Tradition may
also simply be described as Sacra Doctrina. *Sacra doctrina* is an analogous expression that applies to many facets of that activity by which God manifests and communicates himself and a knowledge of his plan because only in this way can we
know the reason we were created and set our lives in that direction. It includes,
on the part of God, an original activity of self-manifestation that culminated in
Jesus Christ who is the revelation of God and the source of that divine gracious
activity by which we can attain the end to which God has freely called us. The
subject of this activity is the Church whose prophetic function, exercised principally through the Magisterium, consists in preserving the authenticity of what
has been and is being "handed on" by the Holy Spirit. By extension, the term
sacra doctrina applies to all the derivative human acts, initiated and sustained by
the Holy Spirit, by which this originating activity is perpetuated and made available, in many forms, to subsequent generations of God's people.[20]

The last "rule" to be mentioned by the document is *"analogia fidei,"* the analogy of faith. The term is found in Romans 12:6 *(analogia tēs pisteōs) preceded by
metron pisteōs* in Romans 12:3. Both expressions seem to refer to testing prophecy
to determine its genuineness and the "faith" referred to is rather the faith of other
prophets (see 1 Cor 14:29–33). However since a norm was already involved even
in this type of charismatic faith, it was not long before the term took on the

---

[17] Gracia, *Old Wine in New Skins,* 94.

[18] Yves Congar, *Tradition and Traditions. An Historical Essay and a Theological Essay,* trans.
Micahel Naseby and Thomas Rainborough (New York: MacMillan, 1967).

[19] *Dominum et Vivificantem* 8 and *Catechism of the Catholic Church,* 78.

[20] This notion has been more amply treated in Chapter 1.

overtones of "corresponding to the overall teaching of the Church," specifically the Creeds. Later still, the expression also referred to the analogical relation between what is known naturally and what is revealed.[21] The *Catechism of the Catholic Church*, commenting on this passage of *Dei Verbum* defines the analogy of faith this way: "By 'analogy of faith' we mean the coherence of the truths of faith among themselves and within the whole plan of Revelation" (*CCC* §114).

One of the most important expressions of this analogy of faith is found in the Canon itself. Attention to this fact would have prevented the tendency in historical critical investigation to understand the "pluralism" of the New Testament to be a conglomeration of conflicting views that would entitle one to continue the centrifugal movement in several new directions.

The final two sentences of §12 speak of the relationship between exegetical work and the teaching office and function of the Church. The first sentence urges exegetes to work according to the "rules" just elaborated so that the judgment of the Church "might mature." A good example of such collaboration can be seen in the way the documents of Vatican II are the fruit of the biblical, liturgical, patristic, and theological work of the previous 150 years, especially that of the *Ressourcement* movement. The final sentence enunciates the principle that the Church has the divine mandate and ministry of preserving and interpreting the Scriptures and other efforts are subject to the authority of the Church's judgment. This principle is well expressed by Thomas Aquinas: "Faith adheres to all the articles of faith because of one reason *(medium)*, namely because of the First Truth proposed to us in the Scriptures understood rightly according to the teaching of the Church *(secundum doctrinam Ecclesiae)*."[22]

Part Two: The Challenge of Integration: The Tensions

The directive of the first part of *Dei Verbum*, that the exegete should employ historical and literary methods in order to grasp what the author intended, and that of the second part, that this be done in a genuinely theological manner, has proved challenging to Catholic and other biblical studies. In this part of my study I wish to point out the tension often found in modern Catholic biblical studies, despite some significant contributions, and then suggest some lines of theological and philosophical effort that can aid in effecting a more satisfactory integration, one that will serve the Church in responding to the Lord's call to holiness.

The tension between the first and second aspects of what is described in *DV* §12 can be attributed, I would propose, to the fact that the methods enthusiastically encouraged and embraced were not sufficiently considered in the light of

---

[21] See Leo Scheffczyk, "Analogy of Faith," in *Sacramentum Mundi. An Encyclopedia of Theology*, ed. Karl Rahner et al. (New York: Herder & Herder, 1968), 25–27.

[22] *Summa theologiae* 2–2, 5, ad 2. For a judicious account of how the Church asserts the meaning of a biblical text, see Maurice Gilbert, "Textes Bibliques dont l'Église a Défini le Sens," in *L'Autorité de l'Écriture*, ed. Jean-Michel Poffet (Paris: Cerf, 2002), 71–94.

their philosophical presuppositions. I wish first to look at the study of history and the use of what is called the Historical Critical Method, though it is in fact a medley of methods. Then I wish to look briefly at the understanding of knowledge and language that must be operative in the interpretative effort.

History

It is a commonplace to point to the inaugural address of Johann Philipp Gabler at the University of Altdorf, March 30, 1787, as the occasion for a program-setting distinction between biblical and dogmatic theology (the title of his address) and the restriction of biblical theology to historical considerations.[23] At one point in his address he states:

> There is truly a biblical theology, of historical origin, conveying what the holy writers felt about divine matters; on the other hand there is a dogmatic theology of didactic origin, teaching what each theologian philosophizes rationally about divine things, according to the measure of his ability or of the times, age, place, sect, school and other similar factors.

Gabler goes on with all the enthusiasm of an Enlightenment-style Christian[24] to speak of the need to "gather carefully the sacred ideas and, if they are not expressed in the sacred Scriptures, let us fashion them ourselves from passages that we compare with each other." After speaking of the historical and philological distance that must be traversed in order to understand the sacred writers, the author goes on to describe how the ideas thus derived must be weighed to see whether they are "truly divine, or rather whether some of them, which have no bearing on salvation, were left to their own ingenuity." Then, finally, the genuine message thus obtained "can then be laid out as the fundamental basis for a more subtle dogmatic scrutiny."[25] Gabler's program effectively separates the very things that *DV* §12 hopes will be integrated in order that historical study be part of a theological undertaking. Underlying this program one can find most of the fallacies that have characterized the historical critical method since its inception. They are well summed up by Brian Daley in a recent article:

---

[23] For an English translation and commentary, see John Sandys-Wunsch and Laurence Eldrege, "J. P. Gabler and the Distinction between Biblical and Dogmatic Theology: Translation, Commentary, and Discussion of His Originality," *Scottish Journal of Theology* 33 (2; 1980): 133–58.

[24] Consciously or unconsciously Gabler is following in the footsteps of Baruch Spinoza: The rule for (biblical) interpretation should be nothing but the natural light of reason which is common to all—not any supernatural light nor any external authority." (*Tractatus theologico-politicus*, 14). For a more protracted consideration of the move toward a "closed system" interpretation of Scripture, see Francis Martin, "Critique historique et enseignement du Nouveau Testament sur l'imitation du Christ," *Revue Thomiste* 93 (1993): 234–62.

[25] All translations are from the article mentioned in the previous note.

"[H]istorical reality"—like physical reality—is assumed to be in itself something objective, at least in the sense that it consists in events independent of the interests and preoccupations of the scholar or narrator, something accessible through the disciplined, methodologically rigorous analysis of present evidence such as texts, artifacts and human remains. . . . As a result, modern historical criticism—including the criticism of Biblical texts—is *methodologically* atheistic, even if what it studies is some form or facet of religious belief, and even if it is practiced by believers. Only "natural, inner-worldly explanations of why or how things happen, explanations that could be acceptable to believers and unbelievers alike, are taken as historically admissible. . . . So God is not normally considered to count as an actor on the stage of history, God's providence in history, the divine inspiration of Scriptural authors and texts, even the miracles narrated in the Bible are assumed to be private human interpretations of events, interior and non-demonstrable, rather that events or historical forces in themselves.[26]

That such is the case can be seen from the statements of some of the biblical scholars themselves. Let this text from Rudolf Bultmann stand for many that could be adduced:

The historical method includes the presupposition that history is a unity in the sense of a closed continuum of effects in which individual events are connected by the succession of cause and effects. (This continuum) cannot be rent by the interference of supernatural, transcendent powers and that therefore there is no "miracle" in this sense of the word.[27]

Many scholars have intuitively overcome the lack of transcendence, even atheism, inherent in the historical critical method and the results of their work have been successful to a greater or lesser degree. However, the restrictions placed on them by the orientation of the method itself have made a genuine integration of their work with attention to the present action of the Holy Spirit, the whole of the canon and the tradition, the analogy of faith, and the teaching of the Magisterium something yet to be accomplished.[28]

There is no doubt that the development of a critical historiography has been of immense help in understanding aspects of the biblical text, and has raised history to the rank of an authentic discipline. The positivistic bias of the

---

[26] Brian Daley, "Is Patristic Exegesis Still Usable?" *Communio* 29 (1; 2000): 185–216.

[27] Schubert Ogden, ed., *Existence and Faith. Shorter Writings of Rudolf Bultmann* (New Yok: Meridian Books, 1960). I owe this reference to the more complete discussion in Alvin Plantinga, "Two (or More) Kinds of Scripture Scholarship," *Modern Theology* 14 (2; 1998): 243–77.

[28] I have been referring to Christian, particularly Catholic, scholars but the same understanding of the limitation can be found among Jewish scholars. See the remarks by Jon

historical critical approach, however, has produced something akin to the results one can find in the physical sciences lamented today by many scientists themselves: We fail to account correctly to ourselves as to what we actually do when we know, and thus falsify the process and the results.[29] I would suggest that in regard to history we must look more closely at what we do when we intuitively "adjust" the results of the historical critical method. Only in this way can we move from the inassimilable presuppositions of the historical critical method to a genuine theological integration of the invaluable work of critical historiography. Faith instinct leads believing exegetes to take account, though as yet imperfectly, of the mystery of Christ, the center of history, and to understand time and the temporality of events in a manner that includes, at least less superficially, an awareness of the interior and vertical dimension of events. Thus, to borrow a famous book title, we must look at Christ and Time, though these will be understood in a different way than that of the author, Oscar Cullman. I will postpone a discussion of Christ for the next chapter and treat briefly here some aspects of time.

Time

I wish now to look at some aspects of the mystery of time and suggest that once the transcendent dimension of time is rescued from the modern study of history, the possibility of the integration we are seeking is more attainable.[30] For modern history, time is succession, a dubious and uneven march toward an indeterminate future. The study of history, now capable of genuine reconstruction and insight, records this march. As we have seen, it resolutely eschews any consideration of transcendence, any search for a causality that exceeds the forces and resources of what is fundamentally a closed system.[31] I would propose in contradistinction that we use the term "temporality" to describe the nature of human existence: Temporality includes succession in a vision of presence. I derive this understanding from St. Augustine. Insisting that the way to an understanding of eternity

---

Levenson, *The Hebrew Bible, The Old Testament, and Historical Criticism. Jews and Christians in Biblical Studies* (Louisville: Westminster/John Knox, 1993).

[29] One could consult the works of Michael Polanyi: *The Tacit Dimension* (New York: Doubleday, Anchor Books, 1967); *Personal Knowledge. Towards a Post-Critical Philosophy* (Chicago: University of Chicago Press, 1958).

[30] In the lines that follow, I am indebted to two studies delivered at a symposium held at the Intercultural Forum of the John Paul II Cultural Center. I am grateful to their authors to be able to utilize their material: Kenneth Schmitz, "The Ingathering of Being, Time and Word and the Inbreaking of a Transcendent Word; Matthew Lamb, "Temporality and History: Reflections from St. Augustine and Bernard Lonergan." Published in *Nova et Vetera* 4:3 (2006).

[31] The relation between this view and the pre-Christian pagan view of reality can be seen in the study by Robert Sokolowski, *The God of Faith and Reason. Foundations of Christian Theology* (Notre Dame, IN: University of Notre Dame Press, 1982).

and transcendence lay in a conversion of life that rendered accessible an *experience* of Being, Augustine describes the fruit of his own conversion: "And in the flash of a trembling glance my mind came to That Which Is. I understood the invisible through those things that were created."[32] From this came an understanding of eternity as not being endless changelessness but rather infinite presence. This gives rise to an appreciation of the intrinsic reality of the *individuum* to which I referred earlier, not as a particular instance of a class but as a unique reality receiving its identity from a relation to its Creator.[33] God, the Creator, who is Eternity, is necessarily present in the action of sustaining all that is. Augustine, responding to the opinion that, since God's will to create is eternal, creation itself must be eternal, answers in this manner:

> People who take that line do not yet understand you, O Wisdom of God and Light of our minds. They do not yet understand how things which receive their being through you and in you come into existence; but their heart flutters about between the changes of the past and future found in created things and an empty heart it remains. . . . [If they consider] they would see that in eternity nothing passes, for the whole is present *(sed totum esse praesens)* whereas time cannot be present all at once *(nullum vero tempus totum esse praesens).*[34]

In this deceptively simple presentation we have the way to recover transcendence in regard to human existence. Temporality, the proper mode of creation's existence, is not just succession; it is succession with the dimension of presence. In this sense, *tempus* is intrinsic to creation: "God, in whose eternity there is no change whatsoever, is the creator and director of time . . . the world was not created *in* time but *with* time."[35] To understand, therefore, time as intrinsic to creaturely existence,[36] and not an exterior and neutral "container" for the changes of the past and future, is to advance toward an understanding of history that includes what Jean Lacroix has already referred to as its "mystery." Augustine and many others have pointed to this dimension of the events narrated in the Bible. The "mystery" is the eternally present Christological dimension of the events of salvation history as this moves through the succes-

---

32 *Confessions* 7, 17. Translation by Matthew Lamb.

33 I refer the reader to Kenneth Schmitz, "Created Receptivity and the Philosophy of the Concrete," *The Thomist* 61 (3; 1997): 339–71.

34 Augustine, *The Confessions,* ed. John E. Rotelle, trans. Maria Boulding, vol. I/1, *The Works of St. Augustine* (Hyde Park, NY: New City Press, 1997). The passage is 11, 11.

35 *De Civitate Dei* 11, 6, translation is that of M. Lamb. *"Cum igitur Deus, in cuius aeternitate nulla est omnino mutatio, creator sit temporum et ordinator . . . procul dubio non est mundus factus in tempore sed cum tempore."*

36 While succession, an aspect of time, is clearly present in material creation, created spirits also have succession in that they go from potency to act.

sion of "before and after." The meaning is to be found, not in the exterior comparison of texts, but in the interior recognition of economic participation. Let two patristic texts suffice out of a countless number that could be adduced. "Holy Scripture, in its way of speaking, transcends all other sciences because in one and the same statement while it narrates an event it sets forth the mystery."[37] The two words "event" and "mystery" refer in turn to the literal sense, the event, and then the same event as it is now seen to have been a participated anticipation of the mystery of Christ. Augustine has much the same to say; "*In ipso facto* [the event itself], *non solum in dicto* [the text of the Old Testament], *mysterium* [the plan of God revealed in Christ] *requirere debemus.*"[38]

One last consideration will conclude this reflection on integrating historical study and authentic exegesis through a deeper understanding of time. Some practitioners of the historical critical method point to the great advantage we now have in being able to establish a "parallel narrative interpretation" as it were of the events narrated in the Bible. There are New Testament exegetes who have used this approach to great effect by trying to reconstruct through critical historiography an event in the life of Jesus and then tracing the inspired interpretative activity of the Gospel writers.[39] Generally, however, as I have said, the tendency is to use the reconstructed event as the norm against which the biblical narration is measured.

If we take the New Testament manner of narrating seriously, then we must acknowledge that the parallel information we can obtain by historical study is always to be at the service of seeking to follow the inspired narrative techniques of the biblical authors. What we have is an action of God in history, in this case in Christ, interpreted by an action of God in the composition of the subsequent tradition and its Scripture. This is what *Dei Verbum* (§2) meant by describing the "economy of revelation" as taking place *"gestis verbisque intrinsece inter se connexis"* so that "the works accomplished by God in the history of salvation, manifest and confirm the teaching and the realities signified by the words, while the words proclaim the works and bring to light the mystery contained in them."[40] It is precisely here that I think we must acknowledge a failure of historical study. Rather than seek to understand more deeply what *Dei Verbum* has already urged us to do in seeking out the intention of the author, we content ourselves with a

---

[37] Gregory the Great, *Moralia* 20, 1 (*Patrologia Latina* 76, 135): "*Sacra Scriptura omnes scientias ipso locutionis suae more transcendit, quia uno eodemque sermone dum narrat gestum, prodit mysterium.*"

[38] *On Psalm 68* (*Patrologia Latina* 36, 858).

[39] I am thinking, for example, of Ignace de la Potterie, "The Multiplication of the Loaves in the Life of Jesus," *Communio* 16 (1989): 499–516; René Latourelle, *The Miracles of Jesus and the Theology of Miracles,* trans. Matthew J. O'Connell (New York: Paulist Press, 1988).

[40] This teaching is admirably summed up by Hans Urs von Balthasar: "The gradual clothing of the events within the folds of Scripture is not only an inevitable drawback (because the people of the Orient of that time did not know, in fact, a historiography

descriptive report of the text, based on pre-established norms of criticism, rather than adjust to the particular nature of the sacred text. What is the "literary form," for instance, of the Gospel narratives that are recounting past events as they exist *now* in the transformed humanity of Christ? Or again, what is the literary form of the Exodus accounts, which, based on the memory of a people and seeking to mediate the experience of God's action in the history of Israel, have a particular mode of narrating that is apt to effect just this mediation? This is surely a different question, one that can only be approached with faith and sensitivity to the authors, redactors, story tellers, and others, who were moved by the Holy Spirit to mediate an event whose actual "historical" existence can hardly be pieced together.[41] A more complete answer to this type of question would involve an understanding of the role of "memory" in the forming of an interpreted event. Once again we return to the fact that the proper dimension of human existence and of salvation history is not mere succession but succession and *presence*. This is the mystery; it is the mode of biblical address and it should be the mode of authentic exegesis.

Considerations for Further Development

We have seen that at the very center of temporality is the Word, the Word made flesh. In dying and rising again this Word, Jesus Christ, has now in principle brought all creation to its perfection. This reality, however, must work out in the world of succession—the world was created with time—and then at some point all creation will reach its goal:

> Then the end will come, when he hands over the kingdom to God the Father after he has destroyed all dominion, authority and power. For he must reign until he has put all his enemies under his feet. The last enemy to be destroyed is death. For he "has put everything under his feet." Now when it says that "everything" has been put under him, it is clear that this does not include God himself, who put everything under Christ. When he has done this, then the Son himself will be made subject to him who put everything under him, so that God may be all in all (1 Cor 15:24–28).

Now, just as temporal existence can have a penultimate and partial intelligibility, but never an independent intelligibility, so too thought and language

---

in the modern understanding of the term), but assuredly also this corresponds unqualifiedly to a positive intention of the Spirit." Hans Urs von Balthasar, "Il Senso Spirituale della Scrittura," *Ricerche Teologiche* 5 (1994): 5–9. Cite is from p. 7.

[41] For this reason, though the approach is not always nuanced I recommend the study by Ronald Hendel, "The Exodus in Biblical Memory," *Journal of Biblical Literature* 120, (4; 2001): 601–22. I have treated Pentecost as a "paradigm event" in Francis Martin, "Le baptême dans l'Esprit; tradition du Nouveau Testament et vie de l'Eglise," *Nouvelle Revue Théologique* 106 (1984): 23–58.

possess the twofold levels of intelligibility. And just as a non-transcendent understanding of history will ultimately distort history itself, so too a non-transcendent understanding of knowledge and language will ultimately distort the reality it seeks to grasp. Space does not allow a complete treatment of these notions, though they are essential to the philosophical and theological bridge-building necessary to bring together modern exegesis and revelation. I will merely point out how such a bridge-building might proceed and leave to another the study of a complete development.

Knowledge and Transcendence

Aquinas says of the interior light of reason that it is itself a "certain participation in divine light;" it is, in fact "nothing else but the imprint of the divine light in us."[42] This is expanded in his commentary on the Johannine Prologue:

> We can understand, "And the life was the light of men," in two ways. We can consider the light as an object, only viewable by men, because the light can be seen by a creature endowed with reason, since only such a nature is capable of the divine vision, as it says in Job 35,11: "He taught us rather than the beasts of the earth, and made us wise rather than the birds of the heaven." For, while animals know some things that are true, only man knows truth itself.
>
> The light of men can be considered as something participated in. For we could never see the Word or the light itself except by participating in that which is in man himself, namely the superior part of his soul, that is, intellectual light. This is what is said in Ps 4, 7 [LXX/Vg]: "The light of your face is sealed upon us," that is the light of your Son who is your face, the means by which you are made manifest.[43]

The light spoken about is the capacity to receive reality, transpose it to the level of intelligibility, and name it. The ancient philosophers appreciated the "divine" quality of such a capacity but had to consider it something "borrowed" by a human being, rather than as actually part of his psychosomatic constitution. It was left to Aquinas to correct Avicenna, a devoted disciple of Aristotle on this point, and to posit the intellectual soul as indeed the form of the body.[44] The anthropological consequences of this are enormous, and affect our understanding of what it is we do when we know.

---

[42] *Summa theologiae* 1, 12, 11, ad 3; 1–2, 91, 2.

[43] Thomas Aquinas, *Super Evangelium S. Joannis Lectura* (Rome: Marietti, 1952). For a development of this notion, see D. Juvenal Merriell, *To The Image of the Trinity. A Study in the Development of Aquinas' Teaching, Studies and Texts 96* (Toronto: Pontifical Institute of Medieval Studies, 1990).

[44] See Anton Pegis, "Some Reflections on Summa Contra Gentiles II, 56," in *An Etienne Gilson Tribute*, ed. C. J. O'Neill (Milwaukee: Marquette University Press, 1959), 169–88.

In the very first article of *De Veritate* Aquinas, who is asking the question "Quid sit veritas?," discusses the relation of being to the intellect. He makes the following statement:

> True *(verum)* expresses the correspondence *(convenientia)* of being to the knowing power *(intellectus)*, for all knowing is produced by an assimilation of the knower to the thing known, so that assimilation is said to be the cause of knowledge *(assimilatio dicta est causa cognitionis)*. Similarly, the sense of sight knows a color by being informed with a species of the color. . . .

As we said, the knowledge of a thing is a consequence of this conformity *(ad quam conformitatem, ut dictum est, sequiter cognitio rei)*; therefore it is an effect of truth, even though the fact that it is a being is prior to its truth *(Sic ergo entitas rei praecedit rationem veritatis; sed cognitio est quaedam veritatis effectus)*.[45]

"Assimilation is the cause of knowledge." And again, "knowledge of a thing is a consequence of the conformity of thing and intellect." And since truth is precisely the "assimilation of the knower to the thing known," it follows that "knowledge is a certain effect of truth." We may call the conformity or assimilation of the knower to what is known "ontological truth" and the knowledge that follows from this "epistemological truth." A person is already modified by being or a being before he can articulate the conformity established through what Maritain calls "the basic generosity of existence."[46] Beings give themselves to us and modify us, thus establishing us in truth whose effect is knowledge.

The "Copernican Revolution" effected by Kant has served to invert this whole understanding of truth and knowledge. Conformity is now between what is considered and the mental structure of the human being considering it. This understanding has, consciously or unconsciously, been the basic conviction of thinkers since the eighteenth century and it explains the non-transcendence of the horizons within which the study of history and of text interpretation are carried out. It has been precisely the work of Edmund Husserl to move metaphysical and epistemological thought out from this "ego-centric predicament" to a position that retains Kant's awareness of the subject but reinstates the priority of the real in the act of knowledge. This is not the place to develop this, but I refer

---

[45] Because this is a controverted text, I give the omitted part here: "The first reference *(comparatio)* of being to the intellect, therefore, consists in its agreement with the intellect *(ut ens intellectui correspondeat)*. This agreement is called 'the conformity of thing and intellect' *(adaequatio rei et intellectus)* and in this conformity is found the formal constituent of the true *(et in hoc formaliter ratio veri perficitur)*, and this is what the true adds to being, namely, the conformity or equation of thing and intellect *(conformitatem seu adaequationem rei et intellectus)*."

[46] Jacques Maritain, *Existence and the Existent* (New York: Doubleday, 1957), 90.

the reader to the work of Robert Sokolowski who has made such a valuable contribution in clarifying and advancing the work of Husserl.[47]

> One of phenomenology's greatest contributions is to have broken out of the egocentric predicament, to have checkmated the Cartesian doctrine. Phenomenology shows that the mind is a public thing, that it acts and manifests itself out in the open, not just inside its own confines. . . . By discussing intentionality, phenomenology helps us reclaim a public sense of thinking, reasoning, and perception. It helps us reassume our human condition as agents of truth.[48]

The challenge remaining in Catholic philosophy is to integrate the metaphysical understanding of knowledge to be found in the Tradition, especially in the thought of Aquinas, with the work of modern philosophy, especially that of Husserl as well as that of Gabriel Marcel and others. As this integration is effected, we will be able to elaborate a genuinely Christian epistemology and thus bring the fixation with texts and words out of its impasse into a place of integration and revelation. We will understand that, in human knowing and communicating, "words are revelatory, not representational."[49]

Language

I have already offered elsewhere a brief critique of some modern understandings of language.[50] I wish here merely to offer a very few words of reflection on the human depth of language, the very medium of our thought and communication, and to indicate how language too is a certain participation in the Word.[51] To take the teaching on inspiration seriously means to understand that, in some mysterious way, the Word enters into a culture and a linguistic grid: He becomes "flesh" in language. This traditional theme was echoed in *Dei Verbum* itself:

---

[47] See, among others, Robert Sokolowski, *Introduction to Phenomenology* (New York: Cambridge University Press, 1999); Robert Sokolowski, *Eucharistic Presence. A Study in the Theology of Disclosure* (Washington, DC: Catholic University of America Press, 1993); Robert Sokolowski, "Semiotics in Husserl's *Logical Investigations*," in *One Hundred Years of Phenomenology*, ed. D. Zahavi and F. Stjernfelt (Boston: Kluwer Academic Publishers, 2002), 171–83.

[48] Sokolowski, *Introduction to Phenomenology,* 12.

[49] I owe this phrase to Robert Sokolowksi in a private conversation.

[50] See Francis Martin, "Feminist Hermeneutics: Some Epistemological Reflections," in *This is My Name Forever: The Trinity and Gender Language for God*, ed. Alvin F. Kimel, Jr. (Downers Grove, IL: InterVarsity Press, 2001), 108–35.

[51] I refer the reader to the excellent study by Olivier-Thomas Venard, "Esquisse d'une Critique des 'Méthodes Littéraires'," in *L'Autorité de l'Écriture*, ed. Jean-Michel Poffet, *Lectio Divina hors série* (Paris: Cerf, 2002), 259–98.

For the words of God, expressed in human language, have been made like human discourse, just as the word of the eternal Father, when He took to Himself the flesh of human weakness, was in every way made like men (§13).

Origen often sounded this theme:

Just as this spoken word cannot according to its own nature be touched or seen, but when written in a book, and, so to speak become bodily, then indeed is seen and touched, so too is it with the fleshless and bodiless word of God; according to its divinity it is neither seen nor written, but when it becomes flesh, it is seen and written. Therefore, since it has become flesh, there is a book of its generation.

You are, therefore, to understand the scriptures in this way: as the one perfect body of the word.[52]

There is much work remaining in order to elaborate a Christian theology of language, but it is necessary in order to complete the integration I have been describing in these pages. It will not be done without a deep sense of the "poetic" quality of language, the fact that it reveals rather than represents. The beginnings of such a theology are implicit in the writings of some of the Fathers and Medieval theologians I have cited here. I wish to close this section with a text that offers a foundation for the continuation of this line of thought. It is from Aquinas's commentary on the Prologue of John:

Though there be many participated truths, there is but one absolute Truth which by its own essence is Truth, namely the Divine Being itself, by which Truth all words are words. In the same way there is one absolute Wisdom, raised above all, namely the Divine Wisdom by participation in whom all wise men are wise. And in the same way the absolute Word by participation in whom all who have a word are said to be speaking. This is the Divine Word, which in Himself is the Word raised above all.[53]

Conclusion

We have been considering some aspects of the contribution of *Dei Verbum* to the holiness of the Church and its self-awareness. I have concentrated this docu-

---

[52] Origen, Fragment of the *Commentary on Matthew* (*Patrologia Graeca* 17, 289 AB), and Fragment of *A Homily on Jeremiah* (*Patrologia Graeca* 13, 544C). To be found in Hans Urs von Balthasar, ed., *Origen Spirit and Fire. A Thematic Anthology of His Writings* (Washington, DC: The Catholic University of America Press, 1984). See also Hugh of St. Victor: "The Word of God comes to man everyday, present in the human voice." (*The Word of God,* I, 2–3 [*Sources Chrétiennes* 155,60]).

[53] Aquinas, *Super Evangelium S. Joannis Lectura.*

ment's description of the manner in which the Sacred Scriptures are to be read and interpreted. We have been immensely helped by the historical and linguistic work that has been done in the last century or so, but it remains for us to overcome the intrinsic shortcomings of these methods in order to bring into full flower all that they can contribute to the life of the Church, gathered to celebrate the Liturgy or receiving a visit of the Word in contemplating him in the Sacred Text. The philosophical work is great but it can be done in the energy of faith that calls reason out beyond itself to heights it could never have suspected. Then we will be partakers of the Mystery, that is, mystics in the profound Christian sense of the term, in union with and sharing intimately in the cross and resurrection of Jesus Christ, the Word in whom all history, knowledge, and language find their ultimate source. Allow me to conclude with these words of Henri de Lubac who knew their truth experientially:

> [S]ince Christian mysticism develops through the action of the mystery received in faith, and the mystery is the Incarnation of the Word of God revealed in Scripture, Christian mysticism is essentially an understanding of the holy Books. The mystery is their meaning; mysticism is getting to know that meaning. Thus, one understands the profound and original identity of the two meanings of the word *mystique* that, in current French usage, seem so different because we have to separate so much in order to analyze them: the mystical or spiritual understanding of Scripture and the mystical or spiritual life are, in the end, one and the same.[54]

---

[54] Henri de Lubac, "Mysticism and Mystery," in *Theological Fragments* (San Francisco: Ignatius, 1989), 35, 69, at 58.

12 The Spiritual Sense (*Sensus Spiritualis*) of Sacred Scripture: Its Essential Insight

THIS CONCLUDING ESSAY is at one and the same time a conclusion and an invitation to seek more deeply for that integration of ancient and modern methods of biblical interpretation that has been the governing principle in all the essays. After trying to broaden our modern tendency to equate *sensus* with "meaning," the study moves on to consider briefly the ancient understanding of the three periods of history witnessed to and embodied in the Sacred Text. These are the time of the initial choice of a people as a preparation for the Incarnation *(umbra)*, the presence in Christ of the fulfillment of that part of God's plan *(imago)*, and the fullness of that plan when God's people are with him in glory *(veritas)*. This basic insight into the Bible's theology of history is then traced through some representatives of the Tradition. Finally, the brief concluding section considers the Body of Christ, and the notions of Analogy and Participation as an initial theological foundation for the spiritual sense.

• • •

The Background of the Term *Sensus Spiritualis*

The basic meaning of *sensus*, which often translates the Greek term *nous*, is given variously as *intellectus, action de sentir,* the faculty or power of perceiving. The notion of "meaning" is found seventh in a list of seven possibilities in a recent dictionary.[1] Thus, in patristic and medieval Latin we find as synonyms of *sensus spritualis*, expressions such as *intellectus/intelligentia spiritualis*: "spiritual

---

[1] Albert Blaise, "Sensus," in *Dictionnaire Latin–Français* (Turnholdt: Brepols, 1954). See also Dominus Du Cange, "Sensus," in *Glossarium Mediae et Infimae Latinitatis* (Paris: Librairie des Sciences et des Arts, 1938); Jacobus Facciolatus and Aegidius Forcellinus, "Sensus," in *Totius Latinitatis Lexicon,* ed. Jacobus Bailey (London: Baldwin et Cradock, 1828).

■ 249

understanding." From an epistemological point of view this is important. For the ancients the accent in the phrase *sensus spiritualis* is on the act of knowing and therefore on the act of coming into contact with the reality mediated by the text. Thus, even when the nuance of the expression would demand that we translate *sensus spiritualis* as "spiritual meaning," we may not forget that the phrase comes with the notion of "understanding" always present. This may seem overly subtle, but it will help us avoid one of the pitfalls of modern liter-ary and biblical criticism, which often restricts itself to what George Steiner characterizes as "words about words."[2] It is important to note, then, that *nous pneumatikos, sensus spiritualis,* spiritual understanding, refer to a Spirit-con-ferred faith experience of the reality mediated by the Sacred Text, and a percep-tion of how that reality shares in the mystery of the Whole Christ.

The New Testament

The foundation for the Christian use of the expression *"sensus spiritualis"* is, of course, the view of the New Testament regarding the work of the Holy Spirit in the Old Testament. There is no need to establish this fact here.[3] An enormous amount of work, however, remains to be done consisting of a careful analysis of the manner in which the various New Testament writings actually view the events and persons of the Old Testament and refer to them in many obvious and subtle ways. I select here but one text, in the First Letter of Peter, which manages to express the presence and activity of the Holy Spirit in the Old Dis-pensation preparing for the New Dispensation, which in turn also awaits com-pletion. It speaks of a "salvation," also called a grace, that was prophesied, then made present in Christ, and yet "is coming at the revelation of Jesus Christ."

> The prophets who prophesied of the grace that was to be yours searched and inquired about this salvation; they inquired what person or time was indicated by the Spirit of Christ within them when predicting the suffer-ings of Christ and the subsequent glory. It was revealed to them that they were serving not themselves but you, in the things which have now been announced to you by those who preached the good news to you through the Holy Spirit sent from heaven, things into which angels long to look. Therefore gird up your minds, be sober, set your hope fully upon the grace that is coming to you at the revelation of Jesus Christ (1 Pet 1:10–13).[4]

---

[2] George Steiner, *Real Presences* (Chicago: University of Chicago Press, 1989; 1991).

[3] Helpful studies include: Pierre Grelot, *Sens Chrétien de l'Ancien Testament. Esquisse d'un Traité Dogmatique,* ed. P. Glorieux et al;, *Bibliothèque de Thélogie, Serie 1, Vol. 3* (Paris/New York: Desclée & Cie., 1962). Paul Beauchamp, *L'un et l'autre Testament. Volume 2 Accom-plir les Écritures* (Paris: Éditions du Seuil, 1990).

[4] So powerful was this understanding of the early Church that Didymus the Blind (d. 398), commenting on this text, was able to say: "Those who lived before the coming of Christ

This threefold view of salvation history—past, present, and yet to come—is implicit in many texts and also found clearly expressed in the Letter to the Hebrews 10:1: "The Law, having a sketch *(skian)* of the good things to come, and not the image itself of the realities *(autēn tēn eikona tōn pragmatōn)*. . . ." The Law possessed only a shadow or sketch, we possess the realities but "in icon," that is, we possess them, not according to their proper mode of existence, but rather in another mode, in signs and symbols, until we are with Christ in heaven. This understanding of the Hebrews text was expressed by Ambrose who spoke of "shadow," "image," and "truth."[5]

Irenaeus and Origen

Despite the witness of the Gospels and Letters, which were on their way to becoming a universally recognized canon of teaching, there was a widespread lack of clarity in understanding the role of the Old Testament. By the middle of the second century two diametrically opposed ways of understanding the Old Testament arose. Both of these were wrong in the premise they shared, namely, that the Old Testament as it stood had nothing to offer Christians. They were also wrong in the opposite solutions they proposed.[6] Marcion took the whole of the Hebrew Scriptures literally and rejected them as being unworthy of the God revealed in Christianity. The *Letter of Barnabas* took the Old Testament to be a great and incessant allegory that must be interpreted in a Christian, often moralistic, key.

The Church, however, under the guidance of the New Testament writings, managed to steer a middle path between these extremes. It was, however, left to Irenaeus (d. 200) to begin a theoretical elaboration of the relation between the Testaments. He was confronted with a widespread Gnostic view of humanity, which essentially denied the goodness of human corporality and thus its historicity, and which saw these as a trap from which only specially endowed people could escape. Basing himself on the reality of the Incarnation, Irenaeus understood human history, especially that related in the Old Testament, to be

---

were less well informed, not because of their wickedness but because of God's dispensation of time. Therefore it is said that the prophets examined how and at what time the salvation of their souls would be fulfilled by the sufferings of Christ and his subsequent glory. They preached these things, knowing that they were not going to be directly to them, but would appear at some future time. Therefore it is wrong to say that their sanctification was somehow inferior to ours." See Gerald Bray, ed., *James, 1–2 Peter, 1–3 John, Jude, Ancient Christian Commentary on Scripture* New Testament, XI (Downers Grove, IL: InterVarsity Press, 2000), 73–74

5 *Primum igitur umbra praecessit, secuta est imago, erit veritas. Umbra in lege, imago vero in evangelio, veritas in caelestibus.* On Psalm 43 (*Corpus Scriptorum Ecclesiasticorum Latinorum,* 64, 204).

6 In what follows I am indebted to the study by Joseph T. Lienhard, "Origen and the Crisis of the Old Testament in the Early Church," *Pro Ecclesia* 9 (3; 2000): 355–66.

recapitulated by the real human life and suffering of the Word of God made flesh, now consummated in glory. Thus, the text that tells us of this history is important because it reveals to us the presence and activity of that same Word initiating and carrying out the plan of the Father:

> At the beginning, God, out of his generosity, formed man. For their salvation, He chose the patriarchs. And to teach the ignorant to follow God, He formed a people in advance. . . . For those who were pleasing to Him, He sketched, like an architect, the plan of salvation. In Egypt, to those who could not see Him, He gave Himself as guide. . . . In all these different ways, He prepared mankind for the harmonious music of salvation (cf. Lk 15:25). St. John therefore says in the Apocalypse: 'His voice was like the sound of many waters' (Apoc 1:15). Yes, the waters of God's Spirit are many, for rich and great is the Father. At every stage the Word ungrudgingly gives his assistance to those subject to Him by drawing up a law adapted and appropriate to every creature.[7]

Ultimately, however, it was Origen who "assured the Old Testament a permanent place in the Christian church not by an abstract theory but by working his way through the entire Old Testament book by book, sentence by sentence, and word by word."[8] It is important, however, to realize that for Origen this painstaking activity was inspired by a profound and mystical understanding of history rather than text. Though his thought was refracted through a Platonic understanding it was not dominated by it. For Origen, the contrast between shadow and reality was temporal rather than cosmic; it was between two aspects of the saving plan of the Creator acting in history rather than between two levels of ideas. Because of the importance of this difference I wish to develop this notion further.

The difference between the metaphysics of Plato and that of Origen is encapsulated in Origen's reply to a remark of Celsus, which refers to the Platonic theory of knowledge by citing enigmatically a brief quote from Plato's Letter VII:

> It has occurred to me to speak about these things at greater length,[9] for possibly the matter I am discussing would be clearer if I were to do so. There is a true teaching/reason *(logos)*, which I have often stated before, that stands in the way of the man who would dare write even the least thing on such matters, and which it seems I am now called upon to repeat.

---

[7] *Against the Heresies* IV, 14, 2. Translation by John Saward in Hans Urs von Balthasar, ed., *The Scandal of the Incarnation: Irenaeus Against the Heresies* (San Francisco: Ignatius Press, 1990), 121.

[8] Lienhard, "Origen," 362

[9] "These things" refers to the need and the difficulty of attaining to a knowledge of the "real," indeed the impossibility of attaining to it save by way of mystical intuition.

For each thing that exists there are three elements by which knowledge of it comes about. The fourth is the knowledge itself; and fifth we must pose the object itself as knowable and really existing. First, then, is the name *(onoma)*, second the definition *(logos,* the expression of the thing in itself), third is the image *(eidōlon)*, and fourth is the knowledge *(epistēmē)*.[10]

Origen ceases to quote Celsus at this point and it is probable that Celsus gives only this brief citation, presumably aware that his audience is familiar with the passage and the platonic theme it sums up. Plato's text goes on to illustrate his meaning through an example. The *name* "circle" evokes a reality in the minds of its hearers. The *logos* of circle can be expressed through nouns and verbs, namely: something that has everywhere equal distances between its extremities and its center. The *image* is a material thing that gives expression to the reality; it could be drawn or turned on a lathe. Such images can be erased or destroyed; they do not affect the reality itself, which is different from them. *Knowledge, understanding, correct opinion (epistēmē, nous, alēthēs doxa)* form a class apart, for they do not exist in either sounds *(onoma)*, or bodily figures *(eidōlon)*, but rather in souls. Of these elements then, it is understanding that most closely approaches the fifth level (the "real circle") in regard to both affinity and resemblance, but this too is deficient since it must proceed by way of nouns, verbs, and so on. What *is*, is beyond definition and name and is *agnōstos*, unattainable by the human mode of knowing: What is knowable and true exists purely in the world of Ideas, a world sometimes glimpsed by those who are faithful to the discipline of philosophy.[11]

Why does Celsus cite this text? In this letter, Plato, already an old man, is summing up a position that he had held his whole life long, namely that access to the real is only through an "ecstasy" of mystical insight and union with the One, the Good, and the Beautiful.[12] Celsus, shocked by the notion of God incarnate and despising the idea that knowledge of God can take place by simply believing

---

[10] Plato, *Letter VII*, 341, a–b. The translation is basically my own in consultation with several other translations.

[11] "But even to the one who has an 'inner affinity' with it, 'the light of understanding' does not come passively but after much effort on his own part; though equally it is as a kind of grace, when 'as a result of continued application to the subject itself and of communion therewith, it is brought to birth in the soul on a sudden *(exaiphnēs)*, as light that is kindled by a leaping spark and thereafter it nourishes itself." Hans Urs von Balthasar, *The Glory of the Lord. A Theological Aesthetics,* trans. Oliver Davies, John Riches, Andrew Louth, Brian McNeil, John Saward, and Rowan Williams, vol. IV, *The Realm of Metaphysics in Antiquity* (San Francisco: Ignatius Press, 1989), 180. (Quotation marks within the citation indicate the text of Plato's *Letter VII*.)

[12] For a complete treatment of this notion and an analysis of other texts where Plato sounds this theme, see André-Jean Festugière, *La Révélation D'Hermès Trismégiste,* vol. IV, Le Dieu Inconnu et la Gnose (Paris: Gabalda, 1954), 79–91.

rather than through the spiritualizing ascesis insisted upon by Plato, sees in Christianity a threat to the whole world order he holds dear. Origen's reply is at least as enigmatic Celsus's objection.

> In keeping with such a presentation we may say that "the voice of one cry-ing in the wilderness" is John introduced before Jesus who corresponds *(analogon)* to the *name* in Plato's text. The second, after John and pointed out by him, is Jesus to whom is applied the phrase, "The Word became flesh." This corresponds to the *logos* of Plato. Plato calls the third, *eidōlon*. However, we who use this word in another sense (idol), would say with greater clarity that there is question here of the imprint *(typon)* of the wounds which occur after (the hearing of) the Word, that is to say the Christ in each one coming from Christ the Word. He who is able will know whether the Christ, who according to us is wisdom residing in "those who are perfect" (1 Cor 2:6), corresponds to Plato's fourth aspect, namely knowledge *(epistēmē)*.[13]

Henri Crouzel has put us all in his debt by pointing the way to an under-standing of this passage in which Origen seems purposely to be evasive.[14] In dependence upon Crouzel's explanation, I will attempt to comment on this text because of the importance it has not only for an understanding of Origen but for the whole Christian understanding of Scripture.

We first note that Origen says nothing explicit about Plato's fifth element, the reality itself as it exists beyond the world of image and thought. It is clear, however, that for Origen this realm of "true reality" is the Word himself:

> One could ask the question whether, in a certain sense, the First-born of all creatures is not himself a world, especially since he is Wisdom, a multiform Wisdom, by the fact that he contains in himself the *logoi* of all things accord-ing to which God made the universe, as the prophet says, "You have made all thing in Wisdom." Thus, he would be a world in himself, a world that is more varied and elevated than the sensible world.[15]

---

[13] *Contra Celsum* IV, 9 (Sources Chrétiennes 147, 200).

[14] Henri Crouzel, *Origène et la 'Connaissance Mystique', Museum Lessianum section théologique* 56 (Paris: Desclée de Brouwer, 1961), 213–15.

[15] Commentary on John CGS IV, 323. This way of speaking contains its ambiguities though Origen is not alone in using such platonic terms. It is interesting that Thomas Aquinas, who roundly condemns Origen's opinions as he had access to them via the tra-dition, says himself: "So God makes nothing except through the conception of his intel-lect, which is an eternally conceived Wisdom, that is, the Word of God and the Son of God. Accordingly, it is impossible that he make anything except through the Son. And so Augustine says in *The Trinity* that the Word is the art full of the living patterns of all things." (*Comm. On John* Lecture 1, No.77). Translation in Thomas Aquinas, *Commen-tary on the Gospel of John,* trans. James A. Weisheipl and Fabian R. Larcher (Albany, NY:

By considering the object of Plato's earnest striving to be a personal and not merely an inaccessible "world," Origen has already subverted, while keeping intact, the schema embraced by Celsus and, indeed, the whole of Greek philosophy. In contrast to this philosophy, and in the light of the biblical principle of creation and the fact of the Incarnation, Christianity puts the accent on the *individuum*, the concretely existing reality related to its Creator, rather than the particular, which is rather an instance of a category, and ultimately for Plato a deficient imitation of the Idea. The *individuum* has a history, it is created not *in* history but *with* history,[16] the particular exists in time, but is indifferent to history. This is the fundamental, though here unexpressed, principle that can help us interpret Origen's reply to Celsus's use of Plato, and indeed understand why Christian thought, based on the realities of creation and Incarnation, is both more transcendent and more immanent than pagan thought both ancient and modern.

The first factor of knowledge in this world, the *name*, is John the Baptist insofar as he represents the whole of the Old Testament.[17] The mystery of salvation or Life, that is, ultimately, union with God in the Word, is already "named" in the Old Testament, but this is not clear until salvation is given an essential expression, a *definition*, by the Word of God made flesh. Origen's thought here is echoing 1 John 1: 1–2: "What was from the beginning, what we have heard, what we have seen with our eyes, what we have beheld, and our hands have felt concerning the word of life—and the Life appeared and we have seen and we bear witness and we proclaim to you the Eternal Life which was with the Father and appeared to us." Contrary to the fundamental principle of all platonic thought, the supra-terrestrial world of Ideas has entered the world of matter: He is Jesus, the Eternal Life.

The *image* of the Word incarnate, the Life which has appeared, is found in the imprint of the wounds *(tōn traumatōn typon)*, "that is to say the Christ in each one coming from Christ the Word," received in faith by each believer. The word *typos* is probably being exploited by Origen to refer at one and the same time to the imprint of Christ's wounds and to the fact that this imprint is itself a "type" or figure of the union with Christ that will be effected in heaven. In either case the notion that the mystical, and in some cases the very real physical, wounds born by the believer are already imprinted by Christ who pre-exists him and has now the glorious wounds as the "Lamb standing with the marks of slaughter upon him" (Rev 5:6). At the same time the glory of the Lamb's wounds

---

Magi Books, 1980), 52. For a good clarification of Origen himself, see Henri Crouzel, *Origen. The Life and Thought of the First Great Theologian*, trans. A. S. Worall (San Francisco: Harper and Row, 1989), 191.

16 *"Cum igitur Deus, in cuius aternitate nulla est omnino mutatio, creator sit temporum et ordinator . . . procul dubio non est mundus factus in tempore sed cum tempore.* Augustine, *De Civitate Dei* 11, 6.

17 See Crouzel, *Origène, Connaissance Mystique*, 214.

make of the believer's wounds the figure of the glory that awaits him. It is possible that Origen is thinking of Galatians 6:17: "Henceforth let no man trouble me; for I bear on my body the marks of Jesus," about which Robert Jewett wrote: "Already it is evident that the body of man, the focus of suffering in this world, was viewed by Paul as the sphere where Christ's rule becomes visibly evident."[18] It is, then, particularly in relation to *image* that we see Origen elaborating a metaphysics that includes the physical: Spiritual and material participation in the mystery of Christ is already a share in the eternal Gospel (Rev 14:6) whose *eikōn* is the reality we experience now in Christ, that is, the temporal Gospel.[19]

Finally, "he who is able will know whether the Christ, who according to us is wisdom residing in 'those who are perfect' (1 Cor 2:6), corresponds to Plato's fourth aspect, namely knowledge *(epistēmē)*." What Plato considered to take place in the soul by way of familiarity and resemblance actually happens through an indwelling of the Logos incarnate, the Christ "the wisdom of God" (1 Cor 1:24). There is thus a continuity and not an estrangement between *the name, the essential expression (logos), the image, knowledge, and the reality itself.* This continuity is established because being at all its levels is a successively profound or elevated realization of the incarnate Logos "in whom are hidden all the treasures of wisdom and knowledge" (Col 2:3).

The importance of Origen's reinterpretation of Plato's Seventh Letter lies in the fact that it demonstrated a maturing of the nascent intuitions of a Justin or an Irenaeus into what would become a consistent worldview. The Incarnation

---

[18] Robert Jewett, *Paul's Anthropological Terms. A Study of Their Use in Conflict Settings,* vol. 10, *Arbeiten zur Geschichte des antiken Judentums und des Urchristentums* (Leiden: Brill, 1971), 251. See also 2 Corinthians 4:10–11: ". . . always carrying in the body the death of Jesus, so that the life of Jesus may also be manifested in our bodies. For while we live we are always being given up to death for Jesus' sake, so that the life of Jesus may be manifested in our mortal flesh."

[19] Henry Chadwick in his translation of *Contra Celsum* (Cambridge: Cambridge University Press, 1953), 323, n. 5, suggests that Origen in his commentary on Song of Songs 2:5 ("I am wounded by love") may be developing what he says here of the "wounds" that make up the "image." This is likely, and sheds light on what Origen may mean by equating this interior reality with the *eidōlon* of Plato. I give a portion of that text here. It should be noted that Origen goes on to speak of being wounded by "wisdom," "might," and "justice": "If there is anyone anywhere who has at some time burned with this faithful love of the Word of God; if there is anyone who received the sweet wound of Him who is the chosen dart; if there is anyone who has been pierced with the loveworthy spear of His knowledge, so that he yearns and longs for Him by day and night, can speak of nought but Him, would hear of nought but Him, can think of nothing else, and is disposed to no desire nor longing nor yet hope, except for Him alone—if such there be, that soul then says in truth: 'I have been wounded by love.'" Origen. *The Song of Songs: Commentary and Homilies,* ed. Johannes Quasten and Joseph C. Plumpe, trans. R. P. Lawson, *Ancient Christian Writers* 26 (Westminster, MD: The Newman Press, 1957), 198.

reveals the true nature of cosmic and mental reality as well as language, and it introduces an understanding of history, learned from the Old Testament and transposed in the New Testament.[20] We will return to this later in the study; I wish now to look briefly at Origen's exegetical practice.

In a recent study Elizabeth A. Dively Lauro helpfully sums up one of Origen's ways of expressing the levels of meaning he found in the sacred text, namely by using the terms, "somatic, psychic, and spiritual":

> [O]ne must begin with the purpose of Scripture for Origen. As direct and sole author, the Holy Spirit has imbued Scripture with a *spiritual* character, the purpose of which is to guide human beings to "perfection" and "salvation." This spiritual purpose of Scripture demands a "spiritual" method of interpretation. Origen's exegesis, therefore, analyzes a Biblical passage in a way that edifies the soul of the hearer and so serves Scripture's purpose by imparting the *knowledge, virtue,* and *wisdom* that lead to perfection and, ultimately, salvation. To this end . . . the somatic sense conveys historical *knowledge* or instruction on *virtue*; the psychic sense inspires the temporal fight for *virtue* against vice; and the pneumatic sense inspires *wisdom* regarding the Incarnation and the Eschaton.[21]

We may observe here that the pneumatic sense, in its primary application, refers not to a different *sense* of Scripture but to a deeper capacity to understand the text and the realities it mediates.[22] What is mediated directly belongs to what, as we have seen, Hebrews 10:1 calls the *skia* of "the good things to come."[23] The further difference between *eikon* and *pragmata* (termed by Origen the "temporal Gospel" and the "eternal Gospel") is one of *epnioia,* our manner of knowing,

---

[20] For a reflection on this aspect of Christian thought, see John D. Zizioulas, *Being As Communion, Contemporary Greek Theologians, 4* (Crestwood, NY: St. Vladimir's Seminary Press, 1985), ch. 1.

[21] Elizabeth A. Dively Lauro, "Reconsidering Origen's two higher senses of scriptural meaning: identifying the psychic and pneumatic sense," in *Studia Patristica XXXIV*, ed. M. F. Wiles and E. J. Yarnold (Louvain: Peeters, 2001), 306–17, at 308–09, italics in original.

[22] "Origen never intended his threefold classification to apply to different 'senses' of Scripture or separate classes of Christian; rather they correspond to different stages on a progressive journey to perfection." Frances Young, "Alexandrian and Antiochene Exegesis," in *A History of Biblical Interpretation, Volume 1*, ed. Alan J. Hauser and Duane F. Watson (Grand Rapids, MI: Eerdmans, 2003), 334–54.

[23] Origen cites this text in his treatise on biblical interpretation (*On First Principles*, I IV, 2, 4) but commentators doubt whether he ever completely integrated his three-level understanding, highly influenced by a Platonic anthropology, with his three-stage historical approach expressed in Hebrews 10:1. See Betrand de Margerie, *An Introduction to the History of Exegesis,* trans. Leonard Maluf, vol. I (Petersham, MA: St. Bede's Publications, 1993), 96–116.

while Origen can characterize the difference between the "shadow" and the *eikon* as on of *hypostasis* or substance.[24]

Origen's reading of the Old Testament is thorough, tending at times to be atomistic, seeking to find everywhere a presence of Christ in the events, personalities, and even the objects spoken of in the text. In regard, for instance, to Genesis 18:5 ("Abraham stood . . . under the tree."), he comments: "What does it help me who have come to hear what the Holy Spirit teaches the human race, if I hear that 'Abraham was standing under a tree' "?[25] Such earnestness and faith deserve emulation even if our understanding of inspiration is not as close to dictation as that of Origen and many early Fathers.[26] Furthermore, our first approach, through critical historiography, is less concentrated on individual components of the text and is, in a certain manner, more sensitive to ancient oriental literary *genres*.[27]

My main point here is to establish clearly that for Origen the primary reality designated by the expression "spiritual sense" is the resemblance between the content of the Old Testament text and the mystery of Christ. This relationship is perceived through an experiential knowledge conferred by the Holy Spirit of the reality mediated in and through the Old Testament now understood in the light of Christ. This Spirit-conferred knowledge is described by Henri Crouzel in the striking image of "prophecy in reverse":

> Spiritual exegesis is in a kind of way the reverse process of prophecy: the latter looks to the future, but the former looks back from the future to the past. Prophecy follows the course of time forwards and in a historical or contemporary event sees darkly the messianic or eschatological fact that is prefigured. Spiritual exegesis follows the course of time backwards and, starting from the Messiah already given to the People of God, recognizes in the old Scriptures the preparations and seeds of what is now accomplished. But this accomplishment is in part prophetic in relation to what will take place in the end time.[28]

The principle that it requires a certain prophetic grace in order to understand the Scriptures has become a commonplace in the Christian tradition.[29] Origen's irreplaceable role in Christian thought is found in his prophetic under-

---

[24] See Crouzel, *Origen,* 68.

[25] Lienhard, "Origen," 364.

[26] It should be noted, however, that the early Christian thinkers never thought of this process in terms that would place the Old Testament prophet in a purely passive or mantic state.

[27] I will explain this remark later on.

[28] Crouzel, *Origen,* 71.

[29] Ibid., 73–74. To anticipate somewhat, we may consider this text of Aquinas who specifically attributes the understanding of Old Testament prophecy to a prophetic gift: "They are also called prophets in the New Testament who expound the prophetic sayings because

standing of what we call today the economy of salvation, and thus bring to greater consciousness and clarity the plan of God in regard to Israel and its Scriptures in that economy now seen in Christ. He was able to articulate the New Testament presupposition that the events and persons mediated to us in the Old Testament are somehow anticipated and partial realizations of the mystery of Christ, now fully present in history, which yet awaits its own completion at the end of history. To this basic contribution, established by authors such as Crouzel and de Lubac,[30] we must add a profound philosophical insight, fully articulated later by the Cappadocians, that was able to preserve and yet completely invert the Greek philosophical system by bringing it, as I have said, into the biblical understanding of creation and Incarnation. Lastly, Origen along with the other great theologians of antiquity, mediate to us their experiential knowledge of the Mystery, its "name," its "Logos," its "image" and its "knowledge." They show us in this way the reality to be contacted in and through the text for the building up of the Church, the Body of Christ.

It should be pointed out in addition, however, that the very authors who have such a profound appreciation of Origen and the theological approach that grew out of his insights are also well aware of the deficiencies and shortcomings of his method. There is, first of all, his lack of terminological precision in speaking about the "literal" and "spiritual" senses of the text. For Origen, in the phrase of Henri Crouzel the literal sense is "the brute materiality of the words."[31] Since Origen appears to bypass what we are intent upon discovering, namely the intention of the human author, it may seem that he pays no real attention to what we call the literal sense. In fact, however, he would accept as actual historical happenings more events in the Old Testament than any modern critical interpreter would be prepared to acknowledge: "For the passages which are historically true are far more numerous than those which are composed with purely spiritual meanings."[32] Fernand Prat responds partially to the difficulty caused by Origen's terminology in his discussion of what Origen intended by the expression *nous pneumatikos*:

> Just so he [Origen] does not attach to the words *spiritual meaning* the same signification as we do: for him they mean the spiritual sense properly so called (the meaning added to the literal sense by the express wish of God attaching a special signification to the fact related or the manner of relating them), or the figurative as contrasted with the proper sense, or the

---

Sacred Scripture is interpreted in the same Spirit in which it is composed." On Romans 12:8, Thomas Aquinas, *Super Epistulas S. Pauli Lectura* (Rome: Marietti, 1953), # 978.

[30] Henri de Lubac, *Histoire et Esprit. L'intelligence de l'Écriture d'après Origène, Théologie 16* (Paris: Aubier, 1950).

[31] Crouzel, *Origen,* 93.

[32] Origen, *Origen: On First Principles,* trans. G. W. Butterworth (Gloucester, MA: Peter Smith, 1973). IV, 3, 4; 295.

accommodative sense, often an arbitrary invention of the interpreter, or even the literal sense when it is treating of things spiritual. If this terminology is kept in mind there is nothing absurd in the principle he repeats so often: "Such a passage of the Scripture has no corporal meaning." As examples Origen cites the anthropomorphisms, metaphors, and symbols which ought indeed to be understood figuratively.[33]

Another of Origen's shortcomings is his conviction, as we saw above in regard to Abraham standing under the tree, that each discrete unit of the text must stand for something. This is due to his philosophical orientation and his overuse of the concept of allegory. Since these are the objections made in antiquity by the Antiochene school, I will defer a discussion of them until we have assayed this school of thought in its strengths and weaknesses.

The School of Antioch

Origen died in 253/54, the result of torture endured in prison during the persecution under Decius. His legacy has left an indelible imprint on theology. In the East, Didymus the Blind was a disciple and Athanasius was deeply influenced by him while the four great Doctors of the Latin Church, along with Hilary and others, evince direct dependence on Origen. Nevertheless his name has been associated with controversy from a very early date.[34] The only aspect of controversy that need occupy us in seeking clarity on the ancient understanding of the spiritual sense of Scripture is that between the followers of Origen, or the Alexandrian school (found throughout the Empire), and the fourth-century Antiochene school whose most prominent though diverse representatives included Eustathius of Antioch, Theodoret of Cyrrhus, Diodorus of Tarsus, and his two pupils—Theodore of Mopsuestia and John Chrysostom.

The two principal objections of the Antiochenes are based on Origen's tendency to search for a higher, allegorical (in the Pauline sense) meaning in small, discrete portions of the biblical text. They countered this by insisting first on the *historia* or narrative logic of the texts and on the *theoria*, by which they meant the contemplative vision of the future of God's plan. While these are serious differences we should bear in mind that this quarrel was between men who had received the same basic rhetorical formation.[35] Origen, concentrating on the unified *skopos* of the Holy Spirit in composing the whole Bible, looked upon the text and parts of the text as necessarily concerned with this *skopos* and was philosoph-

---

[33] *The Catholic Encyclopedia* (New York: Robert Appleton, 1911), Vol. XI. K. Knight, Fernand Prat, "Origen," online edition, 2003.

[34] A good history of these controversies can be found in the article by Prat referred to above.

[35] See Frances Young, "The Rhetorical Schools and Their Influence on Patristic Exegesis," in *The Making of Orthodoxy: Essays in Honour of Henry Chadwick*, ed. R. A. Williams (Cambridge: Cambridge University Press, 1989), 182–99.

ically oriented to look for a higher meaning *(anagogē)*. To this contemplative activity he most often gave the name *allēgoria*. The Antiochenes paid more attention to the intrinsic historical reference of the text (Origen, as we have seen, was serious about historicity in his own way), and to its *historia*, by which they meant the overall logic of the text as opposed to its discrete units. They too looked for *anagogē* but they found it in the discovery of the higher meaning intended by the author and revealed by his use of "excessive" language *(hyperbolē)* to describe a person or event, seeing in such hyperbolic language the author's hint that behind the event or person described there was a deeper and more divine reality. They thus located the contemplative insight into the future relevance of the event or person in the original author considering it as an extended literal meaning of the text. They generally acknowledged the authority of the New Testament authors to see that intention even where their own methods could not find it.[36]

Certain conclusions are evident at this point. First, it should be clear that neither the Antiochenes nor the Alexandrians had any notion of or interest in what we call today the historical critical method. Everyone grants this in regard to Alexandria, but it is also true of Antioch:

> [M]y suggestion that the exegetical debate reflected a difference within Greco-Roman culture about how to treat texts, means that the question of method remains relevant, and also accounts for those features of Antiochene exegesis which sit so ill at ease with attempts to characterize it as if it were the precursor of modern historico-critical method. There was no genuine historical criticism in antiquity. The Antiochenes do take *historia* seriously, but in the sense of *to historikon* [the coherence and argument of the text].[37]

Second, the foundation of the debate lay in the fact that the Alexandrians, following Origen, were *philosophically* oriented and sought a meaning in the realities as they were portrayed by the biblical text, while the Antiochenes were *rhetoricians* more attentive to the *hypothesis* of the text, its basic message, and its *akolouthia* or inner coherence. Both parties made significant contributions to the Christian reception of the Bible and both need correction.[38]

---

36 Theodore of Mopsuestia was reluctant in this regard and earned the censure of later ages. See de Margerie, *An Introduction,* 170–81.

37 Young, "The Rhetorical Schools," 189.

38 For a study that challenges an overly optimistic assessment of Antiochene exegesis, see John J. O'Keefe, " 'A Letter that Killeth': Toward a Reassessment of Antiochene Exegesis, or Diodore, Theodore, and Theodoret on the Psalms," *Journal of Early Christian Studies* 8 (1; 2000): 83–104. In the opening summary the author states: "It [Antiochene exegesis] tended to sever the linkages uniting the Old with the New and weakened the ability of the Bible to function as a Christian text. Rather than seeing Antiochene exegesis as a forward-looking project that was suppressed, we should consider it instead to be a backward-looking project that failed."

Third, both parties, true to their respective assimilation of the Greco-Roman rhetorical principles, saw the Christological dimension of the Old Testament differently. For Alexandria, as I have said, it lay in the realities as they were mediated by the Sacred Text, for Antioch it lay in the vision of the authors of the Old Testament themselves. In the light of what we now understand about the need to reroute historical criticism in the direction of understanding the realities as they were purposely mediated by the Old Testament authors rather than our reconstruction of these realities, the difference between these approaches may not be insurmountable.[39] We can already see the possibility of some reconciliation in the fact that neither school of thought actually expounded the text in strict conformity with its own theoretical description of its method.[40]

Fourth, both schools of thought maintained that there were texts in the Old Testament that referred to the Christ event. For Antioch this was due to the contemplative insight *(theoria)* given to the authors of Scripture by which they perceived that what they spoke about was a figure of something to come. Interpretation meant sharing the contemplative vision of the Old Testament author. For Alexandria it meant entering into the interpretative manner of narrating that we find in the Old Testament itself and seeing the reality so narrated as a participation in the coming Incarnate Word.

Thomas Aquinas

It is certainly of great importance to trace the development of the understanding of the spiritual sense of Scripture, as well as the abuses of the term, and the confusion, exaggerations, and misapplications that often go under the title of "spiritual" or especially its synonym "allegorical" exegesis.[41] However, my goal in this short study is to begin to establish the theology of history that underlies and

---

[39] This new sensitivity to the actual mode of mediation in assessing the event as it is passed on to us is well expressed by K. Lawson Younger, Jr: "While it is perfectly valid (and important) to ask questions concerning which events were narrated, it is equally valid and important to ask questions concerning the *way in which events were narrated.* In fact it is the latter questions which reveal the texts' ultimate purpose. K. Lawson Younger, Jr., *Ancient Conquest Accounts. A Study in Ancient Near Eastern and Biblical History Writing,* JSOT Supp. 98 (Sheffield: Sheffield Academic Press, 1990), 63. Cited in Marc Zvi Brettler, *The Creation of History in Ancient Israel* (London and New York: Routledge, 1995), 1 (italics added).

[40] The divergence between Origen's principles in the *Peri Archōn* and his practice has been frequently noted. In regard to Antioch we read on page 179 of De Margerie's *Introduction*: "It would appear then that it is not so easy to find an example of *theoria* proposed by an Antiochian author that fulfills all the conditions supposedly laid down by the school."

[41] For a balanced account the reader may consult the further study by Frances Young, *Biblical Exegesis and the Formation of Christian Culture* (Cambridge: Cambridge University Press, 1997), especially chapters 9 and 11. Also, Andrew Louth, *Discerning the Mystery. An Essay on the Nature of Theology* (Oxford: Oxford University Press, 1983).

legitimates that understanding of the Scriptures of the Jewish people, which the Christians, following the lead of the New Testament, embrace as constituting the major portion of their own Scriptures. For that purpose I will go to the thinking of St. Thomas Aquinas both because he is a clear exponent of the Tradition and because of his respect for the work of God in the Jewish people.[42]

For this study, I will take what is probably Aquinas's earliest treatment of the question of the "senses" of Scripture, namely the three articles of Question 6 of *Quodlibetum 7*, probably delivered in Paris not later than Advent of 1275.[43] I will comment on these briefly and adduce some other places in his writings that are relevant to our purpose, which, to repeat, is to show that the basic understanding of the spiritual sense of Scripture is that of a Spirit-conferred experiential understanding of the relation between the reality mediated in the text and the mystery of Christ. Question 6 is framed this way: *"De sensibus sacrae Scripturae"* and the articles are: (1) "Whether besides the literal sense in the words of sacred Scripture other senses lie hidden *(lateant)*?" (2) "On the number of senses of sacred Scripture." (3) "Whether these senses are found in other writings?"[44]

In regard to the first consideration, Aquinas invokes as his authorities first the Vulgate of Daniel 12:4, "Many shall pass through and knowledge will be multiple." He then cites Jerome, speaking of the Apocalypse: "In each word there lie multiple understandings."[45] In his argument he invokes the principle that Sacred Scripture is so composed that the truth necessary for salvation is manifested in it, and then goes on to state that the manifestation or expression of the truth can take place "by means of things and words *(rebus et verbis)*" insofar as words signify things and a thing can be a figure *(figura)* of something else. The Maker *(Auctor)* of things cannot only employ words to signify something, but can also so dispose things that they are a figure of something else. Thus in Sacred Scripture the truth is manifested in two ways: In one way the realities *(res)* are signified by words and in this consists the literal sense; in another way the realities (signified) are figures of other realities, and in this consists the spiritual sense. In this way it belongs to Sacred Scripture to have many senses.

In answer to the objection that if Sacred Scripture had many senses there would be a multiplicity of statements in the same utterance, Aquinas responds

---

[42] I recognize that this second point is controverted, especially among some Jewish scholars. While I will not be entering into this debate, I think that what I say here may place it in a broader and more theological context.

[43] For a discussion of the *Quodlibeta* and the dating of the text we are considering, see Jean Pierre Torrell, *Initiation à saint Thomas d'Aquin. Sa personne et son oeuvre,* ed. Pierre Hadot et al., *Vestigia 13* (Fribourg, Suisse/Paris: Éditions Universitaires/Cerf:, 1993), 305–6.

[44] As often as possible I translate Aquinas's latin *allegoria, allegorice,* and so on as "allegory," "allegorically" and so on to give the reader the sense of how thoroughly the Tradition, basing itself on Galatians 4:24, had Christianized the term to refer to a specific mode of *biblical* interpretation.

[45] Get cite [?AU: pls. provide]

that the spiritual sense is always founded upon the literal sense, and thus the fact that it be expounded both literally and spiritually does not produce a multiplicity of senses. To the objection that a plurality of senses would result in the fact that understanding would be confused, he answers with Augustine that difficulty in interpreting Scripture has many advantages, such as avoiding boredom or pride as well as obscuring the text in the sight of unbelievers; in regard to this last he cites Matthew 7:8. The third objection alleges that the presence of any sense except the literal could lead to error. Aquinas answers, again with Augustine, that what is said in a hidden way in one part of Scripture is said openly in another, and thus a spiritual interpretation must have a foundation in some literal interpretation, and in this way error is avoided.

In the fourth objection the statement of Augustine is adduced to the effect that the authority of Scripture has greater authority than any human insight. But is not fitting that Scripture have a sense that has no authority for establishing something *(ad aliquid confirmandum)*. However, only the literal sense is suitable for arguing *(argumentativa)* as Dionysius says, and thus Sacred Scripture has only a literal sense. Aquinas responds by pointing out that it is not because of a defect in the authority of Scripture that one cannot draw an argument from the spiritual sense. It is rather because of the ambiguity in the nature of similitudes that can signify many things and not just one thing, such as the word "lion," which, for different reasons, is applied to Christ and the devil. What Aquinas does not point out, however, perhaps presuming it to be obvious, is that Sacred Scripture is not intended to be merely "argumentative," that is, useful for establishing a truth, especially in discussion with heretics.[46] Scripture "manifests" (note the "disclosure" language) the truth and it does so in an abundance of different ways (for example, the Psalms) in order to lead the believer into a deeper participation in the truth. It suffices for instance to glance at Aquinas's own commentaries on Scripture, which are mostly his editing of disciples' notes taken in class, to see how he actually expounds the Sacred Text, leading his students to a grasp of the abundant truth mediated by the text and freely making use of such expressions as *"spiritualiter"* or *"mystice"* to characterize his exposition.

The last objection states that any meaning derived from a text that does not correspond to the intention of the author is not a proper meaning. Aquinas's answer is twofold. First, the author of Sacred Scripture is the Holy Spirit who can intend many things that exceed what the interpreters of Scripture can make out. Second, it is not unfitting that a human author who is the instrument of the Holy Spirit understand many things in one expression, as Jerome points out in stating that the prophets spoke of present realities *(factis)*

---

[46] For an insight into what St. Thomas means by "argument," one could consult *Summa theologiae* 1, 1, 8 on the "argumentative" nature of Sacred Doctrine. See also, Chapter 1.

in such a way that by their statements they also intended to signify future things. Jerome's statement, endorsed by Aquinas, reflects in some ways the Antiochene understanding of prophecy mentioned above.[47]

In the second article Aquinas treats the four senses of Scripture, listing them as "*historialis vel litteralis, allegoricus, moralis et anagogicus.*" As authorities for this understanding he cites both Augustine and Bede. He then proceeds by returning to the principle propounded in the first article, namely that Sacred Scripture manifests the truth that it mediates *(tradit)* in a twofold manner: through words and through the figures of things *(per verba et per rerum figuras).* That manifestation, which takes place through words, gives us the historical or literal sense, and therefore all that is rightly understood from the signification of the words belongs to the literal sense. The spiritual sense, on the other hand, consists in the fact that certain realities are expressed through the images *(figurae)* of other realities because, as Dionysius says, visible things are wont to be figures of invisible things, and thus that meaning, which is understood *(accipitur)* from figures, is called the spiritual sense. Furthermore, the truth of Scripture is ordained to two goals, namely right belief and right action. This latter sense, namely, right action is called the moral sense also known as the tropological sense. The first sense—that is, right belief—is twofold. Since the state of the Church on earth lies midway between the Synagogue and the Church triumphant, the Old Testament may be said to be a figure of the New Testament while both Testaments are a figure of heavenly realities. The spiritual sense can be founded in the manner in which the Old Testament is a figure of the New, and this is called the allegorical or typical sense, or it can, along with the New Testament, be a figure of the Church triumphant, and this is the anagogical sense.

The first objection hinges on what is meant by *figura*. Many realities are spoken of in a figurative manner, for instance the he-goat of Daniel 8:5 is, in its literal sense, a figure of the Greek empire. In the same way the figures indicating Christ in the Old Testament are to be understood literally, that is historically; they are not to be understood allegorically. Aquinas answers by making a distinction between those imaginary figures that stand for something else and those realities spoken of in a text that are also figures of something future.[48] In regard to the latter he says that those things that happened *in rei veritate* (and not just in imagination) are ordered to Christ as a shadow to the truth (note

---

[47] For a treatment of nuanced manner in which Aquinas accepts the medieval understanding of the condemnation of Theodore of Mopsuestia, and yet his own understanding that some prophecies, notably the Emmanuel prophecy in Isaiah 7:14, have the future event as their literal meaning, see the forthcoming article by Daniel Flores to be published by *The Thomist*: "Aquinas and Theodore of Mopsuestia."

[48] He acknowledges that there are imaginary figures that designate Christ in the literal or historical sense, such as the rock "cut by no human hand" of Daniel 2:34. Actually, the rock "cut by no human hand" refers literally or historically to Israel and spiritually to Christ.

the allusion to Heb 10:1) and designate either Christ or his members constitute a sense other than the historical namely the allegorical.[49]

The second objection wishes to equate the allegorical and the moral sense on the basis of the fact that Christ and his members make up one reality. Aquinas answers by pointing out that the spiritual or allegorical sense of an Old Testament reality applies to the Church as the Body of Christ, whereas as the moral sense refers to the individual acts of the members of Christ. The third objection states that there are many literal statements that regard morals, and thus the distinction between moral and allegorical is not a good one. Aquinas replies that only those moral teachings that take place through the likeness of something done *(ex similtudine aliquarum rerum gestarum)*, and I would add are narrated in Scripture, form a part of the spiritual sense. The fourth objection merely serves as the occasion for clarifying how the allegorical sense applies to Christ as head of the Church militant and the anagogical sense applies to him as head of the Church triumphant.

The fifth objection cites a phrase of Augustine to the effect that in some texts only the literal sense is to be sought. The answer provides the occasion for setting a theology of history. Aquinas begins by stating that not every text of Scripture has all four senses, and for enunciating the principle that most often the spiritual sense is found in an earlier text that somehow expresses something yet to come (recall Crouzel's description of "prophecy in reverse"), and thus all four senses can be found in that which, according to the literal sense, treats events *(facta)* of the Old Testament. In regard to the present state of the Church those things are prior that pertain to the Head in relation to the Body because those things that were accomplished in the actual *(verum)* body of Christ are examples (moral sense) for us, the mystical Body. In Christ, moreover, future glory is set forth for us and thus what is said literally of Christ the Head can be understood, first, allegorically, as pertaining to his mystical Body; second, morally, pointing to how our actions must be reformed; and, third, anagogically, insofar as Christ is shown to us as the Way to glory. Whenever anything is said literally of the Church this cannot be expounded allegorically unless perhaps we can say that those things recounted of the primitive Church can be interpreted morally and allegorically in regard to ourselves. In a similar manner the examples of moral conduct set forth literally in the Sacred Text can be interpreted only literally. Finally, those things said literally of the state of glory are normally to be interpreted literally since they are not a figure of anything but are rather imaged *(figurata)* by everything else.

The third and last article of this question sets forth a remarkable principle in which Aquinas is able to set forth the traditional understanding of sacred

---

[49] The constant use of the term "allegorical" as a synonym for "figural" or "spiritual" ought to be noted, as well as the difference between this use and the later literary use of the term "allegory."

history as being a unique work of God. The question addressed is: "Whether these senses are to be found in other writings?" The authority invoked here is taken from Gregory the Great's *Moralia* 20, 1 (*PL* 76, 135): "Sacred Scripture, in its very manner of speaking, is above all other sciences because in one and the same word, while it narrates an event, it sets forth a mystery." (*"Sacra Scriptura omnes scientias ipso locutionis suae more transcendit, quia uno eodemque sermone dum narrat gestum, prodit mysterium."*) The two words "event" and "mystery" refer in turn to the literal sense, the event, and then the same event as it is now seen to have been a participated anticipation of the mystery of Christ. Aquinas's own answer is worth citing in full since it clearly shows that this manner of interpreting the Scriptures is founded on a faith view of history learned from the Scriptures themselves and not simply an exercise in intertextuality.

> The spiritual sense of Sacred Scripture is derived from the fact that realities, playing out their own actions *(cursum suum peragentes)*, signify something else and that something is arrived at through a spiritual meaning *(sensus)*.
>
> Things are so disposed in their own activities in such a way that from them such a (spiritual) meaning can be understood, and this is accomplished by him only who governs things by his providence, namely God alone. For just as a human being can use words or some fashioned likenesses to signify something, so God uses the very course of events *(ipsum cursum rerum)* which is subject to his providence for the signifying of other things.
>
> The signifying of something through words or fashioned likenesses designed simply to signify effects only a literal sense as we have said. Thus, in no science which results from human effort can there be found, properly speaking, anything but the literal sense. Only in this Scripture whose author is the Holy Spirit and a human being the instrument (can there found a spiritual sense) as it says in Psalm 44 (45): 2, "My tongue is that of a quickly writing scribe."

The first two objections assert that sciences proceed by way of similitudes and that poetry uses various fashioned likenesses to mediate the truth, and thus these two have a spiritual sense. In his response to these, Aquinas returns to his basic principle that only in Scripture, over and above the literal meaning of the words, however image-laden, can the things or events spoken of actually signify other things or events. In response to Aristotle's dictum that he who says one thing says many things, St. Thomas responds that the dictum applies to statements that contain in germ many conclusions that can be derived, but this is not one reality actually signifying another.

It seems clear that for Aquinas there are two basic aspects to the spiritual sense of Scripture. First, this sense of Scripture, often called allegorical, spiritual, or mystical, extending to a moral or heavenly referent, can only be unique to

Scripture. Second, this sense derives from the special action of God in and through Christ by which he created and formed Israel, became incarnate himself in the union between his divine Word and the humanity of Jesus Christ, and formed a Church, the Body of Christ. The goal of this special divine action is the creation of a people who will eternally share in his divine life.

In regard to the first aspect, we see Aquinas very much the schoolman, penetrating and furthering the tradition he had received. Ten years later, when establishing the nature of *Sacra Doctrina* in the first question of the *Summa theologiae*, Aquinas articulates in the tenth article the same basic principle that we have just seen. In answering "Whether the Sacred Writings of this doctrine may be interpreted according to many meanings?," he cites the same text of Gregory concerning the unique dignity of Sacred Scripture in that "*dum narrat gestum, prodit mysterium.*" Aquinas's own answer is basically the same. He responds that God is able to have not only words signify, as humans can do, but also "*res ipsas,*" which, as we have seen, must be taken to mean "events" and not merely "things." He then goes on to say that the first signification, that of the words, belongs to the first meaning (*sensum*), "which is the historical or literal meaning." The signification by which "the realities signified by the words in turn signify other things" ("*res significatae per voces, iterum alias res significant*") is called the "*sensus spiritualis,*" "which is founded upon the literal meaning and supposes it." This understanding is consistent in Aquinas as studies have shown, but this text suffices for our purposes here.[50]

In regard to the unique providence of God in regard to Israel, St. Thomas's second point, we can find remarks such as the following:

> The Jewish people were chosen by God in order that Christ be born of them. Therefore it was necessary that the whole state (*status*) of that people be prophetic and figural as Augustine says in *Contra Faustum* (22, 24).[51] And for this reason even the judicial precepts handed on to that people are more figural than the judicial precepts handed on to other peoples. And thus even the wars and actions of that people are expounded mystically but not the wars and actions of the Assyrians or Romans even though they were by far better known among men.[52]

---

[50] See, for instance, M.-D. Mailhiot, "La penseé de saint Thomas sur le sens spirituel," *Revue Thomiste* 59 (4; 1959): 613–63. Jacques Gribomont, "Le lien des deux Testaments selon la théologie de saint Thomas," *Ephemerides Theologicae Lovanienses* 22 (1946): 70–89.

[51] "First of all, then, not only the speech of these men, but their life also, was prophetic; and the whole kingdom of the Hebrews was like a great prophet, corresponding to the greatness of the Person prophesied." Translation in *Fathers,* Vol. 4, 283.

[52] *Summa theologiae* 1–2, 104, 2, ad 2. Note that Aquinas is speaking here about *realities* (wars and actions), and not only of the words by which these realities are mediated.

It is clear, then, that the life and history of Israel are different from that of the rest of humankind up to the coming of Christ. We will proceed to reflect on this in the concluding section of this study.

Theological Principles Underlying the Traditional Understanding of Sensus Spiritualis

There are two implicit principles that are operative in the traditional understanding of the spiritual sense; both of these must be recovered, and in a process of correlation, be brought to bear on this issue.[53] They are, first, the ancient understanding, and specifically the biblical understanding, of how the past is present, and second, a more adequate theory of cognition and language. Treatment of these must await another study. There is, however, a third basic principle that merits at least brief treatment here. It is implied in the Thomistic text just cited that the wars and actions of Israel must be expounded mystically, that is, spiritually, in relation to Christ. An understanding of this principle can be found principally in reflecting on the Body of Christ.

The Body of Christ

As a guide in this reflection I will consider Aquinas's treatment of the Body of Christ in Question 8 of the Third Part of the *Summa theologiae*.[54] In the third article of that question he addresses the topic whether Christ is the head of all men. As authorities for his positive response he cites 1 Timothy 4: 10: "I mean that the point of all our toiling and battling is that we have put our trust in the living God and he is the Savior of the whole human race but particularly of all believers," and 1 John 2:2 "He is expiation for our sins, and not for our sins only but for those of the whole world." He concludes: "To save men or to be the expiation for their sins belongs to Christ as Head; therefore Christ is the Head of all men."

In his own argument Aquinas points out that the first difference we must note between the natural human body and the mystical Body of the Church lies in the fact that in a natural body all the members are present simultaneously whereas in the Mystical Body the members are not present at simultaneously. This is because, first, "the Body of the Church is constituted by human beings "who existed from the beginning of the world until its end." Second, the members are not all present at the same time because some are only potential members and may remain so until by death they lose even that potentiality. Thus, there are diverse degrees of belonging to the Body of the Church. First and foremost he is

---

53 For an extended discussion of a correct understanding of correlation and its role in theology see, Francis Martin, *The Feminist Question. Feminist Theology in the Light of Christian Tradition* (Grand Rapids, MI: Eerdmans, 1994), ch. 2.

54 For a more ample treatment of this topic in antiquity, see Emile Mersch, *The Theology of the Mystical Body*, trans. Cyril Vollert (St. Louis: Herder, 1952).

the Head of those who are actually united to him in glory. Second, he is Head of those who are actually united to him by love; third, of those who are united to him by faith (as "dead members"); fourth, those who are only united to him potentially but will be actually united; and finally, there are those who are only united to him potentially and will never be united actually.

In answer to the first two objections, one concerning non-believers and the other deriving from the description of the Church as having "no spot or wrinkle or any such thing" (Eph 5:27), Aquinas simply applies to the first the notion of potential versus actual and to the second the diverse degrees in being united to Christ. The answer to the third objection is, however, extremely important for our consideration here.

The objection runs as follows:

> The sacraments of the Old Law [all the liturgical observances] are compared to Christ as a shadow to "the body" as it says in Colossians 2:17. But the Fathers of the Old Testament used these sacraments in their time as it says in Hebrews 8:5, "They used an exemplar and shadow of the heavenly realities." Therefore they did not belong to the Body of Christ, and thus Christ is not the Head of all human beings.

Aquinas answers:

> It should be said that the holy Fathers did not stop at the sacraments of the Law as mere things, but as images and shadows of future realities. For the movement toward an image, in so far as it is an image, is the same as the movement toward the reality as the Philosopher says in his work *On Memory and Recall*. And therefore, the ancient Fathers, by observing the sacraments of the Law, were brought toward Christ through the same faith and love by which we are still brought toward him. For this reason the ancient Fathers belonged to the same Body of the Church to which we belong.[55]

We find the same teaching in Aquinas's commentary on the Letter to Colossians. Speaking about the term *principium (archē)* in Colossians 1:18, he remarks first that "it is the same Church" in the present and in glory, and goes

---

[55] I am indebted here to the study by Colman O'Neill, "St. Thomas On the Membership of the Church," *Thomist* 27 (1963): 88–140. The latter part of Aquinas's response is his translation. The notion that the Jews of Old Testament times belonged to the Body of Christ is not peculiar to Aquinas. Augustine says the same: "Nolite ergo putare, fratres, omnes justos qui passi sunt persecutionem iniquorum, etiam illos qui venerunt ante Domini adventum praenuntiare Domini adventum, non pertinuisse ad membra Christi. Absit ut non pertineat ad membra Christi, qui pertinet ad civitatem quae regem habet Christum." Enarratio in Ps LXI, 4 (*CCL* XXXIX, 774).

on to speak of Christ as the *principium* of justification and grace "in the whole Church because even in the Old Testament there are some justified through faith in Christ *(per fidem Christi)*.[56]

It is important to note with Colman O'Neil, however, that Thomas makes a distinction between the grace of Christ present in the Old Testament and the *state* of that grace that is characteristic of this time of revelation. Availing himself of the distinction we have seen frequently between *umbra, imago, et veritas*, Aquinas distinguishes the first stage as before the Law when individual persons or families were instructed by divine revelation, and the time of the Law. In regard to the threefold distinction itself (shadow, image, truth) we read in *Summa theologiae* 1–2, 102, 2c, that the "truth" is the direct vision of the divine Truth itself and worship will not consist in anything figurative "but solely in the praise of God proceeding from interior knowledge and affection"; as it says in Isaiah 51:3, "Joy and gladness shall be found therein, thanksgiving and the voice of praise." The Old Testament is called "shadow" because at that time "neither was the divine Truth manifest in itself, nor was the way leading thereto yet opened out." The New Testament is called "image" because, though the manifestation of the divine truth, as prophesied in Isaiah, is not as yet present, the Way to it has been made known, and with this manifestation goes a stable form of life (a state) that will perdure until it is perfected by the third stage, the Truth itself.[57]

As O'Neill points out in his study,[58] there are several differences between the New Law and the state of the New Law, between the shadow and the *eikōn* of the realities. The New Law is stable and not to be fulfilled by another dispensation on earth; it is now proposed to the whole human race; it is the Body of Christ, the Church; its sacraments contain Christ or the power of his mysteries and are not figurative only of the heavenly realities; its Scriptures reveal the Way to eternal life by bringing us into contact with Christ now incarnate; it consists in the presence and action of the Holy Spirit who is now himself the New Law.

Analogy and Participation

Our second consideration in making explicit the traditional understanding of the spiritual sense more accessible is to recover the reality of Christ as the center of history, the reality in which all of God's actions find their culmination,

---

[56] Aquinas, *Super Epistulas S. Pauli Lectura,* Ad Col 1:18, Lectura 5, #48.

[57] "It is accepted that the New Testament remains because it is begun here below and perfected in the fatherland." Aquinas, *Commentary on 1 Corinthians 3:1–2,* cited by Bourke and Littledale in the Blackfriars edition of the *Summa theologiae,* Volume 29, 119. I owe some of the translation of the Aquinas passage cited in this paragraph to the same volume.

[58] Colman O'Neill, "St. Thomas On the Membership of the Church," *Thomist* 27 (1963): 88–140.

and participation in whom results in an eternal life of direct union with the Trinity. As Hans Urs von Balthasar expresses it:

> The historical life of the Logos—to which his death, Resurrection and Ascension belong—is, as such, that very world of ideas which, directly or reductively, gives the norm for all history; yet, as not coming forth from some non-historical height above, but from the living center of history itself. Seen from the highest, definitive point of view, it is the source of history, the point whence the whole of history before and after Christ emanates: its center. . . . For the business of theology is not to keep one eye on philosophy, but with its gaze obediently turned toward Jesus Christ, simply and directly to describe how he stands in time and in history as the heart and norm of all that is historical.[59]

Aquinas points out that God is present to his creation in three ways. He is present as cause of all that is, he is present as the object of knowledge and love in those human beings whose level of existence has been raised or intensified by grace, and he is present personally through the grace of union in the covenant between his eternal Word and the elect humanity of Jesus.[60] It is to this third and unique presence known to us only by revelation that von Balthasar is referring in the text above. If we add to that the fact that Christ is the Source of all divine life conferred upon human beings we see that it is not enough to consider how all creatures participate in him as creator, we must understand that special providence working within creation to bring all those human beings who are willing to an eternal goal beyond their capacities.

Thus we answer affirmatively the question once posed by Jean Nabert: "Do we have the right to invest one moment of history with an absolute characteristic?"[61] This does not imply that there is no such thing as a history with its own existence and intelligibility: If human existence were not something "other" the Incarnation would not be union but absorption. Because of Christ's death and resurrection the very essence of human existence has been modified and thus there will come a moment when all of history reaches the goal set for it by God. Enlightenment historiography tends to look at agents rather than subjects and thus restricts its enquiry to a level of causality that, because it seems to imitate that of the physical sciences, has no interior and no genuinely human dimension. But this is not history. History is the action of human subjects and thus necessarily has

---

[59] Hans Urs von Balthasar, *A Theology of History, Communio Books* (New York: Sheed and Ward, 1963; San Francisco: Ignatius, 1994).

[60] *Summa theologiae* 1, 8, 3, c and ad 4, where he mentions the singularis modus essendi Deum in hominine per unionem which he will consider in *Summa theologiae* 3, 2.

[61] J. Nabert, *Essai sur le mal* (Paris: Presses Université de France, 1955), 148.

an interior dimension, what Jean Lacroix calls the "interiority of history,"[62] and what Henri de Lubac has referred to as the "spiritual dimension of history."[63]

This reality of history introduces us into a totally different understanding of time. Rather than a mechanical process moving from past to present and measured by production and progress, history, with the Body of Christ at its center, is a mystery of presence. The mystery of the presence of Christ obliges us to look at expanding what we usually understand by analogy and participation.

Gregory Rocca, paraphrasing Cornelio Fabro, states: "[P]articipation is especially the ontology of analogy and analogy is the epistemology and semantics of participation."[64] Participation is usually divided into predicamental and transcendental. In predicamental participation two realities are said to participate in the same notion: One may be the exemplar of the other. In transcendental participation one reality (God) possesses something *totaliter* ("Whatever is totally something does not participate in it but is essentially the same as it")[65] while another reality shares in that something but not essentially. Here there is efficient causality in addition to exemplar causality. Participation in this case involves a dependence in being between the first reality and the second. As the phrase cited above indicates, this second type of participation is the "ontology of analogy," allowing God's being to be correctly though inadequately spoken of on the basis of those perfections in creatures that participate, through God's efficient causality, in something of which he is the ineffable exemplar.

In the light of the Incarnation a new dimension of reality is made available to humanity. I would wish to call this "economic participation." Just as

---

[62] Lacroix is using the ancient Christian understanding of "mystery" as the divine and Christological dimension of history. I give here the complete text: "Un temps sans mystère, si meme on pouvait le concevoir, serait un temps vide, strictement linéaire. Le mystère est ce qui ouvre la temporalité et lui donne sa profoundeur, ce qui introduit une dimension verticale: il en fait le temps de la révélation et du dévoilement. Ainsi acquiert-il sens." Jean Lacroix, *Histoire et Mystère* (Tournai: Castermann, 1962), 7.

[63] "God acts *within* history, God reveals himself *within* history. Even more, God inserts himself *within* history, thus granting it a "religious consecration," which forces us to take it seriously. *Historical* realities have a *depth*; they are to be understood *spiritually: historika pneumatikōs* . . . and on the other hand, *spiritual* realities appear in the movement of becoming, they are to be understood *historically: pneumatika historikōs*. . . . The Bible, which contains revelation, thus also contains, in a certain way, the *history* of the world. *Catholocisme. Les aspects sociaux de Dogme chrétien* (Paris: Cerf, 1938, 1941), 119. The translation is from Ignace de La Potterie, "The Spiritual Sense of Scripture," *Communio* 23 (4; 1996): 738–56 at 743; emphasis in the text.

[64] "Analogy as Judgment and Faith in God's Incomprehensibility: A Study in the Theological Epistemology of Thomas Aquinas," Ph.D. Thesis, Catholic University of America, 1989 (Ann Arbor, MI: UMI Dissertation Services, 1994), 537. Rocca is condensing the thought of Cornelio Fabro, *Participation et Causalité selon S. Thomas d'Aquin* (Louvain: Publications Universitaires de Louvain, 1961), 634–40.

[65] Thomas Aquinas, *Sententiae libri Metaphysicorum* 1.10.154.

transcendental participation is an ontological reality now seen because of the revelation of creation, so economic participation is an ontological reality because of the Incarnation. Israel's possession of a covenantal relation to YHWH, as Aquinas noted, is unique in the whole of the history of religion. This must be taken seriously. The covenant relation is itself based upon and expressive of acts of God in time, in history, and, as we have seen, these events participate in a proleptic manner in the mystery of the Incarnation, and in its own highpoint in time: the death and resurrection of Jesus. There is thus an economic participation in which all God's acts in human history are related to the supreme act, the cross, which realizes and is *"totaliter,"* the economic action of God, the exemplar and instrumental efficient cause of all the other acts. It is because of this that there is a dependence in being, the being of grace established between Christ and every human being, actually or potentially. Thus, the relation between the Exodus and the Cross, to take one of the most frequent relations established in the New Testament, or the relation between Jesus and Moses or David are *analogical* and not merely intertextual. It was this understanding that led Origen to invert the platonic schema of being and knowledge and replace it with the presence and activity of the Logos incarnate.

Conclusion

It is my contention that this dimension of economic participation—the fact that the events and persons, "the wars and actions," as well as the persons of Israel share proleptically but metaphysically in the reality of Christ—is the basis for the ancient understanding of the spiritual sense of the Old Testament. I would propose that a return to this strict understanding of the spiritual sense is the first step in achieving an integration between the undoubted advances brought about in the study of Scripture by critical historiography and the faith view of history characteristic of the Sacred Text. There is no need to return to some of the vocabulary ("allegory") or the wider use of terms such as "mystical" to designate extended applications of a text, though such practices are common in Aquinas himself in his own biblical commentaries. It is, however, important to regain the sense of transcendence and the experience of the mystery of Christ if we are to grasp and transmit the reality of God's saving presence among us.

The pure white light of Christ, refracted through the text of the Old Testament, illumines that text first in the depth and attractiveness of its own theological and religious teaching. Only by appreciating the intrinsic worth of the Old Testament are we enabled to see it as already suffused by Christ and appreciate the love and reverence with which our forefathers looked upon this gift of God. It was precisely this that led the Church, under the guidance of Irenaeus and Origen and later of the Antiochenes, to make its way through the contradictory and erroneous views of Marcion, the Letter of Barnabas, and others to an understanding of the gift of the Scriptures: "These are my words that I spoke to you while I was still with you, that everything written about me in the law of Moses and in the prophets and psalms must be fulfilled. Then he opened their minds to understand the scriptures" (Lk 24:44–45). It is, finally, by experiencing the ultimate reality prophesied by both Testaments that we begin to know partially the truth of the promise: "When he comes, the Spirit of truth, he will guide you to all truth. He will not speak on his own, but he will speak what he hears, and will declare to you the things that are coming" (Jn 16:13).

Index